Leuante
Sirocho
Ostro
Garbin
Ponente
Maistro
Tramontana
Grego

The McCully Report

Newton A. McCully
Lieutenant Commander, U.S. Navy

The McCully Report

The Russo-Japanese War, 1904–05

by

Newton A. McCully,
Lieutenant Commander, U.S. Navy

edited by

Richard A. von Doenhoff

Naval Institute Press
Annapolis, Maryland

Library of Congress Catalog Card Number: 76-6304
ISBN: 0-87021-371-7

Printed in the United States of America

Publisher's Preface

The McCully Report, a typewritten document, was submitted to the Secretary of the Navy on May 10, 1906. It has been reproduced verbatim, with copy editing limited to italicization of ships' names, correction of obvious typographical errors and inconsistencies in spelling,* and standardization of abbreviations and expressions of time and distance.

Lieutenant Commander McCully's characteristic of not completing or of inverting sentences has been carefully preserved.

* Chinese place names have been spelled in accordance with the *China Postal Atlas*, published by the Directorate General of Posts, Nanking, 1933. Russian place names have been spelled in accordance with *The* [London] *Times Atlas of the World*, Mid-century Edition, 1958. McCully's spelling of Russian proper names has been retained; transliteration of some prenames in footnotes differs from that in the text.

Introduction

The twentieth century has seen turmoil and strife erupt time after time, around the globe. The pages of history are filled with the great battles of two world wars and many lesser conflicts, yet the war that opened the century—and whose aftereffects linger on along the eastern rim of the Asiatic continent—has been all but forgotten, except by historians and a few statesmen.

In that war, which took place between 1904 and 1905, Imperial Japan, an island-based exponent of sea power, won victory after victory, both on land and at sea, over Czarist Russia, a land-based power. By May, 1904, Japanese troops had driven the Russian forces to a point north of Port Arthur. In July, the Japanese Navy decimated the Russian Far East Fleet. Port Arthur fell in January, 1905, and the Japanese completed the destruction of the Russian Navy at the Battle of Tsushima in May. Port Arthur and Tsushima are names that mark the eclipse of significant Russian naval influence in the Pacific until the close of World War II.

Admiral Togo's victory over the Russian Navy has been compared to Lord Nelson's victory over the French Navy at Trafalgar exactly a century earlier. Japanese strategy, technology, and firepower were closely examined by neutral observers at the time, and have since become favorite subjects for naval tacticians. But what of the strategy, tactics, and inherent conditions that led the Russian Navy to ignominious defeat? The old axiom, "Everybody loves a winner," was never better exemplified than in this case. Literally hundreds of thousands of words extolling the brilliance of the Japanese victory have been written and published, while the Russian side of this naval conflict has lain buried in the backwaters and footnotes of history.

The Russo-Japanese War had its origins in a war that had taken place ten years earlier. In 1895, the two ancient imperial regimes of the Far East, China and Japan, engaged in a struggle resulting in the military defeat of China. After the Sino-Japanese War, Japan demanded that the Chinese territories of Korea, Formosa, and the Liaotung Peninsula in southern Manchuria (including Port Arthur) be ceded to her. She was able, however, to take possession only of Formosa, because Russia, with the backing of France and Germany, blocked her annexation of Korea and the Liaotung Peninsula. Japan's hunger for territorial expansion was not thwarted by the Russian move. Armed with a non-aggression alliance concluded in 1902 with Great Britain, Japan went to war with Russia in February, 1904.

Most of the military powers of Europe and of the western hemisphere dispatched observers to report on the conflict between the Czarist and Imperial forces. The representative of the U.S. Navy was Lieutenant Commander Newton A. McCully, who was assigned to the Russian side. There is nothing in McCully's previous career to indicate why he was chosen for this duty. However, his *Report* indicates that he knew the Russian language. Written after his return to the United States in 1905, it was based on a detailed diary he maintained while in Russia; that diary is now in the National Archives.

Most of McCully's report covers military and naval operations in Manchuria, at Port Arthur, and at Vladivostok, and describes the Battle of Tsushima. Some of it relates events that took place prior to his arrival at Port Arthur, and for information on them he relied on official Russian records, which he examined in St. Petersburg in 1905, and on interviews with participants. Of particular interest are the sketches of battle damage to Russian ships, which he made while he perched on a hill overlooking the harbor and examined the ships through binoculars, because the Russians refused to allow close-up inspection of them. McCully had a keen eye for details and he produced a classic example of a comprehensive intelligence report. In addition to describing land defenses, naval operations, ordnance, and troop movements, he recorded voluminous information on railroad construction, agriculture, mining, meteorology, and commerce and industry. His observations of the Russian character and mentality are especially interesting. In getting to the war zone, McCully journeyed all the way across the continent, from St. Petersburg to Khabarovsk, and, when he had completed his assignment, he went by camel caravan across the Gobi Desert to Peking. The sections of his report that describe these journeys assume the trappings of a travelogue, yet they are so detailed and colorful that they are well worth reading.

McCully's general conclusions show that he was very perceptive. However, he had no way of appraising Russia's political situation at that time and he obviously was not aware that the Russian government's inability to support a military operation in the East while threatened with revolution at home contributed to the outcome of the war.

When his report had been completed, McCully submitted it to the Secretary of the Navy, who, in turn, forwarded it to the Office of Naval Intelligence. In 1944 ONI sent it to the Naval History Division of the Navy Department. There are no records to indicate that it was referred to for over half a century. When, in 1964, I became aware of its existence, thanks to the interest of Lee D. Saegesser (now Archivist for NASA), the two-volume bound document was still classified as confidential. In 1965, sixty years after it was written, it was declassified—a first step toward possible publication.

McCully's report could not have been published without the cooperation and support of Rear Admiral E. M. Eller, USN, Retired, Director of Naval History, and Dr. Dean C. Allard, Naval History Division, whose interest in this project is hereby acknowledged. Credit is also due Dr. Robert V. Allen, Slavic Division, Library of Congress, who devoted considerable time to necessary research. Finally, some commendation is due my wife Jan, who exercised much patience and forbearance during the long time that this publication was in preparation.

Richard A. von Doenhoff
Gaithersburg, Maryland

Newton A. McCully, Jr.

(1867–1951)

Newton A. McCully, Jr., was born in South Carolina on 19 June 1867. He entered the U.S. Naval Academy in 1883 and was graduated seventh in the Class of 1887. His career followed the usual pattern until 1904, when he was sent to Russia to report on the Russo-Japanese War. On his return to the United States, he assisted in fitting out the armored cruiser USS *California* at the Union Iron Works, San Francisco, and, after her commissioning in 1907, served as her executive officer. He served on the staff of the Naval War College from 1910 to 1912, and was commanding officer of the presidential yacht, USS *Mayflower*, from 1912 to 1913. In 1914 he returned to St. Petersburg as Naval Attaché. He was detached from that duty in the fall of 1917 and assumed command of Squadron 5, Patrol Force, operating off the coast of France.

In September, 1918, McCully was ordered to command U.S. Naval Forces in Northern Russia. He held that post until June, 1919, when he was detached for duty as Senior U.S. Member of the Naval Inter-Allied Commission of Control of the execution of the Naval Clauses contained in the Versailles Peace Treaty. In December, 1919, he was appointed head of a diplomatic mission to South Russia. He returned to the United States in November, 1920, and was assigned to duty as a member of the General Board of the Navy Department.

In October, 1921, he was given command of the Control Force, and in December, 1922, became President of the Board of Inspection and Survey. In May, 1923, he was appointed Commander, Scouting Fleet, with the temporary rank of vice admiral, and served in that capacity until January, 1925, when, in his permanent rank of rear admiral, he went to Brazil as Chief of the U.S. Naval Mission to that country.

Upon his return to the United States in September, 1927, Admiral McCully was ordered to duty as Commandant of the Sixth Naval District, Charleston, South Carolina. He was transferred to the Retired List of the Navy on 1 July 1931, was advanced to the rank of vice admiral on the Retired List on 16 July 1942, and died in St. Augustine, Florida, on 15 June 1951.

List of Sketches

Contents

February 12—April 21, 1904

Washington to Liaoyang

Office of Naval Intelligence,
Navy Department,
May 10, 1906.

I have the honor to make the following report in connection with duty performed as Assistant Naval Attaché at St. Petersburg, Russia, and while accompanying the Russian Forces of the Far East during the Russo-Japanese War.

At 4 p.m. February 12, 1904,* I received orders, and left at midnight of the same day for New York, sailing the next day on Cunard SS *Umbria* for Liverpool, arriving there February 21. In obedience to telegraphic instructions I remained in London until March 12, while arrangements were being made through the State Department with the Russian Government in order that I might be received as Assistant Naval Attache in St. Petersburg, and be allowed to accompany the Russian Forces in the Far East.

I arrived in St. Petersburg March 15, and the Ambassador** immediately took the necessary steps to assist me in my mission. I made the prescribed official calls on the Minister of the Navy, Vice Admiral Avellan, and on the Chief of Staff, Rear Admiral Rojestvensky,*** and the Chief of the Office of Naval Intelligence, Colonel Stenger. I did not see Vice Admiral Avellan, but was received by Rear Admiral Rojestvensky though not very amiably. Already he had been designated as the Commander in Chief of the squadron to sail in July, and in leaving I ventured to hope that I might have the pleasure of meeting him again in the Far East. He

* McCully was then in Washington, D.C.

** The American ambassador was then Robert S. McCormick.

*** Zinovi Petrovinh Rozhdestvenski (1848–1909).

did not answer, but not very politely grunted and turned away. Colonel Stenger was very pleasant and arranged visits for me to the Nevski Works and the Naval Station at Kronstadt, which I had time to make before permission was granted me by the Russian government to proceed to the Far East.

In St. Petersburg at this time were the military attachés of France, Germany, Austria, Spain, Switzerland, Bulgaria, Sweden, Norway and Great Britain, and Captain W. V. Judson, Corps of Engineers, U.S.A., arrived while I was there. The attachés representing the European powers were presented to the Emperor before leaving, but when Captain Judson and I made inquiry through the Embassador if we should be presented also, we were informed that the Emperor received only those officers with whom he had previously been acquainted. The Americans were the only officers not so presented, but as our principal aim was to go on as quickly as possible, and the function would have entailed a delay, we took no further steps in regard to the matter, and may have suffered somewhat in loss of prestige for not having gone through this formality. All the attachés except the Swiss, Bulgarian, and Americans left on March 22 and 25.

At the Nevski Works were being completed *Jemchug* and *Izumrud,** and under construction were destroyers *Gromki*, *Gremiastchi* and *Grozny*, and one submarine on which work was being done secretly, and which I was not allowed to inspect. *Jemchug* had most of the hull work finished, and engines and boilers in place but no guns or torpedoes yet installed. *Izumrud* had hull work in about same condition, but engines and boilers not yet installed. The three destroyers had been commenced about six weeks before, and were progressing well, frames being up, and plating nearly all on. Another destroyer, probably *Vidni*, that had at first been fitted for gas engines was being converted into a steamer. Work was going on day and night and seemed to be progressing well.

At Kronstadt were *Alexander III*** in commission and complete except installation of torpedoes; gun trials were finished, and she had on board the regular complement of officers, and nearly all the crew, but had to be docked. *Nikolai I* was under reconstruction; *Sis-*

* Small cruisers.

** Battleship.

soi Veliki and *Navarin** were under repairs and receiving modern guns; *Svietlana*** was under repairs; besides were a number of old type destroyers and torpedo boats.

At the Baltic and New Admiralty Works on the Neva in lower St. Petersburg were under construction battleships *Borodino, Orel* (pronounce Ahreole) *Kniaz Suvaroff,* and *Slava;* cruiser *Oleg* (pronounce Olleck) and armed transport *Kamchatka.* At this time it seemed possible that all these ships might be ready by September. On account of the shallowness of the dredged channel to Kronstadt, armor was not placed on the battleships at the shipbuilding works, but at Kronstadt. The Neva was frozen over with three feet of ice, and was not likely to be open until the middle of April.

From March 15–31 was near the end of the St. Petersburg winter, the snow melting and being cleaned off, and the use of carriages beginning. The temperature was quite mild, there was twelve hours daylight, and weather was generally very favorable for expediting work on the naval reinforcements. The Emperor visited all the ships under construction, and by personal addresses, and offers of rewards urged the workmen to increased efforts. On April 1 the Neva was still frozen over, but the ice had begun to look "sick," trams had ceased to run across it, and workmen were busy cutting it up preparatory to floating it out when the thaw came.

In Revel were *Osliabia, Aurora, Almaz* and some of the destroyers. No preparations were yet begun on the three *Oushakoffs, Pamiat Azova* or *Alexander II.* In the Mediterranean was still *Dmitri Donskoi* and some destroyers. I could learn nothing definite of *Vladimir Monomach* or *Nakhimoff.****

Amongst the Russians there seemed a change from the former good relations that existed between Russian and Americans, and particularly between the officers of the two naval services. The government officials were a little more than indifferent to Americans, the naval officers were generally polite but not particularly

* All three were battleships.

** A cruiser.

*** *Osliaba* and *Alexander II,* battleships; *Aurora* and *Almaz,* cruisers; *Pamait Azova, Dmitri Donskoi, Vladimer Monomach, Nakhimoff, Oushakoff*-class were coastal service ships.

friendly, and the newspapers were bitter. Generally America was looked on as a silent partner in the Anglo-Japanese alliance. Military men did not bother themselves with the political aspect of the relations between Russia and America, but had a keen resentment for the reported attitude of the Americans in the affair of the *Variag** at the battle of Chemulpo. The principal comic paper published a cartoon of Uncle Sam blacking the boots of a Japanese officer, who wishes to know how much it is going to cost. "Oh don't bother about that Your Honor, I can send the bill in any time," answers Uncle Sam.

As to the attitude of the Russians in regard to the war, the people seemed very apathetic. There was not much interest taken and little or no excitement. Some incident would occur, cause a little momentary gloom and be quickly forgotten.

---

* On February 8, 1904 the Russian cruiser *Variag* and gunboat *Koryetz*, at Chemulpo, were attacked by a Japanese force of 14 armored cruisers and torpedo boats. In port at the time were the British cruiser *Talbot*, the French cruiser *Pascal*, the Italian cruiser *Elba*, and the American gunboat *Vicksburg*. On 19 February the Russian newspaper *Novoe Vremya* stated that all the commanding officers with the exception of *Vicksburg*'s (Commander W. A. Marshall) protested the attack to the Japanese and that all the foreign ships except *Vicksburg* allegedly aided the Russian wounded and survivors.

Ambassador McCormick reported to the Secretary of State that the incident had aroused hostile feelings in Russia toward the United States; that foreign correspondents in Shanghai and London were promoting anti-Russian sentiments by printing inflamatory articles and editorials, and that these published sources were being taken by the Russian government as statements of policy by the British and American governments.[1]

In contrast to the Russian allegations, the deck log of the *Vicksburg* reported that the Japanese had informed the American ship in advance of the attack and requested that it keep clear to avoid danger, and it also reported that the *Vicksburg* had sent medical aid to the Russian ships and assisted in transporting survivors to the *Talbot* and *Elba*.[2]

On March 30, Captain Judson and I were presented to Count Lamsdorf at the regular diplomatic reception, then made the required calls on the various embassies, received permission on April 1, and left the evening of the same day for Moscow in company with Colonel Audeou and Captain Bardet, Swiss military attaches; Lieutenant Colonel Papadopoff, Bulgarian military attaché; Prince Jaime of Bourbon, an officer of the Grenadier Guards, and some other Russian officers. Our transportation was arranged for us by the Russian military authorities, but we bought tickets and checked baggage as in ordinary peace times.

We arrived in Moscow morning of April 2, and left at 10:30 p.m. the same day on the Siberian Express, running three times a week to Irkutsk without change, by way of Samara, Tcheliabinsk, Omsk, Marinsk, and Krasnoyarsk. Our train consisted of a baggage and a dining car, one first-class sleeping car, one mixed first- and second-class, and two second-class coaches, with a trailer for the train servants. When travelling at the slow speed usual in this trip the cars are very comfortable, but as they are very lightly constructed if speed ever reaches as much as 40 miles per hour they jump and sway and are very uncomfortable if not dangerous. It was only once though that we encountered this experience.

The passenger cars have a capacity of 32 people, being divided into thwartship compartments some for two, some for four, with a side aisle running length of the car. In the dining car the food was served in Russian style but of fair quality.

Besides the attachés, on our train were Major General Kusmin-Kuravaieff of Department of Military Jurisprudence, going out for duty on the staff of the Viceroy; Major General Stolitza, ordered to command of a brigade in the new 3rd Corps; Captain Bilianine of the Railway Gendarmerie and his wife; several officers of subordinate rank, Mr. Gouchkoff and Mr. von Mekk connected with the Red Cross, and representing the Grand Duchess Elizabeth; a few officers' wives and a prominent Chinese merchant.

The Captain of Gendarmerie was particularly amiable but manifested considerable interest in Captain Judson's Russian servant, and seemed also suspicious of Mr. von Mekk, a very intelligent young Russian gentleman who had been seen talking with the soldiers, going and returning, in the attempt to learn something of the conditions in the Far East, in order to facilitate his work with the Red Cross. This suspicion took such definite form that Mr. von Mekk was required to justify himself in a definite way, and to be identified as an agent of the Grand Duchess. It may have been a small matter but Mr. von Mekk seemed to regard it seriously, and first gave me an idea of the power of the Russian Gendarmes, and of the dislike with which they were regarded in Russia. He informed me that this Captain of Gendarmerie could have put him off the train and in detention in Siberia, simply on his personal suspicion if he had not been able to show that he was supported by people in high authority. With persons of little importance an officer of gendarmes can, without reference to higher authority, give them a good start on a journey to some retired place in Siberia. To be on friendly terms with a gendarme makes one liable to be considered as one of their agents. One of their particular characteristics seems to be to show their zeal by compromising or denouncing their own closest relations, and no means are considered extreme by them for securing evidence against a suspected person.

There were no other incidents of importance, and after a rather monotonous trip across a snow covered plain with little timber, and under a leaden winter sky, we arrived at Tcheliabinsk, 2,059 versts* from Moscow at 2 p.m. April 5, or at the rate of about 22 miles per hour. Crossing the Ural mountains, country was fairly well wooded, and some grades quite steep, making two engines necessary. Except here the track was generally straight, bed slightly raised above general level of plain, well cared for and in excellent condition. No special guards seemed to be stationed, and the character of the traffic was leisurely and unhurried.

En route were passed three military trains bound east, one with pontoons and a company of pontooners, one with naval stores, and another with transport wagons, caissons, and field guns. At Tcheliabinsk was a troop train 12 days out from Moscow. Our train remained four hours at Tcheliabinsk and I visited the town, after a drive of three miles over some wretched roads. This is one characteristic in the construction of the Great Siberian Railway which

---

* About 1370 miles; a verst is approximately 2/3 of a mile.

seems most remarkable. It never passes through any of the towns, the railway station being usually from one to three miles from them, and communication from one to the other over the vilest roads outside of China. I was never able to get any reasonable explanation for this peculiarity, but it was the evident design of the railway engineers to construct the line in this manner. Omsk, Irkutsk, Nicolsk are two miles from the station, Marinsk, Kharbin and Kraznoyarsk one mile, Khabarovsk three and one-half miles and the original intention was to have the railway station at Vladivostock two and one-half miles from the town, but the present Emperor, when Tsesarevitch, visited Vladivostock in 1891, and by a personal order fixed the site in the town itself, and this is the only town in Siberia which has the railway station so situated. It is not a question of difficulty of approach, nor of expense in purchasing the land, nor can any motive for corruption be discovered. The reason is either political or military.*

The city of Tomsk, the seat of government of a province, location of a university, head of water communications, and the largest town in Siberia, was passed 55 miles away. Between all the stations and the towns, as at Tcheliabinsk, the roads are invariably miserable, and transportation of freight for this distance costs more than its transportation for 200 versts on the railway. Between the railway station and the town of Nikolsk, I have had to stand on the seat of the telega** to keep dry in passing through some of the mudholes.

We left Tcheliabinsk 6 p.m. April 5, arriving at Omsk at 11 p.m. April 6, or 745 versts in 25 hours, a rate of about 20 miles per hour, and about four hours late on schedule time. So far our train had kept very close to the schedule time, and seemed to take precedence over all other trains, without any particular reason that we

* The engineers of the Communication Ministry laid out railroad routes with economy as a determining factor. Most communities had been located long before by early settlers, but the engineers built bridges where the rivers were narrow or shallow, to reduce cost, and erected stations so as to avoid steep grades or round-about routes. From the station, a traveler got to the town as best he could.[3]

** A crude four-wheel wagon without springs.

could see for doing so, except on account of the mails. The country between these two stations was generally level and seemed rich and well watered, although the water is a little brackish. It is principally agricultural land, large quantities of wheat, oats, rye and barley being exported and besides, there are many creameries along the line making excellent butter, also a considerable item of export. These butter makers in many instances are Danes who originated and established the industry. From the steppes to the southward many cattle are brought down and slaughtered, the meat and beef products exported usually to St. Petersburg and Moscow. At both Tcheliabinsk and Omsk were large numbers of empty box cars, and in the engine houses seemed a sufficiency of spare locomotives.

We left Omsk midnight April 6, and arrived at Kainsk, in the Tomsk Government, at 10 a.m. April 7, or 303 versts in ten hours, still at the rate of 20 miles per hour. Country remains level and uninteresting from the point of view of picturesqueness and, as before, is devoted principally to agriculture and raising cattle, but with the difference that to eastward of Omsk, since the completion of the railway, the exported products move eastward instead of westward. The Russian population of the vicinity, as distinguished from the native tribes, consists principally of Poles, Jews, Finns, and Germans in the order of importance named, indicating settlement by exiles. At Kainsk was a military train bound east with a battery of field artillery, and we met two westbound trains, one a long train of empties, the other the regular Siberian Express.

Left Kainsk at 11 a.m. Country still level and covered with snow, timber scanty, road fairly straight and well built. Road bed was of simple and easy construction, earth being thrown up three feet to six feet above level, topped by a ballasting, sometimes gravel, sometimes stone, kept clean of snow and well polished. Ties of wood and 26″ apart; rails of steel and about 20 pounds to the foot and showing little signs of wear. Each rail is held down on a tie by four spikes, the ends resting on steel chairs, joints matching and double strapped.

Arrived at the small station of Chulim where there were large stores of coal of inferior quality and where we passed a train of 500 Siberian Reservists bound to the front. They had already been one month in the cars and were not half way to Irkutsk from where they had started. They seemed types of simple peasant farmers, rather old and whose principal regret was to leave their families without any assurance of what would become of them. One had taken part in the Russo-Chinese or Boxer War and said that he knew that in this war it would be very different than fighting with the Chinese. Most of the other men seemed to have little idea of why they were called out, where they were going to, or with whom they were going to fight. A little further along from Chulim we passed a sanitary train* of 16 cars with surgeons, nurses and stores, which had left Moscow March 23.

At 9 p.m. April 6, crossed the River Ob on substantial steel bridge of the usual type met with on the Great Siberian. Here was first observed extraordinary precautions for guarding the line, due perhaps to the approach of the line of railway toward the frontier of the Chinese Empire. On each pier of the bridge was posted a sentinel and next morning guards were observed patrolling the track. Each small bridge or culvert was guarded by a special detachment of from four to eight men, their living quarters being recently constructed huts indicating that these posts had not been long established. Estimating roughly, there seemed for this portion of the railway about five men to the verst, including reliefs, besides the regular track walkers and signal men who average perhaps one to each verst. Met another train of 30 empties proceeding westward and passed the long railway construction train bound east.

At 2 p.m. April 8, arrived at Marinsk, 630 verst** from Kainsk, or for this distance having traveled 23 versts or about 15 miles per hour. At Marinsk were large stores of wire, railway ties, and flour. After leaving Marinsk the snow began to melt, in places the earth being visible. At Bogotol, 120 versts eastward of Marinsk, a locomotive repair shop and a number of locomotives under repair. Here we passed an ammunition train which a month later, on May 8, just managed to get into Port Arthur after the Japanese had landed and begun operations against that place. From Kraznoyarsk, country changes in character, becoming more broken,

* Hospital train.

** 630 versts = 420 miles.

rolling and at times hilly, as the railway line crosses the foot-hills of the Sayanski mountain range, part of the Altai system. There is more timber, but that near the railway is not heavy enough for lumber, though suitable for fuel, cross ties and telegraph poles. Krasnoyarsk, one of the large towns along the line, was passed during the night. In this vicinity, there being much less agriculture, more attention is being paid to mining.

Between Kraznoyarsk and Irkutsk are many coal mines. The coal is of an inferior quality, though used on the railway and on the Baikal steamers. We arrived at Olginskaya at 9:45 a.m. April 9, giving a rate of speed from Marinsk, of a little over 15 miles to the hour. The railway follows the general lay of the land, cuts being slight and embankments low. Train drags slowly up one low hill and speeds down the other side, sometimes about 50 versts an hour, when the motion of the cars was very violent, and where the line curves straining the road bed, shown by a slight displacement in the ties. The ground being still frozen at this time of the year more liberties could be taken as to speed, but during thaws such speeds would be dangerous. The road though light seems excellently constructed and cared for. Track kept clean and snow banks in cuts trenched for drainage in preparation for the spring.

Another peculiarity of the road besides that mentioned in regard to passing the towns at a distance, are the curves in the line over level stretches. Sometimes the road will make almost a letter S on ground quite level and where there are no obstacles.* From Krasnoyarsk to Irkutsk the road is well guarded by regular troops of the Railway Guard in addition to the usual track watchers and signal men. On account of spring freshets many dry ravines are bridged over and gullies passed by culverts, the number of these

* The Trans-Siberian Railway crosses swamps, wooded lowlands, rolling hills, and some mountainous sections; as a result, S-curves were frequent. To build a firm foundation for the rail bed in the swamps was too costly for the distances involved, consequently the route followed natural foundations wherever possible. In hilly and mountainous sections, the speed of construction forced the engineers to risk safety by building sharper curves and steeper grades.[4]

being large in irregular country, and it is necessary to guard each by special detachments with semaphore stations and signal men. The railway guards in this district consist of both infantry and cavalry, and signal men and track watchers are armed with revolvers, but there is no artillery. On the grades, between Kraznoyarsk and Irkutsk, two engines are necessary, for trains of more than 25 cars. At Cheremkhova, 120* versts to westward of Irkutsk, is stored about 30,000 tons of Siberian coal and at nearly every station were stores of wood fuel, cross ties and telegraph poles.

We arrived at Irkutsk 4 a.m. April 11, 885 versts** from Olginskaya, a rate per hour of 14 miles for that distance. On the way between these two stations were passed two eastbound troop trains and one coal train, and we met bound west two passenger trains and one freight train of empties. By this time enough could be seen of the working of the railway to reach the conclusion that whatever might be the cause, it was not being worked to its full capacity. With the sidings then in existence, 248 in number, for a distance of 3,048*** versts between Tcheliabinsk and Irkutsk, averaging 12-3/10 versts or eight miles apart, the actual distances varying from four to 20 versts apart, giving time intervals of twenty minutes between trains.

Captain Judson who had considerable experience with railway work estimated that six trains per day might be run each way. Certainly there were not so many. No new sidings under construction were observed. The average rate of speed including stops, over the distance was 24 versts or 16 miles per hour for our train, which arrived nearly in schedule time. All other trains were much later, about three weeks being necessary usually for a military train from Moscow to Irkutsk. Very few troops seemed to be moving, trains for stores and field equipment being more numerous. Besides Reservists no infantry whatever was seen on the way out. From Russia was being sent field artillery, forage carts, sapper and pontoon trains, railway construction trains, and trains of

---

* 120 versts = 79 miles.

** 885 versts = 584 miles.

*** 3048 versts = 2011 miles.

ammunition and stores. Omsk and Irkutsk were the principal military depots, many Cossacks being assembled at the former place and many troops of all arms being assembled at the latter place.

The night before arrival in Irkutsk was the Russian Easter Festival. At all the small stations along the route preparations were being made for the celebration and we were invited by our Russian fellow-passengers to assist at their celebration in the dining car of the train. The car was very prettily decorated and the table loaded with many good Russian things to eat, besides the consecrated Easter cake. The function began with the religious service conducted by a Russian priest, one of our passengers, a hymn was then sung in an excellent and expressive manner and then was the feast of kissing. Every one kissed everybody else, the handsome wife of the Captain of Gendarmerie, the attachés and the Chinese merchant not being excepted. The customs of kissing and smoking are said to have been established by a prikaz* of one of the emperors and all the Russians seem not to be enthusiastic disciples of both practices. Two bearded men will prepare for the function of combing away their mustaches, the Emperor kisses each man of one of his guard regiments at the Easter Festival, and officers frequently kiss their soldiers for whom they have any particular reason of attachment.

Beside the old post road route and the railway, there is a system of water communication between Irkutsk, Kraznoyarsk, Tomsk, Tobolsk, Tiumen and Omsk. This system from Lake Baikal follows the Angara to the Upper Tungus, down that river to the Yenisei, through a branch of that river at Yeniseiisk, by lock canal to the Ket, a branch of the Ob, down the Ob to the junction with the Irtish, and up that river to Tiumen. This route is open for about three months only and until now accommodates only small vessels. Navigation extends up the headwaters of the various rivers in connection with this system, as far as Minusinsk on the Yenisei, Binsk on the Ob and Semipalatinsk on the Irtish. To the eastward of Irkutsk navigation extends across Lake Baikal, up the Selenga River, into Mongolia, and if it would be possible by dredging rivers and constructing canal of 40 versts, it might be further extended

* Imperial order or proclamation.

up the Khilok to the Shilka near Chita, and down the Amur to the Pacific Ocean.

During the latter part of the war, when it was impossible to secure railway transportation for merchandise, the water communication was much in use during the summer by commercial people and in winter the post roads. One gentleman I knew could obtain no transportation by rail for himself and rode horseback from Omsk to Lake Baikal. The military authorities used only the railway and toward the end of 1904 confined its use to strictly military traffic.

From Irkutsk there is a run of about 60 versts* to Baikal Station, on Lake Baikal, at which place, when we were there, all troops and stores were detrained, the lake being frozen over, but ice no longer strong enough to support trains. Until a short time before rails had been laid upon the ice, on embankments of packed snow, and passenger and freight cars were taken across, hauled by light engines, or by horses. The ice was never strong enough to support the heavier locomotives used on the main line, some being lost in the attempt to run them across. It is probable that the lack of locomotives on the eastern side of the lake explained the delay in the transportation up to that time. This idea is strengthened by the fact that some engines were taken apart on the western side and shipped across in pieces, then set up again in the eastern side, and the fact also that few spare locomotives were observed to eastward of Lake Baikal, though there seemed plenty of box cars.

From Baikal Station we crossed the lake, both passengers and baggage in troikas or three-horse sleighs. Troops were marched across and stores were transported in one-horse sleighs, each capable of taking about one thousand pounds and of making the trip across and back in one day. On western side of lake railway ran down close to the shore on which was constructed a great platform with an inclined way leading down to the ice. The stores were discharged on the platform and then chuted down on to the ice and loaded on the sleighs. In April 1904 the lake shore presented an intensely busy scene. Thousands of sleighs coming, discharging, others loading up and returning. The distance across the

* 60 versts = 39 miles.

lake was about 40 versts, or 27 miles, and we made the trip with our sleigh in five hours, including a stop for about three-quarters of an hour at the half-way station in the middle of the lake. The temperature there was 23° F.

The horses used in the sleighs were small, Mongolian ponies and the work must have been excessively hard for many ponies lay dead along the route across the lake. Two batteries of artillery were marching across at the same time we made the trip, part of one of them entraining with us in the eastern side at Tankhoe Station. Midway in the lake was a house and compound forming a half-way station at which both men and animals could rest and be fed.

The ice was still thick and strong with occasional large cracks or "toros," but surface was somewhat cut up and slushy due to the wheels of artillery carriages. The ice breakers usually begin their trips about the end of April, the *Baikal** in 1904 making first trip on May 3. Work was going on on the circum-Baikal line round the southern end of the lake, this section being finished in September. Tankhoe, the station where we entrained again, was on portion of completed line, 55 versts south of Missovaya which was the former junction of the trans-Baikal section of communication.

As far as Lake Baikal there were 10 telegraph wires along the line, and at Baikal two wires cross the lake on the ice, the others laid in cable. From Moscow to Irkutsk locomotives use coal, but after passing Baikal engines were usually woodburners.

Our train left Tankhoe at 10:40 p.m. April 11, consisting of baggage car, one first-class, one mixed first and second-class, two sec-

---

* On December 30 1895 the Russian government contracted with Armstrong's Walker Shipyard in England for construction of a ferry for use on Lake Baikal. The vessel was 290 feet long with a 57-foot beam, constructed of wood belted with 1" steel plates, and a two-foot inner sheathing of timber supposed to enable her to break four feet of ice. After erection, the ship was dismantled, shipped by steamer and rail to Lake Baikal, reassembled, and launched on July 29 1899. She began service in April 1900, but was too clumsy and ungainly to work in thick ice and was used only in summer, or when the ice was thin or rotten.[5]

ond-class and 12 box cars with stores, officers' horses and a few soldiers. The rolling stock on the line to eastward of the lake was very much inferior to that of the Siberian Express between Moscow and Irkutsk. There were no dining or sleeping cars and passengers usually carried their bedding with them and ate at the railway eating-houses. Our party was added to by Major Generals Nadéyine* and Litzinski and some subordinate officers. We arrived at Verkneudinsk, 209 versts from Tankhoe, at 10:15 a.m. April 12. From Tankhoe to Verkneudinsk nine wires followed the line from Verkneudinsk eastward only eight. The country is hilly and well covered with timber of moderate size, road well built and in good condition and of same character as westward of Baikal, makes many turns with moderate grades, ground covered with snow, weather cold.

From Verkneudinsk eastward the railway follows first the course of the Khilok, then passes over the divide of about 1,500 feet elevation above level of Lake Baikal and separating the watershed of the Pacific from the Arctic Ocean. At Petrovski Zavod, 300** versts from the lake, is a large iron works employing about 4,000 men, capable of turning out a large variety and amount of iron and steel manufactures. The raw material is obtained in the vicinity, where there are many iron and coal mines as yet only partially developed. In same vicinity are several Portland cement factories, producing considerable quantities of that article, which forms the return load for the sleighs transporting stores across Baikal. Between Verkneudinsk and Chita is the most attractive portion of the entire railway line. The houses and people seem of a much superior class to those seen anywhere else, the soil is fertile and well wooded, country rolling and watered with clear water streams giving many pretty views, and climate is much milder than to westward of Verkneudinsk, the snow almost completely disappearing. The railway buffets were provided with food superior to that found anywhere else and at most reasonable prices. Everything indicated that this region was the most prosperous and habitable portion of Siberia. It reminded one very much of portions of the United States in Oregon and Washington. It was

* Major General Mitrofan A. Nadéyine.

** 300 versts = 200 miles.

first colonized by the exiled Dekabrists,* people implicated in the attempted revolution of 1825 and comprising many of the noblest families in Russia.

After crossing the divide there are some steep grades and two tunnels, little or no timber, country rolling and principally used as pasturage. Immense numbers of splendid looking cattle were seen grazing, looking sleek and in fine condition, although just having passed through a severe winter. Many new sidings were under construction and at each station were large stores of wood fuel, cross ties and telegraph poles.

After leaving Baikal no attempt was made to follow the train schedule. Trains ran from station to station when the track was clear, only one train being allowed on a section at one time. Before leaving a station the conductor would receive a heavy iron bar three feet long, which was the symbol that he had the right of way with his train. On reaching the next station this bar would be deposited in a box giving an automatic signal to the station left that the line was clear and releasing another similar bar there. When the signal was given that the section was clear the bar was released and could be given to the conductor of another train. This system had the merit of simplicity and nearly absolute security, but a delay in one train would mean necessarily a delay in every train on the line.

---

* During the Napoleonic Wars, young officers returned to Russia with political impressions gained in visits to other European countries. They formed two secret societies during 1816–18, for the purpose of liberalizing the existing autonomous government. Few substantial concessions were granted by Czar Alexander I, so both societies considered revolutionary tactics inevitable.

In December 1825, when Alexander I died, his older brother Constantine would not accept the throne. The younger brother, Nicholas, would not accept that decision and swore allegiance to Constantine. Deliberations over a successor lasted two weeks and the young radicals, called Decembrists later, raised the guard regiments against Nicholas in an attempt to force him to appoint a liberal ministry. Their move failed when Nicholas accepted the throne and arrested the revolutionaries.

One instance where our train was delayed six hours will show for how trivial a cause the entire operation of this line was temporarily tied up under this system. At the station of Khilok after an examination of our locomotive, the station master decided that a new locomotive was necessary for our train. No preparation had been made beforehand and it was necessary to fill the boiler and then get up steam hurriedly on the new engine. In doing this a tube was blown out, and it was decided then to put our former locomotive on the train again. In the meantime the driver of this engine had gone to the town some distance away, and it was some time before he could be found. We finally started, but traffic had been delayed for a considerable distance on either side of us.

At 4:30 p.m. April 13, we arrived at Chita, 728 versts* from Tankhoe, or at the rate of nine miles per hour, including stops. Between Tankhoe and Chita there were 39 sidings, an average of one for each 13 miles, but many new ones were under construction and in June 1905 there were 79 for the same distance, or an average of one for each six miles. On the road we passed one train of Siberian Reservists, one train of stores, and one train with a battery of artillery, caissons, horses and forage carts. Chita is a large town and forms a considerable military depot, about 10,000 troops being there at the time, with large quantities of stores and many empty box cars. It was the principal military hospital station for seriously wounded and sick who were unlikely to return to duty.

We left Chita at 6 p.m. April 13, road bed still of same general character, line curving often with considerable banking and cutting, but with few grades of importance. Country at first almost bare of timber, principally used for grazing, and many fine cattle seen, lightly wooded about headwaters of Shilka, new sidings under construction and nine telegraph wires followed line. At Karimskaya, 90** versts to eastward of Chita, is junction with railway line to Sretensk and steamship line from there down the Amur. From Karimskaya on only five wires followed the line, country rolling and without timber, and fine grazing land. Arrived

---

* 728 versts = 480 miles.

** 90 versts = 59 miles.

at Manchuria station at 10:30 p.m. April 14, 447 versts* in 30½ hours, or about ten miles per hour, with 22 sidings. In June 1905 number of sidings increased to a little over twice that number, and number of telegraph wires increased from five to ten.

At Manchuria connection is made with the Chinese Eastern Railway operated under different conditions from the line on which we had just been travelling and constructed in a superior manner. The station of Manchuria had a customs house for examination of goods coming into Russia from Manchuria and since the beginning of the war had increased very much in importance. Many new sidings laid down, engine houses and living quarters constructed, large amount of stores accumulated, many empty cars and a number of locomotives under repair. It seemed to be intended as a center of railway construction and repair and as a point where troops and horses might be detrained for a few days in order to rest.

From Tcheliabinsk to Manchuria the general character of construction of the railway was the same, rails rather light, road only partially ballasted, generally with gravel, buildings in the vicinity of stations of logs and keeping also the same general character. From Manchuria to the eastward the road remains the same standard Russian gauge of five feet, but the rails are heavier, the rolling stock is superior to that between Tankhoe and Manchuria, the road is better ballasted, good ballast being available all along the line, and the railway stations have superior accommodations. These instead of being built of logs are built of either stone or brick, with large and spacious rooms, artistic design, a slight Chinese touch given in the finish of the roofs. They were constructed apparently with the intention of permanent occupation.

At several of the stations were large brick buildings about 150 feet by 80 feet intended ostensibly as theaters and provided with stages, lobbies and audience room, but also equally well suited as barracks. On the front of these buildings, in colored brick, were the Russian imperial arms in relief and inside the audience rooms were provided with mess tables, the lobby was fitted with soup boilers and bread bakeries with capacity for feeding one thousand

* 447 versts = 298 miles.

men. Many new barracks and other buildings for railway employees were either finished or under construction. At each station a distinguishing mark was the water tower of permanent construction, about 50 yards to one side of the railway line, fitted with loopholes for rifle fire and to serve also as a signal and observation station. At all principal stations and at various other points along the line were small forts or compounds called "impans." These were about 60 by 120 feet, surrounded by loopholed wall with bastions at corners diagonally opposite and containing quarters for the garrison, well, sink and sometime signal tower. Near these forts was usually a signal torch about 20 feet high and one foot in diameter, consisting of a stake rapped with straw to which was suspended a bottle of kerosene oil to assist in ignition. At all stations floated the Russian flag.

Between Chita and Manchuria was passed one train with transport material, horses, and carts, and one train with a battery of artillery. At Manchuria station was another transport train, and another with artillery.

At 11:30 a.m. April 15, we left Manchuria, our car forming part of a military train with part of a battery of artillery. Train was made up as follows: one large French locomotive (Cie de Fives Lille) burning wood and coal; one small, wood-burning locomotive of Russian manufacture; one flat car with water tank; two third-class cars, one second-class, and one first-class; 12 box cars for artillery men and horses; one third-class car for petty officers; 15 box cars for artillery men, horses and stores; five flat cars with forage carts, caissons and cooking wagons, and one refrigerator car, or in all 39 cars. The soldiers of this detachment were all reservists of Buriat type, and as yet had only the cap in the way of uniform. These Buriats are Mongols and Buddhists, somewhat larger as a rule than Japanese, but many of them could be easily mistaken for them. They formed a considerable portion of the Transbaikal Cossacks, and as in this case were also in the artillery, though the gunners would be Russians, and selected men at that.

After leaving Manchuria the country is generally level, suitable for grazing, being burned off in places to afford better grazing in spring, of which we now began to observe the first signs. The roadbed is straight, well built and ballasted, and in excellent condition. From station Hailar, the terminus of one of the caravan routes across the desert to Pekin, the railway begins ascent of the Khingan mountains, following the course of the Hailar River, with many curves and some rather steep grades, country hilly with considerable timber, but all of small size. This is one of the most difficult sections in the construction of the Chinese Eastern Railway.

At 11:00 a.m. April 16, 360 versts* from Manchuria, arrived at the summit of the Khingans, 3,500 feet above sea level, and marking divide between watersheds to the Pacific and to the Yellow Sea. The road at this place passed through a tunnel nearly three miles long, very recently completed, and avoiding some extremely heavy grades in this vicinity. At 12:15 p.m. arrived at Buhédou,** a station of considerable importance, there being here one of the large theaters or barracks, a number of completed houses, and 37 substantial new houses of brick or stone under construction, but no work going on at the time. On each side of the station are large brick yards furnishing the brick used in the construction, fuel being obtained in the vicinity. The construction of the road and stations in this vicinity seemed very recent, probably due to change in route, country mountainous and covered with snow, many soldiers and workmen engaged in work on new sidings, and large stores of wood fuel were accumulated.

After leaving Buhédou, road descends some rather steep grades, following generally the course of the Yali River, a tributary of the Nonni. Along this portion of the line, the bridges were temporary wooden structures, in some places the permanent steel bridges being partly completed, but no work going on. At a point 574 versts*** from Manchuria, a day or so previously, two Japanese disguised as lamas had been captured about 30 versts to southward of the line, being there evidently with the intention of attempting to destroy the line. They had with them maps, fuzes, tools and gun cotton, and were accompanied by some Chinese, who were promptly hanged. The two Japanese were sent on to

* 360 versts = 237 miles.

** Now Pokotu.

*** 574 versts = 379 miles.

Kharbin* on our train, were courtmartialed and sentenced to be hanged, but later, by order of General Kouropatkin, were shot. One was a Christian, the other a Buddhist and both said to be officers of the Japanese Army. This was the only attempt, of which I could learn anything, made by the Japanese to interfere with the railway between Manchuria and Kharbin.

In the beginning of the war it was supposed to be impossible to guard against the many attempts of this kind that it was imagined would be made, but this section was so carefully guarded that there was not a single instance of successful interference with the operation of the railway over it, during the war.

From Manchuria to Kharbin was generally considered the most vulnerable against attack and structurally, the weakest section of the railway, and the most important to keep open, so extraordinary precautions were taken to prevent any successful attack. Here the railway skirted the borders of the Chinese empire from which the most probable attack might be directed, and along this section were the great Khingan tunnel and many small bridges in the Khinghans, and the two large bridges, one across the Nonni near Tsitsihar,** and the other across the Sungari, near Kharbin, the wrecking of either one of which would have been an almost irreparable disaster. About each 10 versts were the compounds or impans previously mentioned, with garrisons of 20 to 30 men, and each bridge was guarded by separate Cossack posts. Foot patrols patrolled constantly the railway line itself, and mounted patrols covered the country for a distance of 40 miles on each side, with occasional excursions down into Mongolia.

Originally there were not so many inhabitants in this part of the country, and this number had become still fewer, since the residence of any Chinamen in the vicinity of the railway and outside of the stations was discouraged. The presence of any human being, not living in the small stations where they were under strict police control, was a suspicious circumstance and radical measures used against any one not able to demonstrate that his presence was legitimate. In regard to an attack from the direction of Mon-

---

* Kharbin = Harbin - now Pinkiang

** Now Lungkiang

golia, there were many practical difficulties to be encountered. Although little inhabited and that only by Mongolian herders and nomads, there are certain well-defined routes across the desert, and to cross by any other direction is dangerous on account of lack of water and interference from various free lances always existing in badly governed countries. Along the trade routes Russian agents were posted to note any suspicious circumstances. A party intent on wrecking the railway must have a certain amount of baggage, and on account of the limited variety of topics or incidents amongst members of the caravans, and the monotonous regularity of their character of trade, manner of locomotion, and customs existing for centuries, the least little thing out of the ordinary excites attention and discussion.

Due to the sparsely settled character of the country, the bad roads or almost entire lack of them except along the trade routes, even a very small caravan must approach the railway very slowly and leave traces by which the patrols if at all vigilant may discover it. Of the party with the two Japanese, only one person happened to be observed by the patrols, who immediately pursued him and through him found the party. The entire guarding of the railway east of Baikal was performed by the railway guards, a special body of men on exactly the same status as regulars, and recruited from various regular army corps. They numbered about 35,000 men for the portion of the line to eastward of Lake Baikal, and comprised infantry, artillery, cavalry, engineers and sappers.* The officers of this corps exchanged into it from other regiments, being required to pass a special examination in the construction, operation, care and repair and construction of railways. Amongst a great many officers it was considered a very desirable billet in war time.

From the Khingan Mountains the country is generally plain without trees, and given over to grazing, with few inhabitants, and only small stations. Across the Nonni and Sungari are large and important steel bridges, and specially guarded. At each end of these bridges was a small fort armed with field pieces and mounting a searchlight, and garrisoned by one company. On each pier

* Members of the Engineer Corps who dug tunnels and trenches, and built fortifications.

was posted a sentry day and night, and at night two men were posted in a watch boat moored at the foot of each pier. About 20 miles to westward of Kharbin* cultivation begins, but not to any great amount.

At 8 p.m. April 17, we arrived at Kharbin having made the 876 versts** from Manchuria in 56 hours, or at the rate of about 16 versts or 10 miles per hour. Between these two stations in 1904 were 35 sidings or one for each 25 versts, though this number was more than doubled by June 1905. In Kharbin the weather was very mild, even warm during the day, the nights cool, and snow entirely disappeared. Before construction of the railway a small Chinese town existed in the vicinity about seven miles from the river, now called old Kharbin. During construction of the railway the Sungari was much used for the transportation of material, and another town gradually grew upon the river bank at the landing place, where the railroad crossed. Between old Kharbin and the river town, on higher ground the railway station was built and about it was constructed buildings for administration officials, church, bank, hotel, hospitals, barracks, and quarters for officers. So at Kharbin are three towns, Kharbin Pristann or River Town, where practically all the commercial business is done; official Kharbin where official business is done; and old Kharbin. The Russian population outside of the military element was about 20,000 but town was growing rapidly.

The Sungari here is about a half-mile wide over the river bed, the bridge is 1,200 meters long, of steel trusses resting on 12 stone piers 100 meters apart, level of bridge about 100 feet above stream. The river is frozen over from latter part of December until first part of April, but is not navigable for lack of water by the regular sternwheel steamers, except from May 1 until end of October. During the flood season in June and July, and as long as navigation continues, it is well lighted and buoyed and connects with the regular steamer lines on the Amur. The usual type of steamer is the wooden stern-wheeler of American model, about 200 feet long, 40 feet beam, and drawing three to five feet for-

---

* Now Harbin.

** 876 versts = 578 miles.

ward, two to four feet aft and 10 knots' speed. A few of the steamers are paddle wheel, and some are of steel. The wooden steamers are constructed in shipyards on the Amur, but the steel steamers are constructed abroad and shipped out in sections.

The Department of Roads and Communications superintends the traffic, and has a number of steamers for guardboat service, supervision of the lighting of the river, and acting as revenue cutters. Some of these during the war were converted into river gunboats, manned by naval crews and naval officers and placed under military control. Above Kharbin the river is navigable by small launches and lighters as far as Kirin along the Sungari, and up the Nonni as far as Tsitsihar.

In Kharbin in April, 1904, there did not seem any very large body of troops, everything was moving leisurely and without excitement, and the only particular activity noticeable was in the construction of hospitals. The country in vicinity is level, without timber and under moderate cultivation by Chinese farmers.

At 10 p.m. April 18 left Kharbin on military train of 38 cars, with a battery of 4th Transbaikal Cossacks. The country continued practically level, dotted with Chinese farms and farmhouses about which would be a few trees, and preparations were being made for the spring sowing. The railway crosses the Sungari again about 120 versts* to southward of Kharbin, and country in that vicinity is rolling, and there are a few moderate grades.

Along the branch of the railway toward Mukden** the small compounds or impans were more numerous, there being one about each five versts and close to the track, and at stations there were two, one on each side of the track. The walls of these were constructed of stone or brick, loopholed for rifle fire, provided with watch towers, and they were located at such distances that they were in sight of each other. The original idea of these was for them to serve as refuges for the Russian population along the line in case of attack by the Chinese bandits, and in war they were posts or stations of the railway guards. They were almost of the same identical model as the Chinese farm houses of the vicinity,

* 120 versts = 79 miles.

** Mukden = Movkden, now Shenyang

where all the principal buildings are grouped together inside an earth wall 12″ to 18″ thick, about 8′ high, with bastions at corners. The Russian compounds were 80′ by 120′, surrounding wall of brick or stone 18″ thick at bottom, 12″ at top, loopholed, and earth banquette* for riflemen, and was entered through an arched gate with armored doors. Inside was one large house with accommodations for 20 to 30 men, one wall of the building forming part of the surrounding wall, windows of building protected by sandbags. Several other smaller buildings were for stores, and quarters of Chinese servants, and cooking quarters.

In each compound was a well, and the wall on one side passed over the mouth of a sink. The watch towers were of frame and about 50′ high. Most of the compounds seemed of recent construction, and no provision was made for the use of artillery from them, or to resist its fire.

From Kharbin to Mukden the line is similarly constructed to the portion between Manchuria and Kharbin, but not so well ballasted. The country is generally level, the only cuts and banking being in vicinity of Sungari to southward of Kharbin, but grades nowhere required the use of more than one engine. Several of the smaller bridges had been damaged by freshets, and in one place our train crossed on a temporary cribwork construction. The damage seemed to be due usually to undermining of the foundations of the stone piers which had not been sunk deep enough. The large bridges across Sungari and Hunhe, and across the Taitze at Liaoyang were strongly and excellently constructed. There seemed at least 10 men to the verst for guarding the line, and all bridges were defended by special detachments.

At 10 a.m. April 21, arrived at Mukden, 506** versts from Kharbin, or at the rate of 8.4 versts or about six miles per hour. For this section were 23 old sidings, and 28 new ones had been constructed, giving an average of one for each 10 versts or 7.5 miles, and gangs of Chinese workmen were at work all along the line repairing and strengthening it, and constructing new sidings. Some of the new sidings were not yet provided with telegraphic

---

* Parapet or trench.

** 506 versts = 334 miles.

connections, so consequently were not yet of much use. On the way south we passed one train of sick and wounded going north. At Mukden the attachés were received by General Kossoloff, commanding the post, who informed us that headquarters were not established at Liaoyang and that we were expected to proceed there to be presented to the commander in chief, Adjutant General Kouropatkin.

As first constructed the railway passed about eight miles to westward of the city of Mukden in accordance with the Chinese requirements to avoid the ancestral tombs, but the road now passed only three miles away, the Chinese being still reluctant to allow a railway to pass close or through their towns. About the railway station were the usual grey brick houses of the railway, civil, and military officials. The Russian government, by the terms of the contract, had jurisdiction over the territory for 50 versts* on each side of the railway, but were not supposed to interfere with the internal administration of the towns or with the relations of the Chinese amongst themselves. For this purpose regular Chinese police were organized, being always subordinate to the Russian police, and having no jurisdiction over Russians. No considerable force seemed stationed at Mukden, and even yet there was little change from ordinary peace conditions, except in the extraordinary delay of the trains.

At 5 p.m. April 21, left Mukden, arriving at Liaoyang at 8 a.m. next morning, or 63** versts at the rate of 4.2 versts, or about three miles per hour. This was quite the usual time required between these two places due principally to lack of sidings at Liaoyang. So it can be seen that even if greater facilities for communication had existed on the Great Siberian between Moscow and Kharbin, advantage could not have been taken of it at this time due to conditions south of Kharbin. As mentioned before, new sidings were under construction all along this section, and these did not seem a difficult matter provided materials could have been obtained. At Liaoyang many of the sidings consisted simply of rails spiked down to ties laid on the level ground, and could have been constructed in one working day.

---

* 50 versts = 33 miles.

** 63 versts = 42 miles.

The war now was over three months old, Port Arthur was still open, and large quantities of stores might have been received by that route. One of the first things that impressed us, seemed the absolute necessity of double tracking the line between Kharbin and Liaoyang, beginning with the section between Mukden and Liaoyang. Perhaps the difficulties were too great to be overcome, and we could not acquaint ourselves with these for lack of official information, but the matter of track laying did not seem very difficult, and labor was abundant.

It was here that the blocks in transportation were usually occurring, and this continued right up to the day of the battle of Mukden. The line was almost straight the entire length, the country level, and the larger bridges could have been left with single tracks at a slight cost in time. It seemed like another illustration of the Russian lack of serious consideration of velocity, the function of space and time. From Kharbin to Mukden were six wires along the line, from Mukden to Liaoyang there were seven.

At Liaoyang we were met by an officer of the staff of General Kouropatkin, and were received by him the same day. He welcomed us cordially, stating that for the present no one would be allowed to go on to Port Arthur, for us to have "patience, la grande patience," and perhaps in a few days or a week we might be allowed to go on there, the ostensible reason being the depression that still existed there on account of the said fate of the *Petropavlovsk* a little over a week before. An officer, Captain Count Ignatieff, was detailed to attend the attachês, and we were instructed that all communications for the commander in chief would be made through him.

Already present in Liaoyang were Lieutenant General Sir Montague Gerard and Colonel Waters, British military attachês; Brigadier General Sylvestre, Major Cheminon, and Captain Bousset, French; Lieutenant Colonel Lauenstein, and Major Baron von Tettau, German; Colonel Marquis de Mendigorria, and Captain de la Cerda, Spanish; Lieutenant Colonel Csiserics and Captain Count Szypticki, Austrian; Captain Edlund, Swedish; Captain Nyquist, Norwegian; and Lieutenant Camperio, Italian Navy, who had come by way of Inkow from Shanhaikwan, as both military and naval attachê for his Government. All attachês lived in the train and messed together at the railway station, as guests of the commander in chief. A couple of days after our arrival Major Home of the British Army arrived by way of Inkow from India, and on April 27 Major Schönmeyer arrived in company with Commander de Cuverville, the French naval attaché, who continued on same day to Port Arthur.

April 21—May 8, 1904

Liaoyang to Port Arthur

On arrival of General Kouropatkin on March 30 1904, Army Headquarters were shifted from Mukden to Liaoyang, situated at junction of roads from the Yalu and the Kwan Tung Peninsula. The town is directly on the Taitze River, which passes close under the northeast corner of the walls, and on level ground near the foothills of the mountains, which sweep round five to six miles southward, ending in a spur projecting into the level plain, the hill of Choushan forming point of spur, 350′ high and bearing southwest 5.2 miles from the city.

About the town the country is perfectly level, thickly cultivated, and dotted with small Chinese farms and villages. Around it is a Chinese wall 30′ in height, 20′ wide at base, 12′ across top, outer face sloping slightly, inner face vertical, and both faces formed of brick, space between filled with earth. The inner wall was in poor condition in several places, outer face in good shape. The walls formed approximately a rectangle 2,000 by 2,500 yards, short sides running NNE–SSW, longer sides ESE–WNW, with one principal gate in each face. Inside the town was of usual Chinese character, but buildings inferior to those of towns like Tientsin or Shanghai.

The population was 20,000 to 30,000, engaged in usual Chinese business. The stores were well filled with the produce of the country, beans, peas, rice, onions, millet, dried meats, potatoes, etc., and prices were very reasonable. Eggs in St. Petersburg were 30 kopecks per dozen, in Liaoyang 24 kopecks, chickens and pigs were plentiful, though very few cattle. Horses or ponies for sale were exceedingly scarce and expensive, an ordinary Mongolian pony costing 60 to 80 roubles, and one attaché paid 500 roubles for one of the best.

About one and a half miles from the western gate was the railway station and about it the Russian town, barracks, étapes, and headquarters of General Kouropatkin. There did not seem to be more than 10,000 to 12,000 troops all told in the vicinity of the city, living in the Chinese town, in the barracks and étapes, and in bivouac.

From 500 to 700 reservists arrived daily, were shaved, uniformed, drilled a few times to acquaint them with the new rifle, then despatched to various stations to southward and southeastward. They would usually remain about one week at Liaoyang, drills consisting of marchings, manual, and bayonet exercise at dummies. There was no skirmish drill, taking cover, or target practice. The Cossacks exercised breaking their horses, many being still only partly broken. On April 25 there was a small review by the commander in chief, of about 2,500 cavalry, 44 field guns, two companies of sappers with pontoon wagons, forage carts, ambulance carts, cooking wagons, but no infantry.

At Ansanchan a few days later we had an opportunity to see a battalion of infantry manoeuver, and they executed the manual and marchings in splendid style, and were a magnificent looking lot of men physically. In open order and skirmish drill, they seemed overweighted and slow and took cover poorly. The cavalry consisted entirely of Cossacks of the Transbaikal, mounted on small, shaggy, Mongolian ponies, in fair condition, and the men seemed excellent horsemen.

The artillery seemed excellent, the guns being 75 cm, 35 calibers, top carriage resting on slide and recoiling against rubber buffers in trail. Guns are of Canet-type,* but Russian construction, and rapid fire, block opening and closing with one movement. On trial is a spade of special type, holding gun quite firmly, jumping up only a little when firing. Slide has small angle of train, and two sights used; one for direct, the other for indirect fire. Pointing for indirect fire is accomplished by the use of a circle similar to ship's azimuth circle, graduated into 600 divisions, and called the "ouglamère." The vertical sight for direct fire has 130 divisions, each division representing 20 sazhen or about 40 meters. Shrapnel fuzes could be cut for 2,600 sazhen or 5,200 meters, though guns had range of 6,000 meters. Only shrapnel were served out to the

* These were 75mm field pieces.

field guns, and these were not effective if enemy had protection of the mud walls usually surrounding Chinese houses.

I heard many Russian artillery men regret bitterly not having high explosive shells, and in the beginning of the war, the Russians were often at a serious disadvantage on this account, though after the battle of Mukden, high explosive shells were furnished to the field guns. In the limber with the gun were 38 cartridges, fixed ammunition and smokeless powder, and in the caissons were 76 more, each cartridge weighing 13.5 pounds.

The artillery men were chosen men, amongst them some excellent gunners. The horses for practically all the batteries were large Siberians, though there was one battery drawn by Mongolian ponies. These ponies though small were most willing, and would work until they dropped, simply under the voice of the driver, without having recourse to the whip. Besides they were accustomed to the forage of the country, on which the Russian and Siberian horses did not thrive so well.

Each battery of field artillery consisted of eight guns, eight caissons, and four reserve caissons. Each gun or caisson is drawn by six horses, with a section leader and five men to each. A full battery then consisted of eight guns and limbers, 12 caissons, 120 horses and men, forage carts, forge, cooking wagon and spare horses for battery and officers. Three men rode the battery horses, and two men on limber. A colonel commanded four batteries, with a captain and one or two lieutenants for each battery, and each officer had one or more spare horses for his personal use, and a mounted soldier as attendant. With each gun was a forage cart also used for ambulance purposes, and one cooking wagon accompanied the battery. For each four batteries was one blacksmith's forge. So each battery might be considered to consist of about 150 horses, and 139 men.

The mountain guns were of same caliber as the field guns, and used same ammunition, but were shorter and lighter. The recoil was taken up by two cylinders, one above and the other below the gun, and sights were the same as on field gun. Initial velocity 970 feet-per-second, extreme range 4,000 meters. Gun and carriage weighed 1,080 pounds, and could be transported on horseback divided up between five horses. Each horse of ammunition train carries 10 cartridges in two bags, one on each side. I did not see any of these batteries in action so know nothing as to their efficiency. Toward latter part of war, only the gun itself was carried on horses, the carriage and mount being hauled.

With the cavalry was a lighter gun called the "Argentino," 47 mm caliber, on carriage drawn by four horses, range 4,000 meters, very mobile and firing rapidly. Very soon after the beginning of the war the Russians found their ammunition supply insufficient, the turning movement on the Japanese right flank at Bensihou during the battle of the Shaho failing through this cause, the guns having exhausted their ammunition supply inside of an hour, and being compelled to retire at just the moment when they were most needed to assist in the attack. Means were taken to remedy this by means of flying parks of Chinese carts. Generally the defects of the Russian artillery seemed lack of ammunition supply, lack of high explosive shells and mobility, and in the beginning poor handling. It was superior to the Japanese in range, rapidity, and mechanically.

The forage carts, also used as ambulance carts, were two-wheeled carts, European model, capacity 800 pounds, drawn by one horse, wide tires, carts furnished with body and canopy, and construction simple and strong. There were also some forage wagons drawn by two horses, and similar to American Army wagon. Cooking wagons were in two sizes, for one horse, and for two horses. These were unquestionably efficient, and excellent. Some forage carts were transformed into cooking wagons by the simple expedient of lashing a kettle in the cart. Pontoon wagons carried the pontoons, two wagons to each pontoon, four horses abreast to each wagon.

One of the first institutions established was the camp bakery. The furnace was at the level of the ground, rectangular in shape, about 4′ × 7′ and constructed of brick or stone in the simplest way. At one end was a pit for the bakers and firemen, and the other the chimney. The fuel used was usually the stalks of kowliang* and

* Similar to sorghum cane; a staple in North China and Manchuria.

when furnace was sufficiently heated, fires were drawn, interior cleaned out, and the dough in large loaves placed inside with shovels. The furnace was then closed up and the bread left to bake.

The dough is made of rye flour mixed with water, with the addition of a small amount of the dough (about one-third), of previous bakings which has been allowed to sour. The bread is heavy but excellent, and most nourishing. A soldier with a loaf, which weighs about 10 pounds, a little tea and sugar is equipped for three days. I have eaten some of this bread three weeks after the baking and found it still excellent. With tea, and if one could have a little butter, it makes a very satisfactory meal.

The ration of the Russian soldier includes one pound of meat per day, cooked in the soup, and served out with it, but it depends largely on circumstances if he gets this, though the bread he must have. With bread and tea he is satisfied, add soup and he is happy, a little tobacco rolled in a piece of newspaper and he is in luxury. I have seen men three days without an issue of bread and they seemed as patient and uncomplaining as cattle. A Chinaman appeared with a wagon of bread, and a mass of soldiers flowed over him like a wave, wolfing the bread in a jiffy.

In the field, makeshifts for baking ovens are constructed in the side of a ditch, and very good bread turned out. At the principal bakeries far in the rear this black bread after baking was cut into small cubes, a little larger than sugar lumps and again heated in special ovens until all moisture was driven out, and each cube seemed like a small piece of very hard and dry toast and called "sukharri." It was then sacked and served out to the troops in place of our hard tack or sea biscuit, and with the tea or soup made a superior substitute.

The hospitals in Liaoyang in April 1904, were in excellent condition, but very evidently insufficient in capacity. Kharbin was the principal hospital base, with capacity for 12,000 wounded, increased toward end of the war to 50,000. At the railway station stores of all kinds were accumulating and being piled up. These consisted principally of rye, rice, grain of various kinds, and forage. A portable flour or grist mill was later provided, mounted on two flat cars and did excellent service.

To the southward of Liaoyang the principal military post was 28 versts* away at Ansanchan. At Haicheng, 57 versts,** and Tashihkiao, 80 versts,*** were also considerable military detachments, and a division guarded Inkow, Newchwang, and the Liao Ho river as far north as Davan, 90 versts**** away. At Kaichow and Kinchow were small posts, on the Yalu about 22,000 men, and at Port Arthur 37,000 including the sailors. Altogether at this time south of Kharbin and besides the railway guards and those at Port Arthur which constituted the 3rd corps, were two corps of Siberian troops, the 1st and 2d, and a new 3d corps was being formed from the reservists arriving and detached regiments. The total number of men under General Kouropatkin available for operations in the district Liaoyang, Yalu, Newchwang was about 75,000.

While I was at Liaoyang from April 22 to May 5, reinforcements arrived very slowly, about four military trains per day coming in with field artillery, transport material, stores, Transbaikal Cossacks, and about 700 reservists. Some days no reservists whatever would arrive. A military train consisted of 40 cars, capable of transporting half a battery of artillery, one battalion of infantry, or two sotnias† of Cossacks.

The trains were usually made up as follows. For artillery, locomotive and tender; one box car for baggage; three box cars for stores and forage; 10 box cars with eight horses and four men each; two flat cars with forage carts and cooking wagon; one second-class car in the middle of the train for officers and servants; one box car for officers' horses; three flat cars for guns, caissons, and limbers; 12 box cars with eight horses and four men each; three cars with ammunition and forage; one box car for soldiers only; one third-class car for petty officers; and one trailer for train servants.

A troop train for battalion of infantry consisted of one baggage car, 12 box cars for soldiers, two flat cars for forage carts and cooking wagons; one second-class car for officers and servants;

---

* 28 versts = 19 miles.

** 57 versts = 38 miles.

*** 80 versts = 53 miles.

**** 90 versts = 59 miles.

† A sotnia consisted of approximately 100 men.

one box car for officers' horses; three cars for ammunition and stores; 16 cars for soldiers; one third-class car for petty officers, and one trailer for train servants. In this train would occasionally be one or two passenger cars. A military train was hauled usually by one locomotive, two being necessary on grades between Kraznoyarsk and Irkutsk, between Tankhoe and Verkneudinsk, crossing the divide between Verkneudinsk and Chita and crossing the Khingan Mountains. On the light grades between Kharbin and Mukden and just to southward of Sungari, two locomotives occasionally necessary.

The regular box car on use on the Siberian railway had interior dimensions 20′ 4″ × 9′ 4″ × 7′ 8″—8′ 00″, with sliding doors 6′ 4″ wide on each side at center of car. Four small windows, two on each side near ends, afforded ventilation, a wood stove in the center heated the car, and a lamp suspended over head gave light at night. Sides of car were double thickness and tight, roof covered with tin, body resting on springs over car wheel axles, four wheels to each car. On an average of each six cars there was one fitted with brakes set up by hand. These cars with brakes had a short extension of about two feet roofed over but open to the weather, in it riding a guard or train servant. These extensions were fitted with steps, and formed passage-ways by which the trains might be crossed when many stood at the same station or sidings. Across each end of the car inside were two flats of boards placed crosswise, the lower flat 1′ 6″ from floor, the upper flat 2′ 6″ above that and on these the men slept as a regular thing.

The theoretical plan by which the car was intended to afford sleeping room for 40 men included the extension of these flats at night by boards carried across on each side of the stove, from one flat to the other. This plan is shown in sketch No. 1, and it would have been possible of course to have placed 40 men in the car, by excessive crowding, each man being allowed floor space of 6′ 4″ × 16″. In practice this was not done, there being usually about 35 men in a car, and I have never seen over 37. Some men complained to their sergeant that they were overcrowded in one of the cars and he informed them that if they kicked he would put the eight horses in their car also (all cars being marked outside "8 horses, 40 men").

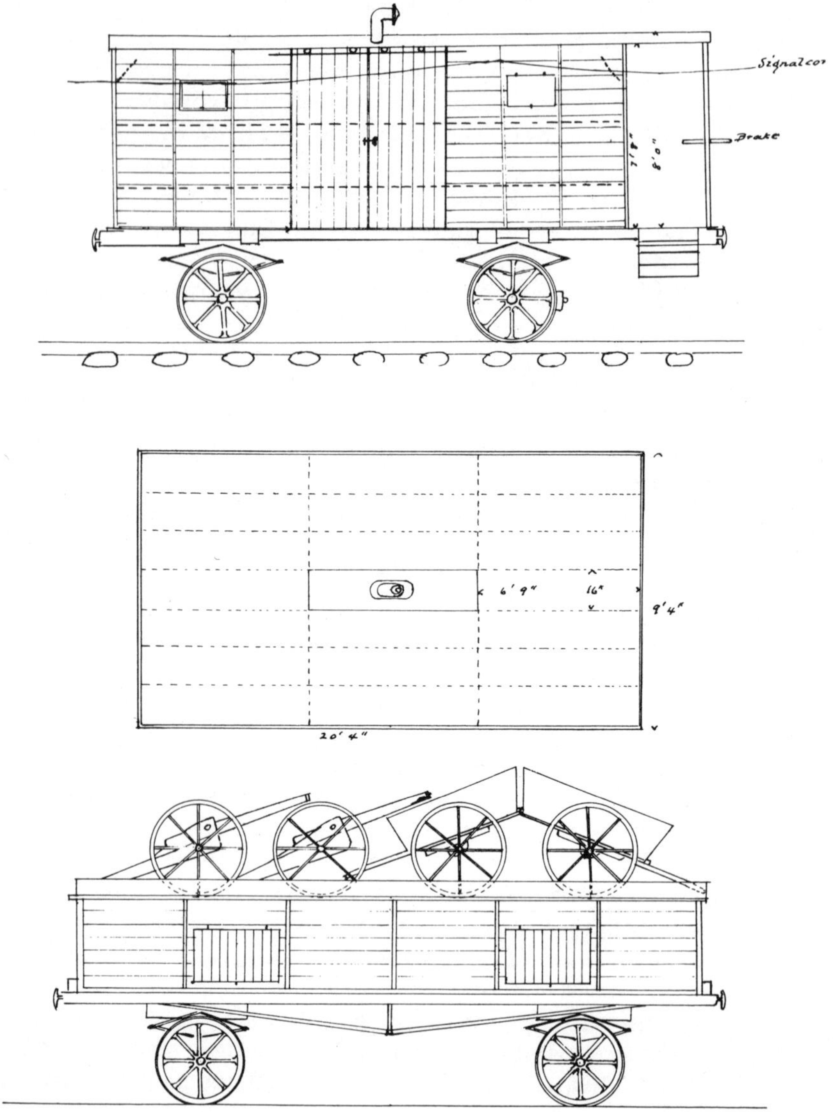

Sketch No. 1 Cars in use on Great Siberian Railway. (top) Ordinary type of box car for transportation of troops. (center) Floor plan of sleeping accommodations, one tier, 20 men. (bottom) Modified type of flat car adopted late in the war.

I have made several trips under these conditions when no other means offered, and found the accommodations restricted but bearable. In cold weather everything is closed up and warm enough, but the odors are very bad—in very warm weather the cars are uncomfortably warm. Underneath the lower flat the men kept fire wood, and their equipment. At each end of car was an inclined shelf in which was kept bread, tea, sugar, cooking utensils, etc. Straw mattresses were provided at first, but later on there did not seem to be any.

While being transported the issue of provisions was confined apparently to bread, tea, and sugar, and an attempt made to give the men soup once a day from the cooking wagons on the train. When the trains reached the large eating stations the men were given a good meal, but these did not occur often enough. However the men seemed contented enough, and certainly looked in splendid condition on arrival. In the cars the teakettle was going constantly and at each station were "kipiatoks" where boiling water was ready to be served out.* The men were given their Easter feast at Buhedou as we passed through, the meal being prepared in the theater. It consisted of "stschee" or cabbage soup with a piece of meat, a dish of boiled "kassia" or broken buckwheat, a big slice of the consecrated Easter cake, like sweet bread, and a colored hard boiled egg, with all the black bread desired. The soup and kassia were excellent, and the meal altogether very good indeed. A second helping was given any one desiring it.

The tea pot is a necessary part of the equipment of every Russian soldier and besides serves the excellent hygienic purpose of inducing him to boil his water before drinking, a fact which had much to do with preservation of the health of the army. The soldiers and all Russians are very fond of sugar, and its issue seemed to come next in importance to bread and tea.

The quantity of tea drunk by Russians is enormous, as they sip it almost continuously from morning till night. In a house the samovar comes before the bed in order of importance of household

---

* The term "kipiatok" means boiling water. The author may have been mislead to assume it meant a room or vessel in which water was boiled.

furniture. Travelling or on the march every opportunity is seized for a "stakann chaiou" and even while on the firing line officers will drop to the rear for a little while to have a glass of tea. I have seen an officer in the field drink nine tumblers of tea after dinner and place three more at his head when he went to sleep for consumption during the night. It is a habit that one adopts rather easily, and seems harmless, but it may be that the excitable, nervous and almost hysterical temperament of many Russian officers may be due in a measure to it. If tea drinking is injurious, it is an abuse in Russia more than any other one thing. The tea issued to soldiers is very coarse, but the officers have an excellent taste in it, and one can usually buy excellent tea almost anywhere in Russia.

Although white bread is not served out to the soldiers, they often buy it and look on it as one ordinarily does cake, but not as replacing the black bread. In each car was a concertina, and the men seemed fond of music, and if the train stopped for any length of time, they would amuse themselves by singing or dancing the national dances. Generally the methods of transportation and feeding the men en route were crude, but well adapted to the circumstances and the character of the men, and placed the men on the field in very good condition.

In the same sort of cars but without stoves, eight horses were transported. These were tied, but not otherwise supported, heads toward center of car, four at each end. On floor in center of car was laid straw and on it slept the men accompanying the horses.

The flat cars for transport of carts, caissons, wagons, and guns were ten feet longer than the box cars but of the same width, on the sides being hinged boards about one foot high to prevent things falling off. Toward the end of the war these were improved by building up on the floor to a height of four feet, carrying in this space ammunition and stores, and on top the carts and wagons, this very simple and practical expedient increasing considerably the carrying power of the railway. All cars were regularly and systematically inspected and bore on them the date and place of inspection with estimated time for which car might still remain serviceable.

The locomotives used to westward of Baikal were generally of French or Russian manufacture. Eastward of Baikal were observed locomotives of Cie de Fives Lille, Societe Anonyme, Nevski Works, Kharkoff Works, Obrianski Works, and a few small Baldwin compounds, first bought for section Port Arthur to Kharbin.

In Liaoyang both officers and men had only the uniforms of peace manoevres, no khaki seen, and almost impossible to buy it. Nearly all officers brought with them uniforms "de grande tenue," and this was a good deal worn. Requirements about uniform were not rigid, the only articles absolutely necessary being the uniform cap, or the sheepskin parka. Many officers and men made an attempt at a sort of service uniform retaining the characteristic Russian blouse belted in at the waist and made of pongee for officers, or cheap drilling for men. The taste of the soldiers seemed to incline to colors, pink, lilac, blue or green, which however soon lost their color if washed. Everyone wore the regular Russian boots, which are very comfortable in cold weather, but unbearable in hot weather. I took dinner with two officers formerly of the Guards one evening, and they were wearing their very handsome full dress uniforms, and when I went to see them off in their train, their sleeping accommodations were on the straw between their horses in a box car. If they had been in khaki it would not have seem so incongruous.

Although none of the Guards regiments came out as a body, still very many officers of the Guards volunteered, and took service generally with the Cossacks, or joined some of the staffs. On account of his prestige, gained in the Boxer War, General Rennenkampf* had a large proportion of these officers with him. Nearly all those officers that I met going out and in Liaoyang finished their service and returned to St. Petersburg before I started back in May 1905. They were delightful fellows to meet, and splendid looking men, but their efficiency was not rated high. Some of the dragoon regiments had the nearest approach to a service uniform,

---

* As a colonel, Paul Rennenkampf commanded a unit of the so-called Zabaikal'skii Detachment during the Boxer Rebellion. During the period from 25 July through 10 September, his forces were frequently in action, sometimes against greatly superior opposition, and took the towns of Mergen, Tsitsikar, and Girin—the later three weeks in advance of official expectations.[6]

consisting of a heavy blouse of dust color, and blending very well with the prevailing colors of the country.

While in Liaoyang the manner of life of officers and soldiers was very quiet and orderly. Drinking shops were plentiful, there were two or three café-chantants, and quite a number of women camp followers. All these were officially recognized, and kept under fairly strict military control. In my opinion there was not more disorder from these causes than would have been found in an American army under similar circumstances, and as far as the soldiers were concerned there was very much less.

There did exist however, a frank disregard for conventionalities not common with Americans or British, and which might have led a superficial observer to believe that there was much more immorality than really existed. If a Russian behaves unconventionally he seems quite unconcerned as to the point of view from which others may regard his behaviour, and the superficial view probably included most of the instances credited to the influence of wine, women and song, and closer investigating would probably have discovered little more. In the restaurant of the railway station where the attachés and many newspaper correspondents messed, one might see some of the women as guests of honor at a table where the hosts were a general commanding a brigade, a colonel count, a colonel baron, a prince, and some lesser lights.

Besides the commander in chief some of the corps commanders had also their private trains, and the Baronesses Stackelberg and Kaulbars accompanied their husbands* to the front, MMe. Stackelberg taking with her some milch cows. The wives of many officers volunteered as Red Cross or hospital nurses, and after coming out were as much as possible with their husbands. In some cases I believe the marriage relations antedated the ceremonies. In a general way the weakness of Russians seems to be much more women than wine, but even then there was too much warm sweet champagne. Nearly all officers and even the men seemed well provided with money which was spent "en prince" as regards the officers and with no regard to its value.

Even in April, 1904, it could be seen that Liaoyang was being prepared as a very strong base, but still without hurry. The loca-

* G. K. Stackelberg and Nikolai Vassilievich Kaulbars.

tion did not seem very well chosen tactically, the town being commanded by low hills from southwest to southeast, these in turn being commanded by higher hills further away, and the town having at its back a considerable river, crossed by vulnerable bridges, making an obstacle to mobility and a danger to retreat. About the town, about one and one-half miles from it, was a fortified line ringing it around, with a number of small earth forts of the same type, connected by trenches and fronted by barbed wire entanglements and pits. Large numbers of Chinese were engaged in work on the defenses, in construction of new barracks, sidings, and repairs to the railway. They were paid the high wages of 30 to 40 kopecks per day, and received their money at the end of each days' work, otherwise they would do nothing. The influence of the work and good pay went far toward reconciling the Chinese toward the Russians, their philosophy being that they paid well and even if they did sometimes kill a man, yet men were quickly born again.

From the moment of arrival in Liaoyang it was clear to me that I should get into Port Arthur, if it were possible, and all my energies were directed to that end. A damper was first put on my wishes in the first interview with the commander in chief, but the German naval attachés, Captain Hopman and Lieutenant von Gilgenheim, were reported to have arrived there on April 19 by the Port Arthur newspaper, and Commander de Cuverville passed through Liaoyang on April 27 and went on there, and I pressed my request more vigorously. The military authorities declined to admit that this was so, and did not seem inclined to allow me to go on. Finally the Viceroy* telegraphed on May 1, refusing me permission, but saying that I might go to Vladivostock if I liked. I then made official written request to have it made a matter of record, and on May 4 when there were already rumors that the Japanese had landed, permission was granted for the Italian attaché, who had not made request, and myself to go to Port Arthur. I received the permission too late to take the train that day, but started on the next train about midnight the next day. The Italian attaché was undecided until the last moment, but though he had made all preparations, finally decided not to go with me. The Viceroy quitted Port Arthur

* Admiral Eugenii Ivanovich Alekseev.

very hurriedly in the morning of the same day, leaving behind some of his staff, who had not time to catch the train, and started for Mukden. The Japanese had meantime landed, and the railway was expected to be cut almost any moment.

The weather during my stay in Liaoyang from April 22 to May 5, was mild and spring-like, with occasional rain showers. The fruit trees were in bloom, the country had begun to show green and the crops were sprouting. The rains were not heavy, and the ground quickly dried out, and when the wind rose, it was exceedingly dusty. On the morning of May 2 was a slight snow fall, turning into rain, which quickly dried up, and that same afternoon was very dusty. The temperature during the night was quite cool, and during the day when the sun shone was very warm.

Before starting on the train, the night of May 5, I was given an unstamped permit simply to visit Port Arthur, my general permission from Count Lamsdorff to accompany the Russian Army having been demanded by the authorities on my arrival in Liaoyang, and not returned to me. In giving it up, on the request of Count Ignatieff of General Kouropatkin's staff, I asked that it might be returned to me if I should leave the headquarters of the commander in chief. He promised to do so, but when I asked for it before leaving, he informed me that it had been lost. I never believed this for a second.

However, I left that night with such papers as I could get, on the regular train which was five hours late in starting, and arrived at Tashihkiao at 4 a.m. May 6, meeting there the train of the Viceroy bound north. On the train as passengers was a naval officer and his wife, a Russian newspaper correspondent, Mr. Borodarchin, and several army officers all bound for Port Arthur. We left Tashihkiao at 8:30 a.m. and arrived at Sunyoshen, about 40 miles to the southward, and near the shore of the Gulf of Liaotung and to southward of Inkow, at 12:30 p.m. While waiting there a train came in from the southward, having been fired on and struck a number of times about 9 a.m. that morning while passing through Pulantien, the station at the head of Port Adams.

The effects of the fire on the train indicated that the steel sides of the first-class passenger cars were proof against small arms fire at the ranges used, about 500–1,000 yards, but that the sides of the second- and third-class and box cars could be penetrated. Some attention has been attracted to this incident, as being an attack on a Red Cross train. The train was a regular passenger train, with ordinary coaches and passengers, and did not fly the Red Cross flag. Several box cars with sick and wounded from Port Arthur were attached to the train and these had the Red Cross sign painted on them. These were hit quite often, and two sick men inside wounded. No one was hurt in the passenger cars, except by fragments of glass.

The officers of the train reported that the line had been cut by the enemy, and that the Russians were retiring to the northward. It was decided to send our train back, and most of the passengers remained in it and returned to Liaoyang. At Sunyoshen was a battalion of the Second Siberian Rifles under command of Colonel Kusmin, and two companies of Primorski Dragoons under Captains Boutakof and Botkine. Colonel Kusmin decided to proceed to the southward immediately, entrained the troops and kindly allowed some of us to go on the same train, amongst them being the newspaper correspondent, the naval officer and his wife, two army officers, and myself. About 30 miles to the southward of Sunyoshen, at Wafango we met another train with refugees, and the naval officer and his wife returned on that to Liaoyang. At Wafangtien seven miles further, where we arrived at 9 p.m., was the southernmost post of the Russians at this time, the rest of the line as far as Puluntien having been abandoned and all troops, railway guards, and volunteers concentrated here. An attack was expected any moment, and every one seemed quite anxious as there were only two battalions of infantry, besides the railway guards and volunteers, one sotnia of Cossacks, two squadrons of dragoons, and four field guns, or about 2,700 men in all.

From Tashihkiao the railway first passes through country almost level, but south of Sunyoshen it first becomes rolling, then quite hilly, the road making numerous curves with considerable banking. As a rule the line followed the valleys, but crossed a number of small streams, and the dry beds of others. All these showed signs of freshets, and in several cases they were crossed on temporary structures. The defects in the construction of the original bridges seemed to have been insufficient or insecure foundations, the stonework of the piers still remaining in good condition, but the piers themselves toppled out of plumb. The temporary structures in these cases as in others, consisted of a clay bank on each side crossing it by cribwork.

During the evening spent at Wafangtien railway station, we had a number of exciting rumors but at midnight definite orders came to General Nierhoff, commanding the detachment, to abandon the station next morning early, and concentrate at Kaichow, 65 miles to the northward, by May 10. The plans were for the women, children and civilians to go out first with the volunteers and railway guards, artillery to follow on the next train, infantry to march out, and the cavalry to bring up the rear, protecting the sappers in the destruction of the government buildings, bridges and railway line. An engine and one car with gun cotton party was to be left for the use of the sappers.

When it was finally decided to abandon the station, the buffetier, who had sold out everything except liqueurs and some tinned asparagus, invited the officers to make free with the buffet, and after this we did not pay for drinks. During the evening I became better acquainted with my friends of the Primorski dragoons, and was invited to join them next day in the rear guard. Count Stenbock Fermor placed one of his spare horses at my disposition, and General Nierkoff very kindly authorized me to accompany the squadron of Captain Boutakoff.

We spent the night in the railway station and early next morning the movement began in accordance with the instructions given the night before. The railway station and other government buildings were mined, and stores and coal piles soaked with kerosene preparatory to destruction. Again it seemed that my chances of getting into Port Arthur were gone. However, about 11 a.m. the cavalry had not yet begun its movement, and quite suddenly its orders were countermanded, and we learned that we were to go south until the enemy was met with and then to keep in touch with him, and my hopes rose again. We started immediately, and I left my baggage in the care of a railway employee to send it to Port Arthur if he could, if he cound not to return it to Liaoyang. I wore only field equipment and took with me besides, papers and a small provision basket, these being in the troop forage cart.

We followed the railway down a wide, fertile valley with hills of considerable height on each side, with advance guard ahead and flankers on each side along the crests of the hills. As we marched down, the Chinese abandoned their villages and could be seen running for the hills. A few of them were captured and interrogated, all uniting in declaring that a battalion of infantry accompanied by a squadron of cavalry had occupied Pulantien.

At one small village, about half way, we halted for a little rest and to eat. The officers and soldiers made free with anything to eat and drink in the Chinese houses, but there was no looting or wanton destruction. I remarked that the Russians did not hesitate to eat or drink anything they found, and that it might prove inadvisable, but was informed that the Russian theory was that a man with a good stomach could eat or drink anything.

Afterward the medical officer in charge of the Port Arthur hospitals, Dr. Bunge, made a similar remark, and there may be something in it. Certainly these dragoons and their officers were as fine a looking lot of men physically as I have ever seen. They were well uniformed and equipped, wearing the khaki colored Russian blouse, which blended well with the prevailing color. Their horses were the large Siberians in excellent condition, although these squadrons had been campaigning since February.

In general spirit, intelligence, and equipment these dragoons were much superior to the Cossacks I had seen so far. The men came from the Primorskaya Province, the district along the sea from Vladivostock to the northward, and many of the officers came from crack regiments, where the financial burdens had become too heavy for them to continue with the regiments and they had volunteered to transfer temporarily in order to recoup. These dragoons were the best cavalry serving with the Russian Army, but there was only one regiment of them. They were commanded by Colonel Wolkoff, of whom I heard a good deal from various directions, and never anything good, though later on in the war he was decorated and promoted for excellent service performed by squadrons of his regiment.

While in the Chinese village a few of the inhabitants gradually drifted in, and were questioned but well treated, and still others came, though none of the women showed up. All agreed with the information so far obtained, which was now looked on as authentic. We were joined here by a sotnia of Cossacks, under Count Armfeldt, with them being Lieutenant Colonel Denisoff, who assumed command of the party.

The march was continued to the southward and when within three miles of Pulantien we received from the captured Chinese precisely the same information that it was occupied by a battalion of infantry and a squadron of cavalry. The place was approached very carefully and from the summit of a nearby hill it came in view, with not a Japanese to be seen. An engine and car with sappers came down about this time, for the purpose of destroying the line, as it came along firing the stores at the different compounds on the line.

The town was entered and found absolutely abandoned, the railway station and houses gutted, and the houses in the military compound destroyed by fire. A small bridge a little to southward of the line had been blown up, but not seriously damaged, and the telegraph poles near it chopped down and wires cut. Empty shells and small portions of a yellow picrate compound were scattered about, and from the evidences left, it was plain that the raid had been accomplished by a small party of cavalry who had made a hurried job and then disappeared. Our party camped in the deserted buildings and the sappers finished the destruction of the telegraphic equipment at the station.

About 5 p.m. an engine and two cars were seen coming up from the southward. At first we thought they were Japanese, but it was soon discovered that they were Russians, and were a party of sappers under Lieutenant Esslinguerre, sent up by General Stressel to destroy the line from Pulantien southward. As none of the enemy was in sight, it was decided instead to repair the line, and restore communications. Work was begun, but soon Japanese were seen on the hills near the town, the dragoons made ready to attack them, and the Port Arthur train was ordered back immediately. I caught it after a lively sprint of about a half mile and we began backing down to Port Arthur. As the squadron baggage had not yet come up, I had now with me only what I wore.

I have described this trip in detail as I was fortunate enough to have first hand information of all the facts and it is particularly interesting as showing some of the causes of the Russian lack of information of the enemy's movements. The Japanese began landing at Pitzewo on May 4, the main force being landed on the 5th and 6th. From the moment of their landing all touch with them seems to have been lost, the telegraphists and signalmen at Pitzewo promptly abandoning their stations, and the cavalry outposts retiring.

No resistance whatever was offered to the landing. A raiding party of not over 50 men was able by an unopposed march of 21 miles to get in on the line, destroy the bridge, force a body of about 30 railway guards to abandon their compound after a loss of only one wounded man, and to start a force of 2,700 men and four guns on the retreat northward, without ever being nearer them than 20 miles, and when they themselves were getting away from the center of disturbance.

Not until nearly the last moment was it decided to order the Russian cavalry down to get in touch with the enemy, and then it was regarded by every one, on account of lack of information, as a desperate sort of expedient with probably no valuable returns. To southward of the point of attack there did not seem to be any more information than to northward. It was not known where the enemy was, nor how strong, and General Stessel had given unqualified instructions to the office of sappers in charge of gun cotton party to destroy every bridge to northward of Kinchow, and to remove the railway guards. On his own responsibility the officer decided not to carry out these instructions, by doing so permitted a day or so later the entry into Port Arthur of a much needed train of ammunition.

From 10 a.m., May 6, until 4 p.m., May 7, the station of Pulantien was abandoned by both belligerents and was thoroughly looted by the Chinese. During that interval of time and over an area covered by a circle of 20-mile radius from Pulantien, neither side had apparently any information of the other. Certainly the Russians had not, and if the Japanese had it would seem to have been their duty to more thoroughly wreck the line and to prevent any possible further communication with Port Arthur. Within a mile to the northward of Pulantien station was a larger and longer bridge, which was easier to wreck and harder to repair and this was not touched. The bridge that was wrecked was repaired in a few hours, the dragoons kept the Japanese off the line long enough to get one train full of ammunition into Port Arthur, and another train full of refugees out, and then retired and Port Arthur was finally isolated by land. This train load of ammunition was an exceedingly valuable contribution to the defense of the besieged fortress, and was particularly valuable to me as it brought in some of my baggage.

I arrived in Port Arthur at 7 a.m. May 8, and was immediately taken charge of by a sergeant of gendarmes until my identity and status had been determined. I was assigned quarters in a small Chinese house, belonging to the government, and near the gate of the navy yard, and took up my residence there with a Russian sailor detailed as my attendant. I messed at the Naval Club, where most of the naval officers spent their time when on shore, and where the naval other attaches, Lieutenant Commander Hopman, Lieutenant von Gilhenheim and Commander de Cuverville, had rooms. We were treated as guests of the club, and in the club met with every courtesy at the hands of the Russian officers.

All the war vessles, except those under repair, seemed in excellent condition, officers and men fairly confident and in good spirits, and apparently ready on completion of the injured vessels, to take the offensive with energy. The Admiral alone seemed not to possess this spirit. On arriving at the town destined to be of such great interest, and viewing the fine fleet moored in the harbor, looking businesslike and apparently efficient, and smoking up as if ready to get out any moment, I felt something like a thrill of confidence and enthusiasm for my Russian comrades, and as far as I was concerned personally, that my difficulties were over.

February 8—May 8, 1904

Port Arthur

In Port Arthur on February 8, 1904, the general public knew only that Baron Rosen had received from the Viceroy a note, couched in most peaceful terms, and that it probably would be delivered immediately to the Japanese government.

The telegraph offices were very busy and there were various rumors. The captains of the ships had heard rumors that negotiations had been broken off. Rear Admiral Vitgeft,* chief of staff of the Viceroy, called on Rear Admiral Stark, commanding the fleet, in the evening, and when leaving the flagship, about 11:30 p.m. spoke of the negotiations being broken off, but that they were expected to be resumed in a few days. At 11:40 p.m. the Japanese torpedo boats attacked.**

The Russian fleet*** was at anchor in the outer roads in irregular formation, *Bayarin* and *Askold* on the left near Lutin Rock, then in the outer line in order from left to right *Petropavlosk, Tsésarévitch, Poltava, Retvizan* and *Pallada,* and *Novik.* Inside of these were the remainder of the fleet consisting of *Peresviet, Pobieda, Sevastopol, Diana, Bayan,* and *Angara.* A merchant steamer, the *Columbia,* was at anchor inside the fleet on western side of entrance. All ships had anchor lights up, the range lights and lighthouse were burning, and no nets were out. *Pallada* at extreme right was guardship, and was using search light. *Novik* only had steam up. All ships were riding heads to southwestward to the current which runs along the shore at that stage of the tide.

At 11:37 p.m. *Pallada*'s lookout observed moving lights a little to westward of south, and turned her searchlight on them. Four torpedo boats of a type similar to the *Skori* were seen approaching in

---

* Rear Admiral Vil'gel'm K. Vitgeft (born 1847).

** Time used in reporting incidents at Port Arthur is Russian; about one hour earlier than time used by Japanese.

*** *Askold, Boyarin, Diana, Novik* and *Pallada* were cruisers; *Angara* was a transport; all others were battleships.

column, coming closer and closer, and then turned sharply to eastward. The flash of a torpedo tube was seen, and the wake of a running torpedo close to the ship, and then another flash and the run of a second torpedo, also passing close to the ship, and one of the boats was distinguished as differing from the Russian boats which were built up between the two middle funnels.

Then the battle alarm was sounded by both *Pallada* and *Bayan* just inside her, which had also observed the torpedo boats, the crews went to quarters, officer of deck of *Pallada* opening fire from gun nearest at hand. Almost immediately the *Pallada* was struck on the port side abreast third funnel near water line, between frames 68 and 78, a column of flame and water shooting high in the air, some of the water coming on board and drenching the officers and crew on the upper deck in the vicinity.

The shock to the ship was not violent, she first lifted easily a little, then settled back as if on springs, and listing about five degrees to port. Two other torpedo explosions were heard, and on the other ships alarms were sounded, nets rigged out, and fire opened. Flagship signalled to *Retvizan* "At what are you firing?" and *Retvizan* answered "I am torpedoed, send assistance." Apparently the attacking boats had suffered some loss and retired, three boats being picked up in the light of projectors for a few moments, the fourth not being seen. *Pallada, Retvizan,* and *Tsésarêvitch,* all were struck, and got underway making for shallow water; while they were going in, the attacking boats approached a second time but accomplished nothing. *Novik* got underway immediately, being directed by flagship to pursue the attacking boats, and after sighting and losing them several times during the night returned at 4 a.m.

About 2 a.m. hostile boats again approached but were driven off without difficulty, and about 3 a.m. the moon rose on a surprised, confused, damaged and partly disillusionized Russian fleet. At the time of the attack the Viceroy in the palace was reading a book and asked his orderly to find out the cause of the firing. The orderly returned with the information that it was a fleet exercise, but soon more trustworthy and accurate news was received, and the town awoke. Parties of men were sent to scour the town for officers and men on shore leave, wherever they happened to be, and send them to their ships. Civilians did not know what had happened nor could they learn.

For the rest of the night the fleet remained awake, uneasy and alert, and the breaking of day was eagerly welcomed. When clear enough to see, a powerful fleet still remained, but on the beach at the entrance, one on each side, were their two best battleships, the *Tsésarévitch* with her bows high in the air, the stern down until her name was awash, and the *Retvizan* listed to port and bows deep in the water. *Pallada* ran aground lightly a little to westward of lighthouse. About 8 a.m. a Japanese squadron composed of *Chitose, Kasagi, Takasago,* and *Yoshimo* was observed to pass about ten miles out from west to east, apparently reconnoitering and inviting pursuit. *Boyarin* and *Novik* were sent after them to keep in touch, and the cruisers headed off to southeastward.

In the opinion of Russian naval officers, Rear Admiral Stark was an excellent officer, and very much the victim of circumstances. It is with good reason believed that he had forecast events more accurately than some of his superiors, and had prepared and submitted plans for the disposition of his fleet, which would have met the approaching conditions with some probability of success. These plans were disapproved by the Viceroy as likely to be mistaken by the Japanese for a threat, and to provoke the conflict, which it was desired to avoid by diplomatic negotiations.

When relieved, on the pretext of ill-health, Rear Admiral Stark was requested to turn over his papers to the staff of the Viceroy, but declined, as in them he considered rested his complete answer to any charges that might be prefered against him, and once in the hands of others, he was too familiar with Russian methods to expect that his papers would ever again be available for his purposes. No official steps were ever taken against him as being in any way responsible for the initial disaster to his squadron, which should exonerate him to some extent from much of the blame awarded to him by public and press opinion.

February 8 was the name and fete* day of Mme. Stark, the wife of the Rear Admiral, and she had a reception for her friends, but a

* Fete day—festival of a saint for whom one is named; celebrated like a birthday.

function which in no way had any bearing or effect on the unhappy incidents which followed afterward the same evening. Junior officers had shore leave as usual, and many were on shore amusing themselves as their comrades in other services are accustomed to do in time of peace, for as far as any one knew, only a diplomatic game was being played. A circus performed that evening, but next day the trick horses were confiscated by the military authorities for the use of the troops.

In the beginning of the war the ships of the Russian Navy were distributed as follows: At Port Arthur the battleships *Petropavlosk, Tsésarévitch, Retvizan, Peresviet, Pobieda, Sevastopol, Poltava;* cruisers *Askold, Diana, Pallada, Bayan, Novik, Boyarin;* gunboats *Otvajny, Gremiastchy, Ghiliak, Bobr, Zabiaca, Razboinik, Djidjit;* mine vessels *Amur* and *Yenisei;* transports *Angara* and *Kazan;* destroyers *Bezstrashni, Bezshumni, Bezposhadni, Bditelni, Vnimatelni, Vnushitelni, Vlastni, Grosovoi, Vuinoslivi, Boevoi, Boiki, Burni, Lieutenant Burakoff, Skori, Smyeli, Ryeshitelni, Raziastchy, Rastoropny, Serditi, Silnyi, Storojhevoi, Steregustchi, Strashni, Stroini* and *Statni,* of which 15 were serviceable; torpedo gun vessels *Vzadnik* and *Gaidamak,* and one small, obsolete, hand-power submarine. At Chemulpo: *Variag, Korietz,* and transport *Sungari;* at Newchwang* gunboat *Sivoutch;* at Shanghai gunboat *Mandjour;* at Vladivostock *Rossia, Gromoboi, Bogatyr,* torpedo boats 201, 202, 203, 204, 205, 206, 208, 209, 210, 211 (No. 207 being lost on the way from Port Arthur to Vladivostock), small gunboats *Yakut, Aleut, Tungus,* and *Kamchadal,* and small icebreaker *Nadiozhnik;* en route Suez to Jibuti Admiral Virenius' squadron of *Osliabia, Aurora, Dmitri Donaki,* volunteer fleet steamers *Saratoff* and *Orel* and seven destroyers with four more in the Mediterranean; at Athens gunboat *Khraby;* in South Atlantic cruisers *General Admiral;* at Kronstadt *Alexander III* and five old destroyers; at Libau the *Almaz;* and the vessels under construction and repair.

The Japanese concentrated their principal fighting force consisting of battleships, armored cruisers (except *Asama*) and some of the cruisers, at Masampho** on February 7. The *Chiyoda* was at Chemulpo, and the *Asama, Naniwa, Takachiho, Tsushima, Niitaka, Akashi, Suma, Idzumi,* and *Akitsushima,* covering a detachment of

* Newchwang; now Yingchow.

** Korean place names were changed after the Japanese occupation transports with troops, were on their way to Chemulpo, and at this time near Mokpho. On February 6, about 3 p.m. ships of this detachment sighted off the Korean coast a Russian steamer, the *Argun*, bound from Dalny* to Nagasaki, stopping and seizing her several hours before the Japanese Minister in St. Petersburg presented his government's decision announcing the rupture of negotiations.

At almost same identical time, the *Fuso* at Fusan seized the *Mukden*, the *Saiyen* seized the *Nonni* in the Korean Straits, and two other Russian merchant ships, the *Rossia* and *Manchuria*, were captured between Kwantung and Korea. In American papers were published the facts of the despatch of transports and troops to Chemulpo, but this news did not appear in any Russian papers, and the Russian government did not seem to attach any importance to the news.

Before noon of February 7, the Japanese main fighting fleet left Masampho for Port Arthur with the third squadron of cruisers and five divisions of destroyers, steaming full speed, and arriving about 60 miles southeast of Port Arthur at sunset February 8. The same afternoon Japanese warships appeared off Chemulpo, and *Korietz*, encountering them, turned back into Chemulpo. The *Nissin* and *Kasuga* passed Admiral Virenius' squadron at Port Said on January 14 arrived at Singapore, and left there February 6 for Yokohama.

The main fighting fleet stood off and on Port Arthur during the night of February 8–9, but sent the destroyers in to attack the Russian ships, three divisions of four-funneled boats going to Port Arthur and the other two divisions searching Dalny. At 9:10 a.m., February 9, the fleet was 18 miles southeast of the entrance to Port Arthur in column, battleships leading and standing to northwest at full speed. This column soon met the third squadron which reported that Russian fleet was at anchor off the entrance, and then fell into column with battleships and armored cruisers.

At 10 a.m. *Novik* returned, under the impression that there would be no attack by the Japanese fleet, but at 10:35 *Boyarin*

ended in 1945. Masampho is now Masan, Chemulpo is Inchon, Mokpho is Mokpo, and Fusan is Pusan.

* Dalny is now Dairen.

showed up returning at full speed, firing her after guns, and hoisting signal "Enemy approaches." Immediately after her followed the Japanese fleet in order *Mikasa,** *Asahi, Fuji, Yashima, Shikishima, Hatsuse, Idzumo, Azuma, Tokiwa, Yakumo, Iwate,* gunboat *Tatsuta,* and third squadron of four cruisers *Chitose*-type. Russian fleet prepared to get underway. At 11:10, when five miles southeast of Golden Hill, the head of Japanese column turned to port heading about west, and a flash signalled the first gun of the action, shell falling in entrance. Russians now getting under way answered before anchors were up, using ranges of 8,000 yards, and headed to southwest in reverse order and irregular formation, *Novik* and *Bayan* leading and nearest the enemy.

Admiral Stark, who had been ashore consulting with the Viceroy, boarded his flagship, the *Petropavlosk,* after she had gotten underway. The Electric Battery on shore, of five 10″ modern long-range guns, joined in with the fleet, and made good practice, but fired slowly. The 11″ mortars on Golden Hill, and the 6″ guns from batteries Nos. 8, 9 joined in, but the mortars had range of 6,000 yards only and were of no use. The *Tsẽsarẽvitch* and *Pallada* aground near lighthouse also fired a few times, but the Russian ships under way did by far most of the shooting and made most of the hits, their fire being at first concentrated on *Mikasa.*

As the fleets approached each other on slightly converging courses the firing was very lively, the Japanese apparently directing the fire of the 12″ guns at the batteries near the entrance, and using the 6″ and 8″ guns against the Russian ships. There was no evidence of fire control from either side, and if anything the fire of the Russians seemed to be more accurate.

The *Novik* approached head of enemy's column going full speed and steering zig zag courses, using her guns and threatening Japanese flagship with torpedoes. She approached to within 3,500 yards and was not struck once, all shots going over her. She did not go close enough to use her torpedoes, but it is said to have done damage to one Japanese battleship with her 4.7″.

The *Bayan* which with the *Poltava* had the reputation for best shooting, kept closer to the enemy than rest of fleet except *Novik*

---

* Admiral Togo's flagship.

and also went full speed, but was hit nine times with heavy shells, most of the hits being in after part of ship, showing the Japanese had not allowed sufficiently for her speed. At 11:30 the Japanese column continuing to southwest, the Russian ships turned together to eastward, nearest range between fleets being about 4,500 yards, the Japanese rear apparently suffering considerably as they passed flank of Russian column.

Bayan continued course parallel to Japanese fleet until recalled by flagship. After turning to eastward the Russian ships suffered very little from enemy's fire, and at 11:50 firing ceased, the fleets being out of range of each other. Admiral Stark signalled "Thanks to fleet for good shooting" and returned to anchorage, the *Novik* which had been hit by a heavy shell after turning to eastward beaching temporarily.

In early part of action *Petropavlosk* was hit once in the bows, having two men killed and five wounded (See sketch No. 2); *Askold* struck once on after funnel, damaging that, killing one man and wounding several others in upper deck; *Diana* was hit once on port side forward near water line; *Pobieda* struck on armor, port side; *Poltava* hit twice by heavy shells, once on starboard side of after turret, once on upper part of armor belt starboard side, taking off step for heel of boom of torpedo net, but neither shot doing more than barely mark the armor. Under gangway on port side were a number of penetrations through the ship's plates, by fragments of a heavy shell striking water near ship and bursting on impact; one 12-pdr. penetrated ship's plates over captain's pantry, port side aft, burst inside and damaged pantry; another small caliber shell struck further aft, point of shell remaining in plate.

Sevastopol was hit once on upper deck forward but with little damage. Toward end of action a heavy shell struck *Novik* on water line under starboard after 4.7″ gun, bursting immediately on striking side, or perhaps as it struck the water, and made an elliptical hole 2′ × 4′, and a similarly shaped depression in the thin plates of the side, 4′ × 10′, edges of hole turned into ship, and outside of ship near hole marked by numerous fragments. The captain of the 4.7″ gun over hit was killed, and fragments marked up gun along chase, but all fragments were small and gun still perfectly serviceable. Inside the ship and in line of hit one officer's stateroom on star-

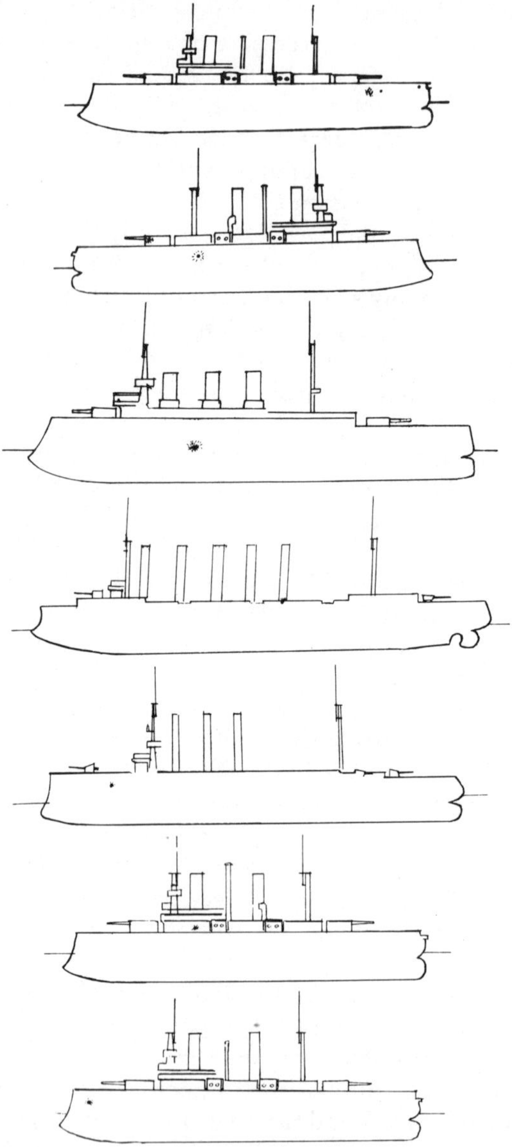

Sketch No. 2 Damage to (from top to bottom) *Poltava* (port side), *Poltava* (starboard side), *Pobieda, Askold, Diana, Sevastopol* and *Petropavlosk* (all port side).

board side was wrecked, and the fragments damaged rooms on other side, but no pieces got through port skin of ship. No fragments got through protective deck, but much water came in and ship got considerably down by the stern and was beached until extent of damages was ascertained, then going into dry dock, where repairs were completed in 10 days, repairs inside made by ship's force.

The *Bayan* suffered most but even then was still in good condition for fighting, speed affected only very slightly and artillery undamaged. She had nine direct hits by heavy shells, but had over two thousand hits from fragments, mostly in funnels and upper works. All ships had many scars from fragments of shell either bursting aboard, or on striking water near them.

Beginning with the *Bayan*, hit "a" was made by 8″ or 6″ HE* shell very near the water line on the taper of the 8″ belt armor where it was about 5″ thick, directly over submerged torpedo tube (See sketch No. 3). Armor plate was forced in slightly, but no bolts started and no leak resulted. A 12-pdr. gun just over impact was so damaged along the tube by fragments, that at the next shot 3′ of the muzzle part of tube was blown off. Hit "b" was on 3/8″ steel plate forming outside of hammock nettings, and was made probably by a 12″ shell, which burst immediately on impact, most of the fragments going outside and destroying a wooden whaleboat hanging at the davits just above.

The plating outside was blown away for a distance of 8′ fore and aft, and the inner side of netting ruptured for a somewhat less distance. The hammocks in the nettings were blown out over the deck, some catching fire, but stopping most of the fragments getting through outer plating. A steel cutter placed on deck inside nettings, with the principal idea, as stated by Captain Viren,** of giving additional protection to engine room, but also reducing target above rail and giving better protection to boat itself, was struck by several fragments which penetrated port side of boat, but not the starboard or further side. The deck house amidship was not struct, though fragments struck higher up along funnels. At foot of main mast on upper deck was a small deck house of ¼″

* High explosive.

** Robert N. Viren (born 1856).

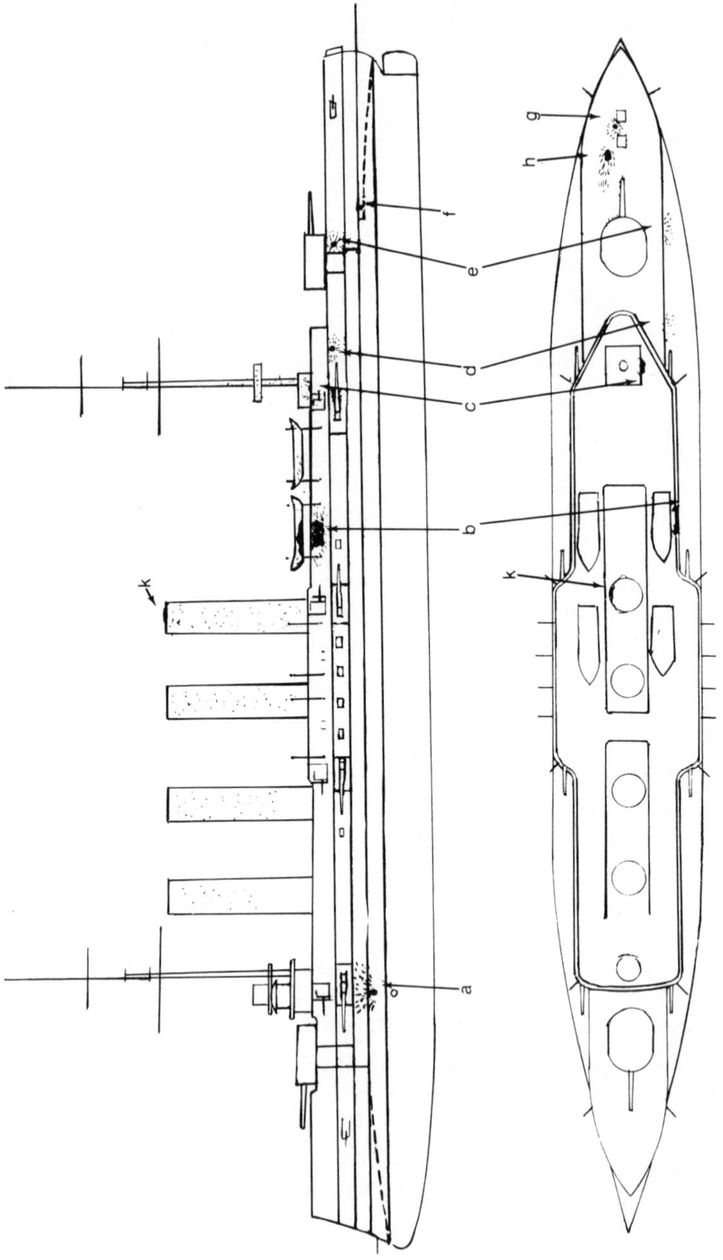

Sketch No. 3 Battle damage to *Bayan*, based on information from Captain Viren and personal observation.

steel, lined inside with a sort of thick linoleum, or other protection, between the steel plating and linoleum being an air space of about 3″. In port side of deck house were two windows, in starboard side a door, and during the action a man was stationed inside making notes.

A heavy shell probably 8″ or 12″, hit "c," struck port side of deck house, just under window, making similar burst to "b," blew a large hole in deck house and in deck underneath, wrecking inside, and tearing man to pieces. The military mast of ½″ steel plates was scarred but not penetrated, and only one small fragment got through starboard side of deck house. The fuze of the shell was recovered between the lining and the plates on starboard side, and the man's note book was picked up little injured. Most of the fragments fell outside, some getting through the deck, and one small fragment striking a box of ready ammunition in which were six cartridges for the 12-pdr. gun. The sides of box were penetrated and the fragment also pierced the case of one of the cartridges causing a low order of explosion which did not blow off cover of box or scatter the other cartridges, and causing none of them nor the shells to explode.

Hit "d" was probably made by 6″, about 16′ abaft after 6-inch gun on port side, and struck just below upper deck, and on outside plating of side which is recessed here to allow train of this 6-inch gun, and has a small glacis or gallery deck on the level of the main deck. A hole about 20″ in diameter of irregular shape was blown in plating, and fragments coming inside cut up bulkheads in vicinity on port side, a very few pieces penetrating bulkhead amidships over engine room, bulkhead on starboard side practically undamaged. Outside of ship the plating in vicinity of impact was marked by numerous fragments and the gallery deck underneath penetrated by some of them. The after 6″ gun was trained at the time about 30° forward of the beam, and the port left open. Fragments coming in through this port killed all the gun's crew of five men, and ranging forward along the deck wounded 30 more.

Hit "e" was very similar in character and position to "d" but 30′ further aft, and just outside captain's office. This office was wrecked inside, and the bulkhead of thin sheet steel much cut up. In observing effects of these shells inside, the large fragments seemed to have very little velocity, while the small fragments had enormous velocities. One small fragment pierced the web of a deck beam over head, ¼ inch thick, the hole of the size of one's little finger, and in a direction almost at right angles to line of flight of shell at impact. Under the port quarter and just at water line, was a hit by a 6″ AP* shell making a clean hole in ship's plating** and bursting in an empty cofferdam extending inside along water line. Few of the fragments got through inner wall of cofferdam, the larger pieces lodging in it. As ship rolled, a small amount of water came in through this hole, but not enough to make it at all a source of uneasiness.

Hit "g" was a plunging hit as *Bayan* turned near end of fight, and was made by either 6″ or 8″, more probably the former. This shell exploded on striking the stanchions forming rail of hatchway just abaft impact, and cut wooden deck up considerably, fragments marking all after part of ship, one very small piece getting in muzzle of after 8″ gun. The gun was fired without injury, but a deep score followed line of rifling. Hit "h" was very near "g," similar in character, and received almost at the same time. This burst on striking the deck, and though it may have been due to either 6″, 8″, or 12″, it is most likely that it was 8″. The turret and after part of ship were covered with marks from fragments, the deck was much torn up, and blown through, the cabin below considerably damaged, and the deck of cabin of one-inch steel penetrated by several of the larger fragments. A trolley beam for ammunition supply under upper deck beams was cut cleanly in two.

Hit "k" was a heavy shell coming from starboard side, just grazing top of funnel, bursting and blowing off funnel cover which went sailing off to leeward, blast and fragments from this shell coming down the funnel damaged the economizers of the Belleville boilers, but not very seriously, since they were repaired in three days. Funnels, tops, ventilators, boats, masts and all upper works were marked by fragments which usually penetrated outer casing only of funnels and were not repaired; some men in tops were wounded, and wireless system temporarily placed out of commission.

---

* Armor-piercing

** Marked "f" on sketch No. 3.

In going out to action all boats were kept on board, and few preparations made for clearing ship beyond giving guns clear arc of fire. Placing the steel boats on deck had some very good points in its favor. The danger from fire was not increased, and being behind the rail, the size of target for HE shell was not increased, the boats gave some protection to parts of ship inboard of them, boats themselves were better protected, and those uninjured were ready for use if needed. Repairs on the hulls of steel boats damaged by fragments were effected with great expedition. Edges of holes were trimmed down, and small metal discs large enough to cover hole, with rubber washers inside were clamped close to skin on each side by a bolt through the center, and nut. The *Bayan*'s steam launch was struck by over 30 fragments and was in service next day.

During the fight the *Bayan* used both HE and AP shell both furnished with bursting charges of pyroxyline (gun cotton?), and in the proportion, one AP to two HE. On impact of these shells very little smoke was given off from the explosion. The Japanese shells on explosion gave off a thick black smoke, explosion developed intense heat and they must have used some AP shells since one hit with that class was recorded. The Russian smokeless powder was in thin, narrow strips, giving a faint yellowish-brown smoke on firing, and was considered very satisfactory, but many officers did not like their bursting charges, as giving off too little smoke for tracing hits, and explosive effect not sufficiently violent. Although having suffered much more than any other ship, *Bayan* was nowhere seriously damaged, and would have been able to put up as good a fight at the end as in the beginning. This ship was always in excellent condition, and always well handled.

The losses in personnel of the fleet during the action of February 9 were 14 killed, five officers and 69 wounded, of which *Bayan* had nine killed and 35 wounded. On shore one man was killed in a battery not engaged, and five men were wounded in Electric and Golden Hill batteries. A number of 12″ shells fired by the Japanese at the batteries fell in vicinity of the Old Town, three striking in the East Basin, one falling near head of dock, one striking the *Kazan* moored in East Basin but failing to explode, one striking water front of the town, another falling nearby in a garden but failing to explode, one falling on Peripolichnaya or Quail Hill, and quite a number in the harbor. The Russians felt with some reason that this brush had resulted favorably to them, since with a decidedly inferior force they had met their enemy, had done apparently better shooting, and suffered very little damage themselves. Hits had been observed on *Mikasa, Hatsuse, Fuji, Yakumo* and *Iwate*, some indicating that fires had broken out and steam pipes cut. The Japanese also learned something, for they never again came so close to the entrance with their heavy ships.

The injuries from torpedoes were as follows: *Retvizan* struck forward on port side, between transverse bulkheads and abreast forward turret, below armor and about 10′ below water line (See Sketch No. 4). Outer and inner skins were broken through, several frames ruptured and 10 requiring renewal, thwartship bulkhead buckled, and armor shelf with lower edge armor bent slightly inboard. One thwartship compartment below protective deck was filled with water and some water got into compartment above from buckling of hatch openings, and consequent leakage on account of bad fit of hatch covers. The size of damaged portion was 30′ × 12′, hole about six feet in diameter.

Tsêsarêvitch had similar injury to *Retvizan* but aft, and abreast after edge of turret, and abaft the torpedo bulkhead fitted as protection against effects of mine explosions (See sketch No. 4). The injury did not seem so extensive as that of *Retvizan*, the blow being taken directly over a transverse bulkhead, which was badly buckled, allowing two compartments below protective deck to be filled. Six frames were replaced in vicinity of injury, and the steering gear was damaged, but protective deck was little damaged.

Pallada was hit directly over auxiliary coal bunker, nearly full, and in which was a magazine for 12-pdr. cartridges (See Sketch No. 5). Apparently torpedo struck about two feet below water line, blow somewhat cushioned by wood sheathing, and coal in bunker offering still further resistance to internal damage. An irregular hole seven feet in diameter was blown through skin of ship, protective deck ruptured, and about injury an elliptical depression measuring 20′ × 12′, greater force of explosion acting on upper portion of hole. The inboard bulkheads of coal bunkers were bulged, and leaks developed in the joints, considerable water com-

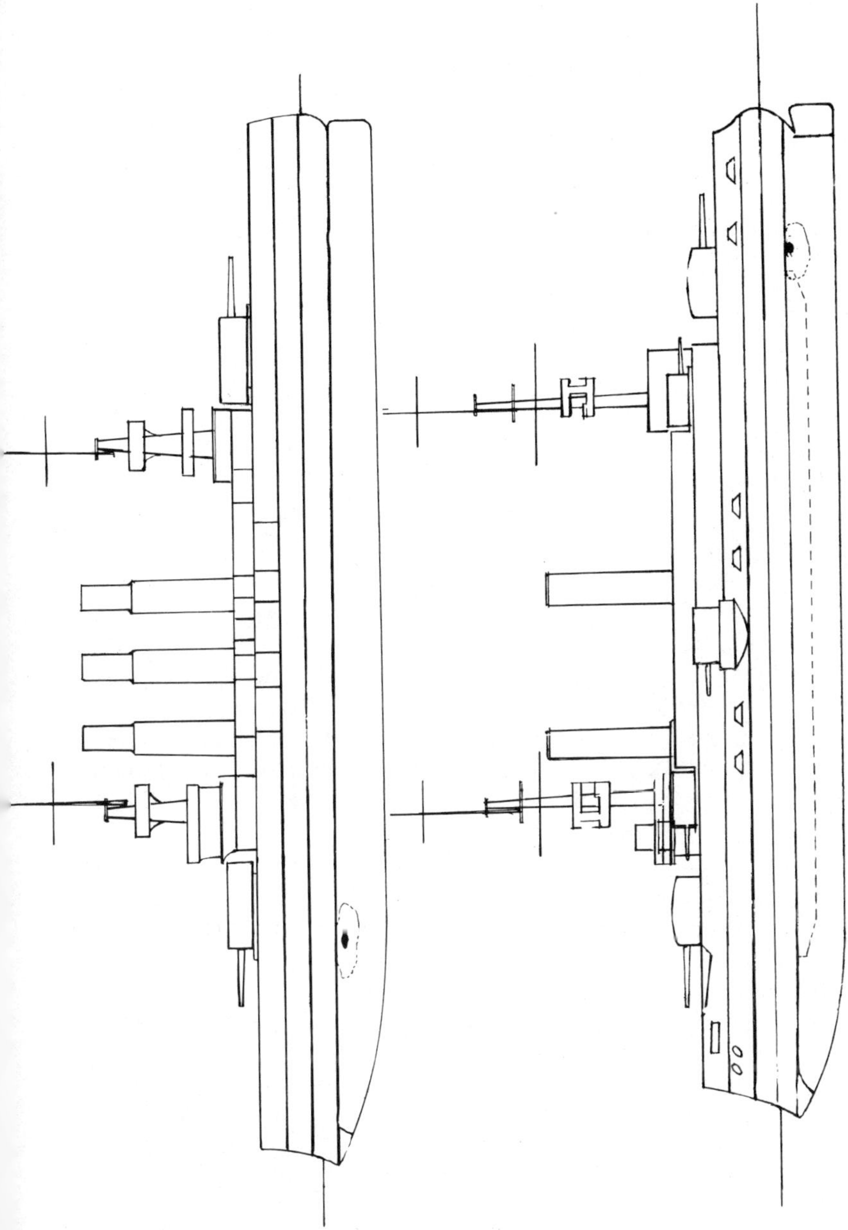

Sketch No. 4 Torpedo damage to *Retvizan* (top) and *Tsesárevitch* (bottom).

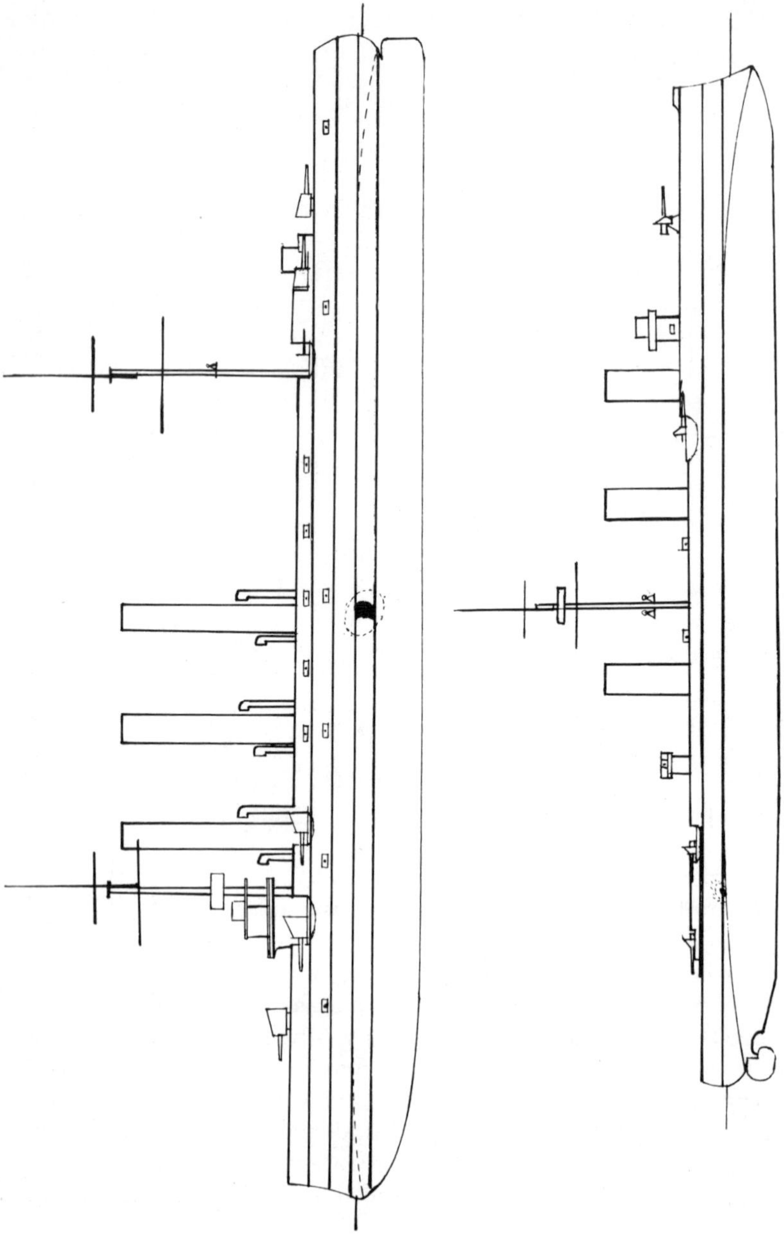

Sketch No. 5 Battle damage to *Pallada* (top) and *Novik* (bottom).

ing aboard and filling one engine room. Under the shock of the blow some of the 12-pdr. cartridges in magazine exploded, causing still others, about 50 in number, to explode also, force of explosion mild, but the burning gases finding their way up through the ammunition chute leading from magazine to battery deck, blowing off door in chute, and escaping out onto the deck amongst the men asleep in their hammocks. A fire was started from the hammocks, paintwork, and clothing, one man being killed, and four other men so badly burned that they died in hospital shortly after. The fire threatened considerable danger, but was soon got under control. A number of cartridges in the magazine were uninjured, and some of the powder from the ruptured cases did not burn, but was afterwards washed off and used in filling other cases. When *Novik*'s repairs were completed, *Pallada* went into dry dock and was repaired in about three weeks (See sketch No. 5).

At the beginning of the war Lieutenant General Stessel was temporarily performing the duties of Commandant of the Fortress of Port Arthur, and had under his command only one division of infantry, consisting of four regiments besides garrison and field artillery. Of this infantry division all were not present, some guarding the railway line to the northward. The place was insufficiently provided with ammunition and stores and the defenses far from complete. In the first six months of the war more work was actually done in preparing the land defenses of Port Arthur than had been done in all the six years of possession previously. It is extremely probable that if the Japanese had landed their First Army at Dalny where it would have been unopposed, instead of at Chemulpo, that they would have captured Port Arthur inside of three months with a small portion of the losses which they suffered later on.

After February 8, General Stessel began energetic measures for the increase of the defenses. All English and Americans were required to leave the town, and many others did so voluntarily. The Chinese too left in thousands, but later on many of these returned. For a few days Port Arthur and nearly all in it were panic stricken. The peninsula was placed under martial law, work commenced on new defenses and preparations made for the siege which was expected to be commenced soon. Prikaz after prikaz was issued, amongst them that celebrated one which even at this early moment contemplated a demand for surrender.

On this same day and about the same time at Chemulpo a Japanese fleet consisting of *Asama, Naniwa, Takachiho, Chiyoda,* two smaller ships and eight torpedo boats attacked and caused the destruction of the Russian detachment there consisting of *Variag, Korietz* and *Sungari,* with loss of one officer and 49 men killed, four officers and 51 men wounded. Having no other knowledge than the published accounts of the fight, I mention it only for the reason of indicating the Russian view of this affair. They all regarded the conduct of the Russian officers and crews with a sort of sacred enthusiasm, Captain Roudneff was given the St. George cross, attached to the suite of the Emperor, and ordered to command the new battleship *Andrei Pervozvannyi* and every man taking part was regarded as an unqualified hero, each being rewarded with a decoration and distinguished marks of approval, so making official sanction of the act of blowing up their own ships, a thing the Russians throughout were always too ready to do.

The mental attitude of the Russians seemed to be always, when in doubt, blow up the ship, so solving all difficulties, and the treatment of the survivors of the Chemulpo affair strengthened them in this view which is supposed to date from an incident in the Turkish wars, when a Russian commander surrendered his ship, in the time of Emperor Nicolas I. The ship was recaptured and destroyed, as having had her decks polluted by the tread of a conqueror, the commander was disgraced and his family and descendants forbidden to ever hold any office of trust or confidence in the Russian Empire. Another effect of this fight was the resentment left in the minds of Russian military men against the Americans. They were perfectly willing to credit the enmity of the American public opinion and press to the activity of the Jews, and as having a political character in which they were not personally interested, but each officer seemed to feel an individual resentment to Americans after that date and on account of the incidents occurring that day. Another incident worthy of notice seemed to have been the disabling of the *Variag*'s steering gear, as being the more immediate cause of the unfortunate result. Injuries of this character occurred later in noteworthy instances.

At Dalny also unfortunate occurrences took place next day. The mine vessel *Yenisei* while laying mines a mile to the westward of Sanshandao about noon of February 11 observed a mine which had broken away from the moorings and was floating. The vessel was stopped, and began firing at this mine to destroy it, when she drifted down on a mine previously placed which struck her under the forward part and exploded, damaging the ship so severely that she sank after 15 minutes with captain, three officers and 92 men; five officers and 92 men being rescued, several severely wounded.

When news of this disaster was received at Port Arthur, the *Boyarin* was despatched to Dalny to render assistance to *Yenisei.* While going at full speed near Dalny she too struck a mine which exploded with such violence that the masts were broken and fell, as happened also with *Yenisei,* and the injuries were so serious that the captain decided to abandon her, and the crew was transferred to a destroyer. This abandonment was premature as the ship remained afloat for more than a day longer, and finally was driven ashore in a blow on Sanshandao Island where she sunk. Her commander was an officer who had distinguished himself at the attack of the Taku Forts in 1900, for which he had been rewarded with the St. George cross, the decoration most eagerly desired by all Russian officers.

So for the first 48 hours of the war the Russians had lost *Variag, Korietz, Sungari* (transport), *Yenisei, Boyarin,* and were temporarily deprived of the services of their two best battleships, the *Retvizan* and *Tsésarévitch,* cruisers *Pallada* and *Novik,* and having *Bayan* considerably damaged, besides losing a number of merchant vessels and two volunteer fleet steamers, with troops and munitions of war. The losses suffered by the Japanese were not accurately known, but it was believed that they were much in excess of what they were willing to acknowledge.* For the Russians, their most serious loss was in their self-confidence, due to the dash and initia-

* The Japanese had three officers and seven men killed, 11 officers and 40 men wounded. Damage to ships was minimal; some ships were untouched, but the fighting top of *Mikasa* was severely damaged, the admiral's cabin in *Hatsuse* was wrecked, the wardroom in *Iwate* was smashed.[7]

tive of their enemy, and this was a loss from which they never recovered during the rest of the war, and led in several occasions later to still more serious material losses.

On February 10, all the Russian fleet including *Tsésarévitch*, withdrew into inner harbor, except *Retvizan* only which remained beached on eastern side of entrance under Golden Hill for a month longer, as it was not considered safe to move her. Various measures were taken to repair her temporarily, to allow of her being floated off, but none seemed successful at first. The part of the ship in vicinity of injury was wrapped in cables, to support collision mats, but without sufficient success to permit moving. After two weeks, a caisson was constructed similar to those built later on, but when in place and pumped out it was too weak and collapsed. Another much stronger one was then built and placed, and the ship finally floated off and moored in the West Basin on March 9.

On February 20 the order of the Emperor was published, designating Vice Admiral Makaroff* to command of the fleet, and the Viceroy authorized Rear Admiral Stark to act temporarily in that capacity in case of absence of Viceroy with land forces, and Rear Admiral Lojinski** was assigned as chief of naval staff of commandant of fortress.

Having suffered severely from a delay in opening fire on the night of February 8, the actions of the Russian naval officers now inclined to the other extreme, and several small merchant steamers, the *Fuping, Ipsing, Pronto*, and *Chingming*, were hastily fired on by Russian vessels while about to leave or while leaving the harbor, in the first day few days after February 8.

Until February 25 the only activity undertaken by the Russians consisted in scouting trips by the torpedo boats in the vicinity of Kwan Tung Peninsula. Apparently the Japanese did not attempt anything either during this time beyond scouting trips off the entrance by cruisers and torpedo boats, and perhaps preparation of their naval base in the Elliot Islands.

In the early morning of February 24 began another busy day for Port Arthur. About 2:45 a.m. were first observed several torpedo boats on which the *Retvizan* and batteries opened fire. At first it

* Stepan Osipovich Makarov (born 1848).

** Mikhail F. Loschinskii (born 1849).

was not guessed by the Russians the effect of this movement, their belief being that the torpedo boats intended attacking *Retvizan* still lying at the entrance. Several large merchant ships were also observed approaching the entrance at full speed, and it was believed that they were fire-ships or "branders" coming in with the same aim. For this reason the Russians always spoke of the attempts to block the entrance as "brander" attacks. It was not for some time that the real object of this attack was apparent to the Russians.

These "branders" in the first attempts were unarmed merchant vessels of about 2,000 tons, stripped of all unnecessary gear, manned by small crews, and equipped with mooring gear to fix them in position, and explosive cartridge arranged to sink them there and block the entrance, similar to the attempt of the *Merrimac.** As the "branders" came in they were met by a heavy fire, and were evidently confused by the search lights, as those beached showed little or no effects of gun fire, and it seems trustworthy that only one man of the crews was killed.

The "brander" fleet consisted of five merchant vessels, *Hokoku Maru,* 2,800 tons, *Buyo Maru* 1,000 tons, *Bushiu Maru,* 1,200 tons, *Jinsen Maru,* 2,300 tons, and *Tiensin Maru,* 2,900 tons. The *Hokoku Maru* landed on west side of entrance directly under lighthouse, bows in on the rocks, fire breaking out on her and burning until next day. Bows were at normal draft, but upper deck astern was awash. In this portion of her above water could be observed only a few hits by small guns. One brander, probably *Jinsen Maru,* ran on reef about three miles to southwestward of entrance and two others, *Buyo Maru* and *Bushiu Maru,* sank off entrance in approximate positions shown on sketch, either by their own crews or from striking mines. On being sunk or running aground, steamers launched small boats and the crews escaped. Russians claimed to have seriously damaged one torpedo boat during the night.

* During the Spanish-American War, the U.S. Navy attempted to trap the Spanish fleet in Santiago Harbor, Cuba, by sinking a ship in the channel. Under Richard P. Hobson, a crew of volunteers sailed the collier *Merrimac* into the harbor entrance on June 3, 1898, but Spanish gunfire blocked the attempt. The ship was scuttled by her crew, who were then captured by the Spanish.

By daylight the torpedo boats, eight in number, retired to the support of the larger ships off the entrance, 12 in number, formed apparently in two divisions. *Askold, Bayan* and *Novik* were sent on a reconnoitering expedition, exchanging a few shots at long range with the ships off the entrance, neither apparently doing any damage. On the night of February 24–25, three divisions of Japanese destroyers investigated Dalny, Pigeon Bay and entrance of Port Arthur. These last were observed from shore and fired on by *Retvizan* and sea batteries. Beyond planting mines, if that were their business, they accomplished nothing else.

Two divisions of Russian destroyers, four boats each, one under Captain Matussievitch,* the other under Commander Prince Lieven** were scouting along shore in vicinity of Liaotishan and encountered an equal number of Japanese destroyers, when there was quite a lively skirmish. The fighting was principally with guns, the boats approaching each other very closely and considerable confusion resulting. In this confusion the *Vnushitelni* and one other destroyer separated from rest of fleet, which returned safely into Port Arthur. The two straying boats were detected early next morning trying to make the harbor, by the Japanese division consisting of *Takasago, Chitose, Kasagi,* and *Yoshimo,* and *Vnushitelni* was cut off, being forced to take shelter in Pigeon Bay under fire of the cruisers at long range. There her commander beached her and blew her up, though she was quite uninjured and had not even any wounded aboard.

When it was learned in Port Arthur that Japanese cruisers were attacking two Russian torpedo boats, the *Bayan, Askold, Diana* and *Novik* were sent out to distract their attention, about 9 a.m., but only succeeded in attracing the attention of the main Japanese fleet of six battleships, six armored cruisers and four protected cruisers. These approached the harbor and fired on the Russian cruisers which, with the batteries, returned the fire, making some hits on Japanese ships, but were compelled to seek refuge inside, and then the Japanese fired a few rounds with the heavy guns at the town and batteries, doing little or no damage on account of the extreme range of 17,000 yards.

* Nikolai A. Matusevich (born 1852).
** Prince Aleksandr A. Liven (born 1860).

On March 8, Vice Admiral Makaroff arrived and assumed command of the fleet, and on March 9 the *Retvizan* was brought inside and moored in West Basin. Apparently, as by regular fortnightly intervals, the Japanese were preparing another attack. A little after midnight of March 10 torpedo boats were observed off the entrance and were fired on by the forts. At 2:40 a.m. a division of four torpedo boats consisting of *Vlastni, Vuineslivi, Bezstrashni* and one other under Captain Matussievitch was sent out on a scouting trip and steamed along the western shore around lighthouse on Liaotishan.

About 15 miles from entrance and while to westward of the lighthouse, this division encountered, about 4 a.m., the third flotilla of Japanese destroyers, and there ensued a sharp skirmish. The guns were used mainly, but Lieutenant Kartseff of *Vlastni* claimed to have sunk a Japanese destroyer with torpedoes, and with apparently good reason, though he may have mistaken explosion of steam pipes on *Akadsuki* for explosion of torpedo. The Japanese were said to be superior in force, but anyway the Russian detachment was not able to hold its own, and was forced to run in for the harbor.

Another division of four destroyers, *Silnyi, Raziastchy, Ryeshitelni* and *Steregustchi,* had also gone out and first two boats returned safely, but while *Steregustchi* and *Ryeshitelni* were returning, about 7 a.m., they were intercepted by a superior force of Japanese destroyers, and *Ryeshitelni* was damaged but got away by superior speed. *Steregustchi* had steam pipes cut, was surrounded and overpowered, and after losing all four officers and all the crew, except four, was captured and sunk while being taken in tow by *Saganami.* Lieutenant Sergieieff, who commanded *Steregustchi* and was killed early in the fight, only arrived in Port Arthur on February 28, and this was one of his first cruises on his destroyer. The commander of the *Ryeshitelni,* Captain Kornileff, was severely wounded and died a month later. Besides loss of *Steregustchi* with four officers and 41 men, Russians had two men killed, four officers including Captain Matussievitch and 14 men wounded, and Japanese loss was one officer and nine men killed, and 14 wounded.

When the desperate condition of *Steregustchi* was observed from the shore, Admiral Makaroff, at 8:30 a.m., on the *Novik,* accompanied by *Bayan*, steamed out to its assistance, but could accomplish nothing owing to presence of five Japanese cruisers and 12 destroyers near *Steregustchi*. A few shots were fired at the Russian cruisers which answered assisted by the Electric and Tiger Tail batteries, but on account of great range no damage was done and firing ceased. Japanese fleet consisted of battleship division of five ships, two armored cruisers, four protected cruisers, and two other ships not identified, with 12 destroyers.

The Russian cruisers being unable to afford any assistance to *Steregustchi*, returned to harbor, and the Japanese armored division of seven ships took up a position to westward of Liaotishan between the lighthouse and Pigeon Bay and began a bombardment of the town, batteries and harbor, lasting from 9 a.m. till 1 p.m. About 154 shells were fired mostly of 12″ caliber, but some also of 8″. Most of the shells fell in the Western Basin, 20 on and near Electric Battery, eight in the New Town, one near railway station, and two on shore near the torpedo boat slips on Tiger Tail Peninsula. During bombardment, the division of four cruisers remained about 10 miles off the entrance, apparently for the purpose of observing effect of fire. The material damage done was insignificant, though the people of the town were much disturbed and many of them, along with a great many Chinese, fled.

The practice might be considered good at the ranges used, of about 17,000 yards, and there were killed one man and two women, a Chinaman, an ishvostchik, two soldiers wounded, and one officer and two soldiers contusioned in Golden Hill Battery, and one soldier wounded in Electric Battery. One shell fell in water near *Retvizan*, bursting and killing two men in steam cutter alongside, and wounding 20 men engaged in working on caisson. (Shortly after, *Retvizan* taken into East Basin, 12″ guns removed and repairs begun). Nearly all shells striking on shore burst, and about two-thirds of those that struck the water, these sending up a column of black smoke and spray. Several times it was noticed that two shots fell near together, as if both guns from a turret had been fired. There was a distinct feeling of physical discomfort when a shell burst within 50 yards of any person, some people getting sick at the stomach, and several having severe nervous shock. The constant aggressive tactics of the Japanese were beginning by now to have a distinct influence on the morale of the Russian fleet, which from this time on seemed to suffer a gradual deterioration with both officers and men, particularly in the case of the senior officers.

On March 17, Lieutenant General Smirnoff arrived from Russia, having been 19 days en route and assumed duties of commandant of the fortress of Port Arthur, relieving General Stessel who was assigned to duty as Commander in Chief of the fortified region of Kwan Tung.

In the early morning of March 22, began the prelude to another aggression by the Japanese, consisting as usual in activity of their torpedo boats about the entrance. Shortly after midnight they were detected by the searchlights ashore, and after being fired on by shore batteries, and the guardboats *Bobr* and *Otvajny* at the entrance for about 20 minutes, were driven off. Again about 4 a.m. three destroyers approached, were detected and fired on, and, after about a quarter-hour, were compelled to retire, though they had evidently made an attempt to use torpedoes in the meantime, for next morning two were picked up on the beach.

At 6:30 a.m. the Japanese fleet, 17 ships and eight destroyers, appeared to southward off the entrance, and Russian fleet started out, with *Askold* in advance flying flag of Admiral Makaroff, followed by *Bayan, Novik, Pobieda, Peresviet, Poltava,* and *Petropavlovsk*, and some torpedo boats. Russian ships remained under shelter of the sea batteries and Japanese fleet made no move to attack them, but divided into three sections, cruisers remaining off the entrance, one division to southward, and one to southeastward, while the armored ships took up position off Liaotishan and between Liaotishan lighthouse and Pigeon Bay, and began firing on vicinity of lighthouse at 9:20 a.m. At 9:40 *Sevastopol* began with indirect fire over the hills at the Japanese fleet off Liaotishan, the *Fuji* and *Yashima* answering by firing on the town. Japanese fired about 100 shots into the town and 108 at Liaotishan, as before doing very little material damage. *Sevastopol* wrecked mount of starboard forward 12″ gun, damage that the Navy Yard was unable to repair, and that gun remained out of commission for the rest of the war. Bombardment ceased at 11 a.m., and Japanese fleet retired to southeast, Russian fleet reentering harbor. During bombardment

Russians lost nine killed and 11 wounded, and town and batteries suffered insignificant damages.

The Japanese seemed surprised to encounter their own tactics of indirect fire used against them and were somewhat at a disadvantage, for while they could not see their target, the Russians could accurately plot every shot falling near the Japanese vessels, and claimed to have made at least one good hit, several shots falling near *Fuji*. Still, at the ranges used, a hit from either side that would do material damage would have been due to pure chance. The Russians now were constructing heavy gun batteries on Liaotishan, two 6″ naval guns being placed on the highest peak near wireless signal station, and other batteries placed near lighthouse and on point to southward of Pigeon Bay.

On March 26, Admiral Makaroff made a cruise with five battleships, four cruisers and eight torpedo boats, visiting first the Miao Tao Islands, and extending the cruise about 20 miles to the eastward without encountering the main Japanese fleet. While out on this cruise a small steamer, the *Kanyu Maru* of 75 tons, was captured while towing a junk and it was attempted to tow her in, but the bitts carrying away, both steamer and junk were sunk by gun fire and the crew consisting of 10 Japanese and 11 Chinese brought to Port Arthur. On steamer and junk were found parts of wireless outfit, two mines, and some Japanese in Chinese dress.

In the evening, the fleet returned and moored inside in usual berths, the *Otvajny* and *Bobr* mooring close inside entrance along with two destroyers alongside. The moon had hardly set, about 2 a.m., when torpedo boats were discovered about the entrance. The search lights were turned on them and fire opened from the batteries and guard ships.

Soon were made out a group of torpedo boats apparently leading in another group of four large ships, indicating another attempt to block the entrance. After being discovered and kept under the rays of the search lights, the torpedo boats hauled off to one side and the four large ships continued straight in at full speed. This attack of the branders came very nearly being successful. Further out at sea other Japanese ships turned their searchlights on the entrance and lighted it up faintly, being of considerable assistance to the branders.

The *Silnyi* was particularly well handled that night, using both torpedoes and guns with nerve and judgment. On the leading brander she fired with torpedoes, striking it at the forefoot near water line on port side, exploding and blowing a hole about four feet in diameter, the bows marked by fragments and interior of ship considerably damaged. This brander was the *Fukiu Maru* under Commander Hirose, who was engaged in the first attempt, and was heading fair for the entrance and only a short distance away, but as a result of the hit, whether from force of explosion or damage to bows, turned a little to starboard and beached under the signal station.

The brander astern followed lead of *Fukiu Maru* and beached in same place, about 50′ to one side. The third brander was also struck by torpedo from *Silnyi* and sank about 150′ astern from the first two. The fourth ship, the *Yoneyama Maru*, having on board a Japanese who had acted for some years as a pilot for Port Arthur and knew the channel well, sheered in time and ran her nose against the starboard quarter of *Hokoku Maru*, beached on west side of entrance, under lighthouse, and was blown up either by the crew or by torpedo from *Ryeshitelni*. She sank almost athwart the channel, the entering range bearing over the after part of her, and reducing the width of the channel by about 100 feet.

The *Silnyi* lying off the entrance, now encountered five Japanese destroyers and torpedo boats, waiting to pick up the crews of the branders and had a hot fight with them for several minutes. Some of these destroyers were of the two-funnel type, and *Silnyi* was at first in doubt whether they were Russian or Japanese, and made the recognition signal to one of them with a lamp.

The Japanese boat, which was very close aboard, instantly replied with all her guns, and *Silnyi* was seriously damaged, steam pipes being cut, and engineer and six men killed, Lieutenant Krinitzki and 12 men wounded. *Silnyi* was then beached under signal station, and next day taken into basin for repairs. As soon as attack developed, Admiral Makaroff in a steam launch went on board the guard boat *Bobr* outside, and personally superintended the operations of the night. *Ryeshitelni* was engaged also with guns and torpedoes, claiming to have torpedoed *Yoneyama Maru*, and was lightly injured.

In the attack the branders carried each two 37 mm Hotchkiss revolving cannon which were used against the torpedo boats, guard ships and searchlights, some of the shells falling in the town. It seems somewhat remarkable that a boat from the *Yoneyama Maru,* sunk almost exactly in the entrance, was able to escape, but it did with most of the crew. Besides the damages from the torpedo, the *Fukiu Maru* seemed to have suffered practically no effects from gunfire, and nearly all her above-water body could be plainly seen. The brander next to her on the beach, the *Chiyo Maru,* and also showing most of the above-water body, likewise suffered little damage from gun fire, only a few hits from small caliber guns being discoverable.

The brander just astern of these two, the *Yohiko Maru,* had upper deck and rails awash and little could be seen of her upper works, but these showed no signs of effect of gun fire. The *Yoneyama Maru* had upper deck awash at low water, and apparently had been hit several times, but no accurate observations could be made. Altogether the guns seemed to have been able to accomplish very little under the circumstances in either the first or second brander attempts.

About 4 a.m. the Japanese torpedo boats withdrew, and firing ceased, but opened again for a short while about 5 a.m. on torpedo boats apparently engaged in rescuing the crews of the branders. At 6 a.m. Japanese main squadron was sighted to the southward and batteries fired a few shots at them, but they soon withdrew to the southeast and out of range. On *Yoneyama Maru* after sinking was observed a signal hoisted apparently to indicate that she believed she had succeeded in blocking the channel. The weather that night was misty and at times during the attacks foggy. About 8 a.m. *Bayan* and *Novik* went out to observe the enemy and so indicated to him that the channel was yet clear.

These determined attempts by the enemy to block the entrance impelled Admiral Makaroff to take extreme measures to prevent the accomplishment of their plans. Four large merchant steamers in the harbor, the *Shilka, Kharbin, Edward Beire* and *Khailar,* were sunk on each side of fairway so as to mask all except a narrow channel. These steamers on eastern side of entrance, together with sunken branders, protected a small area inside of which the guard ships afterward moored, and which protected them from attacks by torpedo boats. During some of the later attacks on these guard ships, which were reported by the Japanese as struck by torpedoes, they evidently mistook a hit on the sunken ships for hits on the guard ships.

The continued activity of Japanese torpedo boats about the entrance indicated placing of mines, and sweeping operations were occasionally undertaken to clear the channels, though this maneuver did not reach its full importance and development until after the sinking of the *Petropavlovsk.* The water batteries of two or three small caliber rapid fire guns were placed alongside entrance on each side, guard ships were always kept moored on each side just inside the entrance, and the larger steam cutters were equipped with 11″ torpedo tubes and torpedoes and cruised at night off entrance.

On the night of April 12, at 6:30 p.m., two divisions consisting of eight destroyers were sent out on a scouting expedition under Captain Bubnoff and Commander Elisseieff, with orders, if meeting the enemy, to attack him. One of these boats was the *Strashni,* lately put in commission and commanded by Commander Yurasofski, recently arrived from Russia, and having had very little experience in torpedo boat work. This, like the cruise of the *Steregustchi,* was one of the first cruises made by the *Strashni* and the second trip by her present captain. That night the *Diana* was guard ship near the entrance, and Admiral Makaroff, whose custom was always to place himself near any probable scene of action, spent the night on board.

During night the lights and silhouettes of boats were seen about three miles out, and the captain of *Diana* suggested to the admiral that they were probably engaged in placing mines. The admiral seemed to agree with this idea and said "We will drag for them tomorrow morning." The *Bayan* was under orders to get out at daylight in support of the torpedo boats, and very fortunately was on her way out when, just at daylight, the signal station reported a Russian torpedo boat attacked by superior force and in distress. During the night, which was thick with occasional rain, the Russian destroyer division cruised well to eastward toward Elliott Islands, then to westward, and about 11 p.m. the *Strashni* became separated from her consorts and about 2 a.m. picked up a Japanese division of four boats which she mistook for her own.

On the other side, two Japanese boats attached themselves to *Strashni* division in her place, cruising with division until 3 a.m., then separating. Russians did not fire on the two boats because although it was suspected that both could not be Russians, it was uncertain until next day if one of them was not the *Strashni.* The *Smyeli* also got mixed up with Japanese boats, but her officers were more experienced and during the night identified them as enemies and quietly slipped away in the darkness, next morning being near *Strashni,* but unable to give assistance against superior force, and herself barely escaping from pursuing boats.

The *Strashni* accompanied her enemies until near daylight, when they approached some Japanese cruisers which received them in a friendly way. *Strashni* knowing no Russian cruisers were out, having now doubts, hoisted her flag, to which the answer from the other boats was a broadside at close range. She fired a torpedo at cruiser and turned to run, but the chase lasted only a few minutes until the forward torpedo was struck and exploded and the steam pipes cut, when she necessarily stopped.

By this time her commander and all the officers, except Lieutenant Melleieff, and many of the crew were killed or wounded, and the boat helpless and sinking. Lieutenant Melleieff himself manned one 3-pdr. gun and kept up fire as long as possible on the Japanese boats, which with superior artillery, continued to play on him at very close ranges. The boat sank and those of the crew left alive were in the water. The *Bayan* was sighted coming up, and soon arrived at the scene of the wreck, placed herself between the swimming men and the Japanese ships, and while engaging them with the starboard battery, lowered a boat on the port side, and rescued five men of the *Strashni's* crew, one badly wounded. Hoisting her boat, she then turned and covered the retreat of two other torpedo boats which were making for the harbor chased by four Japanese destroyers, all the time engaging a division of six Japanese cruisers of which two were armored, approaching from southeast, at ranges from 10,000 to 6,000 yards. This was one of the many gallant things to credit of *Bayan,* and for which her commander, Captain Viren, was decorated with St. George cross. The particular merit seemed to consist in the fact that on one side of *Strashni* were approaching at full speed six Japanese ships and on the other side *Bayan* alone, and it was uncertain whether if *Bayan* continued to the rescue, if she too might not be cut off, for at the moment no other Russian ship had left the harbor, and the *Strashni* had sunk about six miles out, or just outside the limit of effective range of shore batteries. She received many new decorations from fragments of shells, but only one direct hit.

When Admiral Makaroff learned of desperate plight of *Strashni*, he first ordered *Diana* to support *Bayan*, and then almost immediately gave orders for fleet to get underway and boarded the *Petropavlovsk* as first ship to go out, her captain being in the habit of handling her going in or out without tugs and so having the advantage in mobility over other ships of the fleet. *Diana* and *Petropavlovsk* joined *Bayan* and approached Japanese cruiser division of six vessels, exchanging shots at long range, the Japanese retiring and at 8:40 a.m. being joined by a battleship division of four vessels, and the Russians being gradually reinforced by *Askold, Novik, Poltava, Peresviet* and *Pobieda* as they came out, column being formed with cruisers at the head in order of *Askold, Bayan, Diana, Petropavlovsk, Poltava, Peresviet, Pobieda* and *Novik*, and heading to southeast with *Vsadnik, Gaidamak* and five torpedo boats on left flank. Russian fleet turned to the eastward and reformed, *Petropavlovsk, Poltava, Peresviet,* and *Pobieda* in one column, and the cruisers in another column headed by *Askold*, then headed back for entrance.

In returning, and when about three miles southeast of signal station on Golden Hill, at 9:43 a.m., *Petropavlovsk* ran on a mine, one of 30 placed by the division of Japanese torpedo boats the night before, and which Admiral Makaroff intended to drag for that morning, but in the haste to give aid to *Strashni* had not been able to do.

There were three explosions, first the muffled explosion of a mine under starboard side forward, shock very slight, with a column of water and black smoke, then another almost immediately after of much greater force, with greenish yellow smoke, evidently from the magazines of the ship itself, and flame reaching to forward bridge. Evidence of a commission of naval officers leads to believe that the magazines and 12″ shells both exploded. In the gun cotton room were 15 mines with about 180 pounds of gun cotton in each, and these too must have gone up as a consequence of magazine explosion. This explosion was direct cause of ship's sinking, the whole forward part of ship being wrecked and enveloped in flames, mast and funnels falling, bridge wrecked, forward turret hood blown off into the water, and ship practically breaking in two. Bows dipped and ship listed heavily to starboard, stern rising in the air and screws still turning. There was a final explosion a little later probably of some of the ship's boilers, and in less than two minutes from the time of the first explosion, nothing remained of *Petropavolovsk* but a few swimming men and floating wreckage.

At first it was the general impression amongst the Russian fleet that a submarine had been at work, and firing was begun at everything that looked like a periscope. The other ships lowered boats and picked up survivors, and following *Peresviet* started again for harbor, when *Pobieda* too struck a mine which exploded almost exactly amidships on starboard side and between lower edge of armor belt and bilge keel (See sketch No. 6). The hole was approximately of a square shape about seven feet each way, and plating was depressed maximum two feet for a distance of 30′ fore and aft and 10′ vertically. Upper side limited by armor shelf, lower side by bilge keel, and after edge of hole being along transverse bulkhead. Outboard side of 6″ magazine in coal bunkers was bulged in to a depth of one foot, but not broken through, considerable credit being given to protection afforded by coal bunkers which were nearly full. Without difficulty *Pobieda* was taken into dock, and listed to port to await construction of caisson.

Far beyond the loss of the battleship to the Russians was the loss of their energetic and fearless admiral. Officers and men gave him the completest confidence, and under him still believed in the possibility of ultimate victory. From the moment of his arrival, affairs seemed to move. He organized a system of indirect fire to reply to the Japanese bombardments, kept the torpedo boats moving and acquiring experience even if at a somewhat high price, took the fleet out on cruises about the entrance to let them at least become accustomed to being afloat in the presence of the enemy, sank the merchant steamers in such a way as to make the blocking of the entrance almost impossible, and kept on fairly good terms with the

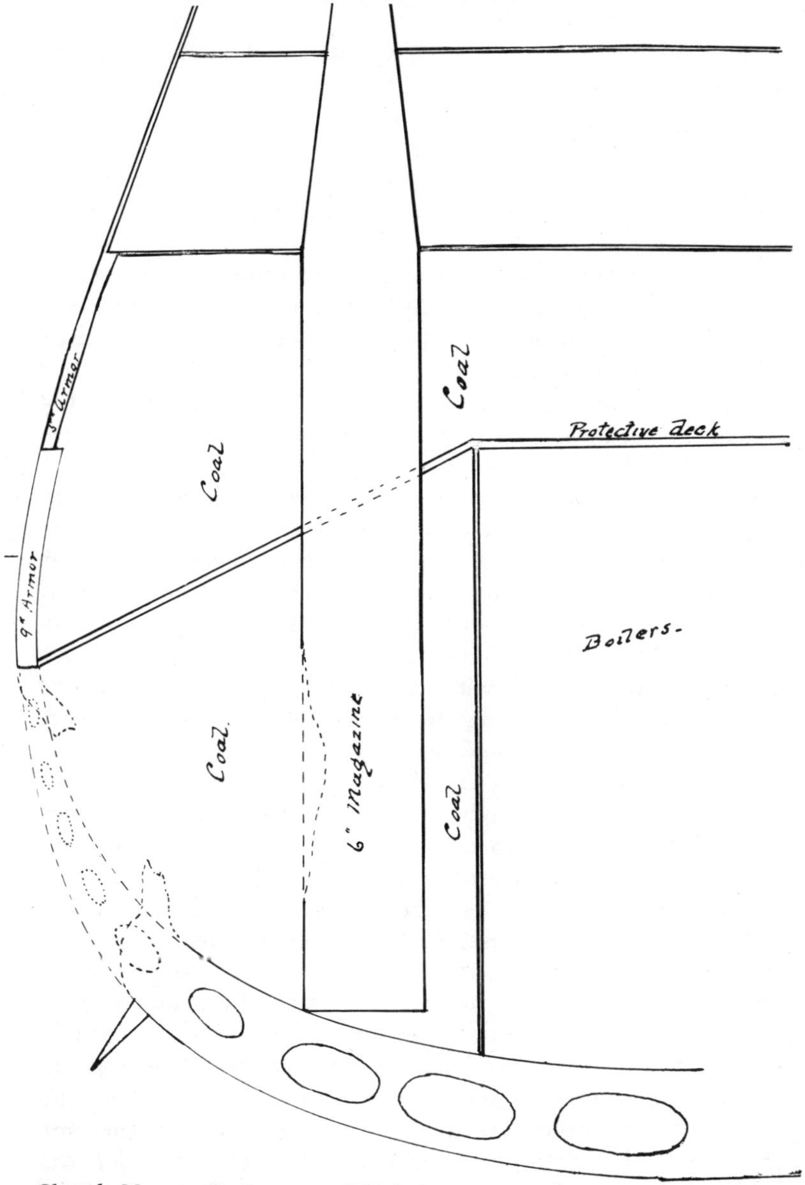

Sketch No. 6 Damage to *Pobieda* by mine explosion; information from officers attached to ship.

army, where his prestige was acknowledged and respected. In the night attacks he was in the first line in gunboat, torpedo boat, steam cutter or whatever might be at hand, and he would hoist his flag in the first ship getting out of the harbor. Often he would pass the night in one of the guard boats at the entrance, doing so even on Easter night, when the Russians have a big religious celebration.

An incident I learned of him was that when one of our ships, the *Minneapolis*, came into Kronstadt, he came out in the boat with the boarding officer, without revealing his identity and incognito, noted the manner in which she came to anchor, and observed details that later on when he came to pay official visits might not have been evident. He was quite a young man still, having been born in 1848 in Sitka, Alaska, then having lived at Nikolaevsk on the Amur, and afterward appointed midshipman in 1868. His loss, too, came at a time when the injured ships were approaching completion, and when the spirit of the fleet again began to run high with the anticipation of victory when they should meet the enemy with their entire fleet and under his leadership. This was a blow from which the morale of the Russian fleet never recovered.

The admiral was evidently killed by the second explosion, one of the rescued sailors testifying that he saw him lying face down, bloody, and insensible in the wreck of the forward bridge. Besides Admiral Makaroff, amongst the lost, were Rear Admiral Molas, chief of staff, four commanders (one of them being Commander Krown of the *Mandjour* disarmed March 30 at Shanghai, and who had made a visit to Japan and was out on *Petropavlovsk* unofficially and not on duty), and 21 officers, besides the priest and the painter Verestchagin. Seven officers and 73 men were saved.

Among those saved from the *Strashni* was a coal passer named Tennison. Some time later he was sent from the Seaman's Barracks to the *Vlastni*, and when questioned by one of the officers said he had been first on the *Boyarin*, then on *Vnushitelni*, then went to the *Strashni*, all three vessels having been lost. This rather staggered the officer who decided that he did not want a man with so much bad luck. The man protested and wanted to know why they were not willing to receive him, asserting that he was a good worker, but the officer had to decline. His story of the *Strashni* was that in the morning of April 13, when they found they were in the midst of the enemy they started to run back.

"Did you make good speed?"

"Oh, yes, we made good speed."

"Did the Japanese boats make good speed?"

"Oh, yes, they made good speed too, but after a little while our steam pipe was cut, and the torpedo exploded, and as it was very warm in the fireroom I went on deck to get cool. Many men were killed and the *Strashni* was sinking aft and I saw Lieutenant Melleieff was fighting a 3-pdr. gun by himself. Then a shell came and splashed water over me and I was cold and went down in the fire room to get warm, but soon *Strashni* sank and we were all in the water. We thought the *Bayan* was a Japanese ship, and Lieutenant Melleieff said 'Well, better die.' Then he sank. After that the *Bayan*'s boat picked five of us up, but I am a good worker, why don't you want me on the *Vlastni*?"

After the *Petropavlovsk* disaster, the Russians became rather mine-struck, and more attention was paid to mining operations. They engaged constantly in sweeping for mines, over the anchorage at entrance, and themselves placed many mines, over spaces not reserved for anchorage and channels. In vicinity of wreck of *Petropavlovsk* was dragged up next day a group of four mines of the Japanese model and stamped with Japanese stamps.

During the morning of April 15, fourteen Japanese ships could be seen off Port Arthur, amongst them for the first time the *Nisshin* and *Kasuga*, their first appearance in action. They were sent immediately to westward of Liaotishan, and had their gun trials in another long-range bombardment of Port Arthur, and of sea batteries of Liaotishan, firing about 185 shots. Bombardment was as usual very disagreeable, but without material results, Russians having five wounded soldiers, but seven Chinese were killed by a shell which fell in the midst of some crowded houses on Peripolichnaya. *Pobieda* and *Peresviet* answered with indirect fire, but apparently also without effect.

On April 15 the Emperor ordered Vice Admiral Skrydloff to the command of the Pacific fleet, but the admiral was for some time busy making speeches, listening to addresses, and receiving icons, so that he did not get started from St. Petersburg until May 3.

This is somewhat in contrast with the movements of Admiral Makaroff who received the Emperor's order on February 14, and arrived in Port Arthur March 8.

On April 16 the Viceroy returned to Port Arthur and on April 17 hoisted his flag on *Sevastopol* as commander in chief, pending arrival of Admiral Skrydloff.

Until May 2 there was little doing, except the continual dragging for mines, a few scouting trips with torpedo boats, and almost every night activity of Japanese boats about the entrance. These would come in, apparently for obtaining information and placing mines, would be fired on by batteries and then run, probably sending in a few shells at the shore projectors. The larger Russian ships kept inside. On April 22 was a serious accident to one of the boats dragging for mines, the boat being blown up, and an officer and 22 men killed.

During the night of May 2–3 was the last, most elaborate and thoroughly planned of all the attempts to close the entrance. Ten branders were prepared, provided with machine guns and two with projectors, and each was assigned a number and the position in which it was to be sunk, and the Japanese ships assisted with their projectors to light up entrance. The Russians too had made more complete preparations. Three guard ships were at the entrance, the *Ghiliak, Gremiastchy,* and *Otvajny* with three torpedo boats secured alongside, one moored alongside sunken brander *Yoneyama Maru,* right across the entrance, the others on each side just inside. Additional water batteries of small caliber RF guns were placed along the beach, and steam cutters armed with automobile torpedoes and tubes cruised just outside the entrance. Besides the ships sunk by Admiral Makaroff to mask the entrance, booms and chain spans covered the intervals, and extra mines were placed.

But of more value than all the Russian preparations to defeat the Japanese plans were the weather conditions. A strong wind from southeast was blowing, making a nasty sea, and the night was thick, though moon showed occasionally. The weather was so bad that the Japanese had decided to postpone the attempt, but for the same reason communication could not be made with the officers commanding the branders and the attack was carried out anyway. As an illustration of how desperately it was carried out, two of the branders passed through the hail of shells from the ships and batteries, escaped the mines and torpedo boats, charged the booms, broke through between the sunken ships and beached themselves close under the lighthouse and a little to westward of the *Hokoku Maru* and *Yoneyama Maru*.

The first sign of the approaching attack was as usual the appearance of a group of five destroyers about 1 a.m., to the eastward of the entrance apparently as a diversion. These were fired on by the shore batteries and compelled to retire. The first brander showed up almost immediately after, advancing straight for the entrance, but was stopped and sunk outside the booms. At 1:45 two more appeared, also being stopped and sunk by the gun fire and from fouling the already sunken ships.

Then at 2:25 came yet four more almost simultaneously, two of which, the *Otaru Maru* and *Sagami Maru*, broke through the barrier, beached themselves and sunk, but still failing to close the channel. Another brander, of large size, painted gray, and having figure "3" on bow, at first came in straight for the entrance, but either suffering damage or becoming confused swerved to the eastward, then turned and came in again, running up on rocks under Electric Battery. This was probably the *Asagao Maru*, and all of her hull and upper works could be easily inspected, and no signs whatever observed of effects of gun fire. The *Askold*, moored in usual berth off the city landing, took part in the firing.

As these last branders came in they kept up an uninterrupted fire from their machine guns on the torpedo boats, guard ships, and projectors, but doing practically no damage whatever. The last group of these branders came in at 2:40, one being sunk well out by fire from batteries or by mines, and the other two, realizing the impossibility of accomplishing their task, turned and stood out to sea.

The branders used in the third attempt were the *Mikawa Maru*; *Sakura Maru*, 2,978 tons; *Totomi Maru*, 1,953; *Yedo Maru*; *Otaru Maru*, 2,548; *Sagami Maru*, 1,926; *Aikoku Maru*, 1,773; *Asagao Maru*, 2,464; *Fusan Maru*, 2,501; and the *Kokura Maru*, 2,596, of which the first struck wreck and was blown up, two got inside wreck line, four more were sunk, one beached and two escaped. Occasionally destroyers could be seen until daylight engaged in the attempt to rescue the crews of the sunken ships, but owing to the bad weather and vigilance of the Russians they had very little success.

Some of the branders launched boats and attempted to get away, but under the fire of machine guns and riflemen from shore, only one succeeded in doing so. Even some of the generals took rifles and tried their markmanship on the boats full of men attempting to escape under the light of the projectors. This was done on the theory that these men being select men from the fleet and probably their bravest, they could not be spared. One boat crew pulling out tried the subterfuge of feigning death, falling over the thwarts and stopping rowing while in the glare of the searchlights, then rowing again as soon as the lights were off. This availed them little however for the machine guns soon converted their sham into a stern reality.

The next morning 30 men were picked up by the Russians, clinging to the masts and spars of the sunken ships; nearly all them being wounded by the continued fire of the riflemen. The Viceroy this night, taking a leaf from Admiral Makaroff's book, took station on the advanced guard boat and remained there until the attack was repulsed. During this attack the Russian batteries seem to have made better practice than during the two previous attacks. Some of the batteries claimed to have sunk two Japanese torpedo boats and probably did get one. Out of the 148 officers and men sent in by the Japanese only 65 returned, nearly all the others having been killed or drowned, making the attempt an exceedingly costly one, and apparently at last convincing the Japanese that the blocking of the entrance was a feat beyond their power. Certainly it is a most difficult thing to accomplish, and their failure to succeed may be attributed to the same causes which made their torpedo boat attacks abortive, lack of cool judgment, and probably poor eyesight.

As if merely waiting the outcome of this attack, the Japanese now began on their final plan for the reduction of the difficult fortress. On May 4 gunboats made a reconnaissance of Pitzewo, and the next morning the landing was begun. On the receipt of this news the Viceroy did not wait to collect his staff, but at 11 a.m. left very hurriedly on his special train for the north. M. Plancon, his diplomatic agent, and General Kuzmin-Korovaieff, his chief of administration and jurisprudence, were left behind along with some lesser lights of the staff. On the approach of the Japanese to the landing at Pitzewo, the signal station post was prematurely abandoned and they landed without encountering any opposition whatever, the cavalry post retiring without firing a shot. Their transports were for several days an inviting target for attack by torpedo boats, but Admiral Vitgeft thought it too far for them to go from their base.

In leaving Port Arthur, the Viceroy published the following order No. 34: "In leaving Port Arthur to go to the active armies in accordance with an order of His Imperial Majesty the Emperor, etc."—in which he thanks the officers and crews of the ships for their services. In another order he designated his chief of staff, Rear Admiral Vitgeft, as temporary commander in chief of the squadron, with instructions to hoist his flag on one of the battleships.

It was well the Viceroy had left so quickly for within 12 hours after his departure a small detachment of Japanese making a forced march from Pitzewo and nowhere meeting with any opposition, had made an attack on the railway line, and interrupted communications. In commenting on the abandonment of Pitzewo in Order No. 170, General Stessel officially notes the fact that all persons connected with the civil department (including telegraphists), left their posts a considerable time before the enemy had even landed. They were to be courtmartialed and all civil officials who might abandon their stations were warned that they would be sent before a drumhead court-martial if they did not on each single occasion have General Stessel's personal authority to do so.

The Japanese were at serious disadvantages in landing at this place, and a small force could have hindered them materially, and probably caused considerable losses before the landing was secured. It could have been foreseen that the vicinity of Pitzewo might be selected as the landing place, as the only one available on eastern side of Liaotung, the western shore being eliminated as too dangerous as long as there were any ships at Port Arthur capable of moving. Besides, so far, the Japanese were but repeating the operations in the Chino-Japanese war of 1894.

May 8—June 26, 1904

Port Arthur

On May 8, 1904, Lieutenant General Stessel commanded the 3rd Siberian Corps, and all the defenses of the fortified region of Kwan Tung, subordinate to General Kouropatkin, commander in chief of all the Active Forces in Far East. The 3rd Corps was composed of the 4th and 7th Rifle Divisions and one regiment from the 2nd Division, with two brigades of artillery, and one squadron of Cossacks, all Siberian troops, and supposed to be the best regiments. Lieutenant General Smirnof was commandant of the fortress, and as yet took no active part in the defense, but according to the Russian War Regulations would have absolute and independent control of all operations if the troops should all be withdrawn into the fortress, and the fortress besieged. The total number of men, including the crews of the ships, was 49,000, of which there were available for active operations outside the fortress 32,500 including the sailors from the Seamen's Barracks, and a naval brigade from the fleet of 1,500 men.

Rear Admiral Vitgeft was commander in chief of the naval forces, the command falling to him as the senior on departure of the Viceroy, May 5. He always laid stress on the fact that he was only temporarily in command, which he construed to limit his authority in directing operations, and kept up this pose until the end. Rear Admiral Prince Ukhtomskii* commanded the 2nd Battleship Division, Rear Admiral Lojinski was in charge of the naval part of shore defense controlling boom defenses, mining and sweeping operations, and directing movements of gunboats, mine vessels and destroyers. Rear Admiral Matussiévitch was in command of Seamen's Barracks or "Ekipazh," and Rear Admiral Grigorovich,** commandant of the navy yard. Captain Reitzenstein,*** flying

* Prince Esper E. Ukhtomskii (born 1861).

** Ivan K. Grigorovich (born 1853).

*** Nikolai K. Reitzenstein (born 1854).

broad pennant of a commodore on the *Askold*, commanded cruiser squadron. *Novik* belonged to cruiser squadron, but when acting with shore defense formed part of Admiral Lojinski's command. Flag of temporary commander in chief was hoisted on *Sevastopol*, whose captain, von Essen,* acted as chief of staff.

On my arrival the following ships were present: battleships *Tsésarévitch*, *Retvizan*, *Pobieda*, *Peresviet*, *Sevastopol* and *Poltava*; cruiser squadron *Askold* (flag), *Diana*, *Pallada*, *Bayan* and *Novik*; gunboats *Ghiliak*, *Gremiastchy*, *Otvajny*, *Bobr*, *Rasboynik*, *Zabiaca* and *Djidjit*; mine vessel *Amur*; transport *Angara*; torpedo gun vessels *Vzadnik* and *Gaidamak*; destroyers *Boevoi*, *Boiki*, *Burni*, *Lieutenant Bourakoff*, *Bezstrashni*, *Bezshumni*, *Bezposhadni*, *Bditelni*, *Vuinoslivi*, *Vlastni*, *Vnimatelni*, *Grosovoi*, *Storozhevoi*, *Rastoropni*, *Skori*, *Serditi*, *Silnyi*, *Ryeshitelni*, *Raziastchy*, *Smyeli*, *Stroini* and *Statni*; a small government steamer *Silatch*, used for surveying purposes; hospital ship *Mongolia*; Russian steamer *Kuzan*, Norwegian steamer *Sentis*, two small Russian steamers, five steam dredges, nine small steamers for dumping dredged material, several tugs and water boats, three floating cranes, two submarines, and a number of coal barges, lighters and junks.

Of these *Retvizan* and *Tsésarévitch* were in East Basin, repairs to injuries produced by torpedo attack approaching completion. (Russian naval authorities in Port Arthur refused to allow me ever to inspect injuries to any ships.) *Retvizan*'s forward 12″ guns were landed and all her 6″ guns and some 12-pdr. had been placed in the land defenses. *Pobieda* was in East Basin also waiting completion of caisson to begin repairs on injuries from striking mine on the day of *Petropavlovsk* disaster. All of her 6″ guns and 12-pdrs. were placed in the land defenses. The starboard forward 12″ of *Sevastopol* was lying on the dock, the mount having been wrecked in attempting high angle fire in answer to Japanese bombardment. In its place in the forward turret was mounted a wooden dummy gun kept covered by canvas. *Peresviet* and *Poltava* and all the cruisers seemed in good shape. The gunboats *Bobr*, *Gremiastchy* and *Otvajny* were in fair condition, but had old batteries with short guns, using brown powder. *Chiliak* was of modern type and more efficient, but carried

---

* Nikolai O. von Essen (born 1860).

only light guns. *Razboynik* and *Djidjit*, old wooden sloops with steam and sail, were in ordinary* with batteries removed, and moored in West Basin. *Zabiaca* of similar type was moored close to railway station, battery removed and sent to the land defenses, but still in commission with crew on board. *Vzadnik, Gaidamak*, and 12 destroyers were available for immediate service, nine other destroyers having slight repairs and overhauling going on, and one, the *Statni*, uncompleted and not yet in commission.

Of these destroyers *Boevoi, Boiki*, and *Burni* were an English type, the first constructed in England, the other two in Russia. *Bestrashni, Bezshumni, Bezpochadni, Bditelni* and *Lieutenant Burakoff* were German boats, the last taken from the Chinese at Taku. *Vlastni, Vnimatelni, Vuineslivi* and *Grosovoi* were French boats, and the remaining 12 were of practically the same type, nine of them being constructed by the Nevski Works in St. Petersburg, sent out by rail in sections, and put together in Port Arthur. The *Burakoff* only could make 30 knots, all the others being 26 to 28 knots, with actual speeds of only 20 to 25 knots. The English, German and French boats had one 12-pdr. forward and five 3-pdrs., but the Nevski boats had only one 12-pdr. and three 3-pdrs.

The Russian destroyers then were inferior in both speed and armament to the Japanese destroyers which were all 30-knot boats with a battery of one 12-pdr. mounted aft and five 6-pdrs. according to information, but as a matter of fact based on observation of them in action, they seemed to have a 12-pdr. forward also. The mine vessel *Amur* was in excellent condition and of great value. *Angara* and *Kazan* were later on converted into hospital ships, and there was a good deal of discussion about what to do with the *Sentis*, though it ended by keeping her in Port Arthur, the Russian government assuming responsibility. The steam dredges were at work in the West Basin, the dumping steamers taking mud out to sea.

One of the submarines consisted of a cylindrical body with conical ends, motive power furnished by hand, and of entirely obsolete model and unserviceable. However, experiments were made with it, and results quite widely advertised in the newspapers as being

---

* Laid up, out of commission.

completely successful. The other submarine was a steel shell about 20′ long, tortoise shaped, with a conning tower on top in center, and underneath a frame work intended probably as torpedo launching apparatus. No idea of the motive power could be obtained, and from its shape it was difficult to decide what it might be, if indeed it possessed any. It was shipped by rail from St. Petersburg, arrived in Port Arthur about the end of April, but not put together until July, and as far as could be discovered, it was never placed afloat, nor were any attempts made to utilize it.

About the middle of March caissons were finally completed for *Retvizan* and *Tsésarévitch*, and then repairs were commenced. The idea of using these was obtained by adaptation of a similar method used previously in repairs on destroyers, when the large dock was not available, the torpedo boat dock being too small, and its successful execution reflected great credit on the Russian naval constructor in charge of repairs. The caissons were constructed of wood, framing made of heavy timbers, and of a size sufficient to cover injury to ship's bottom, and extended from near the keel to well above the water line. On the back and bottom of caisson the frame consisted of 14″ × 16″ timbers spaced two feet apart, and crossed by ties of 8″ by 12″ beams bolted across them inside. Heavy diagonal braces at all the angles. The ends were made to fit lines of ship at sections of contact, edges padded with oakum and canvas to prevent leakage where they bore on the skin of the ship. The sides and bottom of caisson were covered with 2-inch boards pitched and caulked, then outside covered with tarred paper and canvas placed over the paper to protect it against damage. Side of caisson fitting to ship was left open, caisson slung from crane, carried alongside ship at location of injury and then lowered into place. At bottom of caisson was wire span, from which a wire hawser led underneath ship and up on deck on other side being used to assist in hauling caisson down into place and holding it there.

After being adjusted over injury, pumps connected up with water inside caisson, and it was pumped out, divers being sent down to keep a lookout for leaks. As water in caisson fell, the difference in pressure forced caisson close against ship's side and when water was entirely out, the water pressure held caisson in place very securely, though preventers were still kept on. As previously noted, the caisson first constructed for *Retvizan* was too weak and collapsed, but the second was completely successful, and was afterward adapted to Sevastopol and used in making repairs to her after striking a mine on June 23.

Other small caissons were made for repairing the destroyers, and when they were in place, both destroyers and battleships could be moved about the harbor without difficulty or danger. It was necessary to build a special caisson for *Pobieda*, her injury being amidships, and owing to the experience gained with the first two ships, her repairs were finished in much less time than those of *Retvizan* and *Tsésarévitch*. The caisson was fitted to *Pobieda* and pumped out on May 22, and repairs completed on June 16. The repairs were made by filling the hole and maximum depression with wood, and plating over with thin plating, very similar to manner of repairing *Oregon*'s injury in 1902.*

The *Sevastopol* struck a mine on June 23, injury underwater on port bow, and although she could have been placed in the dock, it was elected to repair her with a caisson, adapting for her the caisson that had been used on *Retvizan* and so leaving the dock free for repair and overhauling of destroyers. This caisson required little change to make it ready, being placed on ship July 5, and repairs completed August 7. The destroyer *Serditi* had her bows stove in by a collision one night in July, and had a caisson fitted under her forefoot with which she could be towed about the harbor at five or six knots.

On the outbreak of the war, the navy yard was in no better shape for the demands likely to be made on it, than were the strength of the garrison and defenses, and the provisioning and supply of the town and garrison. Although the Russians had chosen to make Port Arthur the winter base of their active fleet, little had been done to prepare it for such duties beyond dredging out the Western Basin sufficiently to give berthing room for the

* The author was in error as to the date. The battleship *Oregon*, operating in Asiatic waters during the Boxer Rebellion, hit an uncharted rock in the Straits of Pechili on 28 June 1900, and was aground for a week before being refloated. On 17 July she went into a drydock at Kure, Japan, for repairs to her hull.

fleet. Everything about the yard was in much the same condition as when turned over by the Japanese on March 29, 1898. The large dock had been increased to 452′ in length, but the torpedo boat dock remained of the same dimensions, and was too small to accommodate any of the destroyers. The large new dock 577′ × 77′ × 34′ on south side of East Basin had been hardly begun, there was a great deficiency of skilled workmen and of ship plates, old boiler plates being used to repair *Retvizan.*

In March 1904, 252 workmen were brought out from Russia, and later on others, until about 800 were added to the working force. Much of the skilled labor in the navy yard, and all the unskilled labor was Chinese. In the shops the machines consisted almost entirely of those which were installed by the Chinese prior to the war with Japan. Most of them bore the date 1888 and were of French construction by the Fives Lille Company. Some were of Russian manufacture and a few of English, the latest date on any of them being 1899. The foundry was capable of small castings only, repairs to damaged mount of *Sevastopol*'s 12″ gun being impossible to carry out with yard facilities. Forge shops could handle light forgings only. Stores of provisions and grain were satisfactory, of coal there was 35,000 tons good Welsh, but oil stores were insufficient.

Immediately on breaking out of war, steps were taken to remedy some of the existing deficiencies. Shafts were sunk on each side of entrance to completed dock, with the intention of increasing the width of entrance and depth over sill. Work was begun enlarging the torpedo boat dock in order to accommodate the destroyers, and a large number of men were employed on the prosecution of excavation in the new dock. On this work were employed 600 Chinamen and blasting went on daily, the excavation being done almost entirely in rock. The waste material was carried off on a light railway and used for filling in the fresh water lake to eastward of East Basin.

In May Admiral Vitgeft stated that the dock would be completed in 3 months, but this was plainly impossible, and in August when work stopped on account of bombardments, the work on the old docks was only 50 per cent completed, and only 75 per cent of the excavation alone of the new dock was finished. The caisson for the new dock could not be constructed at the navy yard, and was to be forwarded from Russia, so it could not possibly have ever been of any service to the Russians until after close of the war. On the point of Tiger Tail was a building slip with three ways on which the nine destroyers sent out from the Nevski works had been put together. The last one of these, the *Statni*, was in the water, hull finished, engines and boilers on board, and was completed in July. In the navy yard regular working hours were from 7 a.m. to 7 p.m., with two hours off in the middle of the day. Work on repairs of ships went on both day and night.

The West Basin, as dredged out, had a berthing capacity for seven large ships. In the entire harbor was berthing space for ten first-class ships, and five second-class ships, and for a considerable number of small vessels. At the southwestern part of West Basin were some wharves, and on shore were under construction several large buildings, with the intention of making this an addition to the naval station. Until the middle of May active operations continued with the dredges, waste being dumped well outside entrance. After this date the dumping steamers were converted into trawlers and placed under charge of naval officers, and were from then on until the end engaged in sweeping for mines, and occasionally in laying mines.

The Old Town of Port Arthur was that portion in vicinity of East Basin, and was the only town existing during the Chinese and Japanese occupations. The town was irregularly laid out, with still the same streets and houses as existed during the Chinese occupation, and had neither sewerage nor water system and was only partially lighted. The streets, with exception of that encircling the navy yard, were of usual Chinese character, some paved, most unpaved. In dry weather the place was all dust, in wet weather all mud. In the Old Town lived all the officials of the naval administration, and most of those of the military and civil administrations, and though every effort had been made to discourage business in this town, it was still the principal business center, but each large firm was required to have a branch in the New Town. About a mile to the westward of the Old Town was this New Town, established by prikaz, in order to leave the first for military and naval purposes only.

The New Town was well laid out, with wide streets and parks, and all modern improvements in contemplation. As it was situated along the northern shore of the West Basin, where at low water the bottom is dry for a half mile from water front, business was very much handicapped. It was intended to overcome this disadvantage by dredging out along the northern shore until a deep water front could be provided, but this had progressed so far only as a narrow channel reaching about halfway from the deep water of West Basin to the shore. The town so far was only about one-fourth built up, and few of the streets finished, and very little business done there. It was necessary to use compulsion to transfer a business from the Old Town to the New, and merchants used all the means customary in dealing with Russian officials to obstruct the transfer. Previous to the war Port Arthur had been a free commercial port, and also free from operation of the censors customary in Russia, so having decided advantages over Vladivostock, whose merchants resented the distinctions made, and in their own interests were not sorry to see the place go.

From the beginning of the war there had existed some friction between the army and navy, the military authorities asking from the navy men, guns, ammunition, electrical and mining equipment. This friction was kept under control during the time that Admiral Makaroff was in command of the fleet, and as long as the Viceroy remained in Port Arthur.

After the town became isolated the conflict between the two services became more bitter. The 4,800 sailors in the Seamen's Barracks were under the control of the military authorities and it was difficult for the naval authorities to obtain men needed for the purposes of the navy yard and fleet. The batteries of *Razboynik*, *Djidjit*, and *Zabiaca* had been landed and were manned by men from the fleet. The 6″ guns and 12-pdrs. from *Retzivan* and *Pobieda*, while under repairs, had been transported to their positions,placed and manned by the sailors. The search lights and electrical outfit, in part furnished by the navy, were also manned by them. Detachments of men from the fleet under naval officers were digging trenches and constructing fixed defenses of elaborate kinds. The signalling and observation points were also manned by men from the fleet and their officers. In short, all positions requiring personnel of more than ordinary intelligence, were filled by naval men. Army officers criticised severely the inaction of the fleet and some openly denounced it as being gun-shy.

There was no cordial intercourse between Admiral Vitgeft and General Stessel, and when official communications were necessary between them, naval officers dreaded being the intermediaries, as General Stessel would vent his ill humor with the fleet by swearing at and blackguarding them. The navy had always been the petted service, and a mitchman (ensign) in the navy received 260 roubles per month, or more pay than a captain in the army. There were smaller causes, such as differences caused by birth, and a feeling between the Russians of pure Russian descent and those of German descent, which combined with unfortunate outcome in this war, and blended with the existing weaknesses in the Russian character, prevented any harmony inside either service, or between the two. One could not praise any official person to a Russian, and feel his praise approved, and it was much more likely that it would provoke the exposure of some of his weaknesses.

Besides the ships under repairs, the other ships of the fleet and the officers and men seemed in very good shape. The ships were clean, and looked efficient and the men were neat and under excellent discipline. Officers had their morale somewhat shaken, crediting the Japanese with perhaps higher qualities than they deserved, and criticizing their commander in chief more severely than he merited up to this time. All fighting ships except gunboats and destroyers had wireless telegraph outfits.

Battleships and cruisers were painted a dark grey or cinnamon color which looked almost black in the shadow, and after exposure to the weather for some time. *Novik*, gunboats and destroyers were painted a dull khaki, harmonizing well with the russet color of the coast. Later on larger ships painted funnels and masts this color, retaining cinnamon for the hulls and this was serviceable since the Russians, operating along the shore, almost always presented their brighter colored side to the enemy.

The Japanese torpedo boats were painted a light shade of drab and on a cloudy or dull day were almost undistinguishable, unless showing above horizon. At night in the search lights they looked almost white.

On shore two wireless stations were established, one at the Signal Station on Golden Hill and the other on the highest peak of Liaotishan. These, as far as I could learn, were never in communication with the outside world, though they kept touch with the ships when they were out, and when their messages were not interfered with, and claimed to have caught some Japanese messages, one with the information that Admiral Togo had been wounded.

After the landing at Pitzewo on May 5 and 6, and the first attack on the railway, the Japanese outposts were driven back for a short time, allowing the train with ammunition to get in, and another train to get out with the last of the refugees, and the rest of the Viceroy's staff. The naval attachés had an invitation from Admiral Vitgeft to take this train, but had not time to catch it. However the Japanese sent out stronger parties to the westward and southwestward from Pitzewo, and railway communication with permanently interrupted on May 11, a train from Dalny getting as far as Pulantien but being obliged to return.

The landing at Pitzewo being inconvenient, Japanese cruisers and torpedo boats investigated the coast to the southward with the idea of locating a better one. Kerr Bay was reconnoitered by destroyers on May 11, men were landed and destroyed a telephone line. Next day *Itsukushima Miyako* and four torpedo boat flotillas entered the same bay at 7:45 a.m., searched the shores, and began sweeping for mines. Three mines were picked up by the 2nd Flotilla, and another was discovered, but while being picked up it exploded and blew up No. 48 torpedo boat.

On May 14 a squadron of six ships composed of cruisers and gunboats accompanied by one division of destroyers and two torpedo boat flotillas appeared off Kerr Bay with the apparent intention of making a landing. Boats with landing parties were sent under escort of the torpedo boats and destroyers and covered by the fire of the larger ships. Russian detachment of about 350 men opened fire on landing party with rifles and two field guns, and it was driven back with considerable loss, and some injuries to *Akadsuki*. The larger ships ceased firing on the shore at 4:45 p.m. and moved out, *Miyako* striking a mine and being blown up and sunk.

The Russian version of this incident was that after most of the ships had withdrawn, *Miyako* returned and took up anchorage near buoys placed by torpedo boats. While swinging at anchor during night she fouled a mine and was destroyed. When this news was received in Port Arthur, it was given out that it was the *Asama* that had been sunk. This was based on the report of a naval officer who had been sent to Kerr Bay and visited the wreck, sounding over it, observing the tops of two funnels, two masts with light fighting tops, and measuring the distance between the masts, which apparently identified the sunken ship as *Asama*. Admiral Vitgeft firmly believed it to be the *Asama*, and stated so officially.

On land the Japanese, leaving a small force to hold Pitzewo, advanced to southward and southwestward, and took up a line across the peninsula, passing through station Sanshilipu. To the southward the principal Russian force was stationed in the vicinity of Kinchow, their outposts in contact with the Japanese near Sanshilipu, and Kerr Bay guarded by a detachment of infantry with four field guns. On the north the Russians had reoccupied Vafandian and their outposts to southeastward were in contact with the Japanese outposts 10 versts to westward of Pitzewo. A cavalry detachment scouted to within five versts of Pitzewo, but retired when fired on by field guns in position.

From May 8 till May 14, each day ships of the Japanese fleet cruised off the entrance to Port Arthur. On May 11 four battleships were seen, on May 12 three battleships and two cruisers, May 13 again four battleships, but on May 14 there was no Japanese ship in sight, the port being left absolutely unguarded. The usual route for these blockading ships was just out of range of shore batteries, about 10 miles away, and back and forth on a line running ENE—WSW. At 7 a.m. the *Amur* and 12 torpedo boats went straight out to sea with orders from Admiral Vitgeft to lay mines six miles off the entrance. Weather was fairly clear but horizon hazy, with light southerly airs. It may have been the intention of the admiral to lay the mines for action against vessels coming in at night, or that he thought it too dangerous for the *Amur* to go further out than six miles from the entrance, but otherwise it was difficult to understand the reason for placing the mines at this distance.

Since February 9, none of the larger Japanese ships had ever come in closer than 10 miles except at night, and these were either small cruisers or gunboats covering operations of torpedo boats, or assisting the branders. However, the captain of the *Amur*, Commander Fedor Ivanoff,* on his own responsibility steamed further to sea and placed 50 mines in two lines, one mile apart, at intervals of 100 yards from each other, and across the usual track of the Japanese vessels. During entire day no Japanese vessels were observed, and at 1 p.m. *Amur* and destroyers returned to harbor. The admiral was so angry at the disobedience of Captain Ivanoff, that he ordered him relieved from command. Before the order was carried into effect the results of the mine expedition were demonstrated and Captain Ivanoff was allowed to retain his command, was promoted to next higher grade and received the St. George cross. During the night of May 14–15, the Japanese approached the entrance with a number of torpedo boats, but kept well out and made no serious demonstration.

In the early morning of May 15 a Japanese division of three large ships appeared off the entrance and began cruising up and down as usual. This was the 2nd Battleship Division under Rear Admiral Nashiba, and consisted of *Yashima, Shikashima* and *Hatsuse.* Twice this column passed safely over the mine field, but at 10:10 a.m., from the shore was seen a mine explosion near the leader of the column, the *Yashima,* which then stood out to sea with a considerable list, and began to launch boats. The column slowed down and fell into some disorder, but at 10:40 the injured ship succeeded in getting back on an even keel, and the two three-funnel ships approached as if to form column again.

At this moment an explosion with column of water and smoke was seen to rise near the *Hatsuse* followed almost immediately by a second explosion showing smoke only, the explosion being heard distinctly on shore, and in approximately a minute the *Hatsuse* had gone down.

In conversation with a Russian sailor on the signal station, I asked him how quickly the *Hatsuse* went down, and he answered "More quickly than *Petropavlovsk.*" Asking him how he judged, he said "I was on *Petropavlovsk,*" and it turned out to be the quartermaster who had saved the life of Captain Yakovleff. The other two

* Fedor N. Ivanoff (born 1860).

ships, as the Russians had done on April 13, opened fire in all directions at objects floating in the water, under the same impression that explosions were caused by submarines. The damaged battleship made off to southeastward while *Shikashima* remained in vicinity of disaster for an hour longer, and a squadron of cruisers and gunboats came down from the northeastward to render assistance.

At 12:15 the Russians sent out two destroyer divisions of eight boats each under Captain Bubnoff* and Commander Elisseieff,** which approached within range of the Japanese ships but attempted no attack. The *Novik* came out and anchored off entrance, and the other Russian cruisers began to make preparations to go out. The destroyers returned at 4:30 p.m. without any casualties and reentered port. That night about 20 miles to the southeastward we could all see Japanese searchlights working for nearly two hours and clearly indicating the location of the enemy's fleet. It seemed to the attachés the decisive moment for sending out every destroyer able to move and fire a torpedo to do or die, and as naval men we were sick to see instead at such a time, twenty-one destroyers tied up in harbor.

On shore, May 15, a reconnaissance in force was made to the northward of Kinchow by General Fock with eight battalions and 17 guns. The Japanese were found five versts to the northward of Kinchow also advancing and with a strength of 24 battalions and six batteries. A skirmish followed and the Russians retreated on the Nanshan position, leaving Kinchow occupied by a very small force, and with loss of three officers and 23 men killed and 156 wounded. Kerr Bay was abandoned, the detachment skirmishing with Japanese outposts as it retired.

In the meantime between time of landing at Pitzewo, Japanese fleet had appeared at various points about the Liaotung Peninsula, firing on the beach and railway when it could be seen and threatening a landing. Inkow had been threatened, shore and railway near Kaichow fired on, Kinchow Bay occupied, and on May 17 a detachment showed up off the prominent point 15 miles south-

---

* Mikhail V. Bubnov (born 1859).

** Evgenii P. Elisiev (born 1864).

west of the Nanshan position, and attempted to make a landing in cove to southward of this point. Detachment consisted of two cruisers, two gunboats, and some torpedo boats, and 12 ship's boats were sent in about 2 p.m. as if to land. Not having reckoned on the stage of the tide, the boats grounded while still well out, and not being able to land returned to their ships.

Shortly after this General Stessel and staff coming down from a visit to the positions near Kinchow, discovered the enemy's ships, and stopping the train disembarked their horses and decided to proceed to Port Arthur on horseback. The train was sent on ahead and got through without difficulty, but the party of horsemen were more rudely treated. The gunboats approached the shore and opened fire on them with heavy guns, and on their taking shelter in a little valley, they shelled the valley. It was several hours before the distinguished party was able to proceed in safety.

During the night of May 19–20 which was dark but clear, there was a demonstration off the entrance, the object apparently being to lay mines. Four gunboats or mine vessels and two destroyers approached the entrance from the eastward about midnight, were discovered and fired on at 12:45 by the sea batteries and guard-ships *Ghiliak* and *Otvajny*. In return they fired on the shore projectors, but did no damage.

I was on my way up to the church, which was within the night limits assigned to me, and happened to be in range with the projector and the destroyer, five shells passing near and killing two men and some horses quartered on the hill 100 yards away. The practice of the batteries at these boats was very good, shells striking very close and one apparently making hit. The Japanese boats could be plainly seen two to three miles away, looming up very brightly and about them tall plumes of spray from falling shells.

Trawling for mines continued energetically every day, mines being picked up continually. On May 21 *Bezshumni* while out guarding the trawlers, had a mine explosion under the port quarter, apparently caused by disturbance to mine from effect of screw current. From the extent and character of damages, the mine could hardly have been in direct contact with the screw or the boat's hull, as there were no violent local damages, and boat returned to harbor under her own steam. The explosion must have occurred very near and probably just underneath the port screw, which was badly damaged. The deadwood amidships as far as keel line was bulged out to starboard, the stern was lifted by force of explosion and deck plates of upper deck just forward of second funnel were buckled, and required renewal. Port shaft was bent, and had to be straightened, and boat did not complete repairs until middle of July.

At Nanshan the two armies were preparing for the first serious test of strength. The Japanese had succeeded in bringing up three divisions with about eighty guns and these were massed along the railway to northward of Kinchow and on the slopes of Mount Sampson. The neck of low ground here is only one and three-fourth miles wide from shore to shore but approaches on both sides are very shoal; 12 feet can be taken to within three miles of the summit of Nanshan, so that the position there was vulnerable from the sea on both sides. On the southeast side the Russians had a battery on Liushutun Peninsula which closed the harbor of Talienwan to the Japanese vessels, and served as a support to any Russian vessels coming up to cooperate with the right flank. To northwest on their left flank the Russians had batteries of field guns only. Two more of the 6″ naval guns had been commandeered and were on flat cars bound for Nanshan to be placed on shore and guard against attack from the sea, but were not started in time to be of any use and were never removed from the cars. The Russians had two batteries of field guns from the 4th Brigade of artillery, about 50 other guns mostly captured from the Chinese and of various models, in emplacements on Nanshan, and several machine guns.

The defense was entrusted to General Fock with the 5th Regiment East Siberian Rifles, two companies of the 13th Regiment, a company of Okhotnicki (mounted scouts) from the 16 B.C., and the artillery mentioned, or a total of about 4,600 men. This position was considered by General Kouropatkin of the most vital importance, and its weak defense severely criticized. Supported from the sea it is almost impregnable, but even without such support, its defense from attack from the sea could have been much better provided for. Naturally the position is the key to the defense of Port Arthur and certainly a point that it would be indispensable to hold until the last possible moment, particularly as relief was expected from the army in the north. However, such were the measures taken for the defense.

It was one occasion also when the small old-fashioned gunboats *Sivoutch, Mandjur,* and *Korietz* might have proved of great value to the Russians, if even these craft, already in eastern waters, had been concentrated with the rest of the fleet. It is probable that the incident of the attempted landing at Inchenzi and the fact that General Stessel was present in person, and under fire, unduly impressed a man of his character with the danger of such an attempt, and the Russian forces were distributed all around the coasts of the Peninsula at every place that a landing might be attempted.

On May 25 was more or less skirmishing along the fronts, and during the night Kinchow was abandoned, and all troops concentrated in the Nanshan position. That night was a severe rain and wind storm, and next morning at 5 a.m., the battle began with artillery duel. The Japanese gunboats *Tsukushi, Saiyen, Akagi, Chokai,* and 1st Flotilla of torpedo boats came in as close as possible and fired on the Russian left flank, the *Akagi* and *Chokai* doing most of the work on account of their heavy guns, and light draft. On the Russian right flank the *Bobr* under protection of the batteries of Liushutun did excellent work, and caused heavy losses to the Japanese left flank.

This little, slow, superannuated gunboat, with her obsolete battery of one 9″ and one 6″ short BLR,* and smoky powder, with her machinery in bad condition, alone of all the fleet in Port Arthur represented the navy in the battle of Nanshan and she was sent evidently as her loss would have mattered little. Accompanied by two destroyers she had set out from Port Arthur the night before, and about 10 a.m. took position near Liushutun, and bravely blazed away until the battle was practically decided, and then still alone tottered back to the haven of rest. Before starting back her commander, in council with his officers, had decided in case of attack to beach her and blow her up, but beyond a temporary derangement of the machinery, he was not troubled.

* Breech-loading rifle.

This battle offered a chance for some effective work by the fleet, placed as it was between the two points subject to attack by the Japanese, and, besides the wireless system, having a complete system of communication by semaphore and signal stations all round the coast of the Peninsula. The battle lasted nearly all day, consisting after the artillery duel in direct frontal attacks, the Japanese advancing in heavy columns, and not deploying until they had suffered severely from the artillery fire. About 2 p.m. the Russians brought up another regiment, the 14th East Siberian, but too late to have any serious effect in the battle, and in the afternoon and evening the positions were abandoned. To the southwestward of Nanshan was a range of hills six miles long, running from Liushutun to western shore, and forming the second line, also of very great strength, and this too was abandoned. It could hardly have been done because of too great extent, because the next position taken up by the Russians was on a line about 15 miles long, across the Peninsula in its widest part. Besides apparently a stronger position, holding the Nangalin line would have facilitated communication with the north, covered Dalny, and left still available the resources of Kwan Tung in forage and cattle.

When it is considered that a Russian Force of 4,600 men at Nanshan held a Japanese army of 40,000 and inflicted a loss of over 4,000 on it themselves losing only 690 men while there were 25,000 more Russian troops not engaged, it seems reasonable that a larger and somewhat better disposed force could have held it long enough to allow of the completion of the repairs to the Russian battleships, when the fleet might, under the conditions, have become a greater factor in cooperation, and again have eased somewhat the difficult task of the relief column from the north, defeated at Vafango on June 14.

In an official proclamation to the troops, the commandant of the fortress referred to this battle as follows: "For guarding Kwan Tung our forces were divided into different detachments stationed at various gulfs and other positions. One of these positions was Kinchow. Yesterday the enemy with overwhelming strength bore on this point, but our army repulsed all attempts, and did not yield the position. In view of instructions not to exhaust themselves in advanced positions without purpose against superior forces of the enemy, and in accordance with orders, the position at Kinchow was abandoned, so that the defenders of it might unite with the garrison of Port Arthur, and arm in arm, and shoulder to shoulder, defend our stronghold Arthur. In honor of the brilliant army at Kinchow, our war comrades, we shout a thunderous hurrah." The last paragraph paid a well deserved compliment.

After this battle the army became even more bitter against the navy, saying that they could defend the front if only the navy would keep the Japanese off the army's back.

The land forces defending Port Arthur took up a new position across Kwan Tung, and passing through Inchenzi. Dalny was abandoned May 27, and 600 more people came into Port Arthur, 200 of them women and children. Several merchant steamers, some dredges and a floating crane were brought into Port Arthur, making the trip by night.

A small steamer used in mining operations, in charge of a mitchman started down and while on the way sighted some Japanese torpedo boats, and the officer commanding ran her ashore and blew her up. While being court-martialed, he was asked if the Japanese fired on him. He answered that they did not, but that they might have. All officers of *Bobr*, except one who was taken ill when the gunboat received her orders to go out, were decorated, and received well deserved honors.

On May 30 was a night demonstration off the entrance, the exact object of which was not clear. About midnight, four Japanese vessels and two destroyers came up from southward to about three miles from entrance and fired on *Ghiliak*, the guard boat, moored alongside *Yoneyama Maru*. *Ghiliak* and batteries returned fire and they retired. A few small caliber shells fell in the town, and *Ghiliak* was hit once.

On June 4, at 6:30 p.m., a group of eight destroyers came down from eastward about four miles off shore, as if on reconnaissance. No. 22 fired a few shots at them, on which they sheered a little further out, turned and went back. One of the trawling steamers ran on a mine and was blown up.

On June 6, about 11:30 p.m., firing began on two-masted, one-funnel ship approaching from southward, which quickly turned and ran out. This was evidently to distract attention of searchlights and gunners, for almost immediately another ship, apparently a merchant vessel adapted for laying mines, came down from northeastward at full speed close along shore about 2,000 yards out. She was promptly picked up by searchlights and was plainly seen to be hit three times by shells from No. 22, badly damaged and stopped, then staggered off to southeast and was joined by two destroyers. Two Russian destroyers out that night claimed to have come up with her and to have sunk her or another one with her, and the batteries also claimed to have sunk her. Whatever her fate, she did not completely fulfill her mission which was apparently to lay mines in channel close along shore to eastward or near entrance.

During this affair an accident happened to a gun in battery No. 22 in which one man was killed and several injured. The Japanese vessels had fired a few small caliber shells into this battery, and in an official order General Stessel stated that he had made a personal inspection of the gun, and found it was caused by the heavy fire of the enemy, and recommended the commanding officer of the battery for the St. George cross. It seemed remarkable that a heavy sea battery of five 6″ guns on a 300′ elevation protected by shields and earth works could suffer from the "heavy" fire of one mine transport armed with 1-pdr. HRC* at a distance of 2,000 yards at night. The mine vessel was evidently firing at the searchlight near the fifth gun which was the gun injured.

At end of May repairs of *Retvizan* neared completion and work began replacing her 6″ battery. On June 5 all her battery was on board, except some of the 12-pdrs., the caisson was removed and she began coaling. All ships repainted upper works, funnel and masts a dull khaki color, and *Novik* and gun boats painted as well the hull same color.

June 8, at 2 a.m., batteries were firing on torpedo boats off entrance, and about 10:30 to 11 p.m. again fired on some which came close in. During night of June 9 a small steamer brought in mail and despatches, and gave them to destroyer off shore. News said to be excellent, and that General Kouropatkin had come down from the north, fought a great battle with the Japanese, defeating

---

* Hotchkiss revolving cannon.

them and taking 20,000 prisoners. In the club was a great celebration, the General's health drunk with much enthusiasm and many new subscriptions turned into the fund for the construction of the battleship *General Kouropatkin.*

June 10 and 11 were very foggy, and the 10th there being a skirmish at long distance between destroyers, battery joining in but no damage done. At 6:30 p.m. eight destroyers went out of entrance, coasted up and down along edge of fog, then anchored for the night under Liaotishan. The destroyers remained out until June 12, when they returned having captured three junks. At 11 a.m., June 14, *Novik* and 10 destroyers went out to eastward and had a long range skirmish with 15 Japanese destroyers off Lunvantai, range 7,000 yards, then fired on Japanese land positions to eastward of Siaobindao and returned at 4 p.m. On June 16, *Novik, Amur* and five torpedo boats made reconnaissance of Pigeon Bay, returning at 5 p.m., and *Amur,* while entering, fouled wrecks at entrance and so damaged her screws that she was of no further use during the war. A Norwegian steamer was stopped and examined, but her papers being in order, was let go.

During night of June 17 firing was heard and flashes of big guns could be seen out to sea to southwest, but it was not connected with the movement of any Russian ships. *Bourakoff* returned from Inkow, with large bunches of information but which was not served out. On June 18 *Novik, Gremiastchy, Otvajny,* and nine destroyers under Rear Admiral Lojinski flying his flag on the *Novik,* went out to eastward and fired on Japanese left flank and returned at 5 p.m.

On June 22, Japanese mine vessels again approached entrance apparently with intention of laying mines, but were discovered and fired on from 2:30 to 2:45 a.m. At 5 p.m. six Russian destroyers were seen coming down from eastward about one mile off shore and followed by five Japanese destroyers and three torpedo boats about four miles off shore, firing going on between the two flotillas. *Otvajny* went to their assistance and Japanese turned about and steamed slowly back to eastward. Russian destroyers came in and tied up for the night. From 10:40 to 10:50 p.m. batteries and guard boats opened fire on torpedo boats attempting to lay mines.

By June 8 repairs to *Tsésarêvitch* were completed, the caisson taken off, and Admiral Vitgeft shifted his flag to her, and appointed Rear Admiral Matussiévitch his chief of staff. *Sevastopol* hoisted out her dummy gun and replaced it with the real gun, the mount still remaining out of commission. *Pobieda*'s repairs were completed June 16, and she had returned to her some of her guns, but General Bielui kept eight of her 6″ guns, and 16 of her 12-pdrs. in the land defenses, saying they could not be spared. The fleet was ready to go out any day after June 16, and evidently had that intention. However, when I asked if in case it did go out, if I might accompany it, they seemed surprised that I had acquired the knowledge, and the chief of staff asked me who told me that the fleet was going, apparently thinking that the fact could not be discerned from observation. He informed me that the fleet had no intention of going out. Still the intention was plain, though I barely thought it possible until *Pobieda* had all her guns. For several days officers had no night liberty and all the ships were smoking up and getting ready.

In the early morning of June 23 the long expected movement commenced. In an official proclamation the admiral stated that "The squadron having finished the repairs to the ships injured by a cunning enemy before notification of war now goes to sea in accordance with orders of the Viceroy to assist our comrades of the Army in the defense of Port Arthur. With the help of God and of St. Nicholas the Wonderworker, Protector of sailors, we will endeavor to perform our duty to our consciences and oaths before our Sovereign, and beat the enemy already weakened by the loss on our mines of some of his ships. The little gunboat *Bobr* has given an example of what can be done even in very difficult circumstances." Many of his captains hesitated to accept the admiral's plans of action, whatever plan he may have had in going out, condemning them as absurd.

The weather was clear and fine with light airs from the southward, daylight about 5 a.m. *Novik* was first out at 4:30, followed by *Diana*, then *Askold*, then the battleships and torpedo boats, *Tsésarévitch* passing out at 6, *Retvizan* at 7, followed by *Bayan*, when all the fleet was out except *Pallada* which had grounded inside entrance and did not get out until 9 a.m. All the fleet anchored outside wrecks, off entrance, while trawlers were being prepared to precede fleet and clear channel of mines. As fleet passed out observed that *Pobieda* had only three of her 6″ guns, and only fourteen 12-pdrs. of her battery of 22. *Peresviet* was shy the forward 6″, and *Diana* and *Pallada* lacked some of their 12-pdr. guns, all gone to strengthen the land defenses.

All ships carried their boats with their gear stowed inside them. Forward and aft on battleships, stanchions and davits were unshipped but amidships all gear remained in place, the guns being given clear arcs of fire, but no other clearing for action. On *Bayan* and *Poltava* life preservers were hung over side rails and skid beams, and on all ships hammocks were stowed about standard compasses, bridges, deck houses and searchlights, and bags of coal placed about bulkheads over engine room hatches. *Retvizan, Tsêsarêvitch,* and *Novik* had no nets, and all large ships carried wireless. Battleships were handled by tugs in getting out of basin, but passed through entrance under their own steam.

At 6 a.m. there were six Japanese destroyers, and four torpedo boats seven miles to southeast from entrance. At 6:30 the four small boats steamed away to the eastward, at 7:10 two of the larger ones took the same direction, and were followed shortly by the other four boats. At 7:15 two Japanese vessels were sighted 15 miles to east-southeast, one with two funnels, the other with three, apparently armored cruiser *Yakumo*. These were accompanied by three destroyers which approached about six miles from fleet and lay there making observations.

Shortly after fleet anchored in outer roads, a mine was found floating near the flagship. It was exploded by being fired on, and then boats began trawling amongst the ships, finding one other mine which was also exploded. Finally about 1 p.m. the fleet began getting underway and at 2 p.m. stood out in column at speed of about four knots in wake of the trawlers. These trawlers consisted of six of the dumping steamers working in pairs towing the drag between them. These were first in column followed by six destroyers, also trawling over intervals between dumping steamers.

Diana led the column, followed by *Askold, Sevastopol, Poltava, Peresviet, Pobieda, Retvizan, Tsêsarêvitch, Bayan,* and *Pallada*. Near head of line were group of seven destroyers besides those dragging, and rear was brought up by the *Gremiastchy* and *Otvajny*. *Novik* was playing one mile off the left flank, making demonstrations against the Japanese destroyers, which about 2 p.m. were seven in number and had run down until they bore off port bow of the column, and 6,000 yards away. At 2:30 four of these boats (two-funnels) in column approached head of Russian column at right angles, going full speed and opening fire on the trawlers. These for a few moments were in confusion, but soon straightened out and carried on their work. *Diana* and *Askold* returned fire of destroyers, and *Novik* came up at full speed also firing on them and threatening to cut them off. It seemed at one moment as if this were sure to happen, but the Japanese boats went left-about nicely in time, and cleared bows of *Novik* by about 2,000 yards, keeping up a continuous fire.

When *Novik* had Japanese boats opened out well on the port bow, she turned with port helm and stood down toward head of Russian column. Like a flash, right-about went the four Japanese, joined by three other four-funneled boats, all after *Novik* and firing rapidly, *Novik* answering with rather deliberate fire. Shooting both sides poor. This little chase lasted but for not much more than a mile, but was quite exciting, and it seemed a rather remarkable thing to see the scout cruiser running back to the fleet chased by seven destroyers which were under fire of the *Novik*, shore batteries, and other vessels of the fleet.

The Russian destroyers, (though superior in number) made no move to meet the Japanese. Three more Japanese destroyers came up from southeast, but the nearest large Japanese ships were not less than 10 miles away. One of the Japanese destroyers was hit by *Novik* and first hung back, then steamed away slowly to southeast. These distances are given as ascertained later, but in the position from which I watched the affair, they seemed much less. I thought that the Japanese destroyers had approached within 2,000 yards of trawlers and head of line and that *Novik* was as close as 1,000 when they crossed her bow, my distance being about five miles away. The battle flags at mastheads of Japanese destroyers could be plainly distinguished as well as the people on their decks. The Russian fleet had up no fighting flags. The time occupied by this incident was 12 minutes, from 2:31 to 2:43. At 2:45 p.m. leading Russian vessel turned eight points to port and column stood on course east-northeast about five miles off shore. As the intention of the Russians became evident there was a great scurrying of Japanese ships about the horizon. They came and went in an uncertain way and behaved rather as if they were much surprised, always keeping from 15 to 20 miles out.

At 4 p.m. head of Russian column turned again to southeast and four Japanese vessels showed up right ahead, consisting of three two-funneled cruisers and one one-funneled vessel. Two large vessels showed up to southward steaming to eastward, one three-funneled, one two-funneled, probably *Yakumo* and *Takasago* or *Suma*. Five other vessels joined the first four, and the two vessels to westward joined this fleet of nine, making, at 4:15, eleven Japanese vessels in sight, all cruisers or armored cruisers, none of the battleships being yet in sight. Evidently the Japanese fleet had been surprised, the ships joining in detachments, and the various squadrons being broken up and not in regular formations.

At 4:50 the last ship of Russian column turned to southeast and the smoke then prevented following any further the motions of the ships, but the last seen of them the Japanese were retiring to southeastward followed by the Russians who had formed in two columns, cruisers on left flank, battleship column in reversed order, *Sevastopol* leading, *Tsĕsarĕvitch* (flag) bringing up the rear. About 7 p.m. trawlers returned to harbor under escort of *Gremiastchy* and *Otvajny*.

At this time in dry dock were *Bezshumni, Ryeshitelni, Smyeli* and *Bezposchadni; Statni* not yet finished; *Bditelni* was being repaired.

At 8:45 p.m. lights and the flashes of guns seen to southeast and very soon came the Russian fleet full speed for the shelter of the batteries, the rear of the column under attack by Japanese torpedo boats and ships answering with a lively fire from all guns up to 6". Flagship was leading the column which seemed in considerable disorder and was using searchlights and signalling. Other vessels also had lights going, but *Poltava* and *Pallada* bringing up the rear, had no lights.

Whereas during the afternoon and in daylight the fleet had required three hours to clear the mine fields, on the return, spurred on by the Japanese destroyers and torpedo boats and led by the flagship they covered the same distance in 45 minutes, and at 9:30 p.m. were all at anchor in the outer roads, except destroyers and *Sevastopol.* The destroyers at first had been kept in the rear where they skirmished with the Japanese torpedo boats and then had been sent inshore to anchor, one group to eastward in Také Bay and another to westward of entrance.

While coming in, the *Sevastopol* had made the alarm signal to the fleet that she had struck a mine, and had beached in the bight at southwest end of Tiger Tail Peninsula. Almost immediately after anchoring, attacks or feints of torpedo boat attacks began and continued at intervals throughout the night, during which there was not an interval of 15 minutes in which there was not firing.

As the Russian fleet steamed to southeast, the Japanese continued to retire, apparently waiting arrival of more of their ships, both fleets in column heading on practically same course. At 6 p.m. the Japanese battleship squadron came up and the Japanese force increased to 19 vessels, of which there were four battleships, *Mikasa, Asahi, Fuji,* and *Shikashima;* three armored cruisers, *Nissin, Yakumo* and *Asama;* and the cruisers *Chen Yen, Matsushima, Itsukushima* and *Hashidate; Takasago, Chitose* and *Kasagi;* and five smaller cruisers, *Akashi, Suma, Akitsushima, Chiyoda* and *Idzumi,* with 22 destroyers and torpedo boats. From 6 p.m. till 6:45, the two fleets tinued on almost parallel courses heading about southeast, in two columns 12,000 yards apart, the Japanese to the left, the Russians on the right.

At this time the Japanese vessels began to fire up as if contemplating attack and their cruisers threatened the cruisers in rear of Russian column. Then when the Russian captains expected the action to begin, the Russian flagship, the *Tsésarévitch,* went about to starboard, followed by rest of fleet and headed for Port Arthur, the admiral signalling "Make highest speed possible." The Japanese admiral then sent his torpedo boats ahead, and the Russians placed their cruiser squadron to right and rear of the battleship squadron and covering them, assisted by 13 Russian destroyers.

The sun set at 7:15, and the moon gave a faint light: Horizon dim and smoky, sea smooth, light westerly breezes. Two divisions of Japanese destroyers made an attack on the cruiser squadron, coming up on the starboard quarter, and firing torpedoes at range of over 1,000 yards, but making no hits, though one torpedo passed close astern of *Pallada*, the rear ship, which she was able to avoid by increasing speed. The Russian and Japanese destroyers had a skirmish in the rear of the Russian fleet, the *Boevoi* being hit a couple of times, and her commander and two men wounded.

When Admiral Vitgeft left Port Arthur he underestimated the forces which the Japanese could bring into line, believing they had left only three battleships, and that only one of these was fit for battle. *Asama* he believed sunk. Arriving in the presence of the Japanese fleet he exaggerated their strength, reporting that he saw five Japanese battleships ready for battle, and crediting them with a larger number of armored cruisers than they had present.

When at sunset the Japanese fired up, and apparently began to make preparations for a night battle, he turned and ran for Port Arthur. In his official report the admiral stated that "As the courses approached, it was seen that the enemy intended to place one cruiser division and the destroyers between our squadron and the harbor, so that by a torpedo attack at night, with a superior force of torpedo boats, some of our ships might be put out of action, and then to attack us by day with all his forces. Giving attention to the collection of all the enemy's war strength, much exceeding our own, and the much greater number of his torpedo boats, I decided to return to Port Arthur in order to act according to circumstances, considering that *such form of action threatened less losses*."

In answer he was informed by the Viceroy that it was not possible for the Japanese to have more than four battleships since the *Hatsuse* had been known to be sunk, and another battleship had been so seriously injured that she would be of no further service in the war if ever again. This was made known to us on apparently reliable authority, a few days after the return of the fleet, and the latter part being found later to be true inclines me to believe that the circumstances of the Viceroy's reply as detailed were also true.

At first it seemed most probable that *Sevastopol*, being the rear ship in regular formation, had been hit by a torpedo from one of the Japanese torpedo boats, but further information cleared up the fact that she received her injury when no torpedo attack was being made, and while she was running a little out of column on the way to her anchorage. The mine exploded on port side forward of *Sevastopol*, about 15′ below water line, doing serious injury in the vicinity of a magazine. Some cartridges exploded, a more serious accident probably being prevented by the magazine almost immediately filling with water.

Captain Viren in the *Bayan* piloted the fleet in over the mine field as he knew it best, then ran out and anchored to seaward of the rest of the fleet, in order to better repulse the expected torpedo attacks.

I was able to witness the entry of the fleet and the first serious attack, from 10:37 to 11:03, when I was forced by sentries to leave post of observation. The first attack was so far at sea that little could be seen of it, but the other attacks were more clearly observed. At first three torpedo boats approached from southeastward, keeping about two miles out from fleet. They were picked up by the shore searchlights, and fired on and retired, apparently without even using torpedoes. In the first main attack the boats approached in groups of two or three at wide intervals, coming from eastward and southeastward, about 20 in all being engaged. While some distance out they were detected by the searchlights and a very heavy fire directed on them from all shore batteries at the entrance and to eastward of it and from all the ships, with 6″ guns and smaller. The boats could be clearly seen, and about them a rain of shells, the spray sometimes completely obscuring the boats, and probably very much interfering with their view. They seemed to approach to a distance of about 1,000 yards, but officers on the ships stated that at no time did they ever come within 2,000 yards.

At all events their torpedoes did not make any hits due probably to underestimate of distance, some bursting on the rocks along the shore, and next morning 17 others were picked up floating near the beach, and on it, having been set to run the full distance, and sinking gear failing to operate. Several times shells could be seen striking the torpedo boats, the flash of the explosion clearly distinguished. One Japanese boat could be distinguished in the darkness, having a red-hot funnel. All seemed to maneuver and fire their torpedoes at full speed. All Russian ships that had nets had them rigged out. Those that had no nets were inside the outer line.

Altogether there seemed eight well defined attacks (1) 8:45—9:10 on fleet underway and coming in; (2) 9:35—9:40, three boats well out, possibly making reconnaissance only; (3) 10:08—10:17, attack at long range; (4) 10:37—11:03, altogether about 20 boats engaged in groups of two or three, shore batteries and all ships keeping up heavy fire; (5) 11:45—11:57, long range attack by detached groups; (6) 12:13—12:20, lively attack by about 12 or 15 boats; (7) just after moon went down about 2:20 a.m., and from then until 2:35, strong attack of between 20 and 30 boats advancing as before singly or in groups of two or three with wide intervals, and generally from southeastward; (8) 2:45—3:15, firing at boats reconnoitering or giving aid to boats damaged in 7th attack. The three principal attacks were 4, 6, and 7, but none scored a hit.

During the night all of Port Arthur remained awake—there really was no night. The firing never died entirely out, and when the principal attacks were being made it was furious, and the reports of the guns and the reverberations in the bowl in which the town is situated made one continuous fearful roar. At times explosions were heard similar to those caused by mines. The next morning at 5 a.m. the fleet was found at anchor in the outer roads in practically the same positions as it had anchored the previous day when it was delayed while anchorage was searched for mines. At 5:30 a.m. *Sevastopol* came in sight out of bight, under tow and head a little down, and listing slightly. At 7:30 she was taken into East Basin, and the other ships followed one by one until all the fleet was again in inner harbor.

The *Peresviet* and *Diana* had gone in earlier and probably without being noticed by Japanese, on account of which they supposed them missing, and reported them sunk. At 5 a.m. could be seen four four-funneled destroyers about 8 miles southeast, four more 10 miles to east-southeast, and four others 12 miles to eastward. A two-funneled, two-masted cruiser, *Suma*-type, was coming up from eastward, and laying off about 10 miles outside.

At 5 a.m. four Japanese cruisers in sight, all with two funnels and two masts, and standing across entrance to eastward, the leading vessel an armored cruiser of *Asama*-type. Six junks in sight about eight miles to east-southeast. Day was exceedingly clear and the hills off Chefoo could be seen. Russians claimed to have sunk during the night two torpedo boats or destroyers. Next morning the bodies of one Japanese officer and two men were picked up on the beach.

On June 26 the Japanese land forces made an advance against the Russian right flank about eight miles to the eastward, firing being heard about 4 a.m. in that direction. When the news was received in Port Arthur, movements of ships to cooperate with the army began. Near the shore about Siao-bin-dao, at 7:30 a.m., were 10 Japanese destroyers and seven torpedo boats. At 8:15 four two-funneled destroyers approached the shore and bombarded the Russian lines, supported by *Hashidate* and *Akitsushima*. Further out were *Asama, Chitose,* and *Kasagi.*

At 10 *Novik, Vsadnik, Gremiastchy, Otvajny,* six trawlers and 10 destroyers went out and approached the Japanese boats. These in three flotillas, the first of four four-funneled boats, the next of four four-funneled boats with signal mast aft, and the last of four two-funneled boats, turned and came down toward the Russians, followed by three of the smaller torpedo boats. They kept about five miles out, but when off Krestovaya were fired on by *Novik* and Battery No. 22, *Novik*'s shots all falling about one mile short, the shore battery doing better, but making no hits. The *Hashidate* came in near destroyers, but kept outside, and *Asama*-division was still further out.

June 26—August 10, 1904

Port Arthur

Four small torpedo boats remained in position off Siaobindao, with a gunboat about one mile off shore. Russian fleet kept close along shore and Japanese turned and kept on parallel course to eastward.

At 11:00 *Bobr* and two more destroyers came out and joined *Novik*. From 7:30 till 11:30 Japanese continued to bombard Russian land lines and Russians fired on Japanese land lines, but the two fleets were kept apart by the mine field between. At 11:30 trawlers came in and *Pallada* went out, anchoring off Electric Battery. *Diana* was also ordered out, but her captain could not be found, and she did not get out until 2:30, when she anchored near *Pallada*. Another Japanese division of two battleships and *Takasago* and *Chiyoda* came up, but remained well out, steaming backward and forward. Long distance firing between *Novik* and Japanese destroyers, but about 4, all Japanese ships turned to eastward, and shortly after the Russians ships came into port.

In the meantime firing was going on on land, and the Japanese succeeded in advancing their lines against the Russian right. As the first news of this attack on land was received at 5 a.m., the Russian ships were very slow in getting out to cooperate with the army.

On June 27, the cooperating fleet got an early move on and by 6 a.m. *Novik, Gremiastchy, Otvajny, Bobr,* 13 destroyers and Rear Admiral Lojinski on *Ghiliak* went out to act on Japanese left flank. Operations were similar to those of previous day, 14 Japanese destroyers, two gunboats, and *Akitsushima* remaining off Japanese left, and fleets maneuvering at distances of about 10,000 yards from each other. Russians fired on Japanese positions and in the evening returned to Port Arthur, tying up for the night. Japanese boats then came down off Russian right and fired a few shots. About this time the method of stationing ships near the entrance was modified. Gunboats were moored on each side as before, *Ghiliak* alongside *Yoneyama Maru*, and in addition either *Diana, Pallada,*

Askold or *Bayan* would moor to eastward of entrance and inside wrecks. On the nights of June 26 and 27 this was done and although these ships were perfectly protected by the wrecks, booms, and their own nets, they apparently offered a bait for Japanese torpedo boats.

About 8:45 p.m. No. 22 opened up on torpedo boats coming in full speed from eastward, apparently four in number. Firing was quite lively for five minutes all along shore to eastward, and one of the boats approached within 1,500 yards of entrance and launched torpedoes against *Diana*, outer guard ship for the night. It seemed quite certain that one of the torpedo boats was sunk, boats being seen pulling away from where it was seen to be in difficulties. However, Battery No. 22 never fired a shot without claiming to have sunk one or more boats.

Torpedoes from these boats struck the wrecks near entrance and exploded, and as some of the wrecks were lying on their sides, with the upper side just showing, the Japanese believed they sunk a ship. They saw the explosion and the bottom of a ship, and naturally concluded that they had caused the damage, and time and time again sent in their torpedo boats to risk being sunk or damaged in an attack on wrecks, and several times reported sinking Russian ships, the *Diana* being "sunk" three times. It was a very pretty trap, and just the kind the Japanese would bite at again and again.

On July 2, news came into Port Arthur of the arrival of the *New Orleans** at Chefoo. This gave rise to a long leading article of three columns in the "Novi Krai," which looked on it as the first step in a bold and impudent movement of one of the Tripartite Treaty (England, Japan, U.S.) to further divide Shantung, by a seizure of the ports of Chefoo and Tsingtao, while Russia was engaged in the war, and China helpless. It was stated that this was a step that Russia could not regard with indifference, and that means must be taken immediately to confound the plans of a cunning and double-dealing enemy (U.S.). This sort of thing would seem to have little

---

* Flagship of Cruiser Squadron, U.S. Asiatic Fleet. The *New Orleans* was a 3700-ton protected cruiser, armed with six 6″ guns, built in 1895.

weight, but with General Stessel, Admiral Vitgeft and the official world in Port Arthur it was as real and true as their Bible. The article begins: "There are reports . . .," but from that moment these reports are treated as established facts and everything incident is turned until all agrees with the preconceived ideas. A denial or disclaimer of any of these ideas would be looked on by them as a natural diplomatic move, or more plainly a lie, which of course they would be too clever to believe.

On July 3, from 1:04 to 1:08 a.m., two Japanese torpedo boats had another try at the trap, this time baited with *Pallada*, and again apparently suffering more loss than they could inflict.

During July 3, 4 and 5 on land, fighting was going on continuously, resulting generally in the Russians losing about 500 men and taking up another line a few versts to the rear, and including Green and Semaphore Hills. At the shore end of these lines was constant activity of both Russian and Japanese gunboats and destroyers. The Russians would send out in the early morning all the movable coast defense consisting of torpedo boats and gunboats. Japanese gunboats and *Matsushima*-division with destroyers would come down and a few shots would be exchanged at long range, no damage to either side.

Then in the evening, about 6 p.m., the Russians would start back leaving three or four destroyers at anchor in Také Bay, and followed by the Japanese destroyers which would try a few shots at the Russian rear, and be fired on a few times by shore batteries.

The *Burakoff* came back from Inkow on July 3 and brought the news of the sinking of the Japanese transports by the Vladivostock fleet and of the arrival in Vladivostock of the four Argentine cruisers purchased by Russia. This was the sort of information in military circles. Among the civilians still more extraordinary stories were prevalent. These were based on "the Chinese say" or "there are reports" or something similar, and each of them that coincided with the Russian prejudices was received as gospel truth. Where extraordinary rumors existed so frequently, and when lying was so common, it was odd to find so many apparently intelligent men placing confidence in ridiculous rumors.

From 10 to 10:20 p.m., July 3, was again lively firing from guard ships and batteries at torpedo boats again nibbling at the bait. On

July 5 fighting along the shore positions was quite heavy, during the day artillery firing constantly and at night infantry attacks by the Japanese. The gunboats assisted with their guns from western part of Také Bay. Apparently the Russians were attempting to recover some of their lost positions, but without success.

On this day the caisson of *Retvizan* was fitted to *Sevastopol* and her repairs were commenced. None of the attachés were allowed to inspect the injuries, the admiral stating that he did not allow his own officers to do so. Still it was learned that though the hole made by the mine in outer skin was small, the interior damage was more than in either of the cases of *Retvizan* or *Tsésarévitch,* from which it might be concluded that the mine struck lower down than in these two cases, the force of the explosion taking an upward course in this case, but fortunately not another *Petropavlovsk* or *Hatsuse* disaster. It was stated that *Sevastopol* could have gone into the dry dock, but it was considered advisable not to take her in and reserve that for the torpedo boats, four of which, including *Bezshumni* not yet repaired, were constantly in.

As the Russian ships started to return in this afternoon about 6 p.m., *Itsukushima, Akashi* and some destroyers approached them rather closely as if to threaten cutting them off, and firing between the vessels was quite lively, but without results on account of the extreme ranges. At this time the tops of hills were covered with fog, and patches of fog here and there about the entrance. All Russian vessels returned safely leaving as usual a few destroyers on guard in Také Bay. The Japanese gunboat *Kaimon* fouled a mine close inshore and was blown up.

On July 6 the trawlers were at work in vicinity of Lutin Rock during afternoon under convoy of *Gremiastchy, Vsadnik* and four destroyers. *Takasago* was 10 miles out to southward, two two-funneled destroyers and four four-funneled with signal masts aft were six miles southeast; *Itsukushima, Chiyoda* and one destroyer 10 miles east-southeast, with *Asama* a little further away in same direction; four large Japanese ships 15 miles to eastward. Two Japanese two-funneled destroyers seemed to be drifting in closer and closer to the beach from the position of the others. They were finally so near that I was surprised they were not fired on.

A Russian officer with me said they were not Japanese but Russian boats. However, about 5:30 there was a flash from the stern of one of them, then from the other, and then they fired a number of shots. In a few seconds their shells began to fall in amongst the trawlers, and there was some excitement. No. 22 and Canet battery opened fire, the first doing some excellent shooting, their shells spraying water over the boats, which then steamed along the beach for a short distance, still firing on the trawlers with their 12-pdrs. They continued on their westerly course until south of Golden Hill, then ran out and joined the other six boats. *Gremiastchy* fired a couple of shots with her old-fashioned bow gun and smoky powder, then all trawlers came into port. During the night torpedo boats again approached the entrance apparently for the purpose of laying mines.

About 4:10 a.m., July 7, Japanese boats again approached entrance from eastward, were fired on and retired. In the afternoon, from 2:30 to 2:50, again there was long-range firing by *Matsushima* and destroyers on Russian gunboats and destroyers to eastward, and in forenoon fighting going on on land. During afternoon two cruisers of *Chitose*-class and 12 torpedo boats were maneuvering about 12 miles to east-southeast of Golden Hill keeping in approximately the same place. It appeared as if they might be dragging over a certain limited space to allow approach of heavy ships for purposes of bombardment or attacking Russian expeditions along east shore.

On July 9 the Russians made up a somewhat stronger force composed of *Bayan, Poltava, Diana, Pallada, Novik, Gremiastchy, Otvajny,* 10 destroyers and the trawlers which steamed slowly out at 6 a.m. toward Také Bay, the trawlers preceding the larger ships. In Také Bay, close under the batteries, the larger ships anchored, while *Novik* and gunboats approached the western shore and fired on the Japanese trenches with shrapnel. At 11:45 *Kasagi, Chitose, Itsukushima* and *Hashidate* with 10 destroyers were 10 miles east-southeast of Krestovaya. Four destroyers of *Sazanami*-class left main group and steamed in twice toward the Russian fleet, turning to westward and opening fire on the group of gunboats firing into trenches, which were forced to discontinue bombardment and give their attention to repulsing attack of destroyers. *Hashidate* also came in, turned and opened fire at about 8,000 yards with 12″ and 4.7″ guns, followed by *Chitose* and *Kasagi*. Japanese had battle flags up, and evidently were attempting to entice the Russians out across the mine field.

Bayan, Poltava, Diana, Pallada, Novik and destroyers answered with slow fire, but no boat made any move to approach the Japanese.

About 1 p.m. *Asama* and *Akitsushima* came down from eastward but kept well out, and about 4 p.m. *Shikishima* or *Yakumo* and four other large, two-mast, two-funnel ships also approached, but also kept well out. About 4:15 Russians picked up anchors and started home, apparently not having been hit. Times of flight of 12-pdr. shells were from 15 to 20 seconds. Shooting on neither side seemed to be very good, Japanese somewhat better than Russians, many of their shells falling very close, Russians shooting high.

About this time began first evidence of shortage of provisions; fresh beef, beer, and kerosene oil running short, and stores having shelves pretty well cleaned out of tinned provisions through the constant buying. General Stessel informed the admiral that the Japanese were landing another division from transports at Dalny and asked the cooperation of the navy. The admiral replied that for himself he would not take the fleet out, but if General Stessel desired he might assume the responsibility and order it out.

At 11:35 p.m., July 10, there was another attack on the *Diana*, off the entrance, by three torpedo boats, easily repulsed by her fire and that of the batteries, which continued until midnight. The baited trap was still working, two Whitehead torpedoes being recovered next morning in entrance near wrecks. The attacking boats answered the fire with the small guns, a number of shells falling in the town. On July 11 again was observed apparent trawling operations in vicinity, 12 miles east-southeast of Golden Hill. Gunboats and destroyers went out, and a few long-range shots exchanged. About 11:50 p.m. torpedo boats again approached the entrance, but apparently on a reconnaissance or to lay mines, as they did not approach very near and quickly retired. On the 12th there was little activity, Canet battery firing a few shots at approaching torpedo boats in afternoon, and that night, about 11:30, there were a few shots fired at torpedo boats which kept well out. July 13, besides a few shots fired at torpedo boats approaching too close in a reconnaissance during afternoon, there was nothing doing. A gun-cotton party was engaged in blowing up one of the branders, probably *Jinsen Maru,* which ran on rocks about three and one-half miles to southwest. The object of this was not quite apparent beyond the general national inclination to blow up anything that they did not know exactly what to do with. After a number of explosions the brander was reduced to a mass of old iron.

At 12:30 a.m., July 14, torpedo boats again approached the entrance apparently on reconnaissance, as if their suspicions had been aroused about the trap laid for them. One torpedo boat towed a sampan in close to the entrance, where the sampan was cast off, and apparently tried to learn something definite about conditions there. Both boat and sampan escaped, apparently with little if any damage. After this the Japanese had evidently discovered the true nature of the trap at entrance and there were no more attacks on the guard ship stationed there. *Novik, Gremiastchy, Bobr* and three torpedo boats went out to eastward at 7 a.m., fired from Takê Bay on Japanese trenches and field works, and all ships returned at 6:30 p.m. The *Bogatyr,* a small mine vessel, ran out under Krestovaya to place mines, but was promptly attacked and driven back.

This was rather a quiet day, although three to five Japanese cruisers were always in sight, nine to 14 destroyers and torpedo boats and several gunboats close inshore to eastward. *Amur*'s battery removed and sent to land defenses, and officers and crew, except ship keepers, detailed to stations in the land defenses. July 15 three Japanese torpedo boats ran in and fired on trawlers at work off Lutin Rock about 3 p.m., and that night there seemed some activity in the direction of Pigeon Bay. Several Japanese vessels remained in this vicinity using searchlights along the beach, and firing on it, and on junks attempting to get out. As that night despatches were received by General Stessel, it is possible they had been chasing the boat with despatches.

July 16 both fleets showed activity, but along lines of previous days, without any incidents of particular importance. This day was a holiday, being General Stessel's name day. During the night of July 15 Russian destroyers were out on a reconnaissance and one of them, the *Rastoropni,* while in Kinchow Bay, observed a steamer apparently having dealings with the Japanese. The *Rastoropni* followed the steamer and about daylight fired a blank shot to compel her to stop. Steamer attempted to escape and destroyer opened fire on her. She then stopped and showed the British flag, and the destroyer ran up close to her, when the Russians claimed she was fired on from the steamer by some one with a revolver, upon which destroyer fired a torpedo, striking the steamer aft and sinking her in about half an hour, southwest from Iron Island. Steamer was *Hipsang*, 1,040 tons, British register, owned by Jardine Mathieson & Co. and running between Newchwang and Chefoo, and her crew of six Englishmen, a Russian Jew and 90 Chinese coolies were brought into Port Arthur on *Rastoropni* and isolated.

Admiral Vitgeft was very angry about the awkward predicament in which the Russians were placed, and tried to pacify the crew of *Hipsang* with money presents. The Englishmen were later on sent out in a junk.

The regular routine of dragging for mines was carried on July 17, but the Russian ships all remained in port. On land there was occasional firing and Japanese destroyers did some firing on right flank of Russian positions. Until July 22 there were few incidents out of the ordinary, regular routine of trawling during the day, daily visits to Takê Bay by gunboats and destroyers, at night three destroyers usually being at anchor in the bay and close ashore.

A group of four destroyers occasionally sent out at night on reconnaissance, but never going far away from entrance. The weather during July had been hot with occasional rains, and a good deal of fog. Some days the fog would be so thick that nothing could be distinguished at a greater distance than two or three hundred yards either on shore or on the water. On other days the fog would lie over the hill tops, covering them about half way down, with alternate patches and fairly clear streaks at sea. Although a few days were quite clear, yet usually the horizon was hazy and visibility was not good either night or day.

Still, at sea in the clear intervals, it could be seen that the Japanese had not relaxed their watch over the entrance, the ships usually present being the 1st. Cruiser Division (*Matsushima, Itsukushima, Hashidate, Chen Yen*); 3rd division 1st. squadron (*Yakumo, Chitose, Kasagi, Takasago*); 2nd. cruiser division (*Asama, Akitsushima, Suma, Akashi, Chiyoda*); three flotillas of destroyers, and two or three flotillas of torpedo boats, the battleships appearing occasionally a long way out, and some of the gunboats acting along shore to eastward.

During the night of the 22nd fourteen Russian destroyers made a somewhat longer stretch to eastward, and appeared off a bay to eastward of Siao-bin-dao. They began firing at random in order to make enemy discover himself, and two searchlights started up, on which they returned to Port Arthur without having met the enemy. Between 6:30 and 6:40 p.m. there was a short skirmish off the entrance at long range between five Russian destroyers returning to harbor, and a group of Japanese destroyers following them along the coast.

An officer of General Kouropatkin's staff came in from Liaoyang with the news that as yet there had been no decisive battle. *Pobieda* received two more 6″ guns probably from *Pallada*, and the army began to mount some of the old Chinese 12-cm. guns in the land defense, and a 24-cm Krupp, originally from the Shanhaikwan forts, was started out toward Krestovaya on a railway laid temporarily, and hauled by several hundred soldiers. An 8″ gun was being mounted on a peak to the northward of the highest peak on Liaotishan, and work was begun fortifying 203-meter hill. To defend it guns were taken from *Angara* which was converted into a hospital ship. The admiral requested the opinions of his captains and their suggestions for the next movements of the fleet, and there seemed little unanimity amongst them. Commander Krinitzki* of the *Silni* was said to have advised taking the fleet out and going to Inkow, there to await arrival of the Commander in Chief, Vice Admiral Skrydloff.

At 10:20 p.m. shore batteries and guard ships opened fire on suspicious looking craft near the entrance. A Japanese torpedo boat came up towing a junk on which were hoisted the Russian and Chinese flags, casting it off near the entrance and then disappearing. About 300 shots were fired by the batteries at the junk, which was hit several times, but not seriously damaged and finally floated up on the beach under Electric Battery. On board the junk were found several facetious communications for the Russian authorities from the Japanese. The guard ship and batteries were

* Evgenii P. Krinitskii (born 1863).

firing for 25 minutes on this junk, in the belief that it was a new scheme for laying mines, and as it proceeded very slowly, it seems somewhat remarkable that it was not sunk by the fire. Later on during the same night, from 2:40 to 2:50 a.m., firing was again carried on against vessels attempting to lay mines, and next day four mines were picked up in vicinity where vessels appeared.

During night of July 23, the destroyers *Boevoi, Grosovoi,* and *Lieutenant Burakoff* were anchored off Point Chapanchui, on western side of Také Bay, guarding right flank of army. The night was very foggy, and about 2 a.m. in the morning of July 24, two Japanese torpedo boats, four destroyers, accompanied by some gunboats or mine vessels, approached them very closely and torpedoed *Burakoff* and *Boevoi.* Torpedoes were fired from the two torpedo boats at about 200 yards range, set for surface runs. *Burakoff* was struck amidship on port side and managed to get close in shore, sinking in about 10′ of water. *Boevoi* got a torpedo abreast forward boiler room on port side, a large hole being blown in side and deck blown up, most of the damage being done above the water line. Boiler room filled with water but collision mat placed over injury and boat successfully towed into harbor, though damages so severe that boat was of no more use during war. Russians fired on torpedo boats, but the affair happened so suddenly and was over so quickly that it is improbable that much damage was inflicted. The batteries could not fire on the Japanese boats on account of the fog.

July 24 and 25 were both very foggy, and July 26 was cloudy with passing showers, fresh northeasterly breezes. For several days there had been indications of another advance by the Japanese on land, with frequent skirmishes. About 3:30 a.m. batteries fired on torpedo boats approaching entrance, and at 4:30 a.m. lively artillery firing began on the advanced lines to eastward, fighting seeming to be principally in vicinity of the high peak called Kunsan, about seven miles to eastward of N.E. Peak. At 8 there was a movement of the fleet in harbor, and *Askold, Bayan* (under broad pennant of Commodore Reitzenstein), *Pallada, Diana, Novik, Gremiastchy* (flag of Rear Admiral Lojinski), *Otvajny, Ghiliak* and 10 destroyers, with trawlers in the lead, followed by *Novik* and gunboats, heavier ships bringing up the rear. Artillery firing was going on on shore in a very lively way, on an average of 600 shots per hour. Both sides seemed to use shrapnel almost exclusively, these bursting high in the air over Russian positions, the smoke from 16 explosions being observed almost simultaneously.

The firing was practically continuous through the day with apparently little infantry work, which seemed to be reserved for the night. The Russian position on right was on steep western slope of a ridge, about five miles to eastward, and in afternoon Japanese guns could be seen in position on western slopes of Kunsan. The fire of individual guns seemed deliberate, but there must have been a large number of them. The heaviest firing was done in vicinity of Kunsan, but fighting was carried on all along the line across Kwan Tung.

About 11 a.m. gunboats and destroyers arrived under Battery 22, and *Novik* opened fire on two Japanese mine vessels employed in laying or picking up mines about six miles east-southeast of Battery 22. There were two of these vessels of about 700–1,000 tons, merchant steamer type, and one seemed to very soon be in difficulties. *Novik* continued a rather deliberate fire on this vessel at ranges of 5,000–8,000 yards, but made no attempt to approach inside of the shorter of these two ranges, although mine vessels were supported only by destroyers and torpedo boats lying a little further out. *Novik* fired 47 times with 4.7″ guns, making one hit, nearly all shells going over from 100 to 1,000 yards, only four or five falling short. The other steamer took the disabled steamer in tow and both gradually hauled out of range.

In sight, off shore, at the time were *Matsushima*-division of four vessels, *Yakumo, Asama,* and three *Chitoses*, and 34 torpedo boats and destroyers. Russian ships remained close under Krestovaya, gun boats fired a few shots in the direction of the land battle, and about 1 p.m. three destroyers of *Silni*-type started down, along beach to eastward on a reconnaissance, being quickly obscured by a rain shower, which soon passed away and these three boats could be seen coming back full speed chased by four Japanese destroyers, lively firing going on. Another destroyer joined the three Russians but turned back with them, and Japanese sheered off on coming under fire of gunboats and stood out to southeastward.

At 1 p.m. *Diana, Pallada, Bayan,* and *Askold* reached Také Bay, but at 2 p.m. *Diana* returned to harbor, the other vessels anchoring under batteries. At 4 the *Matsushima*-division approached from the southeast to about 10,000 yards from Russian vessels, turned with port helm to eastward at 5:20 and opened lively fire on the group with 4.7″ guns. These ships came up in column at full speed, in beautiful order, with battle flags up, and turned one after the other, firing from port guns, making a very pretty sight. Japanese practice very good, shells falling near Russian ships but making no hits. *Bayan* answered with four 8″ shells and *Gremiastchy* and *Otvajny* fired a few shots. *Matsushima* seemed to be hit.

At 5:45 another Japanese column of *Akashi, Suma, Idzumi, Chiyoda,* and *Akitsushima* came up from east-southeast, turned with starboard helm but did not open fire, the Russians then being on their way back. As this column stood out to south-westward and when about 10 miles southeast of Battery 22, *Chiyoda* struck a mine, the explosion being plainly seen, ship afterward listing to starboard and being taken in tow by *Akitsushima,* and heading off to east-southeast. *Yakumo* and *Asama* with three *Chitose*s could be seen keeping about 15 miles out to southeastward, 32 torpedo boats and four destroyers extended in wide circle about entrance. By 7:30 all Russian ships had returned to harbor. At 8 p.m. artillery fire on shore ceased.

On July 27 artillery fire on shore began again at daylight. At 6 a.m. *Novik, Gremiastchy, Otvajny, Ghiliak,* and 12 destroyers started out going to eastward into Takê Bay as on day before, and followed by trawlers and *Pallada, Bayan, Askold* and *Retvizan* which anchored in Takê Bay about 11, while gun boats approached east shore and fired on enemy's positions in vicinity of Kunsan, until 11 a.m., when *Retvizan* also fired a few shots. From 11 to 3, gunboats fired occasionally at Japanese positions nearer beach, then shifted onto positions in direction of Triple Peak.

On shore enormous quantities of ammunition were expended, the Russians firing less than the Japanese. During the night had been several infantry attacks and from the new positions of the lines Russians appeared to have given way somewhat. During the day the lines seemed to remain practically the same, and not to change under the artillery fire. During the night infantry attacks Russians lost 30 killed and 153 wounded.

During forenoon had been in sight *Matsushima*-division, *Akashi*-division, except *Chiyoda,* while *Asama* and *Yakumo* with three *Chitoses* again kept well out to southeast. *Matsushima*- and *Akashi*-division steamed back and forth on NE—SW course about 10,000 yards out, battle flags up, but not opening fire. Russians also sent up battle flags. Inside the line of Japanese cruisers there was a long line of destroyers and torpedo boats in groups of four, completely masking entrance. Amongst these were four *Sazanami*s, two two-funnel destroyers, four four-funneled somewhat smaller, with signal mast aft, four four-funnel boats with overhanging bow, three large torpedo boats of about 150 tons, and 30 other torpedo boats of 50 to 120 tons. Close inshore, to eastward, was a merchant steamer with spars rigged out under her bows, probably picking up mines. At 1 p.m. *Nisshin* and *Kasuga* and four battleships came up from outside Cap Island, but battleships kept well out. At 3 p.m. Russian fleet started to return, when *Nisshin* and *Kasuga* came up 10,000 yards east-southeast and opened fire on *Retvizan* with 8″ and 10″ guns, firing about 20 shots, practice very good, making no hits, but dropping two shells exceedingly close to *Retvizan*, which replied with four shots from her 12″ guns, making also apparently very good shots but no hits. Fleet returned to port, all being inside at 6 p.m.

As *Bayan* was making turn just off entrance she struck a mine under starboard side forward, and was considerably damaged (See sketch No. 7). She had no difficulty in coming in under her own steam and moored in usual berth, head slightly down in water, listing about five degrees. Apparently the mine must have been touched by the bilge keel, for the damage was not as severe as in any other case of mine explosion. The hole was of irregular shape, covered by seven-foot square, depression over side over space of 18′ × 10′, edges of hole being forced five feet inwards. All damage was between bilge keel and armor shelf, the bilge keel being ruptured and ends of break blown downward toward keel. Part of the force of explosion acted upward, axis of depression being inclined about 45° from vertical. Both inner and outer skins ruptured, and bottom of coal bunker blown through. Owing to better system of watertight subdivision, little water came into the ship, and she might still have gone into action.

This day marked the beginning of a strict blockade by sea of Port Arthur, and a close investment by land. Until this time the block-

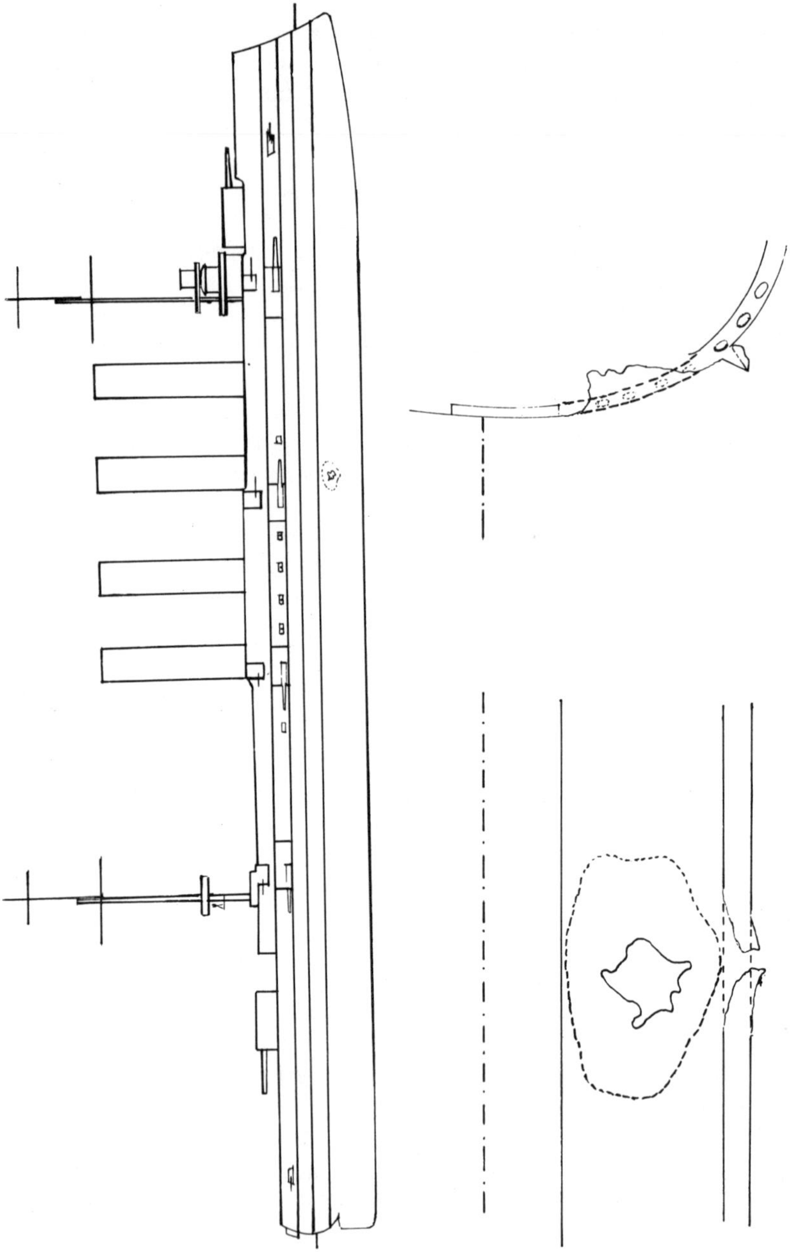

Sketch No. 7 Damage to *Bayan*, by mine explosion. Starboard side view (top), extent of hole in side (lower left), rupture of outer and inner skins (lower right).

ade had been maintained by an irregular force, for some days no large ships whatever being in sight. Usually since May 15 a division of cruisers would be cruising across entrance about 10 to 12 miles out, with occasional appearance of one or two armored cruisers still further out. During the day from four to 12 destroyers and torpedo boats would be in sight laying off about eight miles to southeast of Golden Hill. Off Pigeon Bay a cruiser would be occasionally seen well out. The Russians cruised freely along shore nearly as far as Dalny to the eastward and around Liaotishan to Pigeon Bay, and sometimes up to Port Adams without hindrance. The *Burakoff* made several trips to Inkow without being interfered with.

Junks seem to have had little or no difficulty in getting in or out, neither Japanese nor Russians apparently considering it worth their while to control this sort of traffic. These junks brought in no inconsiderable quantity of fresh provisions, vegetables and rice, also official mail and newspapers. Neither did the Russians seem to consider it worth while to obtain all the advantages that might have been obtained from this traffic. The cargo of the junks would be immediately taken charge of by the military authorities, and compensation paid at rates established by them.

Although many Chinamen engaged in this trade at their own risk on the chance of making large profits, the prices paid in many cases were unsatisfactory to them, and in some cases their junks were seized, so that individual enterprise in this illegitimate traffic was practically discouraged by the Russian authorities, though they assumed the attitude of encouraging it. Russian firms engaged in this business and adapting themselves to Russian methods made large profits. Previous to May there was no blockade of Port Arthur. After the notification on May 26, the blockade might have been considered effective, but was carried out in a very slack manner. Before notification of blockade it seemed probable that nine out of ten steamers intended to supply Port Arthur might have come in safely, with any sort of cargo, contraband or otherwise. From the time of notification until July 27, two out of three should have gotten in.

After July 27 it would have been considerably more difficult for steamers to get in, first on account of the blockading vessels, and second on account of danger from mines, which by this time were liberally sprinkled over the entire vicinity by both Japanese and Russians. It seems remarkable that greater efforts were not made to supply the place in this manner, and not until it was already too late did the Russians resort to this method which would have been of much benefit in enabling the place to hold out.

After the breaking out of the war until my arrival in May, the only steamers that arrived in Port Arthur were some of those that were already on their way before war began. None were especially sent to provide the place. It may have been thought that they would not be necessary, that the railway would be sufficient, or that the Japanese would never dare to besiege the impregnable fortress, or that the fortress was already sufficiently provided, but none of these suppositions would be creditable to men of intelligence.

After the railway was cut it would seem that then extraordinary efforts would have been made, but until late in the year there was not even one attempt. In Vladivostock where the conditions were not dissimilar to Port Arthur in the beginning of the war, ship after ship came in with coal, rice, flour, oil, champagne, and various other necessary articles, in January 1905 nine ships getting in successfully. Many were caught, but in the desperate straits of Port Arthur this should not have discouraged attempts to relieve it.

During night of July 27–28 the Japanese made furious attacks all along the Russian land lines, and next morning Russians began to withdraw all troops to the limit of the fortress under cover of artillery fire which lasted until 11:30 a.m. During night attacks Russians said to have lost 1,200 men in killed and wounded, and Japanese not under four times as many.*

During the day of July 28 troops were coming in all day from eastward and northeastward and taking positions at foot of Dagushan, and along foothills outside of line of fortresses, and all round

* The exact number of Japanese casualties during the action is not known. A Japanese medical officer at the Dalny base hospital estimated a total of 2,500 for the period 26–30 July; most of these occurred during the night action of 27–28 July.[8]

the town. During afternoon there was considerable rifle firing from Russian rear guards, the Russians always firing volleys, the Japanese at will. Over Triple Peak in afternoon the leading Japanese columns appeared, artillery in advance, and on the gallop following closely the Russian rear guard. The 6″ guns from Vantai (Battery No. 33) opened fire on these troops, but range was too great to make effective practice, time of flight of shell one minute four seconds. Japanese followed up and seemed to take positions, near enough for individuals to be distinguished, perhaps three or four miles from line of fortresses. Russian loss in fighting of July 26, 27, 28 and 30 were 7 officers, 248 men killed, 32 officers, 1,553 men wounded, 1 officer and 83 men missing.

The Russian soldiers coming into town seemed in good condition physically, singing and looking quite cheerful and healthy. Uniforms were considerably worse for wear, particularly boots. Horses seemed in excellent condition. A number of artillery horses came in with harness, but without guns. All carriages, rikshas, and many stretchers in use for transportation of wounded, and many hospitals full of them.

By the Russian War Regulations, the commandant of a fortress takes absolute command of all operations when the fortress is besieged. Lieutenant General Smirnoff was commandant of the fortress, and from the moment that the troops were withdrawn into the fortress, General Stessel's duties as commander of fortified region of Kwan Tung, according to the Regulations, were at an end and as expressed to me by a Russian officer, he had only to sit down and look on.

General Smirnoff issued a proclamation published to all the regiments and batteries calling on the defenders to exert themselves to the utmost, and that God was with them against the heathen, and assumed direction of active operations and disposition of troops. He was constantly visiting batteries, and making changes here and there on his own authority and at first it seemed he had complete charge.

The French attaché asked who was now in command of all the forces, and was informed that it was General Smirnoff. If General Stessel's staff were asked they said General Stessel, if General Smirnoff's staff were asked they said General Smirnoff. There was manifestly some conflict, but the weight of opinion seemed to be with General Smirnoff and the War Regulations. In the meantime General Stessel issued no proclamations, and showed little personal activity. For a week he showed himself so little that there were rumors that he had committed suicide. To the already existing dissension between army and navy, was now added internal dissension in the army itself, and that between the two officers of highest rank. How General Stessel finally assumed duties of commandant of the fortress it was not known, whether by virtue of order from higher authority, or whether simply he usurped the functions by virtue of seniority on the ground that there being still some outlying defenses, fortress was not yet isolated, but by whatever means it was accomplished, he was soon again issuing prikazes and telegrams.

Naval operations were now confined to a close blockade by a long line of torpedo boats and destroyers, reaching from the southward of Liaotishan to eastward of Krestovaya with supporting cruisers outside. The inside line was composed of boats in groups of four usually from six to eight miles off shore, a division of cruisers steaming up and down 10 miles out, and four armored cruisers, *Asama, Yakumo, Nisshin* and *Kasuga* laying-to still further out. On eastern end of blockading line were gunboats, and occasionally *Matsushima*-division.

The Russians contented themselves with making reconnaissances with groups of destroyers close along shore, and sweeping for mines. Skirmishing continued along trench lines outside line of fortresses, both day and night, and evidently the Japanese were engaged in taking up positions for the assault of these works. Many people went out in junks, a number being overhauled by Japanese, junks disabled by cutting down their masts and sent back with the warning that any more junks going out would be sunk without notice.

On July 30 batteries Nos. (21), (20), (31), (33), (III) and (66)* were engaged all day firing on presumed location of Japanese batteries, Japanese firing with artillery on Russian trenches about Dagushan. The French and German attachés went to live in Bat-

* For details on batteries see Appendix III.

tery Suvaroff on Tiger Tail Peninsula. This was the battery on the highest hill there, and was a good point of observation for naval operations, but cut off from the land fighting by the water in the West Basin, transportation across which was difficult to get.

I did not ask for the same privilege believing that like all my other requests it would be refused, and also because in my present location I was in a better position to get out to the line of fortresses where fighting evidently was soon to commence. The 8″ gun sent out to high peak on Liaotishan was mounted and tried successfully, and two balloons under construction were inflated with hot air, but there seemed difficulty in manufacturing the gas necessary for an ascension.

For the next few days the naval operations were of little interest, the land operations occupying attention of every one. Russians secured themselves in their trenches on the foothills in advance of the line of batteries, and were busy constructing subpermanent works on 203-meter hill, and on new works in direction of the railway, naming one of them Fort Kouropatkin. The ground was razed beyond foothills and houses, trees and crops cleared. The Japanese advanced generally to 2,000 yards from Russian trenches and kept up desultory artillery fire on them, replied to by the batteries, and by *Retvizan* and *Peresviet* from West Basin, using their heavy guns, and reduced charges. All the ships had stations for assisting in the defense by concentrating their fire on previously designated squares outside the line of batteries. The entrance was guarded as usual by one of the cruisers in the pocket inside the wrecks, the *Ghiliak* moored alongside *Yoneyama Maru*, and the gunboats just inside entrance, but there were no more attacks from this direction.

On August 4 Japanese began firing on the batteries to eastward and northward of the town with field guns, Russians replying slowly. The observation points on the hills where I usually spent the day were also under shrapnel fire whenever people were seen. At night desultory firing of both artillery and infantry going on, and occasional firing at torpedo boats approaching off the entrance and laying mines. Still, in the town itself, life proceeded as usual, concerts going on in the parks, and women and children and many officers out amusing themselves, during the firing as at other times. On August 4 *Bayan* went into dry dock. August 4 was the Dowager Empress' birthday, and was celebrated as usual with parades, speeches, and "Uras." The *Kazan* was also converted into a hospital ship, and painted white with green stripes.

On Sunday, August 7, the Japanese began firing on the town, bombardment lasting from 11:30 a.m.—12, 12:30—1:30 p.m., 2—2:30, 3:30—4:00, and 7 to 8 p.m., about 80 shells of small caliber not over 4.7" falling in the town, killing three and wounding 20 others. The fire seemed directed at the navy yard and most of the shells fell near entrance to East Basin, one of the first striking near the commandant's office. All day lively artillery duel going on on land, Russians firing from (21), (20), (I), (26), (23), (22), (31), (32), (35), (40) and (66), aided by heavy guns of *Retvizan, Peresviet,* and *Pobieda.* Japanese were answering with field guns, but from Northeast Peak nothing whatever could be discovered of their positions—neither flash, smoke, dust nor men. The Russian trenches were filled with men keeping well under cover and the Japanese trenches 1,000 yards in front appeared deserted. Russians were under the impression that an attempt would be made to force the entrance of the harbor, and extra precautions were taken to guard against such an attack. Repairs to *Sevastopol* were completed and caisson taken off. Many Russian workmen in the navy yard declined to do any more work, and the Chinese workmen quit almost in a body. No more work was done on the new dock on southern side of East Basin.

During the day of August 8, beginning early in the morning, Japanese made infantry attacks on trenches at foot of Dagushan, and artillery fire continued all day, from both batteries and ships on their positions. At 7:30 p.m. infantry attacks began again and batteries were very busy, *Retvizan, Poltava, Tsêsarêvitch, Peresviet* and *Pobieda* joining in with 12" and 6" guns. During first part of night violent attacks continued and Russians abandoned Dagushan, troops coming inside line of fortresses. Russians admit loss of 50 killed and 250 wounded, and claimed Japanese lost 5,000 or 6,000.* Lively bombardment of town and navy yard continued all day about 100 shells coming in, and setting on fire oil store house in

* No casualty figures can be found, but it is generally held that Russian estimates of Japanese losses were greatly exaggerated.

navy yard. A fire party from *Amur* made a gallant attempt to extinguish fire, but lost several men from bursting shells which continued to fall in vicinity of burning house. *Novik, Gremiastchy, Ghiliak* and 12 destroyers went out to Takê Bay to fire on Japanese left flank, returning at 6 p.m.

In afternoon while observing attack on Dagushan from authorized point of observation, I was arrested by Cossacks and taken before General Smirnoff who directed me to remain within the limits of the Old Town. I asked then to go with the other attachés on Battery Suvaroff, but this was refused. This reduced me to living in a town under bombardment, absolutely cut off from land operations and without the privilege of even seeing the sea, and as it was a culmination of many other discourtesies and discriminations, I decided to make a protest and leave Port Arthur.

As long as I had been allowed to see anything at all I should have remained and continued to put up with the humiliations that I had to endure from the Russian authorities, but when there was nothing left for me but to live in a bombproof with the civilians and women and children, I thought it best to accept the lot the authorities had endeavored to force on me, and go to some other part of the theater of war.

Accordingly, I made request to General Smirnoff to leave, stating that I had never while in Port Arthur done anything to give the authorities just cause of offense, while they in return had denied me the privileges granted to the other attachés and had treated me with discourtesy and suspicion.

The bombardment continued next day, August 9, on the town and anchorage in harbor, the ships in the West Basin being hit a number of times, *Retvizan* particularly. The shells seemed to be of 12cm and to be fired from a point about 9,000 yards almost north of East Basin. The practice was exceedingly good, being made with no chance of rectifying the fire. The town and harbor seemed to be taken in sections, fire continuing on each section from one-half to one and one-half hours, shells falling in all ellipse, major axis about 1,000 yards, minor axis 200, and center of impact well located. About two out of three shells striking the water burst on impact.

I saw the *Retvizan* hit five times, and *Peresviet* also several times. I learned afterward that *Retvizan* was hit 17 times and that one shell not larger than 12cm struck water near *Retvizan* on port side, and exploded against her sides about 10′ below surface of water, and nearly abreast foremast, blowing a hole with area of 23 square feet, and allowing 200 tons of water to get into one compartment. The flagship had been struck by fragments and the admiral had to close the armored shutters of the cabin windows to keep them from coming into his cabin. These two days forced the conviction on him that the fleet must get out, and that evening there were indications that it again intended moving.

Wednesday, August 10, was fair and warm, with light southeasterly breezes, horizon hazy with occasional wisps of fog in the morning. At 5 a.m. fleet began to move, all being out at 8 a.m., and anchored off the entrance. *Tsêsarêvitch* (flag) then got underway, preceded by trawlers and accompanied by 16 torpedo boats, and steered to southwestward along shore as far as large rock three and one-half miles southwest of entrance, then turned to southeastward followed in order by *Retvizan,* with a slight list to port from injury of previous day, *Pobieda, Peresviet* (flag), *Poltava* and *Sevastopol.* Next came cruiser division *Askold* (flag), *Pallada, Diana,* with *Novik* detached on left flank and hospital ship *Mongolia* in the rear. Gunboats *Gremiastchy, Otvajny,* and *Bobr* followed to mark the turn and cover retirement of trawlers. All ships had battle flags up, and went out quickly and in excellent order, acting as a fleet with a purpose.

Ships kept distance 400 yards apart, and made a very handsome show. *Pobieda* still lacked five of her 6″ guns, and six 12-pdrs.; *Pallada* and *Diana* were short four 12-pdrs. and two 6″ guns each; *Peresviet* was shy one 6″; *Askold* shy two 6″ and *Sevastopol*'s 12″ had not yet been repaired; *Retvizan* was damaged as described. Repairs on *Pobieda* and *Tsêsarêvitch* were only temporary, and *Tsêsarêvitch*'s steering gear was already giving trouble. At 10 a.m. fleet was out of sight in the haze.

In early morning, of the Japanese there were visible only the inner line of destroyers and torpedo boats across entrance, the large ships showing up at 8 a.m., the *Yakumo, Chitose, Takasago,* and *Kasagi* 15 miles to south-southwest; *Idzumi, Akashi,* and *Akitsushima* 12 miles south; *Nisshin* and *Kasuga* 10 miles southeast; and 17 torpedo boats and destroyers. As Russian fleet steamed out to southeast the Japanese ships steamed along to eastward as if to concentrate.

From 12:50 to 1:10 p.m. firing distinctly heard, apparently deliberate fire with great guns. The destroyers left in port were *Boevoi, Serditi,* and *Bditelni* under repairs, and *Ryeshitelni,* and at 1 p.m. the trawlers, gunboats and eight destroyers, *Skori*-type, returned. At 2:30 p.m. a small Japanese torpedo boat steamed alone across the entrance at full speed about six miles out without being molested. At 5 p.m. eight Russian torpedo boats steamed out to eastward and anchored in Také Bay, and *Ryeshitelni* went out during the night to Chefoo with despatches. During the day the Japanese continued bombardment of navy yard, and of bridge between the Old and the New Towns, and Russian batteries kept up desultory fire on presumed positions of Japanese batteries.

At daylight, on morning of August 11, *Poltava, Pallada,* and *Mongolia* in sight well out, anchored off entrance, *Retvizan* first coming inside, then later taking a berth inside wrecks off entrance. At 7 *Peresviet* sighted coming in slowly accompanied by *Sevastopol* and *Pobieda,* all showing signs of action, *Peresviet* considerably battered. About 10 a.m. all ships came into harbor, battleships mooring in West Basin. The killed and wounded, and women* were sent shore, and almost immediately the land batteries again began a bombardment of the town and harbor. The loss of the Russians in killed and wounded was not severe, but their loss in morale was greater, for they believed the *Tsésarévitch* and *Diana* sunk, although they thought the *Novik* and *Askold* had gotten away.

* Russian warships frequently carried female nurses as members of the medical department.

August 10—14, 1904

Port Arthur

At 10 a.m. August 10, when the Russian fleet disappeared from view in the haze, it was steaming slowly, making about four knots, in column regular formation, preceded by trawlers with covering division of destroyers, heading SSE, and crossing mine field. On the left flank of the column was *Novik,* and a division of destroyers consisting of *Boiki, Burni, Vuineslivi, Vlastni, Grosovoi, Bezstrashni, Bezshumni,* and *Bezposhadni,* accompanying the fleet.*

At 9 a.m. admiral had made the signal "Go to Vladivostock," a decision which if made June 23 would have been more easily carried out, and with a fleet stronger by one more ship, the *Bayan,* at this time left in dry dock to repair damages from explosion of mine on July 27.

At 11 column changed course to southeast, trawlers were dismissed and returned to port with covering division of destroyers and gunboats. At this time Japanese cruiser column of seven vessels was on starboard bow, steaming on parallel course to that of Russian fleet, *Nisshin* and *Kasuga* on port beam keeping just abreast, while to the eastward appeared the *Matsushima*-division composed of that ship with *Itsukushima, Hashidate* and *Chen Yen.*

The Japanese battleship squadron of five vessels was also sighted about 11 a.m. coming down from the NNE at full speed from its base in the Elliott Islands, which it had quitted at 8 a.m.** This squadron consisted of *Mikasa* (flag), *Asahi, Fuji, Asama* and *Shikishima* (flag), the *Asama* masqued as the sunken battleship *Yashima*. The Japanese torpedo boats increased in number and appearing at head

---

* The author prepared, from personal observation, a detailed chart showing the disposition of the Russian ships. The extremely small scale makes it impractical to reproduce the chart here.

** The author prepared a series of seven charts covering the movements of the opposing fleets during the Battle of the Yellow Sea. The charts were extremely small scale —each one showing an area of approximately 600 square miles —which makes it impractical to reproduce them here.

of Russian column threw overboard mines or what were apparently such in the track of the Russian fleet. No damage was effected by these devices, but the Russians maneuvered to avoid them and so lost time that permitted approach of full strength of Japanese.

At noon the Japanese battleship squadron bore almost ahead, and steered to south-southwestward to cross course of Russian fleet at speed of 16 knots, the Russians gradually increasing theirs to a little over 14 knots. At 12:15 p.m. Japanese battleships headed southwest as if to pick up cruiser division, then at 12:25 went ships left, forming line, and at 12:30 ships left again forming column in reverse order, and steered course about ESE. At 12:45 p.m. they went ships right-about, and formed column in regular order heading northwest and on opposite course to Russian column.

At 12:50 Russians opened fire at 14,000 yards, answered by the Japanese, and firing continued very deliberately with heavy guns from both sides, ranges decreasing to about 8,000 yards. This firing I heard distinctly in Port Arthur and noted the times. Each gun was distinct, and only about 60 rounds were fired.

At 1:00 p.m. Russians changed course to east, and at 1:05 shifted cruiser column to left flank, the *Askold* having received a hit in forward funnel, and putting forward boiler out of commission. At 1:10 firing ceased, with practically no other damage to either side.

Japanese cruiser division led by *Yakumo,* crossed wake of Russian fleet, then turned to southeast and followed on parallel course, keeping bearing on port quarter of Russians. The battleship squadron also steered a similar course diverging a little, keeping on starboard quarter of Russian columns, and not approaching within 10,000 yards of rear-most Russian ship. The *Nisshin* and *Kasuga* at first kept on port quarter of Russians, and the *Matsushima*-column, steered a parallel course, but being able to make only 10.5 knots was being rapidly left behind. The Russians were now steaming in two columns, cruisers to the left, course clear, making nearly 15 knots, and steering course southeast. They had a considerable lead on the pursuing Japanese, who however were making a little over 16 knots and gradually overhauling the Russians, but keeping beyond effective range of guns. Between 4 and 5 p.m., courses of the two battle fleets began converging and at 4:30 Russians headed east, with head of Japanese column bearing a little abaft the beam of rear ship, the *Poltava.*

At 5 p.m. the battle began again, Japanese opening fire at 10,000 yards, range gradually decreasing. Russians answered, both sides firing at will and deliberately. Neither side made any attempt at fire control. About 5:30 the *Nisshin* and *Kasuga* with Japanese cruiser division led by *Yakumo,* which had again crossed the wake of the Russian fleet, fell into rear of Japanese battleship division. Ranges decreased to 5,000 yards and both fleets now began to suffer from the fire.

Shortly before 6 p.m. the Japanese sent a detachment of armored cruisers, probably *Nisshin* and *Kasuga,* around Russian rear, and at 6 when the fleets were almost abeam of each other and 5,000 yards apart, the *Tsêsarêvitch* at head of Russian column turned abruptly to port, followed at first by other ships of battleship column. Shortly before a shot had struck near heel of foremast and burst, killing Admiral Vitgeft and several of his staff who were standing on the port side of upper bridge, near the conning tower.

Almost immediately after than another shell struck water near the ship and burst, a large piece forming point of shell ranging upward, passing through hammock nettings on starboard side of conning tower, then striking under lip of conning tower cover, which was shaped like an inverted saucer. This fragment continued on along under side of hood displacing all connections, and causing fragments which killed man at the wheel and wounded others. Fragments then fell into nettings on port side, from which it was recovered. Probably from this cause, but also perhaps in some measure due to the defects already existing in *Tsêsarêvitch's* steering gear previously mentioned, the helm was forced over hard to starboard and jammed there, the ship fell out of line, and the Russian column fell into disorder.

Observing this the Japanese admiral detached a cruiser division to follow the armored cruisers around the Russian rear. The ships following *Tsêsarêvitch* under the impression that her turn was another countermarching maneuver turned also to port, as did likewise the cruiser division. Then *Tsêsarêvitch* stopped and made signal "Admiral turns over the command" and it was seen that it was not a maneuver, but an accident, and *Retvizan* turned to starboard as if to charge the Japanese column, and reestablish formation. She approached to within 3,000 yards of it, the Japanese giving way somewhat, but the other Russian battleships, in disorder, could not support her more effectively. The Russian cruiser column led by *Askold,* after turning to port, ran down to the group of Russian ships, passed to westward of them, and then steamed to southward charging line of Japanese cruisers steering WNW. She was followed by *Diana* and *Novik,* but *Pallada* broke away and continued full speed to northwestward.

The Japanese circled about the group of Russian ships, whose exact movements for a short while are very much in doubt, but which about 6:45 again formed column headed by *Peresviet,* which had made signal "Follow me." This signal was made by a hoist on upper bridge railing, both topmasts being carried away by gun fire, wreckage hanging about mastheads, and both day and night signalling arrangements destroyed. The column now took up course about northwest in wake of *Pallada,* Japanese battleships on starboard beam and continuing to pour in a hot fire, to which Russians replied as well as they were able. The *Matsushima*-column, which by this time had been able to come up, was sighted a little on starboard bow, steaming down toward head of column of Japanese battleships.

Tsěsarěvitch was left behind, having had to stop for 40 minutes to make necessary repairs to steering gear, and then steered to southward. *Askold, Diana* and *Novik* also continued to southward, after breaking through line of cruisers. The battle continued between main bodies of the two fleets until dark, then Japanese hauled off to northward and sent in destroyers and torpedo boats. These made several attacks during night on *Tsěsarěvitch, Askold, Diana* and Admiral Ukhtomsky's squadron, but without scoring one hit. The main portion of Russian fleet returned to Port Arthur in early morning of August 11, but *Peresviet,* the ship most seriously damaged, not arriving until 7 a.m. After clearing the line of cruisers, the *Askold* slowed down, and steered course well out from land to avoid torpedo boats.

Next morning Admiral Reitzenstein directed *Novik* to proceed independently in accordance with the plan decided on and communicated to the different captains before leaving Port Arthur, and after examination of the injuries of the *Askold* decided that "in view of the damages discovered, the lack of coal, the reduction suffered in speed, and the probability of encountering rough weather" he would not proceed immediately to Vladivostock, but would go to the neutral port of Shanghai. At the end of the battle the *Askold* was making 20 knots, but the coal consumption was much increased by injuries to funnels.

At 4:30 p.m., August 12, *Askold* arrived at Wocsung, having been preceded a few hours before by the destroyer *Grosovoi*, average speed from scene of action having been 10.5 knots. At daylight on morning of August 11 *Tsésarévitch* was off Shantung Promontory, having been able to make only about 4 knots up to that time, but she arrived at Kiau-Chau at 8:30 p.m. that same day, making average of nearly 11 knots for last 170 miles of run. *Diana* arrived Saigon on August 24, having run 2,400 miles at average of 7.5 knots per hour.

The last orders to the destroyers accompanying Russian fleet previous to the second part of the battle were to remain with the cruisers. During the disorder following accident to *Tsésarévitch* the commander of the destroyer division was called alongside the flagship and asked if he could attack the Japanese. He answered that he would if they could be found, and remained near flagship until after sunset. Five of the destroyers knew nothing of this and, carrying out their instructions, tried to remain with the cruisers, but the *Grosovoi* alone succeeded in doing so. The *Burni* next day ran ashore on Shantung to eastward of Weihaiwei and was blown up by her commander. *Bezchumni* had trouble with her machinery, but managed to get into Kiau-Chau at 5 p.m., August 11. *Beztrashni* and *Bezposhadni* first made a stretch to eastward, next morning being near the islands of the Korean coast off Chemulpo, but turned and headed for Kiau-Chau arriving there about noon August 12.

The *Novik* arrived at Kiau-Chau at 5:30 p.m., August 11, took aboard coal and at 3 a.m. next morning left for Vladivostock. This little ship since the very beginning of the war had been the most active of all the Russian ships. She belonged to two squadrons, the cruiser and the coast-defense, and was continually in demand for work with one or the other. Her speed at the beginning of the war was very nearly the trial speed, but seven months of hard use had lowered it to about 20 knots. She had not been in drydock since February, and her boilers had deteriorated. In the battle of August 10 she received three underwater hits. In going to Vladivostock her commander chose the outside route, going through Van Diemen's Straits, and arriving in Korsakovsk at Sakhalin Island in the morning of August 20, having kept up an average speed of 11 knots, but nearly out of coal.

Having received some coal and a Japanese cruiser being sighted, she left at 4 p.m. the same day, but about 5:15 p.m. was intercepted by the *Tsushima* and in a 45-minute fight was hit five times at or just below the water line, the steering gear being damaged and the steering compartment filled with water. Her commander then returned to Korsakovsk, and despairing of being able to effect repairs ran her into shallow water and blew her up—officers and crew making their way to Vladivostock.

The losses in men were as follows: from fleet returning to Port Arthur, two officers and 38 men killed, 21 officers and 286 men wounded, of which only 50 were seriously; on *Tsêsarêvitch* four officers and eight men killed, nine officers and 40 men wounded; on *Askold* one officer and 10 men killed, four officers and 44 men wounded; on *Diana* four killed and 23 wounded; on *Novik* two killed and one wounded (Aug. 20, two killed 15 wounded), or total for battle of August 10, of seven officers and 62 men killed, 35 officers and 394 men wounded, but most of them not seriously.

There is evidence that the Japanese loss was greater in officers and men killed, and if their wounded were not greater it was most likely due to the fact that many slightly wounded were not reported.* For this reason and the weak finish made by the Japanese, combined with other published information, it would seem that in this battle the Russians shot better, maneuvered better, and from tactical point of view won the battle.

The injuries to the ships were as follows, beginning with *Peresviet* (See sketch No. 8). She was the most seriously damaged and had 16 well defined hits by shells of large caliber. Hit "a" was 2′ below

* Japanese casualties included 6 officers and 29 men killed; 10 officers and 78 men wounded. His Imperial Highness Prince Kwacho, aboard the flagship *Mikasa*, was slightly wounded.

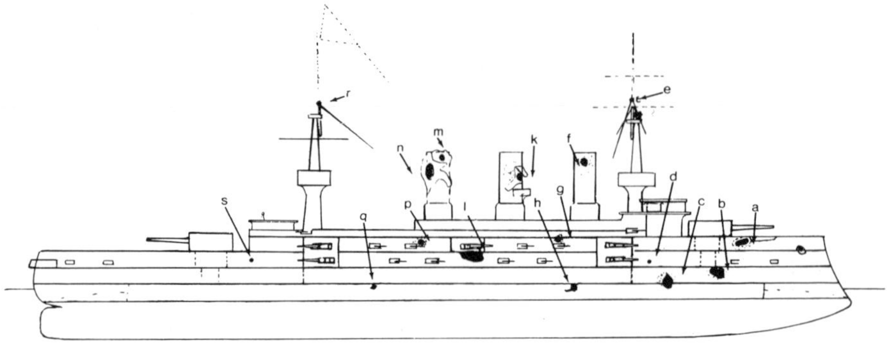

Sketch No. 8 Battle damage to *Peresviet;* based on personal observation. (Key letters "i," "j," and "o" omitted in original drawing.)

upper deck, hole in outer plating about 2′ by 4′, and made by either 8″ or 6″; "b" was a heart-shaped hole, caused by hit from largest caliber shell or 12″, was located 7′ above water line, and measured about 5′ x 6′; "c" was probably another 12″ hit, 2′ above water line and measuring 4′ x 7′. I saw a man step from a sampan into this hole without lowering his head. Hit "d" was a clean hole, by shell not smaller than 8″; "e" carried away foretopmast, signal-yards and wrecked searchlights; "f" was by 6″ or 8″; "g" was 6″ hit, making hole in plating 2′ in diameter and damaging gun beneath; "h" was by heavy shell, probably 12″, at water line, causing lead. Armor was not perforated but an irregular shaped fragment was cracked off near edge of plate. When ship came into harbor she listed to port and placed collision mat over this hit. Hit "k" was by 6″ or 8″; "l"was by 12″ making very large hole in side underneath midships 6″ gun; "m" was by 6″; "n" was by 12″, badly wrecking funnel. From these funnel hits boilers were so much damaged that *Peresviet* could make only 6 knots at close of action, and for a week after arriving in port did not again raise steam on any of them. Hit "p" was by 6″ making hole about 2′ in diameter and damaging gun beneath; "q" was a splash hit on armor by 6″; "r" wrecked main topmast with wireless; and "s" was a clean hole by 8″ or larger. Excepting the funnel hits, these that made large holes in outside plating did little damage inside. The electrical connections were very much damaged inside and the forward turret remained trained to starboard for several days, and until August 14, the wreckage of the topmasts and signal gear still hung about the mastheads.

The *Pobieda* was very little damaged, having eight hits of which two were 6″, one possibly 12″, and the other five uncertain (See sketch No. 9). Boilers were still in fairly good shape, battery uninjured, and no penetrations in armor.

Poltava had nine hits by large-caliber shells, of which two, "c" and "g", were probably 12″; "b", "f", "e", "k" and "h" probably 6″; and "a" and "d" uncertain; "k" was an underwater hit, filling a compartment and bringing ship somewhat down by the stern. On the port side, one of the guns in after 6″ turret had about 6′ of muzzle broken off (See sketch No. 10).

Sevastopol had 14 hits with two, "a" and "q", possibly by 13″, and "b", "c", "d", "e", "h", "k", and "p" probably six inch, and "m," "n", "f", "g", and "l" uncertain. She was not seriously damaged in either hull, guns or boilers (See sketch No. 11).

Retvizan had six hits during action of August 10, of which "c" was probably by 12″, "b", "c", and "f" by 6″, "a" and "d" uncertain, and "g" the hit made by a 4.7″ shell during bombardment by land batteries on August 9, when she was struck altogether 17 times, but this hit alone doing serious damage (See sketch No. 12).

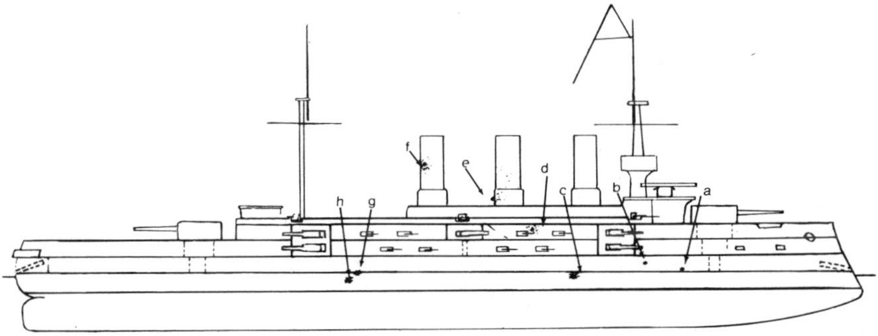

Sketch No. 9 Battle damage to *Pobieda;* based on personal observation. (Keys on drawing are not mentioned in text.)

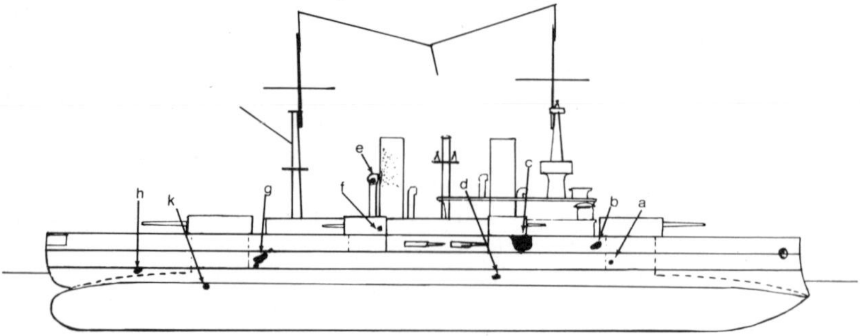

Sketch No. 10 Battle damage to *Poltava;* based on personal observation. (Key letters "i" and "j" omitted in original drawing.)

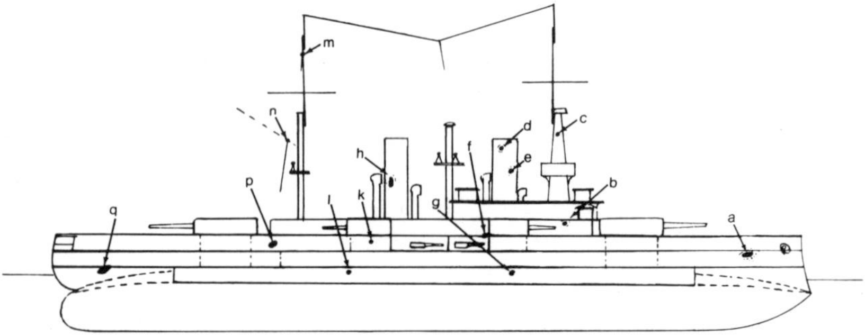

Sketch No. 11 Battle damage to *Sevastopol;* based on personal observation. (Key letters "i," "j," and "o" omitted in original drawing; no keys mentioned in text.)

Hits by shells of less than 6" were not plotted, but there were very few of these, and the damage from them insignificant. The wireless outfits of all the ships were so damaged that they could not be used, all masthead wires cut by the numerous fragments. The torpedo nets of *Peresviet* were completely wrecked on starboard side, being cut to pieces by fragments from shells striking side, and hanging in the water nearby. All boats, and most of the search lights were out of commission temporarily. Steps were immediately taken toward commencing repairs, but the land bombardments continued, and interfered very much with this work.

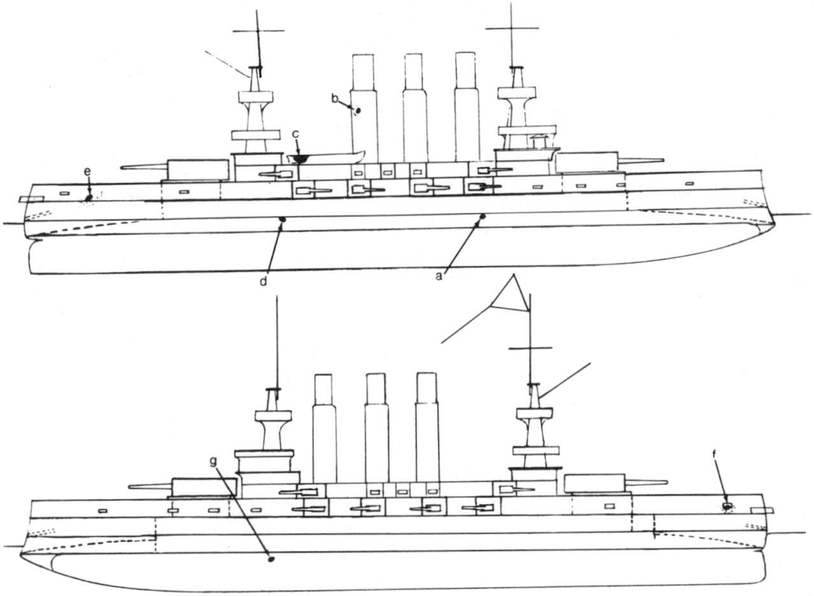

Sketch No. 12 Battle damage to *Retvizan,* starboard side (top) and port side (bottom); based on personal observation.

Though I visited *Peresviet* and *Poltava,* I was not permitted to inspect closely the damages of any of the ships, what information I have being obtained by an inspection with glasses from the shore, about one-half mile away, and from conversations with Russian officers in the fight. The French and German attachés requested permission to inspect the injuries of the ships but were refused.

On August 12, the bombardment from land positions was continued, being directed principally on the ships moored in West Basin, *Sevastopol* and *Pobieda* being hit a few times, and hospital ship *Angara* moored in southwestern part of harbor also hit several times. *Peresviet* answered with her 6″ guns, *Pobieda* with her 10″ and ships began shifting berths to avoid the fire. In the afternoon of August 12, the New Town was bombarded. It was said in military circles that the fleet had orders to go out again immediately, and that Admiral Ukhtomsky had declined to take them out. Besides the bombardment of the town and harbor, the Japanese were also actively firing on the batteries to northward of the town, principally on No. 40. The Russians replied with howitzers from Golden Hill and Battery No. 35 assisted by some of the ships. During August 13 and 14 few shells were fired into the town, more attention being paid to the batteries.

The town of Port Arthur and district about it had suffered five bombardments from the heavy guns of the Japanese ships at sea, beginning with that of February 9, when the fire of the 12″ guns of the fleet had been directed at the batteries and town. Most of the shells fell in the vicinity of Electric Battery, and those marked "q","r", "s", "t", "u", "w", and "y" fell as shown in sketch.* Casualties represented by one man killed and five wounded in the batteries, and the damage by shattering of the window panes along water front due to explosion of "r"; "q" fell in a garden and failed to explode, being recovered by military authorities entire; "s" narrowly missed dry dock, and burst with practically no damage; "t" struck steamer *Kazan* and failed to burst. Others fell in water in the vicinity. In the later bombardments, hit "a" fell in a vacant lot 150′ from a small brick house in which were two men and three women. A crater was made in the hard ground, 12′ across, and 6′ deep, and most of the fragments continued in prolongation of line of flight of shell toward the house, which over a space of 10′ x 25′ was struck by 11 fragments of appreciable size, three being rather large. None perforated the walls which were 12″ thick, but one of the men and two of the women were killed by other pieces coming through the windows. Hit "e" struck near sidewalk of a street built up on both sides, and fragments badly wrecked a low brick wall and porch of a house 50′ away in direction of line of flight. Hit "k" struck between two houses, 30′ from one, 20′ from the other, and wrecked the kitchen of one of the houses in direction of line of flight. Walls of both houses marked by many fragments, no fragments perforating them however. Hit "w" fell alongside *Sevastopol* bursting against her armor, but doing no damage. Hit "o" fell alongside *Retvizan,* which had just been brought into port on March

* The author's sketches of bombardment damage to Port Arthur, mentioned several times in this chapter, were of such small scale as to make it impractical to reproduce them in a book of this size.

9, the day before. Work was going on repairing leaks in caisson and pumping it out, divers were working below the surface, and steam launch was tending them. Shell burst on striking the water, killing two men in steam launch, and wounding about 20 others near by. Another shell falling on shore killed seven Chinamen and those falling near batteries killed six men, and wounded one officer and 16 men, but without damaging batteries. In all there were fired into the town from sea, 499 8″, 10″, and 12″ shells, causing a loss on shore of one officer contusioned, 10 soldiers killed, 23 soldiers wounded, a civilian, two women, an Ishvostchik and seven Chinamen killed, and in the fleet two men killed, 20 wounded. In attempting to reply to one of the bombardments *Sevastopol* wrecked mount of one 12″ gun, which could not be repaired, but which may have been offset by similar damages to Japanese guns and mounts. In bombardments of March 10 and 22, Russians replied by indirect fire from battleships, but though making good practice made no hits. Ranges used by bombarding ships, 14,000 to 17,000 yards. After February 9 all shells that landed on shore burst on impact, and about two-thirds of those that fell in the water also burst. The largest fragment of shell recovered was from a 12″ shell and weighed 14 pounds.

In the bombardments from land beginning August 7, a 4.7″ gun was used located in the Wolf Hills and distant from the town 9,600 meters. From the hills near this position could be seen the southwest portion of West Basin and northern part of town along slopes of Peripolichnaya, but the navy yard and northeast portion of West Basin could not be seen. We had expected the bombardment to begin almost any day after July 30, and just after church about 11 a.m. on Sunday the first shell was heard, falling and bursting at "a", followed shortly after by another which struck very near.

A little later one fell so near the office of the commandant of the navy yard that all the window panes were broken, and building so much damaged, that office force was moved to another building. About 80 shells were fired into town during day. All Chinese workmen quit work in the navy yard, and it was difficult to hold the Russian workmen, severe penalties being imposed on any man stopping work. Three men were killed and 20 wounded. Weather was fair and very warm with light southeasterly airs.

Bombardment continued on next day, August 8, which was cloudy, with occasional light rain, light to moderate northerly breezes. About 100 shells were fired into town, entrance to East Basin being about the center of area bombarded. Several shells fell near flagship *Tsĕsarĕvitch,* and armored ports of admiral's cabin were closed to keep out fragments. One shell, "a" struck roof of oil store-house, flames bursting out immediately, and house destroyed, in spite of gallant efforts of fire party from *Amur* to extinguish it, another shell bursting amongst fire party while they were at work and causing loss of several men. In afternoon about 30 shells were fired at a barracks on foot of eastern slope of Peripolichnaya which was probably in sight from gun position.

August 9 was cloudy and warm, with moderate breezes from southeast. During this day the bombardment was directed at ships moored in West Basin, some of which could probably be seen. The firing was very accurate, and I did not see any shell fall at a greater distance than 200 yards from the ships. About 60 shells in all were fired, of which I saw five strike the *Retvizan,* and it was said that she was struck by 17. Most of the shells burst on falling into the water, but about a third did not. One that struck the water near the *Retvizan,* traveled for some distance under it, and then burst against the underwater portion below the armor, doing such damage that ship had one of the small compartments filled. *Peresviet* was also struck, and now at last it was brought home to the Russians that it was dangerous for the fleet to remain in Port Arthur.

The next day it went out, and the battle of August 10 was fought. In Port Arthur the bombardment continued, most of the shells falling in eastern part of navy yard. In the afternoon fire was directed apparently at the bridge connecting the Old and the New Towns, this bridge also probably being in sight of gunners. On August 11, it was fair and warm, hazy, and light airs from southeast. Bombardment was directed on Old Town, and covered larger area than previously.

On August 12, fair and very warm, with light airs from southeast, bombardment began on the ships moored in West Basin. *Pobieda* and *Sevastopol* were hit, and *Sevastopol* moved up ahead of *Poltava,* and probably out of sight of Japanese battery. Several shots struck hospital ship *Angara* which was probably in sight from the gun position, the line of sight passing through valley of stream between the Old and New Towns. In the afternoon the New Town was bombarded.

During August 13 and 14 there was little firing on the town or harbor, the principal attention of the enemy being given to the Russian lines of defense. After a few shots from the siege gun its sound could be distinctly recognized from the reports of other guns firing, and one knew quite certainly that another shell was coming. About five seconds after hearing the report of the gun could be heard the sound of the projectile in the air, and from this sound it could be decided if the shell was coming near or not.

If it was thought that the shell was coming near there was probably a second or two before the shell landed in which to take such precautions as seemed best. Most people hearing a shell coming near would run, others would dodge behind a wall or tree, but the best plan was to lie down. A shell might strike very near, say within 10 feet or a person and he would be quite uninjured, while another man 200 yards away would be hit. From the point of impact the fragments would generally fly away in form of an inverted cone, point resting where shell struck the ground.

One shell landed within 20 feet of a group of 12 sailors and no man was hit. Several fell within 50 feet of me, earth and pebbles striking me but without injury. The crater in the usually hard ground was about four feet across and two feet deep, the smoke from explosion black and mixed with dust. When striking roof of a Chinese house, which was composed of tiles laid on Chinese mats supported by boards, the shell seemed to burst instantaneously, making a hole in the roof about five feet in diameter, most of the fragments going outside, but enough getting through to wreck any room just underneath.

When striking a brick wall 12" thick a hole about three feet in diameter would be blown through the wall, and fragments of bricks would do considerable damage inside, but few fragments of shell would get in. In neither case of striking roof or wall of a house, were there any signs of the force of explosion inside the house, the roof not being displaced, nor the walls bulged or blown out. All the violent damage seemed in immediate vicinity of impact, but fragments flying to considerable distances. On August

7, hit "b" was on roof of a store house with galvanized iron roof and walls. Shell burst on impact, tearing a hole in roof about two by four feet, and many fragments got inside, and walls were perforated by many pieces flying out. Some fragments did not have sufficient velocity to perforate the thin sheet iron walls, and remained inside of house. In the craters could usually be recovered fragments of considerable size.

One piece I found comprised part of base, and a strip of the wall 8" long by 2" in width. In the angle between wall and base was a small quantity of a black greasy looking mass, with an appearance like vaseline mixed with lampblack. Pieces from the shell picked up some distance away from impact were hot enough to burn wood. One could light cigarettes from them. If a shell struck a coal pile there was no fire, and hardly a mark left in the coal. It seemed at first very improbable that these shells could damage a battleship. During the bombardments from August 7 to 14, about 500 shells of 4.7" caliber were fired into the town, causing a loss of less than 50 killed and wounded, the burning of one building, but forcing the Russian fleet out to battle.

During the days of bombardment life went on with very little change from ordinary circumstances. he stores would be open, officers in carriages driving about, women and children out walking, but not so many as before bombardments began. Nearly every house and store had a bombproof, usually consisting of pit dug in the ground, roofed over with heavy beams, protected by sandbags. In some cases, bombproofs had been chipped out of the solid rock.

General Stessel had a very elaborate one in rear of his house, the pile of sand bags looking like a small mountain. As his house was not near any of the targets of the enemy's guns, no shells had fallen near his house up till August 14. When the shells would be heard coming into the town, the stores would be closed, and clerical force and all civilians would take refuge in the bombproofs, remaining there until firing was over, when things would open up and go on as before. The military and naval people seemed usually very cool and indifferent under fire, and did not visit the bombproofs. The gendarmes had the most difficult duty of staying at their posts in the open; sometimes this required considerable nerve, and probably for the first time in their lives entitling them to a little respect from Russians.

From the beginning of the war until May 26 the Japanese had not declared a blockade of Port Arthur, and when they did it included only the coast from Pitzewo on the east round to head of Port Adams on the west. Newchwang remained open until it was captured on July 25. Until May 15 it would not have been difficult to have partly supplied the fortress from the sea, the entrance being left unguarded occasionally for days at a time. Admiral Makaroff went out with a strong fleet on March 26 and April 11, cruising 20 miles from the entrance and remaining out all day without molestation from the enemy. For leaving the entrance unwatched on May 14 the Japanese paid very dearly with the loss of *Hatsuse* and *Yashima.* After that date it was always watched, but by an inadequate force to prevent ingress to blockade runners if well handled. In dealing with this question both sides seemed to lack energy, the Japanese to prevent, and the Russians to encourage communication by sea.

Junks communicated with Chefoo almost without hindrance until July 27, sometimes as many as seven being in sight at one time off entrance, and once two of them being towed out of harbor by the Russians, casting off and standing out without being stopped by a group of Japanese torpedo boats watching the entrance. Only after July 27 was a strict blockade established with a long line of from 30 to 40 torpedo boats and destroyers six miles out, and with a strong support of cruisers behind them. The Japanese battleships remained at Elliott Islands 60 miles away, and if the Russians had earlier realized the danger of remaining at Port Arthur they might have had a good start on the way to Vladivostock, before the Japanese could have overhauled them. From the ineffectual pursuit by the Japanese admirals of ships damaged in the battles of August 10, and 14, the Port Arthur fleet would have had an excellent chance of arriving safely at Vladivostock.

Attention to the introduction of a supply of fresh meat by sea might have lessened the 14,000 cases of scurvy in December. As to the manner in which the fortress was provisioned, it was always impossible to get definite information. It could be very easily seen that there were large quantities of flour on hand, and in this respect the claims of the Russians to be provisioned for one year was perhaps justified. Before the fortress was isolated by interruption of railway communications little attention had been paid to the supply of fresh meat. Kunst & Albers, a large German firm, in April offered to collect all the cattle on Liaotung Peninsula for supply of the army, but the offer was not considered. When the army abandoned Nanshan the military authorities purchased all sheep, cattle, goats and pigs that could be purchased but which altogether would furnish fresh meat to the army for one month only.

Before August forage for animals had become exceedingly scarce, the animals confined within the fortress having grazed the hills bare and there being little else. A few cabs were still about the town, but the cab-horses were in a pitiful condition for lack of food, the price of which was exorbitant. By August 1 fresh meat was served out to officers once a day only, soldiers and sailors receiving it less often. Ammunition seemed to be plentiful from the manner in which the sea batteries expended it at extreme ranges against enemy's small craft.

The women and children had been allowed to remain in the town, the number being increased by those coming from Dalny when it was abandoned. Any woman, except American, might remain if she had a Russian officer as protector. All women remaining were inscribed in the police register with duties for which they were considered qualified, and liable to be called on at any time by the commandant of the fortress to act as nurses, washerwomen, sempstresses, cooks, or laundry women.

General Stessel was exceedingly strict in dealing with the use of intoxicating liquors. Soldiers and sailors under the influence of liquor were sent to work on the defenses, and officers court-martialed. There was no gayety in the way of café chantants or theaters, and practically no disorder. If any café or restaurant made a little rough house as is quite common in Russia, it was instantly closed and confiscated for a hospital. As a consequence during the entire time the town was always very sober and quiet.

After the sinking of the *Petropavlovsk,* mining and sweeping for mines was extensively carried on by both sides. Rarely a night passed but that the Japanese showed some activity about the entrance, usually connected with mining. Every day the Russians sent out their.trawling caravans to sweep for mines, and other boats to plant them. In this work were engaged all the tenders formerly working with the dredges, with large ships boats and steam cutters. In July the destroyers were also rigged to lay mines, being used at night to lay mines well off the entrance.

The *Amur,* on account of her draft could not be used in laying mines over a field already partly mined for fear of blowing herself up. For this a two-legged derrick to which was slung a mine was rigged over the stern of a destroyer, and she was sent out at night to the place intended to drop the mine. Certain channels as shown in sketch* were kept as clear as possible of mines, and Russians did not plan to mine within the three-mile limit, except very close to entrance to guard against branders. The Japanese attempted to mine as close in as possible.

The Russian mines were of two forms, a small spherical mine with 100 pounds of pyroxyline, and a larger buoy-shaped one with 200 pounds. Both were exploded by electro-chemical means, glass tubes enclosed in lead, and filled with sulphuric acid, and inserted in upper part of mine. The mines placed by *Amur* were of Elia type, automatically adjusting themselves to required depth below surface, in whatever depth of water planted. There were some electric observation mines planted, but I could not learn just where, probably near the entrance, but by far the greater number of mines used by both sides were contact mines. In sweeping or trawling for mines the Russians used a wire hawser between two towing boats, at intervals along the hawser being alternately, a grapnel or an 80 pound shot, seized to the hawser. The hawser was about one cable long with heavy rope pendants at each end, the pendants taken aboard the towing boats. These steamed at speed of four knots, about 100 yards from each other, and if drag picked up a mine, the mine usually exploded, the Japanese mines nearly always doing so.

If mine did not explode it was hauled to the surface, disconnected from its cable and fired at until exploded. A rifle bullet fired into body of mine would cause an explosion of low order, several trials being necessary sometimes, and occasionally the mines

---

* This sketch not reproduced.

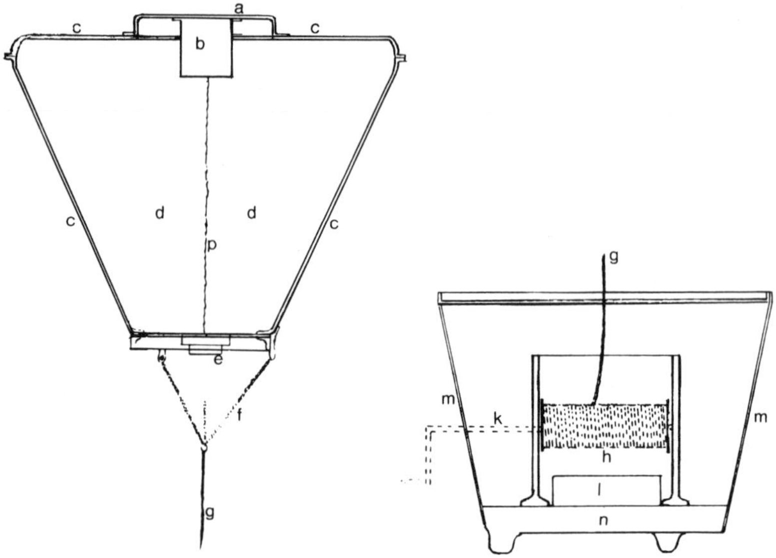

Sketch No. 13 Japanese mine, contact type. (a) cover, (b) exploder, (c) shell or casing, (d) gun cotton, (e) safety mechanism, (f) bridle, (g) cable, (h) cable reel, (k) reel crank, (l) depth regulating mechanism, (m) outer casing, (n) anchor, (p) conductor.

detonating. Sometimes the Japanese mines would explode when no boat was near, and when the only motion they received was due to the waves or swell. The Russian mines were safer to handle and if picked up could be disarmed and replanted. Naval authorities gave reward of 25 rubles for each mine found.

The general type of the Japanese is shown in sketch and is probably a modification of the Elia, having only Japanese stamps on it (See sketch No. 13). It is shaped generally like a truncated cone, broad side floating up, and this particular mine which I saw on the beach contained about 180 pounds of gun cotton, in round perforated discs, but it is said that the Japanese also used shimose. * The mine itself consisted of the shell of ¼″ steel, on top of

* Explosive, consisting mostly of picric acid, invented by Masahika Shimonose Kogaubachi.

which was a small cap or cover carrying the exploder or fuze chamber, which is connected by a short conductor to safety mechanism on bottom of mine. A wire cable of 1/2" diameter is connected to mine by a bridle of three short pieces of chain, then runs to reel in the anchor.

Anchor consists of a disc in solid casting, on bottom three heavy lugs or feet. On top is a box containing depth regulating mechanism, and supports for carrying reel. About this is a thin shell of 1/4" steel. In this shell is hole for a crank with which reel is wound, but which is not shipped when mine is let go.

The mine and anchor are reeled up close together, safety mechanism adjusted, and both let go together. When anchor strikes the bottom reel is released and mine floats toward surface, and reel is locked when mine reaches a level of 10′ below surface. It was not possible to examine the mechanism in detail, but the operation seems to be as follows: In the exploder is suspended vertically a pendulum which, when mine is struck or inclined, makes electric connection with one side or the other. The safety mechanism is on the principle of clock work set to run 15 minutes so that mine is not armed until that length of time after letting go.

The system by which the depth is regulated could not be learned, but probably depends on variation of pressure on opposite faces of a diaphragm similar to manner in which depth below surface of automobile torpedo is regulated.

Hardly a day passed but perhaps from four to 10 mines would be picked up, some within a few hundred yards of the entrance, and again mines were seen to explode spontaneously six to 10 miles off. Some would drift up on the beach, and explode on striking it, or be exploded by the beach guard. Mines that had become detached from their anchors were occasionally found and destroyed. For a certain belt off shore between the three-mile and six-mile limit both sides planted mines, and ships of both sides carefully avoided this danger zone.

Prior to August 14, only one Russian destroyer, the *Bezchumni*, had been injured by accidentally striking a mine, and two small boats had been blown up while picking up mines. As draft of most of the destroyers was about seven feet, it indicated that the mine fields as planted were fairly safe for destroyers, which did quite a lot of cruising over them. The gunboats and *Novik* also cruised considerably along shore line unaccompanied by trawlers and were fortunate to escape destruction. Whenever the larger ships went out, trawlers invariably preceded them going and returning.

In the disposition of their destroyers the Russian authorities did not seem disposed to give them a free hand, or to allow them to take any chances. The flotilla was divided into two divisions of 12 boats each, with an independent commander for each division. As with their admirals and captains of larger ships, these officers as well as the commanders of the destroyers, were constantly being changed. In the beginning Captain Matussiévitch commanded one division, Captain Ginter the other. Commander Lieven relieved Captain Ginter shortly after February 9, and Commander Eliseieff also commanding *Boevoi* relieved Captain Matussiévitch in April and continued to perform this duty until the end of the siege, also commanding *Boevoi* until July 24 when she was torpedoed. Commander Lieven was relieved by Captain Bubnoff in April, and Captain Bubnoff was in turn relieved by Commander Krinitzki in August.

Each division of 12 boats was divided into groups of four, which generally acted together under direction of senior commander of four. This had disadvantage, when senior boat was laid up, of placing that group under a new man or of sending out the senior commander on some other boat than his own. Usually 16 boats were available for service, eight in each division, no greater number having been known to be out while I was in Port Arthur.

Vzadnik and *Gaidamak*, of almost the same type as large destroyers, acted separately. *Vnushitelni* was lost February 25; *Steregustchi*, March 10; *Strashni*, April 13; *Vnimatelni*, May 26; *Lieutenant Burakoff*, and *Boevoi*, July 24; *Burni*, August 11; and *Bezshumni*, *Bezstrashni*, *Bezposhadni* and *Grosovoi* interned—all without having accomplished anything in their line. The admiral thought Pitzewo was too far for them to operate, and the boats when going out had always encountered superior forces, until they believed that the Japanese had many more destroyer than was really the case.

The commanding officers of destroyers were old lieutenants or commanders, few being under 40. They complained that their eyes became so inflamed they could not see, that their feet swelled, their nerves were not good, and the lack of sleep exhausted them physically. As a consequence there were frequent changes in the commands of the destroyers, between February 8 and August 14, only two destroyers, the *Vuineslivi* and *Vlastni,* having retained the same commanders. The Russian boats had less speed and feebler armament than the Japanese and these facts lowered the confidence of their commanding officers.

The Japanese rigged extra funnels on some of their torpedo boats and passed them off as destroyers; and with this trick aided to impress the Russians with the idea of their superiority in numbers. On April 12, eight boats were sent out by Admiral Makaroff with orders to attack the Japanese wherever found, but with such unfortunate consequences next day,* that Admiral Vitgeft did not repeat the experiment, and always prescribed limited cruises along shore. Torpedo boats were placed to guard the Army's flanks, when the Japanese were closing in on the fortress, *Lieutenant Burakoff* and *Boevoi* being lost in this way. They were never sent out with the aim of attacking the Japanese ships or transports. I asked an officer why this was not done, and he said that the Japanese had so many more destroyers than the Russians, that it could not be risked. Inexperienced officers were detailed for the commands of destroyers, officers who had not even had previous experience in that sort of duty, and who could not distinguish their boats from Japanese boats. *Steregustchi* and *Strashni* were lost due to these causes.

Identification signals at night were made by flashing a bullseye lantern. Russian boats often joined Japanese flotillas and cruised with them under the impression that they were their own, and Japanese boats did similarly. The only method they considered a guarantee against this accident was for their boats to cruise together at night in exceedingly close order.

Boats subjected to gunfire were usually first disabled by having steam pipes cut, and Russian officers considered some protection necessary for these pipes, or to build destroyers and torpedo boats

* This referred to the loss of the *Petropavlosk* (sunk by a mine) and the death of Admiral Makaroff.

with gas engines. The forward gun in destroyers so blinded commanding officers at night that it was preferred not to use it. For day work they wished to have two heavy guns, one forward and one aft. Three-pounders were considered too light to form armament of destroyers. Draft of destroyers should not be over seven feet to allow them to pass over mine fields, without danger of striking mines, or of causing them to explode by screw current. Bows of boats should be strengthened to prevent twisting in case of light collisions in close formations, and to ram a suspected boat at night without giving alarm. With the Russians their favorite type of destroyer was the French boat, type *Vlastni.*

The Japanese destroyers and torpedo boats never exhibited any lack of nerve either day or night, but their commanders were badly deficient in cool judgment under search lights and gun fire at night, and seemed absolutely incapable of correctly estimating distances under such circumstances. It must have been extremely difficult to do this in the glare of search lights, and with their boats almost undistinguishable in the spray from falling shells, but they sometimes discharged torpedoes at extreme ranges of 3,000 yards. Bad judgment was shown in attacking at full speed and by single boats or by small groups instead of in numbers, and in approaching the Russian fleet under way, and attacking from astern.

In the handling of their ships, the Russian captains did very well. Captain Jakovleff would enter or leave the harbor without assistance of tugs. Captain von Schultz* of *Novik* would enter, turn his ship with her own engines, and back her down through the entrance to East Basin, and into the Basin. Some of the ships were not so well handled, the French attaché once making the remark as he saw a cruiser trying to get out on June 23 "C'est dégoutant. Je ne puis plus regarder."** *Tsésarévitch* had never had target practice until the battle of August 10, though she might have been given the opportunity enjoyed by *Bayan, Poltava,* and *Retvizan* in some of their expeditions to Také Bay during July. Captains Viren, Ouspensky, von Schultz, von Essen, and Ivanof of *Amur* were commanders with whom no fault could be found. Others, as the com-

* Mikhail F. von Shultz (born 1862).

** "It's disgusting; I can't watch any longer."

manding officers of *Vnushitelni* and *Boyarin*, were very weak, and one commanding officer of a battleship was taken ill the day previous to sortie of fleet on June 23, being relieved by another officer, and recovering and resuming command two days after the sortie.

The subordinate officers were rather apathetic, with little enthusiasm, and inclined to overvalue the Japanese forces and ability. In conversation with these officers, they disputed the correctness in sentiment of the American proverb that "Time is money" and demonstrated how if Russia were victorious the result would prove the superiority of the Russian system of government and military administration.

At the dinner table in the club one evening several Russian officers and the attachés were talking, and one Russian naval officer remarked that the German and American navies were at a disadvantage in comparison with the French and Russian, in that they did not have the glorious naval history possessed by the two later. It was said very seriously, but without any intention of giving offense, and the Germans and I only smiled. Von Gilgenheim made a rather rough joke with one officer saying that they ought to sell their ships in Port Arthur and use the money to pay the Japanese indemnity. The officer might have taken several different views of this suggestion, but only answered with great determination that "Russia will *never* pay indemnity".

Toward the end both von Gilgenheim and the French attaché expressed some very free and open criticism of affairs, and suffered somewhat for it. Owing to the close supervision and lack of facilities, the officers of both army and navy in Port Arthur were extremely quiet and sober in their behavior, though there were quite a number of suicides.

The enlisted men of the navy were clean, well behaved, and under strictest discipline. They were more intelligent than the soldiers, but judging from those detailed to act as my servants, their intelligence was not even then of a very high order. A simple mechanical device would puzzle them very much. The first man had done a great deal of duty as personal attendant on officers, and was supposed to be a very good man for that sort of duty. He was a very expensive luxury, besides being addicted to the use of perfumery and rouge. Finally he became implicated in the disappearance of my papers and was relieved by another man, who seemed a very decent sort of fellow, but who was taken away after a few days, his record showing that he had been convicted of stealing. The third man was a dirty, simple, honest sort of fellow, but had a great affection for a bombproof. My Chinese servant had been arrested as a thief soon after my arrival, and after being beaten several times finally disappeared, I could not find out how. The enlisted men were a splendid lot physically, and had in them some excellent qualities.

The great misfortune of the Russians was in their commander in chief, Rear Admiral Vitgeft. The Russians themselves said that on account of his mediocrity he had been chosen for chief of staff by the Viceroy, who did not wish to have clever or energetic men about him, as being likely to be disturbers. Their idea of the Viceroy himself was that he was an able man, very sympathetic and tactful, but first of all a courtier. He always wished everything to go smoothly and without friction, and if there should happen to be any of either, he did not wish to know of it, or if he was compelled to know it himself, he would not inform the Emperor of it, for fear of disturbing the Imperial serenity. As commander of a ship or in command of a fleet, Russian officers nevertheless had a high opinion of him. Admiral Vitgeft was a typical bureaucrat of very limited intelligence, and an intense dislike to action. He was obstinate, superstitious, and fearful of responsibility, being always oppressed by the idea that he was only temporarily commander in chief and lacked full power.

After the isolation of Port Arthur it is hard to understand how the fiction was still retained. He was exceedingly affable to his inferiors, and looked on the enlisted men as his children. Disliking energy or action in both theory and practice, he spent the entire time in the cabin of his flagship, reported to be fondest of lying in his bunk and reading Zola. In personal appearance he looked older than his age of 57, appearing more like a slow thinking, benevolent old professor, with long grey uncombed hair. In 1899 he was promoted to rear admiral, but the first time he ever commanded a squadron under way was on June 23, 1904 in the first sortie. Obtuse, purblind to actual conditions, hating activity and fearful of responsibility, yet when once forced to a decision, his obstinacy would have impelled him to persist in its execution and, had he lived, he would probably have brought some of the ships into Vladivostock.

The second in command, Rear Admiral Prince Ukhtomsky, was not esteemed as particularly able, but was considered a Russian patriot, and had the credit with the fleet of having forced Admiral Vitgeft to make the sortie of June 23.

General Stessel was a rough, blustering soldier autocratic, energetic, and unscrupulous as to means of bringing himself into notice. Under the spell of his loud voice, violent manner, and absolute authority he had nearly everyone in Port Arthur cowed, army, navy and civilians. Besides his staff, however, he had no friends, and every one seemed to hate him and delight in spreading all kinds of unfavorable stories about him, in regard to his family, his education, his intelligence, and his courage. Openly some most outrageous things would be said of him. How much was true it is difficult to say, but he certainly was a most disagreeable character.

General Smirnoff, the commandant of the fortress, was a more highly educated man, and of considerable force. General Fock was the active fighting man, always in the advanced positions, and in command at Nanshan where he considered one regiment sufficient to hold the position, and with it did indeed make a splendid fight. Amongst the Russians there was a unanimity of opinion in giving to General Kondratenko the greatest credit for the preparation of the fortress to resist a siege, and for conduct of operations after it had begun. I could not learn just why this was so, because General Kondratenko commanded only one division, and though he must have been a good man, yet it seemed that hostility to Stessel and the death of Kondratenko combined to give the latter more credit than was perhaps actually due him.

The subordinate officers of the army were not socially of as good a class as officers of similar rank in the navy, nor were they so well educated, but they were healthier morally and good fighting men, though not capable of a high degree of head-work. In both army and navy could be noticed the predilection for simple methods of fighting, and a mental failure to grasp the more highly developed and modern ways. They did better at close quarters, and on sea would have shown improvement if they had had more leaders like Makaroff who would have taken them there.

On August 14, all the attachés requested permission from General Smirnoff to leave the fortress in order to visit Vladivostock, permission being granted in each case, but it was the intention at that time for von Gilgenheim to remain in Port Arthur a while longer. This day there was a strong attack on the Russian left flank, the Russians yielding ground, and communication with Pigeon Bay being threatened. As this was now the usual point of departure for junks breaking blockade, cutting it off would have made it necessary to leave by the main entrance when the chances of capture would have been very much greater. I chose to go out by junk, as to accept a safe conduct, or to be captured would have been a termination of my mission, and then it seemed as if the fleet must soon leave again for Vladivostock which would be then a very interesting place. So having made arrangements for a junk I thought it best to leave immediately before the Japanese had advanced further, but the other attachés said they could not get ready in time, their baggage being in the battery on Tiger Tail.

Shortly before leaving, Commander Kitkine of the navy had asked me if I objected to convoying a lady, Mme. Chaffanjon and her little daughter, so they accompanied me, also another lady, wife of a Russian officer on *Tsésarévitch* who came in at the last moment. We passed along the rear of the Russian lines, then engaged, and reached Pigeon Bay in the afternoon. I then learned that a Japanese cruiser in sight of the shore had sunk three junks the day before, one of them with an officer I had seen off, and the other two with Chinese and Hindoos. The crew of the junk I had engaged had mostly deserted after getting this news and we had some difficulty in getting another, but about 10 p.m. with cloudy weather and a light easterly breeze, started. Nearly all junks leaving had made for Chefoo, but I had decided to leave my destination to depend on wind and weather, making it the first object to get safely out of sight of land.

In starting I kept close along shore to the northward intending if chased by the Japanese to beach the junk and take my chances on shore, but fortunately we were not discovered, though we passed under the search light of a cruiser which made our sail loom up enormously in the darkness. The Japanese were attacking about the same time, the Russian searchlights were flashing around and the star shells were making it light enough to read by at a distance of five miles. About midnight we had showers of rain, and the breeze holding well we were soon far enough out to be reasonably sure against any interruption.

I had intended to make for Shanhaikwan, but during the night and the next morning observed from their Chinese compass that the "laodah"* continued to steer a northerly course. The little daughter of Mme. Chaffanjon spoke Chinese, and using her as interpreter, I found that the laodah was heading for Tsinchow** at northwest corner of Liaotung Gulf. He insisted on this course, saying that there were many pirates in vicinity of Shanhaikwan, and that he did not want to go there. It made little difference to me, though I thought his reason more probably was that he might have been in trouble about Shanhaikwan and was afraid of the police.

About 6 p.m. August 15, when in sight of Saddle Island we sighted on starboard bow two junks at anchor, which picked up their anchors, made sail and stood down toward us, one crossing the bows, the other heading to go astern. There are many lawless junkmen in the Gulf who rarely attack Europeans however, but taking into consideration the uneasiness of my laodah and Chinese crew, who said the junks were "hung huza" or pirates, I took no chances on their getting too close and headed our junk off to westward. The winds were very light and the two junks followed us for about an hour, our screw sculling along with the "ula."*** At dusk they were about 1,000 yards astern, and one of them fired twice at us with a rifle. It seemed quite certain that this vicinity was not very safe, and I now insisted that we head for Shanhaikwan. This was done and we drifted along during the night with light winds, next morning at daylight being off a low sandy beach, in vicinity of Sand Point.

I had trusted the navigation to the Chinese pilot, who was recommended to me by the Russian officer commanding the beach guard at Pigeon Bay, as being a good pilot for the whole of Liao-

* Pilot.

** Now Tsingtao.

*** Yuloh—a long oar.

tung Gulf. But when he informed that this was Shanhaikwan, I knew he was mistaken, since although I had never been there, and had only a small scale chart with me, I knew the Great Wall came down to the sea at that point.

We anchored and one of the crew went ashore to find out where we were, and on his return we picked up anchor and ran down the coast arriving at Shanhaikwan about 8 p.m. August 16. They are good boatmen, the Chinese junkmen, handling the junks excellently. In a little squall we ran into they were all standing by with all sail made, and in the stronger gusts would handle the sails and helm well to meet the emergency. As the man came off to us at Sand Point, there was a strong current, and he could not make the junk. One of the deck hands on the junk very neatly floated a line down to him in a bucket, and he hauled up alongside.

When running into Shanhaikwan I found they knew the place quite well, but evidently had some reason for not wanting to visit it. I slept on the junk that night and early next morning on going ashore found a couple of Japanese soldiers on the beach sketching and making notes of everything connected with the junk and her passengers. On starting out from Pigeon Bay I had paid the junk man half the agreed price, one hundred rubles, and now gave him the other hundred, and he immediately began filling his junk with vegetables for a return trip to Port Arthur.

I was able to learn later than the day after I left, Commander de Cuverville and Lieutenant von Gilgenheim also started on their attempt to get out with the intention of following the same route I had taken. A junk was secured by paying 400 rubles or twice what I had paid, and just before casting off the Chinese crew demanded a cumshaw* of 100 rubles which was given them in the form of a cheque. They did not get clear of the coast that night, but anchored under Liaotishan until next morning, and a junk supposed to be theirs was seen to be working slowly out to westward shortly after daybreak.

It was never known exactly what became of them, but some Chinaman tried to pass the cheque given them as a cumshaw, and

* Colloquial for Chinese *kam-sia,* a gratuity or gift. General naval use: something obtained for nothing.

from that as a clue, a disconnected sort of story was learned of their movements later. According to this the junk first anchored under Liaotishan for lack of wind, and next morning the Chinese crew objected to proceeding on account of danger from mines, or from Japanese cruisers or some such reason. The attachés insisted and in the dispute shot one of the Chinese crew in the leg, then cut the cable, and made sail themselves. The crew the next night attacked the officers and threw them overboard, and killed the Russian servant of Commander de Cuverville, who was one of the party.

The Chinese testimony was that the officers were drunk, but neither of them was a man likely ever to get in that condition, and the Chinese may have mistaken a certain excitement not strange under the circumstances for that condition. They stated also that the two officers had money and many objects of value about them, but this was very improbable. What gives some air of truth to their story was the mention of the Russian servant being with the officers, and few knew of that circumstance. If they were made away with by the Chinese crew it must have been through some misunderstanding with the crew, neither speaking the others' language, and a probable embarrassment from which I was free, thanks to the little daughter of Mme. Chaffanjon.

For a long time I believed they had been encountered by a Japanese cruiser, which sunk the junk, as they had threatened to do. The Japanese destroyers overhauled junks met with, but the larger ships did not waste time on them and sank them by gunfire all standing. Whether murdered by the crew, sunk by the Japanese, blown up by a mine, or captured by pirates, it is still difficult to say, but the Chinese government officially closed the incident by executing three Chinamen in Chefoo a short time before I passed through there in August 1905.

Captain Hopman, the other German attaché who intended to remain a while longer in Port Arthur, was ordered out by the German Emperor on August 17, took a junk and went out under safe conduct to the Japanese line of blockading ships, whence Admiral Togo sent him to Kiauchow. He had the opportunity of seeing the Japanese ships from a short distance on August 13, and they appeared then ready for action, *Mikasa* included, but with marks of battle about their funnels and upper works.

August 12—September 4, 1904

Tientsin to Vladivostock

After visiting Tientsin in order to communicate with the Department and obtain money, I left there August 12,* en route for Vladivostock. I travelled by train of the Chinese Eastern Railway Company as far as Sinmin, trains running during day only. There had been some disorder along the line between Kowpangtze, where there is connection with Newchwang and Sinmin, line having been attacked by "hung huzas", but our train had no difficulty. I arrived at Sinmin 6 p.m. August 22, visited the Tartar general who furnished me with an escort of six Chinese soldiers as far as the Liao Ho River, where we expected to meet a Russian detachment. I was in company with Captain Leznenko, on his way from the Russian Legation in Pekin to join the active army, and we travelled in the regular Chinese carts, which do not form the most comfortable means of transportation. The roads were in a terrible condition, there having been considerable traffic between Sinmin and Mukden, principally in luxuries and minor necessary articles for officers and soldiers.

At 2 p.m. August 23 arrived on the shore of the Liao Ho, a muddy stream, 150 yards wide, channel 12′ deep and 30′ wide at ferry, current two to three knots and banks low and sandy. Just above ferry is a pontoon bridge thrown across by Russians, but not used for traffic. We were ferried over in scows and took lun-

* There is an inexplicable discrepancy in the chronology here. The author earlier stated that he left Port Arthur on August 14 and arrived in Shanhaikwan on August 16, after which he proceeded to Tientsin, so he could not have been in Tientsin on August 12. The most likely explanation is that he picked the wrong date off his calendar, and actually left Tientsin a week later than stated, or on August 19.

cheon with the officer commanding the Russian post on east bank, and in the afternoon proceeded on our way to Mukden, stopping in a deserted house for the night and continuing next morning.

When about 10 versts* from Mukden our Cossack guide came back with the information that hung huzas were ahead of us. We got out of the carts and proceeded on foot in the direction of a small group of men in the middle of the road three of whom, dressed like coolies and armed with knives, were the hung huzas. When we were within 200 or 300 yards of the group we heard horses galloping behind us and up came three of the Chinese cavalry men, unslinging their rifles and looking quite business-like. The hung huzas promptly disappeared in the kowliang on each side of the road, the soldiers after them. We waited some time to watch the outcome, and one of the soldiers came out of the kowliang and asked us to guard the road while they beat up their men. We remained about half an hour and seeing no developments, started on again, going about 100 yards, when we heard rifle shots in the kowliang and soon out ran the hung huzas, one of them wounded. They crossed the road and took shelter in the grain on the other side, when the three soldiers came out hot-foot after them.

Whether the robbers were caught or not we did not learn, but the soldiers behaved in quite a dashing and business-like way. These Chinese soldiers are very well developed men and are more intelligent than the ordinary Russian soldier. They ride the small hardy Chinese or Mongolian ponies, riding gear very simple and cheap, uniform of Chinese dress lettered and colored alike, and ordinary straw hats. They are variously armed, most that I saw having a 11mm Amberg rifle of 1888, but a few with good modern 7mm Mausers. Their rifles were not in good condition, the sights usually being damaged or destroyed. According to the ideas of the men with whom I talked the sights are not very necessary anyway.

The hung huzas were a subject of considerable interest, and by Russians the term is used indiscriminately referring to any disorderly Chinaman, or any Chinaman suspected of offense. The kind of hung huza we encountered were probably the cheapest kind,

---

* 10 versts = 6.6 miles.

petty robbers, holding up Chinese merchants or any passer-by for a tax of so many cash. They do not bother Europeans as a rule. The junk pirates are a more desperate and unscrupulous lot, but also do not attack Europeans as a rule. However if they begin an attack on Europeans, perhaps not knowing them to be such, and injure any of them, their plan is carry the attack through in the attempt to destroy the evidence.

The organized hung huzas are a sort of irregular police operating in bands, with their districts and amounts of tribute well defined, and accountable unofficially to Chinese officials, who demand their squeeze. These bands in return for the tribute regularly paid on each mow of land under cultivation engage to protect their taxpayers from other bands. Both Russians and Japanese had bands of hung huza under their control, and used as irregular cavalry principally for purposes of obtaining information. They were well armed, drilled after European model, and uniformed; the Russian hung huzas in black coats with white letters, the Japanese in red coats and black letters, some officers from each side accompanying the detachments.

During the months of July and August the entire country between Sinmin and Mukden and to southward of this line about lower part of Liao Ho River was covered with growing crops of kowliang. This resembles very much in appearance Indian corn, planted thickly in rows, and reaching a height of eight to ten feet. It makes excellent cover for military purposes, and until September when it is cut down gives refuge to the bands of petty robbers, which are very active while the kowliang is high. The plant has no ears like the Indian corn but on the top is a tassel, like that of the sugar cane, the grain being threshed out, and used as food and forage, either whole or ground up. The blades are also used as forage, the stalk for thatching roofs, giving stiffening to the mud walls, repairing roads, covering bridges, but principally for fuel. The roots are pulled up, dried and piled, and also used as fuel. Other principal products are beans of various kinds, with their products—bean oil, bean cakes, bean flour, etc. Next in importance is millet, the grain being used for food, the stalks cut up for forage. Other articles grown in small quantities are rye, buckwheat, wheat and Indian corn.

I arrived in Mukden August 24, visited Liaoyang for a few days and had interviews with General Kouropatkin who was particularly amiable, and on August 28, left Liaoyang for Vladivostock arriving there September 4.

Until August, Vladivostock had seen very little of the war. On February 8, 1904, there were present in Vladivostock the armored cruisers *Rossia, Gromoboi, Rurik;* cruiser *Bogatyr;* torpedo boats 201, 202, of 76 tons each and 17 knots; 203, 204, of 175 tons and 20 knots; 205, 206 of 103 tons and 19 1/2 knots; 208, 209, 210, 211, of 120 tons and 18 1/2 knots; small gunboat *Tungus, Yakut, Aleut, Kamchadal;* transport *Lena;* icebreaker *Nadiozhnik,* and some small navy yard craft, with a floating dock capable of taking a ship of 3,000 tons and self-docking, and three floating cranes. Rear Admiral Stackelberg commanded the squadron, which was officially termed the Cruiser Division.

On February 9 at 3 p.m. the Cruiser Division composed of *Rossia* (flag), *Gromoboi, Rurik* and *Bogatyr* left Vladivostock on cruise to the southward under command of Captain Reitzenstein, Rear Admiral Stackelberg remaining on board the flagship as passenger, but too ill for active duty, having been relieved shortly before sortie by Captain Reitzenstein. The squadron first visited Gensan,* then cruised to eastward as far as Sado Island. About 20 miles to the northward of this island, February 12, in heavy weather, the Japanese steamer *Nagoura Maru,* 1,500 tons, en route from Sakata to Otru, loaded with rice, was captured, her crew of 40 with two passengers taken on board Russian cruisers and the *Nagoura Maru* sunk by gunfire. The *Senshio Maru* was sighted about the same time, but escaped during the thick weather. On February 15 the fleet returned to Vladivostock, having made the cruise at average speed of 10 knots.

On February 24 the same ships again went out, under command of Captain Reitzenstein, visited Gensan and Tsushima Straits, and returned to Vladivostock on February 29, without incident. On March 1, Japanese ships were reported in vicinity and squadron went out on a reconnaissance and returned the same day.

* Now Wonsan, Korea.

About 10 a.m. March 6, a Japanese fleet of seven vessels consisting of *Idzumo, Azuma, Yakumo, Tokiwa* and *Iwate,* with two two-funneled cruisers and four torpedo boats was sighted about 10 miles south of Askold Island, heading for Vladivostock. The two cruisers and two torpedo boats remained near Askold, two other torpedo boats along shore to northward of the island, while the five armored cruisers continued on course toward Skrypleff Island. The weather was clear and cold, with strong breezes from northwest, ground covered with snow, Zolotoi Rog or Golden Horn frozen over with two feet of ice, and the Japanese ships as they approached also ice covered. Only the day before the ice in Ussuri Gulf had been broken up and blown out to sea in a northwest gale.

When head of Japanese column bore about east from Skrypleff Island, it changed course to north, then circled with port helm about four and a half to six miles from shore, and about southeast from the town of Vladivostock. Firing was begun at 1:05 p.m. and about 200 shells from 6″ and 8″ guns fired into vicinity of the town, most of the shells falling in the harbor, in vicinity of navy yard, and about the HE* magazines at head of Diomedes Inlet. Bombardment lasted 50 minutes and Japanese then withdrew, disappearing below horizon to southward at 5:30 p.m. The damage done was practically nothing, one woman being killed, and five sailors from Seamen's Barracks wounded. About 60 of the shells failed to explode on impact, either ashore or when falling on the ice in the harbor. Some of the 8″ shells were part of the Russian ammunition captured in Manchuria at the very beginning. The only batteries that could bear on the Japanese were forts Ourossoff, Linievitch, No. 18, and Suvaroff which did not yet have their heavy guns mounted, these being on the trucks in the streets of Vladivostock, and none returned the Japanese fire. Some 8″ shells with base fuzes, and 6″ shells of English make charged with lyddite and nose fuzes were recovered, having failed to explode (See sketch No. 14).

Very few of the people in the town knew the place had been bombarded until several hours after it was over, and the Emper-

---

* High explosive.

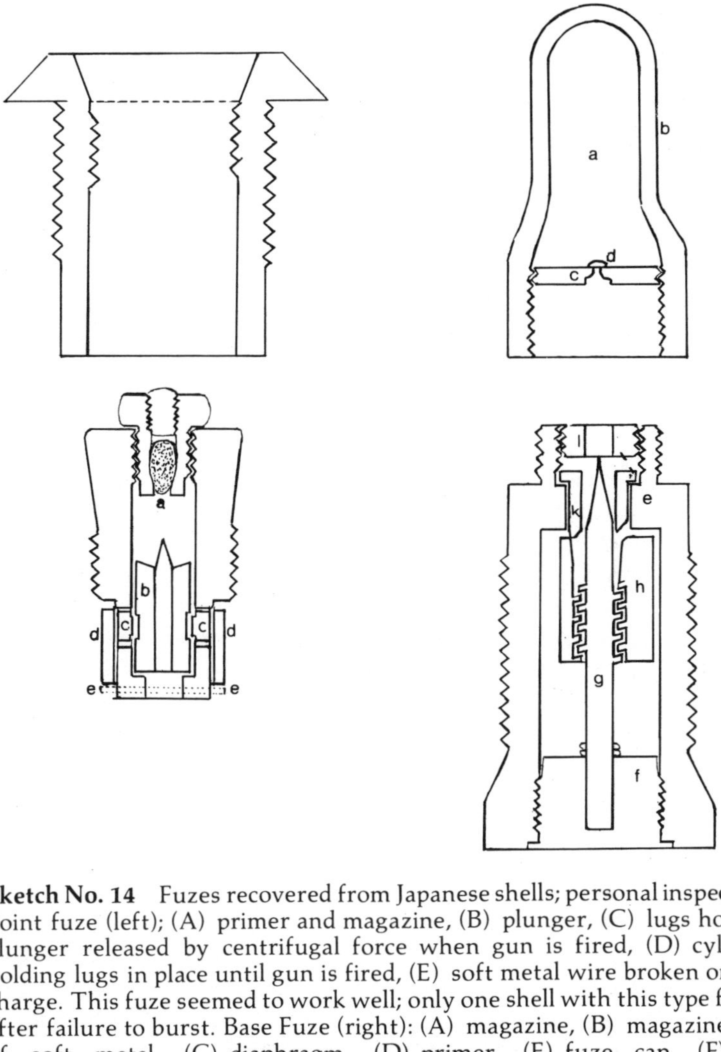

Sketch No. 14 Fuzes recovered from Japanese shells; personal inspection. Point fuze (left); (A) primer and magazine, (B) plunger, (C) lugs holding plunger released by centrifugal force when gun is fired, (D) cylinder holding lugs in place until gun is fired, (E) soft metal wire broken on discharge. This fuze seemed to work well; only one shell with this type found after failure to burst. Base Fuze (right): (A) magazine, (B) magazine case of soft metal, (C) diaphragm, (D) primer, (E) fuze cap, (F) cap, (G) plunger with square heel setting into it, (H) pendulum working loosely on (G), greater weight of metal on one side axis eccentric to axis of (G). When shell is fired (H) does not take up motion of rotation and works to rear of thread, leaving sufficient play for point to strike primer. This fuze did not work well; a number of shells with this type were recovered after failure to explode.

or's telegram received complimenting them on their excellent behavior, then there was quite a celebration. As the Japanese withdrew, the Russian fleet got underway and steamed out, returning next morning about 7 a.m. On March 15, Rear Admiral Yessen assumed command of the cruiser division, relieving Captain Reitzenstein who left for Port Arthur assuming command of the cruiser squadron at that place. On March 30 some Japanese ships were sighted to the southward, and the cruiser division again went out for a couple of hours, under Rear Admiral Yessen for the first time.

The next cruise of the Vladivostock squadron began April 23 when *Rossia, Gromoboi, Bogatyr* and six torpedo boats left Vladivostock, making for Gensan, on the way passing very close in a fog the Japanese squadron under Admiral Kamimura. Arriving off Gensan in the morning of April 25 two torpedo boats were sent in, finding a small Japanese steamer at anchor, the *Goyo Maru,* of 500 tons, with load of fish. Crew were ordered to leave her, and steamer was sunk at anchor, using two charges of 10 pounds pyroxyline each, placed in engine room. Torpedo boats then joined cruisers which about 8 p.m. met small Japanese merchant steamer *Nakanura Maru* of 220 tons, which was captured and sunk, crew being taken aboard Russian vessels.

At 11 p.m. the same night a steamer was sighted coming down from the northward which, mistaking the Russians for Japanese, first signalled "I bring coal for you," then realizing her mistake tried to escape, but was quickly overhauled by *Bogatyr.* She turned out to be the *Kinshiu Maru* with the 10th company of the 37 Regiment Japanese infantry which had made an expedition to Sin-po about 60 miles to the northward for purpose of reconnaissance, and was returning to Gensan. Inspection showed steamer to be a transport armed with four 47mm Hotchkiss guns. The captain and some of the officers were removed to the Russian ship, and many of the crew with some of the soldiers attempted to escape in the steamer's boats, but were picked up and taken aboard along with those people seen on the steamer. Thinking all the people were off the ship, an officer went aboard with gun-cotton party to blow her up. While engaged in this he found a group of Japanese officers in a locked room, who were compelled to surrender. Also about 130 armed soldiers were found in the forward hold who refused to surrender, and the Russian officer returned to his ship.

The Japanese remaining in *Kinshiu Maru* were given one hour to leave the ship, and when they would not do so, about 1 a.m. she was torpedoed, sinking in about half an hour. On being torpedoed the Japanese soldiers opened fire with their rifles on the Russian ships, which returned it with rapid fire and 6″ guns. Amongst the prisoners taken by the Russian were 17 officers, 20 soldiers, 85 coolie bearers and 65 men belonging to crew of steamer. Russian squadron then returned to Vladivostock, again passing on the way Admiral Kamimura, who was returning to Gensan. Admiral Kamimura on arriving off Vladivostock, attempted no operations on account of foggy weather, and when he returned to Gensan learned that the Russian fleet was out, upon which he again went to Vladivostock, but too late to meet the Russians.

On May 14 *Bogatyr* with Admiral Yessen on board went out to swing ship* and try the engines, and when returning in a thick fog, at 12:30 p.m. ran ashore at speed of 10 knots on southern side of entrance to Slavianski Bay, about 20 miles southwest from Vladivostock. Ship was badly damaged, bottom from one-third her length from forward being stove in, and boilers lifted up about two feet out of position. That same day there was a heavy blow, during which the ship rolled 28° to starboard and 17° to port, while resting on the rocks. All stores, ammunition, coal, guns, conning tower, and turrets removed, ship being lightened as much as possible. It was not attempted to blow off the point of rocks inside the vessel for fear of exploding her magazines. The vicinity was mined and booms laid to defend against torpedo attack, and a battery of field guns emplaced on shore near accident. Weights were placed on after part of ship, decks and bulkheads shored up, pumps started and on June 16 she was hauled off by tugs and taken into dock at Vladivostock.

During the month she had been lying helpless on the rocks, no Japanese ships appeared, though it must have been well known

* Swing ship; to determine local compass deviation by bringing the ship's head successively to each point of the compass, and taking bearings of a distant object.

that the *Bogatyr* was wrecked, since even in isolated Port Arthur the fact was known in latter part of May. It seems very remarkable that some attempt was not made by the enemy to find out her true condition and complete her destruction if it were possible. No attempt was made to remove damaged portions of ship, but a new skin was built around it, and boilers left in their dislocated positions, new connections being made all round. Repairs were finished to her on September 11, and she again shipped her battery and took aboard stores.

On May 8, Vice Admiral Bezobrazoff was appointed to the command of the 1st Pacific Squadron, and in June arrived in Vladivostock. At the same time Rear Admiral Rojestvensky was ordered to assume command of the 2nd Pacific Squadron then fitting out in the Baltic, and on May 24 Vice Admiral Skrydloff arrived in Vladivostock, assuming duty as commander in chief of all naval forces in Pacific Ocean.

The composition of the 1st Pacific Squadron is rather indefinite, since most of the ships belonging to it were in Port Arthur. Rear Admiral Yessen commanded the cruiser squadron, composed of the ships at Vladivostock, though at first these seemed to be included in command of Vice Admiral Bezobrazoff, since he went out in command of them on June 12 and 29. Later on, however, though he flew his flag on *Rossia* he would haul it down when the squadron went out, and go ashore, and Admiral Yessen would take command of active operations.

At daylight, on June 12, the fleet composed of *Rossia, Rurik* and *Gromoboi* left Vladivostock and steamed straight for Tsushima, appearing off that island early in morning of June 15, then setting course for Shimonoseki. When northwest of Shimonoseki and about 20 miles away, the smoke of two steamers was seen on horizon and Russians went in chase but failed to overhaul them. Another steamer was discovered about this time and *Gromoboi* went in chase. Steamer did not stop for blank shot, and fire was opened on her, on which she stopped, many of her crew jumping overboard. *Gromoboi* signalled to ship directing crew to abandon her, which they did in two boats, and were received by *Gromoboi* which also lowered boats and rescued some of those in the water. Steamer was *Idzumi Maru,* of 3,000 tons, with freight and troops from the army en route from Talien-wan to Sasebo, and after being abandoned was sunk by gun fire about 8 a.m. Of the people on board *Gromoboi* received 105, 17 of them being officers.

Three other ships were now discovered to the southward, a man-of-war, the *Tsushima*, and the *Sado Maru* and *Hitachi Maru*, the two latter of about 6,000 tons each, the first loaded with railway and telegraphic materials and workmen, war contraband, officers, horses and pontoons, and on the other were about 1,000 soldiers, both steamers bound for Dalny. *Gromoboi* went in chase, leaving *Sado Maru* to *Rossia* and continuing after *Hitachi Maru* which attempted to get away, when *Gromoboi* opened fire, on which the steamer stopped due to injury to engine, and crew was then directed to abandon ship, which at first it failed to do, ship again going ahead and turning as if to ram *Gromoboi*, when fire was again opened on her. Many people began jumping overboard and under the heavy fire, the steamer began to sink. As she went down very slowly, flagship signalled to hasten the operation which *Gromoboi* did by firing torpedoes, and *Hitachi Maru* quickly sank about 11 a.m.

Rossia overhauled *Sado Maru* and after sending boarding officer signalled to crew to abandon the ship, which they did in the ship's boats. *Rurik* then about 1 p.m. fired two torpedoes at her, one striking over the engine room and making hole 14′ long by 9′ high, and the other striking outside of coal bunker forward of engine room. Bunker was full of coal, and this may have been responsible for less damage by this torpedo than by the first one. The hole in this case was only four feet square, though both torpedoes were the same size, 18″, and carried charge of 200 pounds of gun cotton.

While Russians were engaged in sinking the merchant ships, the *Tsushima* had been actively telegraphing by wireless, and smoke of other ships appearing on horizon, the Russian fleet steamed away to northeastward, through a sea of swimming Japanese. It was said that Vice Admiral Bezobrazoff was sickened by the sight and had to go below, and that it was due to his squeamishness on this occasion that Admiral Yessen afterward commanded all the expeditions, except that of June 29. The last seen of *Sado Maru* she was apparently sinking and crew were escaping in boats towards the islands of Tsushima and Ikishima, sea smooth and no wind according to Russian report.

The next day, June 16, at 10 a.m. to northward of Okishima the steamer *Allanton* was met, en route from Mororan to Singapore with cargo of Japanese coal, and was seized as a prize and sent into Vladivostock for action of prize court.* During night of June 19 fleet arrived off Vladivostock, coming in early next morning.

When the Russian cruisers first appeared off Okishima about 6 a.m. June 15, telegraphic information was immediately sent to Admiral Kamimura, probably in Strait to westward of Tsushima, who received it at 8 a.m. and sent a torpedo boat flotilla to guard passage between Tsushima and Ikishima, while he proceeded with his squadron round the southern end of Tsushima, then steering to northward of Okinoshima. All this time the *Tsushima* was in touch with the Russian fleet, at noon reporting them as being about 15 miles south of Okinoshima and proceeding northwestward, and at 1:30 p.m. that they were about five miles south of Okinoshima. The two fleets at this time were not more than 10 miles apart, weather cloudy, misty, with occasional heavy rain. The *Tsushima* lost touch with the Russians, but was able to find and join squadron of Admiral Kamimura who continued search for the Russians, steaming to northward at slow speed during afternoon and night, as reported on account of thick weather, but according to Russians, fine and smooth.

Next morning, June 16, speed of Japanese squadron was increased, and search line formed but no traces discovered of the Russians, then the fleet turned southward and searched along the shores of Japan while the Russians continued leisurely to the northward, on June 19 the Japanese returning to Masampho.** As criticised in the Japanese Parliament the explanation by Admiral Kamimura of his failure to find the Russian fleet was almost as clear as the fog, on which he laid the blame.

On June 14, the day after the cruisers left Vladivostock, a detachment of three torpedo boats, Nos. 203, 205, and 206 also went out in direction of Hokkaido visiting Esashi and vicinity of Hakodate on June 16, destroying several small sailing craft engaged in coast trading and fishing, and acting as a diversion to movements

---

* See Appendix IX.

** Now Masan, Korea.

of cruiser squadron in the south. This detachment returned to Vladivostock on June 21.

On June 29 *Rossia, Rurik, Gromoboi, Lena,* and nine torpedo boats under Vice Admiral Bezobrazoff went out bound for Gensan, arriving there next day about 6 a.m. The torpedo boats were divided into groups of three, the first consisting of 203, 205 and 206 under Commander Vinogradsky, the second of 201, 202, and 204 under Lieutenant Ignatief, and the third under Lieutenant Tigerstedt. The boats entered the harbor, first detachment along the northern shore, second in the middle of the harbor, and the third along the southern side. One of the boats belonging to the second group, No. 204, ran on the rocks in the center of the entrance and remained there, while the others steamed in to about 600 yards from shore, and with 37mm and 47 mm guns bombarded shore and warehouses, and sunk a small steam launch, a sailing vessel, the *Seisha Maru,* of 110 tons, and destroyed some junks hauled up on the beach.

Some soldiers on shore fired on the boats with rifles, but were soon dispersed and the buildings were set on fire, but fire extinguished before buildings were consumed. The firing lasted about one and a half hours and the torpedo boats then hauled off. No. 204 was pulled off the rocks, but was very badly damaged, and although an attempt was made to tow her, she was unable to steer, the towing strap around hull with which all Russian torpedo boats were fitted, parting, and it was finally abandoned and destroyed by blowing up with two charges of pyroxyline, each of 10 pounds, one placed in the engine room, and the other in magazine. For this action a St. George cross was given to the crew of each torpedo boat, deciding by lot which man was to wear it.

On June 28, while attempting to enter Vladivostock from eastern entrance, German steamer *Tiberius* ran on a mine, and only saved herself by beaching in the Golden Horn.

After leaving Gensan the Russian cruiser squadron proceeded to the Straits of Korea, while the torpedo boats under convoy of the *Lena* returned to Vladivostock. July 1, the squadron made prize of the British steamer *Cheltenham* loaded with railway material, bound from Otru to Fusan, and on the evening of that same day sighted a Japanese squadron of seven ships, four being armored cruisers, and accompanied by a number of torpedo boats. The Japanese fired a few harmless shots from a range of 16,000 yards and the Russians turned and headed to northeast, soon losing sight of Japanese fleet.

At about 10 p.m. the Japanese torpedo boats approached the Russian squadron and made an ineffectual attack. Eight torpedo boats came up from port quarter, and three from starboard; weather hazy, and cloudy. These were all detected and fired on by the Russians, and it is said that not one of them came within 2,000 yards of a Russian ship. Admiral Kamimura followed the Russians for a while, but then as he says "the Russians suddenly put out their lights and disappeared from view. We made an exhaustive search but without result." The Russians say that the Japanese ships fired into their own torpedo boats as they returned from the attacks on the Russian ships. Russian squadron called off Hakodate and then returned to Vladivostock, arriving there July 3.

On July 17 the *Rossia, Gromoboi* and *Rurik* filled up with coal, taking deck loads besides, and left Vladivostock bound for Tsugaru Straits where they arrived in early morning of July 20, through which they passed without hindrance and off eastern entrance to Straits began work of overhauling vessels. The Japanese steamer *Kioto Unyu Maru* of 140 tons, bound for Mororan, was searched off Esan and allowed to proceed in consideration of large number of passengers, many of them women; but another steamer, *Takashima Maru,* was sunk in same locality about 6:30 a.m. July 20, and the British steamer *Samara* searched but let go for lack of evidence. The squadron remained off the eastern entrance of Tsugaru during day of July 20, then after sinking two small sailing schooners proceeded southward off Yokohama, cruising at slow speed off the entrance July 22 and 23 making prize of British SS *Arabia,* 4,400 tons, with cargo of flour from Portland, Oregon, and sent in to Vladivostock for adjudication.

Squadron then headed to the westward, cruising as far as Omai Saki, about 100 miles to southwest of entrance to Gulf of Tokyo, and a 6 a.m. on the 24, overhauled the British steamer *Knight Commander,* * 4,300 tons, in latitude 34° 21′ N., longitude 138° 53′ E. Steamer was bound from New York by way of Suez, Singapore,

* See Appendix X.

Manila, Shanghai (left July 20) for Kobe and Yokohama, with cargo of railway and bridge material and machinery. Cargo declared contraband, and as steamer had only four days coal supply, she was sunk by placing three charges of 10 pounds each of pyroxyline in machinery compartments, and exploding them by means of Bickford time fuze.

The German steamer *Thea* of 1,600 tons, loaded with fish and provisions, and under charter to a Japanese company, was also overhauled and sunk as not having sufficient coal to take her into a Russian port, and several small sailing vessels engaged in coasting trade and fishing were also sunk. About 3:30 p.m. on same day British steamer *Tsinan* was searched but allowed to let go, after sending on board the Lascar crew of *Knight Commander.*

The Russians then steamed eastward and next morning about 6:30 a.m., in latitude 34° 53′, longitude 140° 13′, off Nojima Saki, made prize of the British steamer *Calchas,** 6,000 tons, bound from Takoma to Yokohama with cargo of flour, girders, and miscellaneous machinery. Steamer was held and sent with prize crew into Vladivostock for adjudication. Squadron then started on return to Vladivostock, coal supply having become considerably diminished, passing through Tsugaru Straits during the day of July 30, and sighting gunboat *Takao,* old cruiser *Kongo* and some torpedo boats, but again being quite unmolested. Squadron then proceeded to Cape Kruilov, where it remained for nearly a day waiting for foggy weather in which to approach Vladivostock, and then in the evening of August 1, entered the harbor having almost completely exhausted the coal supply.

Had the squadron been able to remain off Yokohama a few days longer it would probably have made a very important capture, as the steamer *Korea* was then on its way from San Francisco with a very valuable cargo, and reached Yokohama on July 29. The steamer *Arabia* was afterward released, though part of her cargo was seized and condemned as contraband. *Calchas* was also released very much later.

On August 12 the squadron again left somewhat unexpectedly with the idea of cooperating with the Port Arthur squadron which was known to be out from despatches of *Ryeshitelni,* and might be

---

* See Appendix XI.

expected in Korea Strait very soon. Squadron steamed straight for Tsushima at full speed, about 13 knots, and at daylight August 14 sighted the squadron of Admiral Kamimura about eight miles away. The Russian squadron was heading south for Korea Strait, and the Japanese about southwest for the Western Channel. Position of the Russian squadron at this time was on the parallel of Fusan and 36 miles northeast of northern end of Tsushima.

At the first moment the Russians thought the ships were from the Port Arthur fleet, but soon identified them as Japanese and turning with port helm stood to the eastward, Japanese executing a similar maneuver. Speed of Russians was 13 knots which was the best *Rurik* could do, and Japanese were steaming a little over 16, Japanese gradually overhauling the Russians, and at 5:25 opened Russians were in order *Rossia* (flag), *Gromoboi, Rurik,* and Japanese *Idzumo* (flag), *Azuma, Tokiwa,* and *Iwate* (flag).

During this stretch Japanese appeared to concentrate their fire on the *Rossia,* and one shell, a plunging hit, fell on the port side of the deck aft, killing the executive officer, Commander Berlinski, on the after bridge, and killing and wounding about 50 men stationed at upper deck guns aft. Japanese were in communication by wireless with other ships, and as both fleets stood to eastward, the *Naniwa* was seen approaching from southeast. Besides, head of Russian column was being forced off to southward due to superior speed of Japanese, on account of which, about 6:10, Admiral Yessen turned with port helm and stood to northwestward.

In making this turn Japanese concentrated their fire on *Rurik* which received one shell near water line on port side aft, damaging steering gear and causing steering engine compartment to fill. The helm was jammed hard aport and *Rurik* could no longer steer. She was directed to repair injuries and proceed on former course to eastward, while *Rossia* and *Gromoboi* continued to northwestward to draw off main portion of Japanese fleet. *Rurik* attempted to carry out instructions, but was forced to signal that repairs to injuries could not be effected, and in the meantime was attacked by *Naniwa,* which later was joined by *Takachiho,* while several torpedo boats were sighted coming up.

Russian fleet again turned with port helm and stood toward *Rurik* which was suffering much from the heavy guns of *Naniwa,* her captain having been killed in the conning tower, and a large part of her battery being disabled. Approaching her, Admiral Yessen turned near her with port helm and maneuvered with *Gromoboi* and *Rossia* so as to cover *Rurik* as much as possible.

About 8:30 the Russian admiral concluding that *Rurik* would be unable to keep up with other ships but that she would be able to take care of herself against *Naniwa* and *Takachiho,* turned to northwest and making about 17 knots headed for Vladivostock, Japanese executing similar maneuver, but the Japanese fleet in reverse order, *Iwate* leading.

Russians had now a slight advantage in speed, and began to draw away from Japanese, who during this time began to increase rapidity of fire, and from 9:30 to 10:00 fired more furiously than during any other period of the action. Generally from 6 o'clock until the end of the battle the ranges had remained almost constantly at 8,000 yards, the least ranges being 6,000 yards from *Gromoboi,* and 5,600 yards on *Rossia.*

Russian fire throughout was at will and deliberate, the Japanese more rapid. The Russians found ranges by taking masthead angles with an instrument called "scholl" in form of a telescope with cross wires. Range-finding officers were stationed in foretops, and ranges communicated by telegraphic connection, until these were carried away early in the action, then by means of messengers. One range-finding party in foretop of *Gromoboi* was entirely carried away by a shell which struck the top, only a portion of one man's body falling on the deck. The hits from which the Russian ships suffered most were the plunging hits on the upper deck which caused most of their casualties, and the funnel hits which damaged the boilers.

At end of action *Rossia* was in quite a serious condition, and could not have kept up her speed much longer. Mines were already placed to blow her up, and the fuzes laid. The *Gromoboi* though suffering more in killed and wounded, was not anywhere in a serious condition, and except from a slightly diminished fire due to loss of men and guns damaged, was still in good condition to either run or fight. Considering all the circumstances it was difficult to understand why the Japanese turned back. Among reasons advanced by the Russians was failure of ammunition, but the Japanese at end of the action were firing more actively than at any other time. Another was to assist cruisers against *Rurik,* but the poor old *Rurik* was down by the stern and on her last legs when the Russians stood to northward at 8:30. Other assumptions were some serious damage to the Japanese ships, or orders to keep Korea Strait covered. If they had continued the pursuit *Rossia* most certainly would have been destroyed, since the Russian squadron was compelled to stop practically all the next night to effect repairs to machinery.

After turning away the Japanese proceeded to where *Rurik* was still feebly struggling against the three protected cruisers. Her captain and executive had already been killed, Lieutenant Zeniloff, the third officer in rank taking command, when he too was killed, the command being finally assumed by Lieutenant Ivanoff, the officer fourth in rank on the cruiser, who was severely wounded.

About 11 a.m. all the *Rurik's* guns were out of commission, 200 men were killed, and 300 wounded, and she ceased firing, after, with a last expiring effort, firing a torpedo from the only tube left undamaged, but accomplishing nothing on account of the range. The intention was to blow up the cruiser but could not be executed for lack of fuze, which was destroyed in conning tower, the remainder being in filled compartment. Instead the bottom valves were opened and cruiser gradually sank. When Russians ceased firing, Japanese also ceased, and when cruiser sank they used utmost endeavor to rescue the crew who were floating about on mattresses, wooden articles, and swimming, all boats having been destroyed. At 4 p.m., August 16, the two Russian cruisers entered Vladivostock, having made average of about 8.5 knots, with little signs of battle along the port side, but many marks left in the funnels and along starboard side.

Rossia carried most of the marks of battle and apparently, being flagship, had received most of the attention of the enemy (See sketch No. 15). Hit "a" was over forward torpedo tube, torpedo being in the tube, and head blown off but no detonation. On starboard side "b" made a hole about 3′ in diameter, and so damaged muzzle of 6″ gun near, that part of it was lost at next discharge and also damaged anchor engine; "c" was hole 4′ in diameter, shell bursting on impact, causing many splinters and putting dynamo

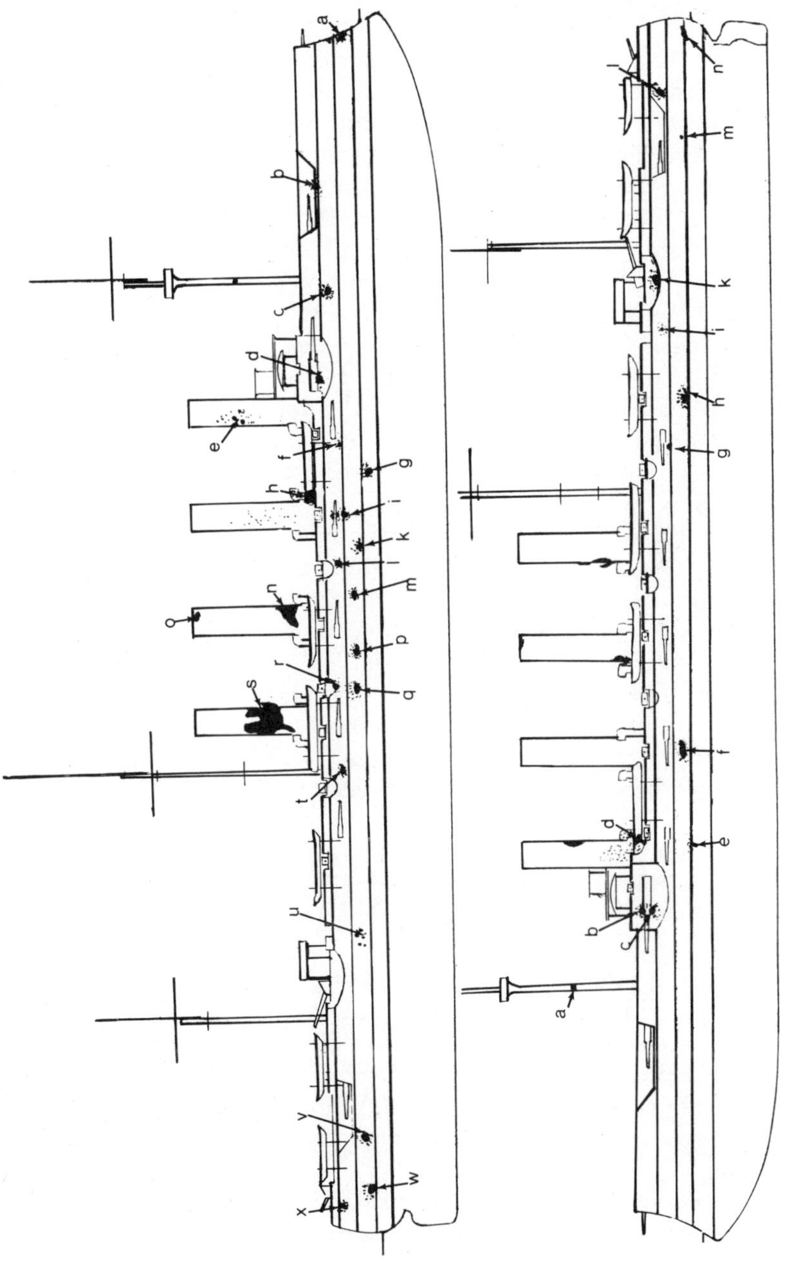

Sketch No. 15 Battle damage to *Rossia*, starboard side (top) and port side (bottom); based on hurried inspection.

on that deck out of commission; "d" was hit by heavy shell on edge of port, putting this 8" gun out of commission; "e" were two funnel hits close together; "f" probably 6" shell bursting on impact, making hole 12" diameter and damaging mount of No. two 6" gun; "g", "j", water line hit, damaging sheathing and opening seams in armor causing leak, which was stopped without much difficulty; "h" was hit on stern of boat, wrecking that badly and fragments marking funnel and ventilators and striking deck at "g"; "i", two hits in side plating close together, each hole about 3′ in diameter, men killed alongside gun, but gun still serviceable; "k" hole about 4′ long exposing coal bunker; "l" hit similar to "i;" "m", "p", "q", holes similar to "k" over coal bunkers; "n" hit at base of third funnel doing considerable damage; "o" hit in top of same funnel; "r" hit under 12-pdr. gun making hole about 20" diameter; "s" is probably result of two hits, funnel badly wrecked; "t" hole 3′ diameter; "u" hits from fragments of shell striking close alongside and bursting on impact with water; "v" is large hole about 4′ in diameter badly wrecking rooms inside; "w" is hole about 5′ largest dimension, just above armor, which in *Rossia* extends all round the stern, no serious damage effected; "x" is hole about 12" in diameter.

On port side "a" was hit in foremast; "b" and "c" were two hits almost simultaneously by 8" shell, striking on edges of 8" gun port, disabling mount of that gun, but gun itself remaining serviceable, though much scarred. All the gun's crew was killed or wounded, and charges brought up for rapid service of gun were ignited, starting a serious conflagration under forecastle. The paintwork, linoleum deck, crew's oilskins, bread bags, all took fire, and for a while the whole forward part of the ship seemed ablaze, flames pouring out of the gun ports and airports as if blown out under pressure from interior of ship.

Paintwork on outside of ship about airports and gunports was burnt off to a distance of 20′ from opening, leaving a whitish color on sides of ship over burnt off portions. Flames extended part way down the ammunition hoist, igniting cartridges on way to the guns, but not reaching magazines. Eight men were burnt to death and fire soon burnt itself out, without use of fire extinguishing apparatus.

Hit "d" is on hammock netting damaging 12-pdr. near by, and wrecking boat; "e" hit on armor damaging sheathing; "f" is a hit by

8″ shell, tearing a hole in side plating over coal bunker 7′ long by 4′ wide, exposing coal in bunker, but not damaging inboard wall of bunker; "g" was a glancing hit by 6″ AP shell on upper edge of 4″ armor, shell bursting and fragments ranging upward, damaging slightly gun just above; "h" was simply a splash on the armor; "i" was a splash on side plating probably made by shell not larger than 12-pdr.; "k" was hit probably by 8″ making hole about 3′ in diameter, and most of the effects of explosion occurring inside of ship; "l", large hole 3′ x 5′, wrecking rooms inside; "m" small hole probably by 6″ AP; "n" hit by 6″ AP fired from astern, striking upper edge of armor and denting it in, leaving a long score fore and aft.

On the deck were three plunging hits, one on the forecastle, one just abaft forward bridge, and the third aft on port side, just abaft 8″ gun. This last was received early in the action before 6 o'clock and practically swept the deck clear of all men aft. The executive officer on the after bridge was killed, and of the 55 men on the after part of the ship, only five were uninjured. Fragments from the shell left scars all over after part of ship, and on account of the extent of the damage effected by it, the 12-pdr. guns on upper deck of *Rossia* were afterwards not manned during the action. *Rossia* had three boilers out of action due to hits in funnels, and lost six men in the fire-rooms from wounds due to same hits. Both forward 8″ guns, the two forward 6″ guns on starboard side, and five 12-pdrs. were rendered unserviceable. All funnels except the second were removed and rebuilt.

On *Gromoboi's* starboard side were the following hits: "a" on shank of starboard bower anchor, 10″ in diameter, cutting it in two and marking side with fragments, of which only a very few got through skin of ship; "b" was a hit in military top on port side carrying away range-finding party of 12 men, part of one man's body only falling on deck; "c" hit on armor, damaging sheathing; "d" hit on rail, damaging boat; "e" hole 4′ in diameter over coal bunker; "f" hit in port of 6″ gun, causing explosion of ready ammunition in casemate, setting paintwork on fire and charring to a cinder the officer and six men in the casemate; "g" hit in second funnel seriously damaging it, so that it was removed on arriving in Vladivostock; "h" three small hits probably from fragments of shell bursting on impact with water; "k" hit in hammock netting; "l," 6″ hit in third funnel not doing extensive damage; "m" hole 4′ in diameter over coal bunker; "n" on armor damaging sheathing only; "o" hit on rail, damaging boat; "p" large hole with local damages only; "q" shot striking and destroying steam cutter and damaging 12-pdr. gun; "r" hit on after edge armor around 6" gun making large hole in side of ship, and another in glacis underneath; "s," 6" hit about 3′ in diameter, damaging quarters inside; "t," 8" hit 4′ in diameter rupturing deck beneath, but not damaging steering gear below (See sketch No. 16).

On port side of *Gromoboi** "a" was a hit on hammock nettings, putting a 12-pdr. gun and a boat out of commission; "b" was a hit on edge of armor making a splash only; "c" was hit on armor over 6" gun making splash and no damage; "d" hit on edge of armor, making hole into coal bunkers and developing slight leak; "e" was a very large hole 6′ x 7′, doing considerable internal damages in vicinity of wardroom; "f" clean 6" hole, made by HE shell which struck chain protection of ammunition hoist inside and then burst, but failing to damage hoist which continued in operation; "g" hole 4′ in diameter made by HE shell fired from astern; "h" was plunging hit, penetrating upper deck and bursting along side of 6" casemate denting walls of casemate but not perforating them; "k" plunging hit on forward bridge, bursting on impact, fragments getting under hood of conning tower, killing man at the wheel, and wounding captain and navigator.

The starboard forward and port after 8" guns were temporarily rendered unserviceable, along with port after 6", five 75mm guns, and three 3-pdrs. The projectors over military top forward were carried away, and all boats along starboard side, and three of those along port side were rendered unserviceable, several being wrecked.

On *Rossia* one officer and 47 men were killed, seven officers and 140 men wounded, many only slightly. On *Gromoboi* four officers and 87 men were killed, five officers and 170 men being wounded. Captain of *Gromoboi* was twice wounded, and second in command took command. *Gromoboi* was not hit as often nor as seriously damaged as *Rossia,* but had a much larger proportion in killed and wounded, particularly in the former due to the two very destructive hits in the fore top and forward 6" starboard, and to the fact that her upper deck 12-pdrs. were massed during the action, and

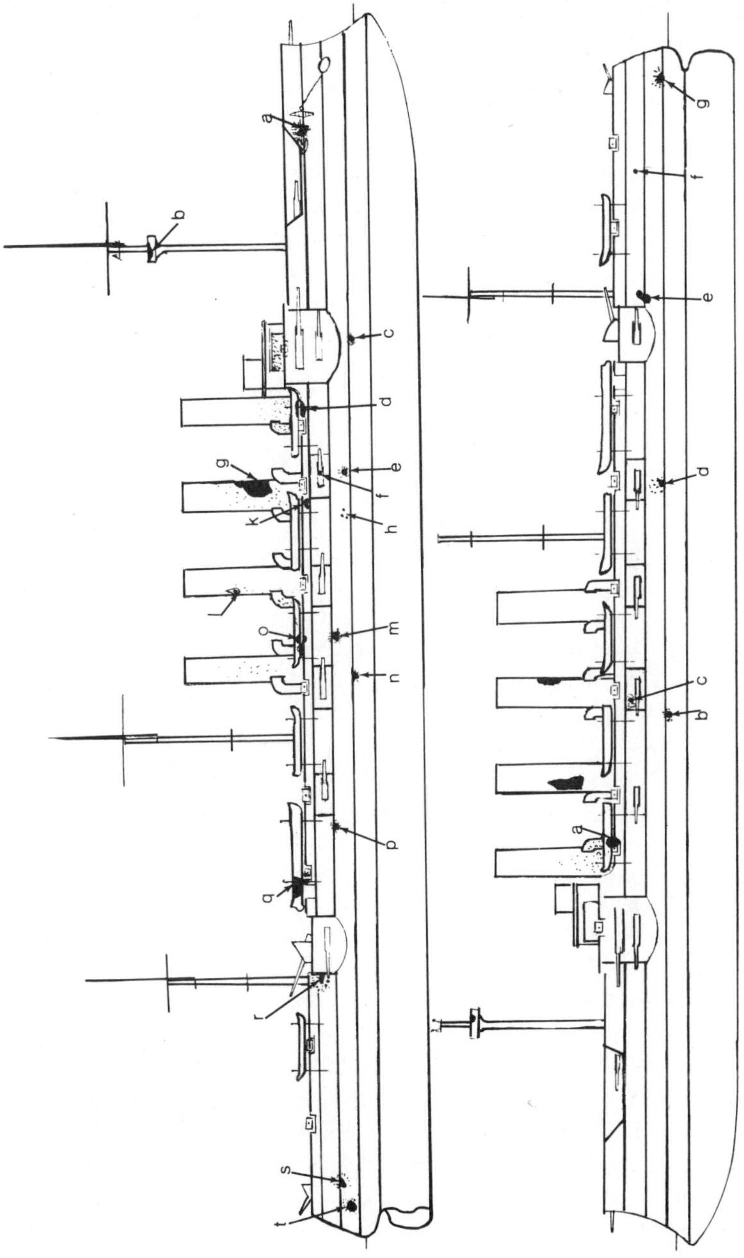

Sketch No. 16 Battle damage to *Gromoboi*, starboard side (top) and port side (bottom); based on hurried inspection.

these exposed crews suffered considerably. There was no perforation of armor in either ship, and protective deck also remained intact, but there were leaks, due to blows on armor, opening up seams. The destruction caused by the plunging hits was exceedingly great, little escaping the large number of fragments.

On *Rurik,* besides the damages due to injured steering gear, she had injuries to machinery from penetrations through protective deck, steam pipes cut, funnels destroyed, and all guns rendered unserviceable. She lost nine officers and 200 men killed and drowned, nine officers and 278 men wounded, so that total Russian loss in this battle was 14 officers, 334 men killed, 21 officers, 588 men wounded, or 957 men out of 2,400, or very nearly 40 per cent, practically all from gun fire.

The *Gromoboi* and *Rossia* fired altogether 200 shots from their 8″ guns, and 1,300 shots from their 6″ guns, or about half of their full ammunition supply. They used both AP and steel shell, both loaded with pyroxyline, and fired deliberately and at will always. During the action most of the wounded that visited the hospital reported there without assistance, in only a few cases was it necessary to call for aids to wounded. From conditions of the ships it seemed very evident that the Russian admiral had remained in action as long as he would have been justified in doing with such a superior force, but why the Japanese did not follow up their success it is very difficult to understand.

Both *Gromoboi* and *Rossia* went into dry dock and had repairs completed in about three months. After completion of repairs Rear Admiral Yessen installed on each of his ships six more 6-inch guns, placing them on the upper deck in broadside in blindages* completely enclosed with 1/2″ steel, replacing as many 12-pdrs. formerly installed. The ships had no difficulty in carrying these extra guns, but there would have been difficulty in keeping them supplied with ammunition. The admiral's idea was to distribute between *Rossia* and *Gromoboi* an increased battery equal to that of the sunken *Rurik.* Below on main deck of *Rossia* around each 6″ gun was constructed a sort of casemate by enclosing each gun with torpedo netting suspended from deck above, to which were secured

---

* Protective cover or screen.

the crew's hammocks. This would indicate a necessity for casemates or other method of protecting the crews of broadside guns, though there still remains the rather peculiar fact that *Gromoboi* with casemates and armor about 6" guns lost nearly twice as many men as *Rossia* which had no casemates, and no armor except along water line, and the latter was hit oftener. After arrival in Vladivostock commanding officers of both *Gromoboi* and *Rossia* were detached and ordered home, Captain Dabitch of *Gromoboi* having been wounded, and Captain Andréef of *Rossia* being exceedingly nervous.

September 4, 1904 to May 13, 1905

Vladivostock and Manchuria

On arrival in Vladivostock on September 4, 1904, Vice Admiral Skrydloff was Commander in Chief of the Pacific Squadron; Vice Admiral Bezobrazoff nominally in command of the 1st Squadron; Rear Admiral Yessen commanded the Cruiser Division comprising *Rossia, Gromoboi* and *Bogatyr;* Rear Admiral Haupt was admiral of the port or commandant of the navy yard, and in charge of torpedo boats, submarines and shore defense afloat; Rear Admiral Terentief was in charge of the affairs of the Volunteer Fleet; Lieutenant General Voronetz was commandant of the fortress. I made official calls on all these officers and was very politely received, but few facilities were given to obtain information, though there were no distinctions made as had been done in Port Arthur.

Present in Vladivostock also were the naval attachés: of Great Britain, Captain Eyres; of the Argentine Republic, Commander Moneta; of Sweden, Lieutenant Lybeck; and of Denmark, Lieutenant Tvermoes. All the attachés lived in private quarters in the town, some distance away from the navy yard, and their excursions were restricted within certain limits, no visits to batteries being permitted. During September Captain W. V. Judson, U.S.A., visited Vladivostock for a couple of weeks. During the month of September weather in Vladivostock was generally fine and very mild, with some rain toward the end of the month. Beyond repairs going on on board the damaged ships there was little doing. There were no expeditions to a distance, but each day some of the torpedo boats would be out on scouting duty, going as far as Olga Bay to the northward and Possiet Bay to the southward.

These torpedo boats were painted in a rather odd manner in irregular streaks along the side, of alternately white and the regular cinnamon color of the larger ships. This color was not easy to distinguish in bright weather or in the rays of the search light, but in the shadow or on a cloudy day showed up very clearly. The entrances were very thoroughly mined, the eastern entrance being no longer used. Ships coming in would report at Askold Island, and a Russian naval officer would pilot them in across mine fields. One ship came in across mine fields without knowing about them and got in safely. Two others fouled mines, and one was sunk. One torpedo boat, No. 201, had fouled a mine near Skrypleff Island, was blown up aft and sank in about three minutes.

On October 3, *Gromoboi* having completed most of her repairs, went out on trial trip. About the same date torpedo boats Nos. 202, 203 were in collision off Popoff Island, and 202 was sunk, all that was saved besides the crew being the flag, for saving which an officer was decorated. Accident occurred off Popoff Island, near southeast end of Russian Island, and boat sank in shallow water, but could not be recovered.

On October 7, the first submarine arrived out from Russia by way of the Transsiberian [railroad]. This boat was the *Delphin* of Russian type and about 70′ long, having little freeboard, making about 7 knots and diving quickly. On October 13, *Gromoboi* which had been out for gun trials, while returning and making about 17 knots, ran on the Two Brothers rocks, over which was about 3 feet less water than the ship was drawing. Bottom was very seriously damaged, 16 frames were broken and ship made considerable water, it being found necessary to send fire tugs alongside to pump her out. In attempting to undock *Bogatyr,* in order to allow *Gromoboi* to go into dock, *Bogatyr* fell over in dock, and was further very seriously injured. About a week later she was taken out, bow supported on pontoons and *Gromoboi* placed in dock to repair injuries from striking rock.

In the middle of October Vice Admiral Bezobrazoff was ordered as commander in chief of the Baltic Fleet with Rear Admiral Haupt as junior flag officer of the same fleet. Rear Admiral Yessen was ordered to command of 1st Squadron, Pacific Fleet, and Rear Admiral Grévé to relieve Rear Admiral Haupt as Admiral of the Port. On October 18, Lieutenant Tvermoes, the Danish naval attaché, was recalled by his government, and about a week later Lieutenant Lybeck, the Swedish attaché, also left for home. On October 22, after having obtained permission, I left Vladivostock for Mukden to spend a month with the army. During month of October in Vladivostock weather was cooler, but still very pleasant, October 21 being the first cold day.

While passing through Kharbin on my way to Mukden I called on the Viceroy, Admiral Alexeieff, who was there and on the point of leaving for St. Petersburg, having been recalled by the Emperor. He received me especially and very amiably, and was apparently a man of great tact and very intelligent. He seemed rather anxious to learn if I intended writing a book.

From Kharbin I travelled to Mukden on a sanitary train, No. 6. This train consisted in order mentioned of engine, 13 box cars fitted with the regular troop flats, and capable of accommodating 24 wounded men each; one refrigerator car with fresh meat and stores; one kitchen car, one dining car converted by knocking out the partitions in a third-class car, one third-class car for the nurses, one mixed first-and second-class for army officer having charge of train and the medical officers; eight small regular hospital cars with eight suspended cots each; one operating car; 12 hospital cars converted from regular third-class cars by knocking out the partitions, 12 suspended cots in each; and 17 empty box cars which were dropped as train proceeded south. On the train were a captain in the army commanding the train, four medical officers, 10 women nurses, and two soldier attendants detailed for each car. These trains are not supposed to receive any passengers, but by a special arrangement Prince Jaime of Bourbon and one Russian officer, besides myself were allowed to accompany the train.

We left Kharbin at noon October 29, and arrived at Mukden 10 a.m. November 1, a distance of 506 versts,* or at the rate of about 4.8 miles per hour including stops, our train seeming to run on about the usual schedule. In equipping the car there are two tiers of cots on each side, 12 cots in all. Cots are suspended by slings from hooks on the inner side of a light flexible wooden beam near roof of car. This beam is suspended by means of a span of 2″ hemp passing over fair leaders on sides of car. At the bottom the cots are secured to the deck by a three-part stay, which prevents too much motion in either direction of length of car or transverse to it. Cots

* 506 versts=337 miles.

have canvas bottoms and straw mattresses, and are very comfortable, except that the inboard side had perhaps too much spring, while outboard side was a little stiff.

The cars were very roomy, with plenty of extra space, and by crowding a little and putting in three tiers of cots might have been made to accommodate 20 men instead of 12. It would seem to be a good idea too if the cots had been arranged so as to be transferable, and save the wounded from shifting from one to the other as sometimes was necessary, and also difficult. The medical officers and nurses were very hospitable and kind, but the soldier attendants were stupid and dirty, the lavatory especially being very poorly kept. Still the wounded seemed to be very comfortable in mind if not in body, since there were no longer any perplexing questions to be solved, and they could smoke, chat, and drink tea all day long.

While at Mukden I visited the front of the Russian lines covering the main position along the Shaho River for a distance of about 30 miles from east to west. The Russians were in position over a front about twice this length, with detachments of cavalry on the western flank as far as the Liao Ho River, and on the eastern flank to a distance of 100 miles east of Mukden. The main positions followed the line of the Shaho River, a small stream from 10 to 20 feet wide, and easily fordable anywhere. The Russians held one position to the southward of this River, a small hill, afterwards named Putiloff from the colonel of the regiment, which on the night of October 16 assaulted and captured it from the Japanese along with eight field guns, five mountain guns, and one machine gun. To westward of the railway the Japanese line crossed the river where it bends to the southward, and at this point, Linshinpu, the lines of the opposing forces were about 300 yards apart.

For the rest of the front the distance between the lines varied from 500 to 2,000 yards. No active operations were in progress, though desultory firing was going on every day with raids by scouting parties during the night. The Russians were busy entrenching, preparing winter quarters, making roads, and laying trolley tracks along the rear of center. The country was practically abandoned by the Chinese, their houses being looted, and large portions of them removed for fuel. There seemed a great deal of wanton destruction, but much more of waste. The stores of fuel of kowliang roots belonging to the Chinese would be scattered about under foot, while the windows of the houses, being made of light frames covered with paper, would be torn out by the soldiers to use in making fires. Removing the windows of course rendered the house uninhabitable. The Russian intendants or commissary officers purchased all the forage and grain that was possible, but still in the vicinity of the army large quantities of kowliang would be cut down and left to rot on the ground, both grain and stem.

The weather during first part of November was quite mild during the day, but very cold at night. Still all day long fires would be kept burning in every direction, and also until late at night, using up the limited amount of fuel available. I have seen one soldier warming himself in the morning beside a large bonfire of kowliang. I have seen a Coassack feed his horse by pouring the grain out on the bare dusty ground, when there was within reach a feeding basket. When a beef was killed, the soldiers left many eatable portions on the ground to the dogs and crows.

It was very difficult to get fresh meat about this time, and it would seem that more care would have been used to make what was available go as far as possible. However, if the Russian soldier is improvident, at least he compensates in a measure for it, by uncomplaining submission to privation. Before the winter was over, fuel, beef and water became very scarce, but there was not as much suffering in the army as might have been anticipated. When I saw the men and horses again in February 1905, they seemed really in excellent condition, due in great measure probably to their naturally hardy physique.

The winter huts used by the soldiers consisted of a pit dug in the ground, about 6′ x 7′ and four feet deep, on each side the earth not dug out to full depth, but left as a sort of ledge for a bed. A thick mat of kowliang stalks was placed in an inverted V shape for the roof and earth thrown on top of them. At one end was the door with a wind shield of kowliang stalks, and at the other end a small fireplace of brick, or simply dug out from the earth. On the beds was laid more kowliang stalks for a mattress and in each hut lived four men. These houses were almost air tight, having no ventilation, and as the soldiers lived and slept in their sheepskins they did not suffer from the cold. The closeness would have been uncomfortable to an American, but it was customary with the Russian peasant, and did not inconvenience them.

It did not seem that the Russians understood as well as Europeans how to adapt themselves to winter military campaigns, the principal idea being to construct as nearly as possible a hermetically closed compartment, to crawl into it, and hibernate. The alternation of temperature on coming out of one of these sweat boxes was extreme, and with any one except Russians or Esquimaux would have caused bronchial diseases. During the Russian or Siberian winters the peasant farmers crawl into their huts, seal everything there, make their bed on the stove, and spend the winter sleeping and eating, going out only occasionally to attend to their cattle. The Siberians accustomed to hunting, adapted themselves more intelligently to conditions of very great cold, and it was principally from amongst men of this character that the active parties were formed engaged in raiding and scouting along the front.

At 3 p.m. November 15, left Mukden on the regular passenger train, arriving at Kharbin 12:30 p.m. November 18, or at the rate of 4.9 miles per hour. Left Kharbin at 10:30 p.m. November 18 and arrived at Vladivostock 7 a.m. November 21, or 730 versts* in 56 1/2 hours or 8.7 miles per hour. Troops in considerable numbers were moving from Kharbin toward Mukden, and many sick were coming north. Toward Vladivostock store and ammunition trains were moving, but few men.

On arrival in Vladivostock found *Gromoboi* in dock, and *Bogatyr* with forward turret and guns not yet shipped, and bow still supported by pontoons. Repairs of *Rossia* were nearly finished and there were seven torpedo boats in the harbor. During the month of November an English ship, the *Carlisle,* had been loaded with ammunition and provisions for Port Arthur, but after getting outside lost her propeller, and after being about three months out was finally brought into Manila. Another merchant ship, the *Peitang,* was purchased by the Russian Government, placed in charge of a

* 730 versts=487 miles.

naval officer, and started for Port Arthur, but after a week's absence was reported in Olga Bay and was brought back to Vladivostock, having met with heavy weather, and deeming it unsafe to proceed. She was overhauled and started out again November 30, bringing up a month later in Tsingtao. Another ship was being fitted out with guns, ammunitions and other stores, but did not get away before Port Arthur fell. During November several merchant steamers came into Vladivostock with coal and sundry stores.

From November 21 until end of the year weather was cold with very little snow, and occasionally high winds making the town very dusty. Ice began to form at the head of Ussuri and Amur Gulfs, and at the head of Golden Horn about December 1, floating ice seen in middle of December, and by December 20 it was thick enough to walk on. Temperature during night would fall to 9° or 10° below 0 Fahrenheit, but air was very dry and the days were not uncomfortably cold, except when there was strong wind. Then the air would be full of dust, and life in Vladivostock was very uncomfortable.

By January 1 the harbor and both gulfs alongside Muravieff Peninsula were frozen over to a depth of from one to two feet. A channel was always kept clear without difficulty by the small ice breaker *Nadiozhnik* and if there were much traffic in the harbor, the traffic itself would keep a channel open without need of the services of an ice breaker. The warships in Vladivostock never have the least difficulty in getting in or out during the winter on account of ice, the fleet consisting of *Gromoboi, Rossia, Rurik* and *Bogatyr* requiring six hours only from the time of beginning to get underway until fleet would be outside. The icebreaker is particularly necessary in clearing away the ice to assist ships in going alongside docks, and in clearing them from the docks in getting out. Ice never reaches greater thickness than 28″, and port cannot be considered at all as a closed port. This impression seems to be so general and firmly rooted, that it is worth while to contradict it most emphatically.

On December 26 four more submarines arrived by rail from St. Petersburg. These boats were of submersible type with considerable superstructure, and side torpedo-launching gear, Drziewicki-type. They were about 100′ long, 11′ beam, and 15′

depth, and their transportation for such a distance was a remarkable feat. Opportunity to inspect them or the carriages on which they were transported was refused, but the general idea is as shown in sketch No. 17. Forward and aft at about 1/4 of the length of the boat from each end, it was supported in a cradle which pivoted on a bed resting on two trucks.

Each truck had eight wheels, and arrangements made on the trucks to allow a small amount of play of the cradle bed in direction of motion of train, and shock taken up on buffers. The two sets of trucks did not seem to be connected in any way, and all strains seemed to be taken up on body of boat. Certainly there were no rigid connections, and I was informed besides that there was no connection whatever between the two sets. This seemed odd, but fairly well established. Under forward end of boat was a small separate truck, with a caboose for the brakeman, and on the rear truck was also a brake. The small detached truck apparently acted also somewhat as a buffer to take up severe shocks. The four boats formed first part of the train, then 13 box cars constituted the remainder, in these being part of the equipment of the boats, the

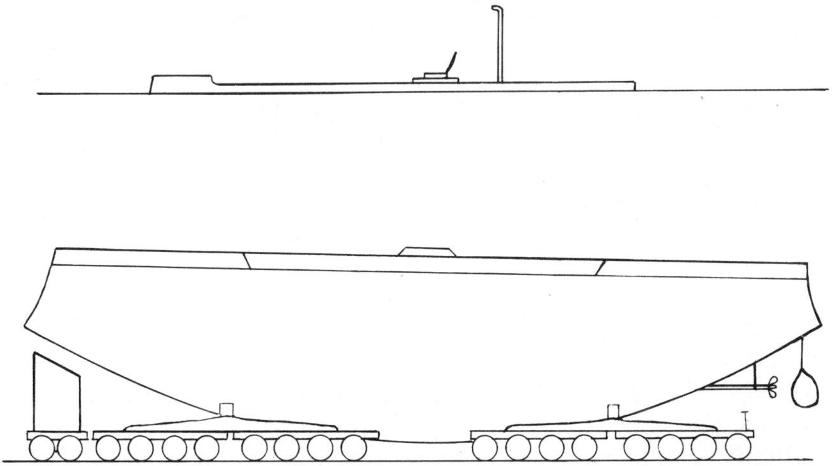

Sketch No. 17 Types of Russian submarines. (top) Small submarine, waterline view. (bottom) Large submarine mounted on rail transport trucks used in overland haul from St. Petersburg.

military guards, and some sailors detailed for duty with the boats. They had left St. Petersburg on November 17 and had been 40 days en route.

Early in January Vice Admiral Skrydloff was recalled, and returned to St. Petersburg, Rear Admiral Yessen assuming command as senior flag officer. Rear Admiral Skrydloff previous to the war had an excellent reputation as disciplinarian, was an able courtier, and was considered a very fair officer. He had been too slow in starting when ordered to take the place of Admiral Makaroff and did not arrive until Port Arthur had been isolated. Then, although still urged to attempt to get in Port Arthur, he was reported as answering that he would prefer orders to Nagasaki direct. Without doubt he had several opportunities to get in by boarding the *Lieutenant Burakoff* which safety made three trips to Inkow. He never went to sea on the Vladivostock ships, which would have been hardly appropriate anyway as there were only three ships which already had two admirals attached to them, both commanding divisions of the fleet under his command. The activity of the Vladivostock ships may be credited to his orders, giving some color to the criticism of an army officer that in time of war there were necessary two admirals for a fleet, one to command it and the other to live on shore and send it to sea.

Judging from the comments of military men, he did not get along any better with the other officers of high rank than did the officers at Port Arthur, not being on good terms with either the Viceroy, General Kouropatkin or with Admiral Yessen. He would refer to Admiral Yessen as "cet animal" and Admiral Yessen returned the compliment by referring to his commander in chief as "sitting in a girl's school entrenched behind his icons." At a celebration of a regiment in Vladivostock to which the attachés were invited Admiral Skrydloff made a speech in which he spoke of the "victories" of the navy, referring to the sinking of the Japanese transports, but added that "while doing honor to these let us not forget the victories of our army." On being recalled he was not well received in St. Petersburg and was much in disfavor with the government.

About this time there were many rumors in Vladivostock indicating a very bad spirit in the fleet. Several officers committed suicide, one of them, Lieutenant Bogdanovitch, under accusation of an attempt to blow up the *Gromoboi* while in dock. Several of the officers of the *Rossia* attacked the executive officer who was very unpopular, and beat him while on board ship. Another officer that I knew mustered his division, and made a disloyal speech before it in which he said he disapproved of the war, and could not conscientiously take any further part in it. He then took off his arms and invited his men to arrest him. The crew of the *Rossia* broke out in a half hearted, irresolute mutiny against their officers, accusing them of devoting all their attention to women, and were only quelled by the use of troops of the 31st Regiment. The workmen engaged on repairs of ships at the navy yard were kept at work by soldiers stationed over them, claiming that their contracts had been broken and that they were being kept over their time.

The medical officers of the army, composed mostly of Jews and students, held a meeting to protest against the conditions under which they were required to serve, with the idea of drawing up a protest to the Emperor, and their meeting was broken up by the gendarmes. One medical officer was reported to have been executed. On the surface little if any of these events could be seen, and the reports may have been exaggerated, but coupled with later events they seemed more probable.

Personally I knew only of two officers who committed suicide, and of the officer who declined to take further part in the war. That the spirit of the officers and men was not good, was easy to discern, and apparently they sought in dissipation, more than was done at Port Arthur, a relief or distraction from the misfortunes of their position. There was more drunkenness, and officers gambled for excessive stakes with money not their own; and this was partly responsible for some of the suicides. One officer whom I knew well had gambled with government funds, lost, and was forbidden to gamble any more under penalty of dismissal.

Shortly after the departure of Admiral Skrydloff Lieutenant General Voronetz was relieved by Lieutenant General Andréef, a cavalryman, after a disagreement with General Kouropatkin. When we called on Russian New Years', January 14, to pay our respects to General Voronetz and offer him our best wishes for the New Year, he rather sadly informed us that his New Year had begun very unhappily for him since he had just received news that he was to be detached, another officer having been ordered to be his "General Stessel" as he expressed it, and he had protested, feeling it to be his due, after planning and constructing the defenses of Vladivostock to have the right of commanding them in case of operations.

Leiutenant General Andréef was commandant for about a month only and was then relieved by Lieutenant General Kazbeck, sent out from Russia, who accepted the post of commandant only when assured that he would have no "General Stessel" over him. The news of the fall of Port Arthur arrived on January 4, three days before the Russian Christmas,* which in consequence was not fully celebrated, the comment of one officer I knew being only "Why could they not have held out a little longer, so that we might have had our Christmas?" snapping his fingers in a provoked way. The civil and commercial population of Vladivostock looked on the fall of Port Arthur almost with equanimity.

As long as the water was frozen over the commandant of the fortress was extremely uneasy over the prospect of the fortress being attacked over the ice. Each day the icebreaker was out, and attempting to keep a broken channel around Russian Island and the peninsula on which Vladivostock was situated. At intervals of about one verst, or two-thirds of a mile, machine guns were stationed with a post of four men, and a small house for shelter. This method of attacking Vladivostock is one worth serious consideration, the defenses not being constructed particularly to resist this sort of attack, and the Russian military authorities having become aware of their weakness in this direction only when the fortress was enclosed in ice.

As mentioned before, the ice lasts from December 20 until March 10, and during the months of January and February is of sufficient thickness to support large bodies of men and to allow, if necessary, of the transportation of field artillery. It usually extends over the entire area of the harbor, and over the two bays, Amur and Ussuri, and sometimes as far out as 10 miles to sea from

---

* Although most of the world had adopted the Gregorian or New Style calendar by 1900, Russia still marked dates by the Julian or Old Style calendar, in which during the twentieth century dates come 13 days later than in the New Style calendar. Russia adopted the New Style calendar in 1917.

Russian Island. Ordinarily the ice line is between Askold Island and Rimsky Korsakoff, during the winter of 1904–1905 having been a little inside of that line, extending from Askold to southern part of Russian Island and from there to Slavianski Bay. When unbroken it is usually about two feet thick, so that a strongly built ship can force its way through it without much difficulty, and on arriving at a suitable place disembark on the ice. The cold is severe particularly at night, but air is usually so dry that it is not so much felt as in a damp climate. A winter campaign against Vladivostock as defended at present offers much better chances than one made in open weather.

On January 15 two submarines of the *Holland*-type, one the *Fulton* and the other a new boat, arrived by rail in Vladivostock, and a week later were placed in the water. *Rossia* went out on trial trips on January 20.

On January 17 the new temporary commandant, Lieutenant General Andreéf, arrived and relieved Lieutenant General Voronetz. Vladivostock was placed on a siege basis, all persons living within city limits registered with the police for duty in case of operations, the men as firemen, hospital attendants, volunteers, watchmen, workmen or to handle coal and ammunition; the women as cooks, nurses, laundresses, etc. Every inhabitant was instructed to be ready to leave at 24 hours notice, the schools were closed, and many people did leave, going to Nikolsk, Khabarovsk, Blagoveshchensk and other places.

During the month of January nine merchant steamers came into Vladivostock, nearly all bringing coal, and all having contraband. Four of the steamers were British, two having been sent out direct from England, three were German, one was Norwegian and one Russian from Sakhalin. Most of the steamers came from Hongkong or Shanghai, one of them coming through Korea Strait, the others by way of La Perouse. The Norwegian steamer *Tungus* arriving January 1, by way of La Perouse, passed through 90 miles of two-foot ice. German steamer *Eva* 31 days out from Shanghai was in the ice of La Perouse Strait for a week, and arrived in Vladivostock January 9. British steamers *Hindoo* and *Lord Antrim*, arriving January 21, were from three to six days in the ice which was generally about two feet thick but in floes occasionally of much greater thickness. British steamer *Ellamy* left Shanghai and made

Vladivostock in six days by way of Korea Strait meeting no difficulties whatever. Steamer *Emma* with refugees from Sakhalin was 15 days in the ice, having much difficulty getting out.

All ships that had been in the ice showed the effects forward in ribbed-out frames, leaking seams, dented plates, etc., but enough steamers came through by the way of La Perouse to show that it is not closed to strongly built vessels during the month of January. None of the vessels coming in sighted any Japanese vessels, and none were sighted off Vladivostock, showing that the blockade of the port was very lax. All these steamers left during February, and there was only one other steamer to get in after January.

The weather during first part of January was very mild, the snow and ice melting, and part of the harbor where there was most traffic, clear of ice. Later on in the month it again became very cold, with strong northwest winds, and very dusty and disagreeable, with very little snow. February was much the same as latter part of January and harbor and gulfs remained frozen over.

In February there began to be evidence of the scarcity of such articles as kerosene, sugar, tobacco, champagne, candles, matches, beer, wines, flour, and fresh meat, the prices of which had by this time doubled the prices in peace time. To be allowed to remain in Vladivostock every civilian had to deliver to a government storage agent a certain amount of flour as guarantee that he would not be dependent on the military authorities in case of siege.

At the coal docks was stored about 60,000 tons of good coal which was expended very carefully. The ships in harbor used for ordinary expenditures while at anchor, coal from the mines in the vicinity of Vladivostock. These mines, about 30 to 50 versts away from Vladivostock, and on the same peninsula on which the city is situated, were furnishing about 1,000 tons of lignite or semibituminous with 70 or 80 per cent of carbon, and 4 to 15 per cent of ash. The railways use this coal on their locomotives between Vladivostock and Nikolsk, and it furnishes the ordinary house fuel for the civilian population of Vladivostock. The coal-bearing formations extend along the shore from 150 miles to the northward of Olga Bay to down near Possiet Bay, and inland for about 80 miles. None of the mines have been fully developed, but some have shown great promise. The price of the native coal in Vladivostock was between 15 and 20 rubles, or between $7.50 to 10.00 per ton.

On February 16 Lieutenant Andréef notified the attachés, Captain Eyres, Captain Moneta and myself, that they were invited by the commander in chief to visit Mukden to witness operations, and as there was some doubt as to their returning to Vladivostock, it would be better to take their baggage with them. This came as a very unpleasant surprise to all us since just about this time it seemed that there might be hopes of Admiral Rojestvensky again proceeding on his way, and we had expected to remain until his arrival. However, we recognized the intent of the invitation, and on February 18 left for Mukden, arriving Kharbin February 20, having made the run from Vladivostock at the rate of 9.3 miles per hour.

We left Kharbin same day and arrived Mukden February 22, making trip at rate of 7 miles per hour including stops. In passing through Kungshuling, there seemed quite a remarkable development of the place into a sub-base of considerable importance. Many new sidings were laid, considerable stores accumulated, and it had become a hospital base second only to Kharbin. Very few troops were moving to the southward and traffic seemed to be in very much better shape than at any time since the war began. We passed two trains with artillery bound to Kharbin. Arriving in Mukden we were informed that we would be presented to the commander in chief on February 27.

On February 23 began the battle of Mukden, with an attack by the Japanese on the extreme Russian left. Fighting continued in this direction for several days, but without any one getting the idea that the big battle had begun. On February 27 we were presented to the commander in chief, General Kouropatkin, who informed us that as there was no fleet left in Vladivostock, and as the operations in the vicinity of a fortress could be of little interest to naval officers, and besides the unfortunate accident of the two attachés from Port Arthur who had disappeared, he had decided that we could not remain in Vladivostock. We replied that there was left in Vladivostock enough of a fleet to still be responsible for serious damage to an enemy, that operations against a maritime fortress were of the deepest interest to all naval officers, and that the Russians could not hold themselves in any way responsible for the sad fate of the two missing attachés. These arguments seemed to have little weight, and the interview was closed very suddenly by important despatches indicating that the great battle had begun.

We were invited to luncheon with the commander in chief and during it he spoke very freely about the coming battle. Amongst other things he advanced the theory that most of the best Japanese fighting men, the samurai, had been killed off by this time in the previous battles. These had been in the habit of leading the common soldiers and in doing so most had been killed so that now the personnel of the Japanese Army was inferior to what it had been in the beginning while the Russian Army had improved, the soldiers in the beginning being practically all Siberians.

In regard to the Japanese the theory may have had some basis, though the subsequent operations did not make it appear so, while as regards the Russians, most of the attachés had gradually come to the idea that the Siberian infantrymen were the best soldiers in the army, and the regiments on the field in the beginning were the best of the Siberian troops. The Russian cavalrymen were superior to the Siberians as a rule, though the dragoons from Primorski province were always looked on as excellent.

According to our interview the incident seemed closed, but as I had received permission from General Kouropatkin himself to go to Vladivostock to observe operations, I submitted a letter with a full statement of the circumstances and asked to return. The other attachés informally made the same request.

About March 1 the principal part of the fighting shifted toward the Russian center and right, and increased in violence on the Russian right indicating the turning movement of the Japanese in that direction.* It was difficult to get any idea of exactly what was going on, the range of visibility being limited on account of the flatness of the country about Mukden, there being no elevated points from which to observe and March 3 and 4 being so dusty that men could not be distinguished at a distance of 200 yards.

---

* The turning movement was a maneuver executed primarily by the 8th Division, 2nd Japanese Army, with supporting operations by the 9th Division and 5th Division, during 1-3 March 1905. The operation was commanded by Lieutenant General Baron Tatsumi, and was combined with frontal attacks under cover of heavy artillery barrages.[10]

On March 3 commander in chief shifted headquarters to Mukden and on March 5 it began to be evident that the battle was going against the Russians. On March 4 Major Mockler, another British attaché, arrived having been 31 days en route from St. Petersburg. Several divisions passed through the city bound to the northward, the heavy guns were loaded on trains and also sent in that direction, and it was learned that the Russians were abandoning their wounded, which they never did unless very hard pressed. The Japanese artillery fire was directed on points three miles from Mukden station, and heavy fighting was going on to northwestward of the station. Several times I went out to try and make some observations of the progress of the battle, but was not allowed to approach nearer than a half mile to the firing line.

On one occasion a soldier came up to me, just in rear of the lines and asked in English if I were an American. He had been a shoemaker in New York for three years and was drafted into the army on returning to Russia. He looked like a Jew and was quite intelligent but estimated all distances in blocks, apparently the only American estimate of distance he was acquainted with. He informed me that the Japanese were about three or four blocks in their front, and accused his own officers of remaining two blocks in rear of the fighting line. He had come back himself to get something to eat for himself and comrades, then returned to the firing line.

Movement of troops continued to the northward and Russians abandoned their first line, taking up positions along the Hunké. In afternoon of March 5 attachés were notified that their train would proceed to the northward, and that they might go with it or remain in Mukden as they chose. As Captain Moneta and I had no horses and had been notified unofficially that we could return to Vladivostock, we decided to take no chances and to go with the train along with several of the other attachés, while most of them remained in Mukden. Captain Eyres, British naval attaché, who owned a horse, decided to remain at Mukden and went into the Chinese city with the newspaper correspondents and American military attachés. Our train left early in morning of March 6, arriving at Tiehling at 10 p.m. the same day. Severe fighting was going on about 10 versts to northwest of Mukden, and considerable transport and troops were already marching toward Tiehling. The heavy guns were sent on to the northward toward Kungshuling.

While at Tiehling train after train of wounded passed through bound to Kharbin, the wounded on these trains suffering very much from lack of attention. These trains were the regular troop trains without other accommodations than the ordinary board flats without cots or mattresses. From one train 16 dead were removed, and the platform of the station had always a heap of stretchers with the dead, amongst them some Japanese. The hospitals in Tiehling were crowded, and only officers and the most desperate cases were received there. In one hospital were several women surgeons, one of whom that day had already performed five capital operations.

In conversation with these surgeons while in company with the French attaché they informed us that they were all republicans, the women being more ardent than the men. It did seem a rather remarkable fact that so large a proportion of the medical staff should be so devoted to republican principles. It is not surprising that the Jews, who form a considerable proportion of the medical staff, should be republican, but it was the same with both pure Russians and Russians of German descent of whom there were also many.

Inquiry as to why there were so many Jewish surgeons, brought out the fact that in Russia Jews are not allowed to live in any except certain towns, unless they have a government diploma as doctor or lawyer. They obtain these by the required course of attendance at the government schools, and then have the right to live in any town, but do not as a rule practise the profession for which they have received diplomas. They must, as surgeons, register in the reserve and consequently, in time of war, must accompany the troops in their mobilization district.

All day of March 9 and 10 which were both very dusty large numbers of troops were arriving in Tiehling Mukden being abandoned daylight of March 10. Captain Eyres, the British naval attaché, two American attachés and the newspaper correspondents were captured in Mukden, Major Macomb alone, of those living in the Chinese city, being able to escape. About 7 p.m. March 10 the rest of the attachés arrived in Mukden, but their baggage had been lost in an attack on the baggage train. During March 11 in Tiehling there was a scene of great disorder, thousands of soldiers straggling through and a train of guns, wagons, cars and carriages, sometimes five abreast, drifting to the northward in no order whatever. Many trains of wounded continued to pass through but transportation was almost blocked and sometimes a train was side-tracked at Tiehling for several hours. Some trains were en route over a week between the battlefield and Kharbin, and the wounded must have undergone great privations.

When a train stopped it was visited by a medical officer and nurses, the dead removed, the wounded inspected and their wounds dressed again if in great need, piles of bloody bandages marking the stopping trains. Some of the wounds seen in the hands and legs of the men had apparently been infected, the members being very much swollen. One man was walking about without bandages and seemed quite lively; I asked if he were wounded too. He answered that he had been five days previously, the bullet passing through his stomach from the right side to the left. He was walking about eating peanuts, without fever, and apparently as well as ever. In many cases the infection was caused by bullets carrying part of the sheepskin coats or wool into the wounds. The bodies of the soldiers too were exceedingly dirty, in some cases the dirt really forming a thin hard scale, which was difficult to remove.

In the beginning of the battle, toward the end of February, the weather was generally cold, February 23, 24, and 25 being dusty with mild temperatures during the day, very cold at night, thermometer going down to 8° Fahrenheit. February 26 was windy with snow all day long. February 27 and 28 were fair and mild, during day thermometer rising above freezing point, but still very cold at night. March 1 and 2 were fair and mild with light breezes, and not so very much dust, some snow on March 2. March 3 was exceedingly dusty with strong breezes from northwest. Temperatures moderated gradually and March 10 and 11 during the day were quite pleasant, thermometer rising to 50° Fahrenheit in shade. If the weather had been severe, as at this season it might well have been, the sufferings of the troops on the retreat would have been very great. Without any standard of comparison it is difficult to say whether the retreat was well conducted or not. The most that can be said is that it is most disagreeable to march with a beaten army, and an experience one would never wish to repeat.

At 8:30 p.m., March 11, our train left Tiehling and at 11 a.m. next morning crossed the head of the column of retreat, 30 versts or 20 miles to the northward of Tiehling. Arrived at Kungchuling at 1 a.m. March 14, having travelled from Tiehling at rate of about 20 miles per hour. We left Kungchuling at 3:15 p.m. the same day and arrived at Yaomine at 9:45 a.m. March 15, travelling at the rate of about 5 miles per hour. About 40 versts* to the northward of Kungchuling, and 247 versts** to southward of Kharbin the railway was attacked on February 15 by a combined force of Chinese and Japanese, and the central pier of a small bridge blown up.

Communications were interrupted for two days only. This was the only serious attack made on the railway between Kharbin and Mukden though there were a few attempts of minor importance, and there were reports of quite a number of attempts between Kharbin and Vladivostock. From March 12 to 15 weather became much colder with snow, on March 15 temperature going to 10° below 0 Fahrenheit. Several trains were passed moving to the southward with troops and stores but no artillery.

We arrived at Kharbin during night of March 15, having made the trip from Tiehling to that place at the rate of about 3 miles per hour. At 11 p.m. March 16 left Kharbin and arrived at Vladivostock at 7 a.m. March 20, having travelled at the rate of 6.1 miles per hour including stops. At Vladivostock the same ships were present as when we had left there, *Gromoboi's* repairs having been completed, and *Bogatyr* again entering dry dock. No merchant ships had arrived during our absence, and there were no reports of Japanese ships having appeared in the vicinity. Lieutenant General Kazbeck had relieved Lieutenant General Andréef as commandant and was exercising at this time command independent of any one except commander in chief.

---

* 40 versts=27 miles

** 247 versts=165 miles.

The harbor of Vladivostock was almost clear, ice being broken up by traffic and drifted out, only the eastern part of Golden Horn still frozen over, and Ussuri and Amur Gulfs still closed. Weather was fair and mild, and continued so during rest of March, about the end of which all ice was out of the harbor, and the bays on each side of Muravieff Peninsula. Weather remained fair and pleasant during April, and besides a very active movement of troops both into and out of Vladivostock was very much increased until it numbered about 60,000 men, new defenses were constructed, and a number of 6″ guns were brought in.

Five of the torpedo boats made a cruise over toward the Japanese coast, destroyed two small sailing vessels and returned. The submarines were constantly exercising and seemed to be in good condition, the large submersible type requiring about 20 minutes to submerge. *Rossia* and *Gromoboi* were ready for sea, having still further increased their efficiency by mounting the bow 6″ gun on the forecastle instead of through the stem, so allowing of beam fire with them. With the six extra guns already mounted, these two ships had been able to increase their broadside fire by four more 6″ guns, or giving them now two 8″ and twelve 6″ in broadside, and making them more nearly equal to the Japanese armored cruisers with four 8″ and seven 6″ in broadside.

Of the naval attachés now only the Argentine, Commander Moneta, and I were left, and though the prospect for obtaining information did not seem very bright, we decided to remain in Vladivostock awaiting the Rojestvensky fleet, as long as possible. The commandant of the fortress, General Kazbek, and the commander of the 1st Squadron Pacific Fleet, Rear Admiral Yessen were always personally very pleasant, but did not seem disposed to give the naval attachés access to any means of obtaining information. Practically we were confined to the limits of the town, sentries being posted everywhere on the outskirts, and on the crests of the hills, and no one but officers of the Russian military and naval services being allowed beyond these.

On April 14 we were again invited to proceed to the headquarters of the new commander in chief, General Liniévitch, to be presented to him, and left Vladivostock on April 19 for Kharbin, arriving there at noon April 22, having made about 6.2 miles per hour. On the road were passed on an average each day 10 trains bound to the eastward, most of them with stores and ammunition, a few with troops, and one with two 6″ and 12 4.2″ howitzers.

On this trip from Vladivostock to Kharbin we were accompanied by Mitchman (ensign) Boutakoff, and from him learned some rather interesting facts regarding the Russian Navy. The Boutakoffs are a naval family, and the young man with us was the twenty-eighth of his family to be in the service, of whom there are three in the Navy at the present time. In Ensign Boutakoff's class which left the naval school after a six year course, in 1902, there were 130 graduates given commissions. Of these 14 have been killed, six died, and four committed suicide, inside of three years. It is quite common to find many officers of the same name in the Navy, in the case of one name there being as many as twenty-six. Usually officers of the same name belong to the same family, except in the case of common names as Ivanoff, Vassilief, corresponding to our Johnson, Jameson, etc., and ordinarily after the names of most officers is an ordinal number indicating the particular officer of that name referred to.

On arriving in Kharbin and reporting to the officer detailed to accompany the attachés, we were informed that with the other attachés we would be presented to the commander in chief on May 4, at Godziadan, the present headquarters of the Army. Since the battle of Mukden all the military attachés had remained at Kharbin having been informed that at present there was nothing of interest likely to happen at the front.

In Kharbin itself there did not seem much activity, not as many officers and troops being evident as on former occasions, but the efficiency of the railway had been enormously increased. For several days observations were made extending over period from 7 a.m. to 11 p.m., and one day observations were made covering the entire 24 hours, and 19 trains were found to have come into Kharbin from the westward, and 12 trains gone out in that direction. About one-third of the trains coming brought troops, the others brought horses, stores, hospital equipment, railway and electrical equipment, sappers' and engineers' equipment, transportation material, artillery and ammunition. About one-half the trains arriving at this time were despatched to Vladivostock, but this was a temporary diversion only. Each day a regular passenger express arrived in Kharbin with mails and passengers, and another left, both making slow time but running close to schedule.

The operation of the railway had improved very much after a year's exercise under war conditions, and its capacity had been tripled. This part of the Russian organization had been improved beyond any expectation of attachés who had made a study and had some experience in railway military transportation, and seemed above any other department to be entitled to the respect and admiration expressed for its efficiency. During the entire war its operation between Moscow and Kharbin was never suspended, the line was never seriously attacked or injured, and the work it accomplished in transporting altogether very nearly one million men for a distance of 4,030 miles, (assuming the distance between Samara in Russia and Kharbin as representing fairly the route over which by far the greater part of the troops and materiel passed), and keeping them supplied during a campaign and after three of the greatest battles in the history of the world, and then at the end still supporting an army of between 500,000 and 600,000 men in readiness for further operations was surely work calling for unlimited commendation. Besides the work for the army the railway at the same time had been used to supply the needs of the navy and many of those of a great part of the civil population who were accustomed to receive by it many things not produced in Manchuria.

Seven submarines had already been delivered in Vladivostock, and while we were waiting in Kharbin an eighth of the *Protector*-type passed through. This had twin screws and was 80′ long by 12′ deep and 11′ beam. A lofty conning tower was carried on a separate car along with other parts of the equipment belonging to the boat. Two destroyers in sections also passed through Kharbin about this time bound for Vladivostock. The boats and conning tower of submarine were completely masked in canvas, and strongly guarded by detachments of sailors and soldiers.

At 7 p.m., May 1, the attachés' train left Kharbin for Godziadan, arriving there at 11:30 a.m. May 3, 307 versts* from Kharbin, or

* 307 versts=205 miles.

having travelled at the rate of 5.1 miles per hour. Godziadan was the position assumed as headquarters after the battle of Mukden, and was 200 versts or 135 miles to the northward of it. It was not made a military base, only a very few extra sidings being constructed, no stores accumulated, and few trains running into the station. The principal bases were Kunchuling and Kwanchenzi, and troops marched to their positions from these stations. Godziadan practically was the location of the special train of the commander in chief.

About noon of May 3 all the attachés were presented to the commander in chief and afterward took luncheon with him. He seemed in very good humor but stated that for the present no operations were expected, the lines of the two armies being at some distance from each other, and that in case of operations beginning the attachés would be informed, but that in the meantime they might remain at Kwanchenzi [or] in Kharbin as they chose.

After the close of the interview the three naval attachés, now including Lieutenant Camperio of the Italian Navy who, however had always accompanied the army, asked for a special interview and requested permission to return to Vladivostock. In reply we were informed that it was impossible, that by the Emperor's express command no attachés were to be allowed in Vladivostock.

As this definitely excluded us from observing further naval operations and it was rather late to begin work with the army, the necessary outfit would have been very expensive, and even the military attachés no longer being allowed at the front, Commander Moneta and I asked permission to return to our countries, and to proceed by way of the Amur River, and then by caravan across the Mongolian desert, intentions which I had already communicated to the [Navy] Department. We stated that we wanted to visit Khabarovsk where General Liniévitch had long been stationed, and a place of which he was very fond, looking on it as the Paris of Siberia. He seemed pleased with the idea, willingly approved it, and going even further gave instructions that all the other attachés were also invited to visit Khabarovsk.

General Liniévitch seemed a rather rough old soldier, his uniform and equipment not quite coming up to the dashing standard of most of the Russian officers. He seemed energetic and good humored, but yet with decided views, and he was admired and respected by his men and officers more than most of the Russian generals, often being referred to as "Little Papa" though he was not a small man. In talking his manner was rather peculiar, all his upper teeth being missing. His ideas were very practical, and for a Russian Army he probably was an ideal commander, after the type of some of their rough and ready successful generals of the past.

It is stated that General Liniévitch rose from the ranks, and in a sense it was true, although he entered as a volunteer who was given a somewhat different status from that of a man serving under conscription. One point about the ideas of General Liniévitch that seemed rather surprising, was that in spite of his character and the predilection of all Russian officers for the bayonet, General Liniévitch did not believe in it. His age was a matter of some question, and was given out as 66, but there was good evidence to believe him much older or about 73.

Left Godziadan at 4:35 p.m. and arrived in Kwanchenzi 3 a.m. May 4, spending the day there. This was now a considerable military base, and a large number of troops stationed there. Many reservists were being exercised by their petty officers, and instead of the drills in the manual and marchings at which they were being exercised at Liaoyang in April 1904, they were being instructed in making rushes in groups of 12, and taking cover. We finally arrived at Kharbin on May 5, and Commander Moneta, who was ill, went to the hospital, arranging to meet me later at Chita. Weather now was clear and springlike, nights being still a little fresh.

At 10:20 p.m. May 8 left Kharbin in company with all the attachés, and proceeded to Nikolsk where we arrived at 11:30 a.m. May 11, having travelled at rate of 7 miles per hour. In April 1904 between Kharbin and Nikolsk, a distance of 628 versts,* were 34 sidings or on an average of one for each 18.3 versts, or 12.3 miles. In May 1905, there were 58 in all, or an average of one for each 10.8 versts or 7.2 miles. Between Nikolsk and Vladivostock and

---

* 628 versts=419 miles.

between Nikolsk and Khabarovsk the number of sidings remained the same.

As the attachés intended remaining in Nikolsk for a day or so, I separated from them here and proceeded direct to Khabarovsk so as to take the first steamer, making the trip up the Amur. The trip of 615 versts* from Nikolsk to Khabarovsk was made in the very good time of 24 hours, or at the rate of 17.1 miles per hour, or at about the rate the trains were accustomed to run previous to the war. There seemed little traffic of importance on the Ussuri branch of the railway, no movements of either stores or troops. Khabarovsk is a very pretty town of about 20,000 inhabitants and the seat of government of the four provinces. As usual it is situated from three to four miles from the railway, and the streets being unpaved are all mud in wet weather, and dust in dry weather. Houses are usually constructed of wood, though there are a few rather handsome buildings of brick.

From passengers on the train coming from Vladivostock I learned that *Gromoboi* and *Rossia* had started out on May 7, and had not returned when they left on Tuesday May 9. As *Rossia* went out she had up a balloon, and apparently it was the intention of the cruisers to join Rojestvensky. The torpedo boats had gone out several days before. I learned afterwards that these ships returned to Vladivostock a few days after and that in returning *Gromoboi* again had an accident, running on a mine.

---

* 615 versts=410 miles.

May 13—September 26, 1905

Manchuria to St. Petersburg

At 8 a.m. May 13 boarded the steamer *John Cockerill* and started up the [Amur] river. The last of the ice had passed down the river a week before and this steamer was the second to start up the river this season, the other steamer having left the day before. The *John Cockerill* was a steel paddle-wheel steamer of about 1,000 tons, 264′ in length, 44 foot beam, and not carrying full load, drew only 3′ 8″. She was built in sections in 1894 and shipped to Nikolayevsk, engines built same year by Société Anonyme John Cockerill, Belgium. Speed was about 11 knots, boilers wood-burning and bunkers at this time on light draught carrying fuel sufficient for one day's steaming only. Besides the *John Cockerill* there are four other steamers of similar size and construction running on regular schedules between Blagoveshchensk and Nikolayevsk.

Trips begin as soon as ice is out of the river in the middle of May and continue until water gets too low, and river begins to freeze in middle of October. As soon as ice is out of the river it begins to rise and continues steadily to do so until after the summer rains in July and August when it begins to fall again. River rises 12 to 20 feet in lower portion below Blagoveshchensk, and 10 to 15 feet above that place. In June and July there is considerable fog. When the river is low no steamer drawing over three feet can get to Blagoveshchensk and not over two feet can be carried above, on account of rocky shoals. When the river is high, no difficulty is met on account of draft. The regular times for these steamers going up is five days Nikolayevsk to Khabarovsk, Khabarovsk to Blagoveshchensk five and one-half days, Blagoveshchensk to Sretensk eight days. Coming down the times are in order five, four, and three days. When the river is high the times may be diminished by about a day for each stage, steamers running by night as well as day.

When we made the trip the river was very low, the channel being usually about 12′ in depth, rarely falling below six feet. Banks were generally low, and between Khabarovsk and the mouth of the Sungari River is split up in several channels by low islands. Current varies from two to four knots, being swiftest at narrowest point and over shoals. There are no "narrows" in the usual sense of the term where the currents are very swift, the width of the river varying usually from 400 to 800 yards between mouth of Sungari and Blagoveshchensk.

At Ekaterina Nikolskaya, 375* versts above Khabarovsk where we arrived about 3 p.m. May 15, we found quite a fleet of river steamers waiting a rise of the river to get over the shoals, about 10 miles above. The weather was very mild, spring just beginning, trees starting to show green, and river rising slowly as the ice of the upper reaches began to melt. We remained at Ekaterina Nikolskaya until the early morning of May 17, then started again, the river having risen about eight inches in the meantime. Approaching the shoals the banks are high, but river does not narrow very much. The character of the bottom is stony with large boulders which constitute the danger. We proceeded very slowly sounding carefully as we went along, but got nothing less than six feet. After passing these shallows, our steamer soon took the lead of the fleet, most of which had from one to three empty barges in tow.

After this point there was little difficulty, though off Poyarkova about 100 miles from Blagoveshchensk, the river is split up by a number of small low islands, and the channels are narrow with sharp turns, with rather swift currents. At times men forward would assist the *John Cockerill* to turn by running out a long pole as a spur and shoving her bows out from the bank. Along the Amur, below Blagoveshchensk, the country is rather uninteresting, about half way to Khabarovsk, at Radde, being some pretty views. All the villages are on the north side of the river and range in size from the Cossack stanitza of 40 or 50 people to small towns of 1,000 to 1,500 people. Along the river bank is a post road, used mostly in winter, and the towns are connected up by telegraph.

---

* 375 versts=250 miles.

The river is also used for sledging in winter, but on account of the numerous turns the distance is greater by that route.

Aids to navigation are plentiful all along the river averaging one every two miles. On the Siberian or northern bank beacons are white and show white lights at night, and on the Manchurian or southern side red, with red lights at night. For narrow channels range marks are established, at sharp turns are watch towers and signal masts to warn vessels when channel is clear or not, and dangerous sand spits are marked by beacons with lights at night. Still the steamers very rarely run all night, usually tying up about 11 p.m., then going ahead again about 4 a.m. next morning.

The inhabitants along the banks are hunters, fishermen, and all do a little farming. Below Blagoveshchensk there is no lumbering. The people seem healthy, fairly intelligent, and happy, though very dirty. Buildings are all log houses, lined up along the bank, with nearly always the church the most imposing, and often brilliant in yellow, blue, and green. No troops whatever seem to be stationed along the river, though of course the Cossack stanitzas have almost the character of military posts.

What few Chinamen seen were the most wretched and miserable of their kind. It is rather worthy of note the deterioration of the Chinamen, as one goes north. Whether demoralized by contact with the Russians, or from other causes, the Chinamen of Mukden for instance are very much inferior to those of Tientsin, Pekin or Shanghai, and those of Kharbin are inferior to the Mukden Chinamen, and those on the Amur still lower. In no place under Russian control was it possible to find the clean, honest, intelligent Chinamen one meets further south. They seem to have completely lost these qualities, and in a measure to deserve the character attributed to them by the Russians as being dirty, thievish, lying, and generally untrustworthy.

A short distance below Blagoveshchensk was passed the site of the former Chinese village of Aigun where the trade route from Tsitsihar meets the Amur River. This village was destroyed and its population of several thousand exterminated in 1900 under the orders of General Grodekoff, then commanding the Russian forces at Blagoveshchensk. Even the Russians speak of this incident still as something that was not very nice. General Grodekoff was rewarded and promoted for the excellent organization of the troops sent down into Manchuria during the Boxer war, and very recently relieved General Liniévitch as commander in chief in the Far East. Another Chinese town above Blagoveshchensk was similarly destroyed, and thousands of bodies of Chinese men, women and children floated down the river for several days. Neither of these towns has ever been rebuilt, and all that is left are the remnants of the walls and watch towers and some charred stakes.

Arrived at Blagoveshchensk 4 p.m. May 19, and found quite a large, clean and business-like town. It is said to be the largest town in Siberia and at all events is the largest town east of Lake Baikal, nicely laid out, well situated on a bluff, some very handsome dwellings and business houses, wide and good streets, and well lighted and with modern conveniences. Off the water front of the town was a large fleet of river steamers loading up preparatory to beginning the season's work. Most of them were wooden stern wheelers of the American model of about 180′ in length, 40 feet beam, and drawing five feet forward, three and one-half aft.

On the way up the river passed two government steamers, the *Khabarovsk* and *Hazimir*. The first was paddle-wheel steamer about 200 feet long, of steel with two funnels and three masts, steaming about 12 knots and carrying six small RF and machine guns. The *Hazimir* was a stern wheeler 150′ long and carried two light guns. Both vessels were under the flag of the Ministry of Ways and Communications, flew pennants, and officers and crew were in uniform. On some of these vessels were naval officers, and shortly afterward Captain Klado was ordered out from St. Petersburg to take charge of the fleet. Besides these two vessels were two more of the type of the *Khabarovsk*, the *Sretinsk* and the *Blagoveshchensk;* and four more of type of *Hazimir* with five other smaller ones. The commercial fleet of the river is composed of the five packet-boats like the *Cockerill* running between Blagoveshchensk and Nikolayevsk, three smaller ones between Sretinsk and Blagoveshchensk; 22 wooden stern wheelers about 180′ x 40′, 14 paddle steamers 200′ x 40′; seven small stern wheelers, and about seventy barges.

On the river Zea and Sungari are also fleets of similar steamers but not so many, navigation extending up the Zea for 420 miles, and up the Sungari as far as Kharbin when the rivers are full. Blagoveshchensk is the business center of this district, the mining industry being most important, but no mines situated near Blagoveshchensk. Next in importance come agriculture, lumbering, fishing, and hunting. There are several shipyards at Blagoveshchensk capable of building hulls and engines of types of vessel used in the navigation of the river.

All the river traffic was hung up temporarily waiting for the river to rise a little more so as to get over a shoal about 20 versts* above Blagoveshchensk. The regular post steamer was not expected to leave until the 23rd, so I managed to get passage on a small stern wheeler, and left May 21. Just above the town river begins to narrow, and banks become hilly. Arrived at the shoal about 3 p.m. and spent three hours getting over, steamer being around several times, but finally succeeding in getting through. A few days later we overhauled a steamer which had started ahead of us and soon were leading the fleet up the river. Our steamer was 157 feet long, 35 feet beam, drew four and one-half feet forward, three feet aft, made eight knots and was built in Blagoveshchensk. She carried 21 first-class passengers, 168 deck passengers, and about 200 tons of flour and rye for the mining stations near Albazine.

In the river was still floating ice and along the banks ice cakes were piled up to a height of eight or 10 feet. From these it could be judged that the ice in winter is about four feet thick. At a point 500 versts above Blagoveshchensk the ice did not begin to break up until May 19, and from that time on river began to rise gradually, but irregularly, some days rising one foot, other days falling a couple of inches. The color of the water remains brownish, and not clear, current three to four knots, the banks are generally low, but more thickly wooded than lower down and country on either side undulating, and apparently well adapted to agriculture until Chernaeva is reached, 400 versts** above Blagoveshchensk. This seems the largest of the small towns along the river, has population of about 3,000, and is center of district where is considerable gold-mining.

* 20 versts=13 miles.

** 400 versts=267 miles.

Above this place country is more irregular, and the principal industry besides mining seems to be lumbering. In the bight which the river makes to the extreme northward, the banks are usually high on one side, low on the other, currents very swift, turns sharp, and river split up occasionally into several channels. Aids to navigation were still in plenty but no steamers ran during the night at this stage of the river. On May 28 arrived at the confluence of the Argun and Shilka rivers, and continued trip up the Shilka. The Argun is navigable for about 120 miles by small steamer, while the Shilka is navigable only during the open season by the general type of Amur River steamers as far as Sretinsk. When the river is high steamers may go further up to Nerchinsk but no aids to navigation are established above Sretinsk. The banks of the Shilka are high and usually thickly wooded, and as we passed through there were many forest fires, making the air so smoky as to interfere with navigation.

At 10:30 a.m. May 31 arrived at Sretinsk, a town of about 5,000 inhabitants, and took the train at 2 p.m. for Chita where I met Commander Moneta, recovered from his illness, and we proceeded together westward. He informed me that another destroyer in sections had passed through bound to Vladivostock, and that some days as many as 8,000 new troops had passed through Chita. Some of these I had met, and was struck with their excellent appearance, being very much younger than recruits I had formally seen.

Between Chita and Verkneudinsk the trip was very pleasant, spring in full season, and the train very comfortable, and confirming the impression received on my way out that this was by far the most attractive portion of Siberia. The number of sidings had been more than doubled along this stretch, having increased from an average of one to each 13 miles, to an average of one to each six miles. Arrived at Verkneudinsk at 3 p.m. June 3, and were fortunate enough to find a small steamer on the point of leaving, going up the Selenga River as far as Ust-Kyakhta or Kyakhta Landing. The Selenga River is not large, but the currents are very swift, channel deep and turns sharp. Navigation extends further up the river beyond Kyakhta into Mongolia for small steamers, but lack of enough trade prevents development. The scenery along the river is very pretty and the trip was very pleasant and comfortable.

We arrived at Kyakhta Landing on June 5, and left next morning by troika for Troitz-Kosavsk, about 10 miles away which is the Russian commercial town. It has a population of about 8,000 Russians, and is two miles from Kyakhta which is on the Russian side of the boundary between Asiatic Russia and the Chinese Empire.

Troitz-Kosavsk is the seat of administration and the center of local business, nearly all the Russian population living there. Kyakhta is practically only the location of the custom house, telegraph company's headquarters and residence of the principal large tea merchants. Outside of the wholesale traffic in tea, there is little else done in Kyakhta. The tea comes into Kyakhta by caravan, across the Mongolian desert, from Kalgan about 200 miles northwest of Pekin. The usual route of the caravans is in a direct line across the desert, but during the season when there is little rain and grass, the oxcart and pony caravans take another route to the eastward to Kerulen, then follow the Kerulen River to Urga and then by the usual route from Urga to Kyakhta. From Kyakhta the larger part of the tea is now sent down the Selenga by steamers, when the river is open—by caravan to the railway at Verkneudinsk when the river is closed. The return freight for the steamer and caravans between Verkneudinsk and Kyakhta is flour and bread.

On our arrival in Troitz-Kosavsk we were unfortunate enough to encounter two holidays in succession, during which nothing could be done in the way of securing transportation further on. Due to the shiftlessness and unreliability of the Russian moujik we met other delays and were not able to start until June 11. Our time had been set for 10 a.m., but due to the many little obstacles constantly arising we did not get away until 3 p.m., but insisting on starting then, simply to make sure of at last having a start.

Our caravan consisted of a tarantass* with a "troika," (three horses) a telega,** with a "para" (two horses) and a dvugolka or two-wheeled cart, the two latter for the baggage, which weighed about 500 pounds, and the forage. Two Mongol drivers, the Russian ishvoshik, and his daughter as cook, completed the party.

---

* Tarantass, a 4-wheeled springless cart.

** Telega, a 4-wheeled cart.

Besides, I had purchased a pony, having heard that it was very difficult to obtain camels at Urga. It seems that the favorite season for camel caravans is the winter time; in the summer the soles of their feet wearing off against the gravel and hard ground so that a camel must have a rest of a month or so after a summer's trip to let his feet grow again. Also in the summer the heat is very severe, and the camels suffer much from it, losing a great deal of weight, and numbers dying along the route. The part of the route usually covered by camels is between Urga, and to within about 30 versts* of Kalgan, the rest of it being accomplished by other methods of transportation.

The distance between Kyakhta and Urga is 285 versts or 190 miles, and we arrived in Urga at 7 p.m. June 16, having made an average of about 34 miles a day. The country between the two places is irregular, but not rough, roads are excellent, and on only two hills are the grades severe. Several small clear water streams were crossed, and elevation gradually increased, from that of Lake Baikal to about 3,000 feet above it. There are no villages but only occasional clusters of Mongol huts, practically all the country being devoted to grazing, large droves of ponies and cattle and great herds of sheep and goats feeding in the valleys. There is only a small amount of light timber, but even this is very valuable, several caravans being passed transporting it toward Urga. Other caravans were met with meal and one with champagne. On the River Iro an American company for quite a time operated gold mines, but they were abandoned, and the machinery is now left to rust.

Considerable game was seen, and wild flowers were abundant, altogether the trip being made through exceedingly attractive country, with many pretty views. For a great part of the distance automobiles could travel at 30 miles an hour, finding difficulties at only two hills on account of the grades. The days were usually pleasant, the usual temperature 80° and at night between 40° and 40° F. En route we passed a caravan of Manchurian Chinese from near Mukden bound for Pekin.

Urga, situated in the valley of the River Tula, is a large Mongol town of about 20,000 people. About twenty Russian merchants

---

* 30 versts=20 miles.

live in the town. There is a Russian Consulate in a fortified enclosure with guard of 30 Cossacks, and a branch of the Russo-Chinese Bank. Our landlord informed us that it would be necessary for the Russian Consul to "visé" our passports, but as we were in China we merely sent our cards. A Chinese "amban" or governor resides at Urga and there are about 300 Chinese Imperial troops in barracks there. Besides being a starting point and base for caravans there is little business in Urga, at the time we were there most of the interest of the people being taken up in religious matters, due perhaps to the presence of the Dalai Lama who had fled there from Lhasa on the approach of the British expedition.* He was a young and quite intelligent man of about eighteen, was absorbed in the study of geography at the time, and expected soon to return to Lhasa. We were informed that he would be pleased to have some foreigners, particularly Americans accompany him, as he feared assassination, and looked to them for a record of what might happen. He had no objections to meeting foreigners, nor to being photographed. We did not feel at liberty to take part in the expedition, though it was most attractive to an adventurous spirit.

The town was flooded with lamas or Buddhist monks, both Mongols and Tibetans, and religious ceremonies were continually going on during the day, and howling of myriads of dogs during the nights. As in Turkish centers these dogs are the scavengers, and more than this, the dead are exposed to be eaten by them. A number of Russians were in Urga as students of the Mongol and Tibetan languages, and it almost seemed as if the place was as much under Russian as Chinese influence.

Immediately on arriving we began negotiations for transportation, having been informed before hand that these would

---

* This was an armed expedition, under Sir Francis Younghusband, sent into Tibet to counter Russian expansionist aims in that part of Asia, as Lord Curzon, Viceroy of India, felt that Russian influence and control in Tibet would threaten British interests in India. The Dalai Lama, upon learning of the British approach, fled to the Gobi Desert in mid-August 1904. The complex issues surrounding the expedition are described in Peter Fleming's *Bayonets to Lhasa* (New York: Harper & Brothers, 1961).

require time. For two or three days it almost looked as if we would be unable to secure camels, but finally struck a bargain with a fine looking old leather-faced, blue-eyed Mongol for camels. From other sources we had secured carts and thought after laying in provisions that all was provided for. On the day of starting however we found that everything had to be furnished by us, and that our man wished to be paid all the money in advance. Inquiring as to what would be our resort in case we paid all our money and the other side failed to carry out their part of the contract, we were told that we would have recourse to their law, which would require the execution of the contract.

We did not have time to learn anything about legal methods of procedure but found out enough to know that careful legal contracts were necessary in an affair like ours, and that there really existed a Mongolian system of justice to which we could make appeal. This was quite a remarkable surprise to us, as we thought we were no longer in a country of legal papers. As it was not in our contract, we had to delay matters to purchase harness for the camels, rope for lashing on the baggage, grease for the carts and camels backs, water buckets, spare articles for emergencies, etc., and compromised with our head Mongol, by paying one half in advance, the other half on arrival.

Between Kyakhta and Pekin there is regular postal communication, and the two places are connected by telegraph. Each week there are usually two light mails carried by post riders, and for letters only, and one heavy mail in a tarantass with three horses, with relays every 45 or 50 versts.* Time for mail from Kyakhta to Pekin by post route is ten to eleven days. Passengers also may travel by this post route on receiving permission from the Russian and Chinese postal authorities, and paying a considerable price, and the new Russian Minister to China, Mr. Pokotiloff, passed us en route.

The telegraph line has two wires in use from Pekin to Kyakhta, owned by the Great Northern (Danish) Telegraph Company, the lower of the two wires being leased to the Chinese Imperial Telegraph Company. The Danish company leased only the lower wire,

* 30 or 33 miles.

as that is the wire usually interfered with by the Mongols who occasionally steal it. For short distances a third wire is strung but is discontinued in sections, on the theory that if some wire must be stolen, it may be taken from a line not in use. However the companies are very little troubled by interferences with the line, about the only casualty being from the rotting and falling of the telegraph posts. There are stations at Kyakhta, Urga, three relay stations across the desert, and one at Kalgan.

On June 24 we concluded negotiations with our Mongols, and after setting a time to start at 3 p.m. got away at 6 p.m. with two carts, two Mongols and eight camels. Some of our camels seemed a little wild, and that same evening about 11 p.m. the baggage camels stampeded on account of some dogs barking and disappeared in the darkness.

A caravan of camels is formed in single file, a Mongol riding by the leader, the other Mongol acting independently. Each camel has a leading cord passing through his nose secured from slipping through by a toggle. The other end of the leading cord is secured to the tail of the camel ahead. Our green camels had been making heavy weather with this arrangement for some time, sheering from side to side and doing a good deal of bellowing. When the dogs showed up, matters were brought to a climax and the rear camels bolted, either breaking the cord or pulling the toggles through their noses. When this happened our caravan stopped, and making a search we found some of the baggage scattered along the desert but had to wait until next day to recover the rest and the camels which fortunately we were able to do. Altogether we had eight camels, three for riding, two for baggage, two for carts and one more for tent and water buckets.

For the first hundred miles out of Urga country is undulating, without timber, and elevation gradually rising. There is considerable grazing and many herds of sheep and goats, and droves of ponies and camels, considerable game also seen, many herds of antelope coming up close to our caravan.

Water seems plentiful, there being occasional springs, and fresh water pools or lakes, and wells at regular intervals of about 20 miles. These wells are very shallow, from six to twenty feet deep, and where they have to furnish water to a large number of herds or caravans are quickly exhausted. The water in them is very cold, the temperature being invariably 40° to 44° F. all across the desert. The weather during this part of the trip was fine, the air being splendid, temperature during the day 80° to 90°, during the night 40° to 50°. The roads were almost level, of hard ground with topping gravel, and good enough for an automobile speedway. About 160 miles out from Urga, the roads become rougher, but still not bad, and we passed some rather remarkable hills in the plain, near which is a large lamasery. Vicinity is called Bogdo-ola, and from this point the real desert begins, thereafter being no habitations, little or no grass, and fewer wells.

Previous to this there had been quite a number of Mongol huts belonging to the herders, and our No. 1 Mongol who seemed to have many friends in the vicinity, was often setting sail and disappearing over the horizon on visits to some of them. On his return he would occasionally be the worse for wear, having absorbed more of the mare's milk liquor than was good for him. This came to be a nuisance as it necessitated our carrying water, assisting in the care of the camels, and collecting fuel, which items we did have in the contract to be carried out by the Mongol accompanying us. We had gotten up a phrase book in Kyakhta with the phrases likely to be most useful to us, and having practised them a few times managed to exchange simple ideas with the Mongols, expressions for this purpose being easier to learn than the corresponding phrases in Russian. Besides, Commander Moneta was rather clever in talking with his hands, and we never seemed to have any difficulty in indicating what we wished to do, or getting some idea of the Mongols wishes. Making them do these things was more difficult—they were obstinate, and very autocratic in the handling of the caravan, and when No. 1 was drunk, particularly so.

No. 2 Mongol seemed a very good natured hard working simple fellow, and other Mongols we met seemed to resemble him, so it may have been not quite ordinary for them to be so disagreeable as No. 1. Our principal difficulty with him, besides his abuse of liquor, was that he would rarely halt the caravan near a well. Usually we would start a 4 o'clock in the morning, run until 11 or 12, halt until 4 p.m. and then take up the march again until midnight. If we did not stop near a well we did not suffer for water to drink, carrying still plenty in the buckets, but there was not enough to bathe in, and this was annoying. Several times we would discover that the halt would be just short a mile or so of a well or we had passed one a mile or so back, and one day the offense became so aggravated that we almost had trouble with the man, and he had to be subdued with a revolver. This was the only unpleasant incident in the whole trip, the route being as safe, well established and free from interference as one of our transcontinental railways.

On June 30, when about 200 miles from Urga, we encountered the first dust storm which was not severe, and lasted only about an hour. It began with strong puffs of wind from north-northwest about the horizon, rolling red dust clouds, and rain showers, overhead cloudy. Tent was struck and camels and carts prepared to weather the storm which found us about 4:30. Wind shifted to northeast and blew with force of 7,* and for awhile nothing could be seen and we were very uncomfortable. Barometer remained steady, thermometer fell from 75° to 58°, wind diminished, a sprinkle of rain fell, and the affair was over.

From 160 to 200 miles from Urga the roads are not good, and entirely different from those for the first 150 miles. They are usually sand with many stones and boulders, and at night the road is easily lost. On account of this riding was impossible in the carts, the camel being particular only about his own route, and leading the cart wheels over boulders two feet in diameter. Riding on the camels was also inadvisable since from the long and late hours of the march and the easy motion one was likely to go to sleep and fall off, so usually during the night marches we walked. The general level of the road seemed to vary very little (barometer changing 0.2″ to 0.3″ only with change of elevation) and after 200 miles was almost perfectly plain, road becoming much better. The surface of the ground here was coarse gravel or pebbles, general color reddish brown, and undulations very slight with nothing whatever growing.

At a point about 250 miles from Urga, which we reached about 7 a.m. July 2, is a lake called Udzur about which is some grass, and a few huts and herds, and we also saw quite a lot of water fowl. Up

---

* A wind speed of from 28 to 32 miles an hour.

to this time besides the antelope seen outside of Urga, we had seen little else but a sort of prairie dog, hawks, crows, eagles, a few rabbits and some small birds resembling sparrows. Where anything could grow there were sometimes a few hardy wild flowers, but these were not often seen. At 280 miles from Urga, there is a system of irregular black-topped hills, rising not 200 to 300 feet above the general level and the roads again bad for short distance, with many lava-like boulders.

On July 4, arrived at the half-way station of Udé, about 320 miles from Urga, and situated in a red, barren, dusty valley with nothing living in the immediate vicinity. At this half-way station on the telegraph line is a small house, a Chinese telegrapher, two Chinese servants and a few chickens. Amongst the Mongols one never sees pigs or chickens. Beside the dog, their only domestic animals are in their herds. These furnish them nearly all their necessities, which are few and very simple.

With all the Mongols mutton is the principal article of food, first roasted, then ground up fine and made into a sort of soup. With flour they make a dough which is rolled out and strips put into their mutton broth where they are cooked. Salt is used if convenient, but does not seem to be a necessity. Tea seems to be a necessity, and usually is drunk without sugar. In the early morning our two Mongols would light a fire, boil water and tea in a shallow pan and while very hot, drink this from wooden cups. At noon they would make their mutton broth in the same pan, drop in a few strips of dough, which would make their dinner. For supper tea would be made as in the morning, but first their shallow wooden cups would be half filled with flour on which the tea would be poured. They would first drink the tea, then eat the dampened layer of flour on top. This operation would be repeated until the flour was consumed.

For ourselves, on leaving Urga, we had purchased about 50 pounds of Russian black bread, a roasted sheep, and had besides some potatoes and tinned provisions. As Commander Moneta remarked, for our camels we had only meal tickets. The Mongols did not like our chow, and shortly after passing Udé, with their usual improvidence they ran out of provisions and wished us to buy a sheep for them. This we were willing to do, but then they wished us to do the slaughtering of the sheep, since it is a rule of the Buddhist religion that their lamas shall not take life, and both our Mongols were lamas.

After Udé the country gradually improved, there being occasionally a little spear grass, and our camels were able to find something to eat, but other small difficulties cropped up. One riding camel wore off the soles of one foot and went through the interesting operation of having his foot half-soled. The Mongols make him kneel, then start to work and place a leather patch over the tender spot, stitching it to thicker portions of the sole. But this did not last very long and it was soon necessary to leave him to recuperate in care of some herders. One of the carts began to show signs of distress, and sections of the iron tire threatened to fall off. This was a carpenter's job, and had to be attended to by us since it was not in the contract for the Mongols to do anything with the carts. Our fresh provisions were exhausted, but it was possible to purchase mutton almost anywhere.

Amongst the Mongols as a rule there seems to be no regular currency, small affairs of business being transacted through the system of barter, the currency commonly used being the pressed blocks of tea, and lumps of sugar. A little candy will also purchase quite a lot of things, and small services were willingly performed for empty tins, bottles, boxes, etc. In larger affairs amongst Mongols, who visit the towns, and with the Chinese who usually handle the tea caravans of ox and pony carts, silver in "shoes" of 50 taels or lan each are used, with smaller pieces which are cut up and payments made by weight as in China.

On pitching camp about noon, apparently there would be no living thing in sight. Soon over the horizon would appear a figure usually on horseback or camelback, though sometimes our visitors would arrive on foot, until there would be perhaps a half dozen who would expect to be invited to dinner with us. We had been informed that this was the custom of the country, and that in turn if we should call at their huts they would assume that we came for something to eat, and would entertain us without question. We found this to be true, but also that afterward our hosts expected pay in tea, sugar, or empty bottles.

On July 6, 385 miles from Urga near the usual route is a salt lake called Lake Iren. On its shores were quite a number of Mongols getting salt and about five or six miles from the road was an old

Buddhist temple of rather odd architecture for this part of the world. About the lake are some fresh-water springs, water somewhat brackish and very cold. A number of cattle and sheep were grazing in vicinity and a large number of water fowl were seen. The roads again became very good, grazing and water quite plentiful, country improving as we went on, and signs of recent heavy rains. On July 8, 162 miles from the midway station of Udé passed another relay station of the telegraph line called Pong-hong, in charge of a Chinese telegrapher. A little south of this, although the country seems fairly good, we saw more dead animals from the caravans than at any other point of the route.

Just before arriving at Kalgan, we shifted from camels to horses, the road for the last 20 miles becoming too rough for the camels. Within the last 100 miles we began to see Chinese habitations and signs of agriculture, and could buy chickens, vegetables and eggs. After shifting to horses for our transportation we made a long easy ascent to the crest of the hills, from which we could look down on Kalgan and China proper. Along the crest ran a branch of the Great Wall, but in ruins. We descended the southern side of these mountains which are about 5,000 feet high by a steep and rough road and on July 13, at 5 p.m., arrived at Kalgan* and took quarters at a Chinese inn until we could get transportation to Pekin. Kalgan is beautifully located, and seems a quiet, industrious, thriving Chinese town, with a branch of the Russo-Chinese Bank, American missionaries and postal and telegraph facilities. What we enjoyed most was the fruit and vegetables which were good and plentiful, and the comforts of a Chinese inn which are not to be despised.

From Urga we had been 19 days en route, travelling altogether 2,100 Chinese li, 970 versts, or about 650 miles at the rate of 34 miles per day. By repeated trials we had arrived at an estimate of the speed of the camels, which padded along with machine like regularity at 2.9 miles per hour. Taking the actual running time, and multiplying it by this rate we found that the distance traversed was only about 20 miles different from the distance as measured on the map. We had met many caravans proceeding north-

---

* Now Changkiakow.

ward, composed usually of pony and oxcarts but also some camel caravans. These usually were freighted with tea, flour, kerosene oil, bean oil, Chinese spirits (samshin) and dry goods. The camel caravans, being more expensive, took only the finer grades of tea, champagne and luxuries.

The usual time necessary for a camel caravan to make the trip from Kalgan to Urga is 25 days, pony carts 40 days, and oxcarts two to three months. The oxcart caravans are much slower, these caravans travelling only by night since the oxen will not graze during the day, and it requires so much longer for them to find sustenance. Then the oxcarts themselves are of the most primitive fashion, made entirely of wood, without any iron whatever used in their construction, and manufactured for about $3.50 each, Mexican money. It is necessary however to fit iron shoes to the oxen to keep their feet from wearing down, and with every pony caravan, a Chinese blacksmith accompanies it to keep the ponies shod. For riding, ponies are not usually shod, it being possible to find softer ground for them to travel on than the regular road. Early in the journey my pony's feet became so tender that, having no blacksmith to shoe him, he had to be sold.

From Kalgan over the hills transportation can only be accomplished by pony and oxcarts, and pack mules; after getting over the crest loads transferred to camels if desired. In Kalgan the police called on us to examine our passports, which was the first time I had encountered that formality in China, and we learned that it was only lately instituted. The people in Kalgan seemed very quiet and friendly, but this attitude changed as we neared Pekin, when it was made quite evident that foreigners were not popular.

On July 15, we secured transportation by mule chairs, starting at 9 a.m. and arriving at Pekin 3 p.m. July 18, after a very pleasant and uneventful trip of about 110 miles through exceedingly pretty and interesting country, but over rough roads until Pekin was neared. At night we would put up in Chinese inns, being very comfortable and well looked out for, and at charges ridiculously small. In the first inn out from Kalgan we had hardly arrived in the little court when half a dozen coolies lifted off our chairs, put the mules in stalls where feed was immediately given them, water brought for a bath, hot water for tea, etc. All this was done in quick one-two-three order, and brought forth the remark from Commander Moneta "At last we are in civilization," and after our experiences of the last year it really seemed so.

Russian influence seems to extend all along the route, even the common people, when they understand any other language at all, speaking a few words of Russian. Besides the telegraph, postal communications, and consular service, there is the Russo-Chinese Bank, exercising a powerful influence all along the line from Kyakhta to Pekin. It is quite probable that a railway will in time be constructed over this distance, and the idea presents no great difficulties. Already a branch is under construction from Pekin to Kalgan, and its extension across the desert or steppe is a matter of not very great time.

The only great difficulty beyond Kalgan is the ascent of the mountain range just near it. These hills or mountains are very irregular with steep grades, and this part will be expensive. Beyond this crest all the difficulties of construction will be extremely small, the great part of the desert being an elevated plateau without water-courses, with few changes of elevation, and these of moderate extent. The line would be profitable, the route being almost direct between the most productive portions of Siberia and those of China, and even now by the exceedingly crude methods of transportation 30,000 tons of tea alone pass yearly through the custom house at Kyakhta. On the desert itself little or no material or produce would be found perhaps for a long time, but Chinese labor for construction of the road should be available, and between Pekin and Kalgan are a number of coal mines in active operation, which we visited during that part of the trip.

After arrival in Pekin I received instructions from the Department, and proceeded to Shanghai from which I sailed August 12, leaving the steamer at Genoa, and going to St. Petersburg to pay my respects to the Minister of the Navy and then returned to the United States, arriving here October 20.

May 27—29 1905

Battle of Japan Sea*

The Second Pacific Squadron, or the squadron under Vice Admiral Rojestvensky, at 6:30 a.m., May 27, 1905, was 28 miles northwest of the island of Ukushima, and steering a course for the eastern channel of Korea Strait. Squadron was in two columns, about 1,200 yards apart, the right column headed by *Suvaroff*, and left column by *Nikolai*. *Jemchug* and *Izumrud* were in advance and flanking line of march of main squadron. Between the columns and near the rear was a column of four transports, and bringing up the rear were two tugs, followed by *Almaz*, *Svietlana*, converted cruiser *Ural* with two hospital ships on flanks. Fleet was steaming at its best speed of 10.8 knots, weather hazy with fresh southwest breezes and moderate sea, current of one and one-half knots to northeastward. At 6:30 a.m. the Japanese cruiser *Idzumi* was sighted on the port hand, and distant 12,000 yards, but soon disappeared in the haze.

At 9 a.m. a column of five Japanese cruisers, *Matsushima* leading followed by *Itsukushima*, *Hashidate*, *Naniwa* and *Takachiho* was sighted coming from the westward, but after maintaining a parallel course to Russian fleet for a short while also disappeared in the haze. At 10:30 another squadron composed of *Kasagi*, *Chitose*, *Niitaka* and *Tsushima* (there were present two vessels of this type, but one may have been *Otowa*) was seen approaching, and Russians formed in single column, *Suvaroff*-column taking the lead. Japanese approached to range of about 7,000 yards, then steered parallel course to Russians, some shots being exchanged but without damage.

At noon Russian column headed north 23° east to leave Okishima on starboard hand. In the meantime the Japanese cruiser

* Battle of Tsushima.

columns were keeping in touch and reporting their movements to Admiral Togo who had left Masampho about 7 a.m. and had then stood to eastward passing to northward of Tsushima Island, crossing Eastern Channel, then turning and steaming to westward until 1:20 p.m. when Russian fleet was sighted.

When the Japanese fleet was sighted by the Russians, Admiral Rojestvensky, with the First Division, took position a little to right of the line of march of main column, so placing the head of the column in echelon. Japanese main squadron stood down toward head of Russian column until at 1:50 the Russians opened fire at a little short of 10,000 yards range. Japanese column immediately changed course to northeastward, steering a slightly converging course with the Russians, who began to ease away, so forming practically a single column. Russian firing was at will and deliberate, and shooting seemed to be fair. Japanese did not answer until range had decreased to about 6,500 yards, when they began, their shots being in considerable error in range but falling well together. The range was secured in a short time and they began firing much more rapidly than the Russians, apparently concentrating fire on *Suvaroff* and *Osliabia,* both of which suffered severely, fire breaking out on the *Suvaroff* at 2:15 but soon being extinguished, and at 2:20 *Osliabia* listing to port also with fires on board. *Borodino* also received injury, falling out of line for a short time, but returning almost immediately. The Russian cruisers with transports and auxiliaries were running in the lee of the fighting line, and taking no part in the action until 2:30 when *Idzumi* came up from vicinity of Okishima and began firing on the transports. The Japanese cruiser divisions of nine vessels also steamed across rear of Russians and headed as if to attack the transports. The Russian cruisers under Rear Admiral Enquist turned to starboard and interposed between their transports and the Japanese cruisers, firing taking place at ranges of 10,000 yards and over and Russians suffering very little.

At 2:40 p.m. *Osliabia,* severely injured, fell out of line, took reverse course, and shortly turned over to port and went down bows first. Russian officers state that entire armor plates had fallen from her side, also that her forward turret was missing. The construction of this ship was much criticised in the Russian Navy as being very poor, water-tight bulkheads not water-tight, and armor inferior.

At 3 p.m. the Japanese by superior speed had passed the head of the Russian column and were bearing heavily on it, the *Suvaroff* having suffered very much. The Russian column then turned in a wide circle with the port helm and steered to northwestward, the Japanese going ships left-about with the six leading ships, followed later by the other five armored cruisers, one of them, the *Asama*, having been damaged and falling out of line. Firing continued at ranges of 4,500 to 7,000 yards, but the smoke from the fires and funnels of the Russian ships blowing down on to the Japanese obscured their view, and rendered the practice more or less ineffective. About 3:20 p.m. the Russians turned to the northward with the port helm, attempting in this way to get away in that direction by cutting across Japanese rear. The speed of the Russians had, however, become reduced to less than 10 knots on account of the injured vessels, and even at this speed their movements were hampered by the slowness of some ships of the third division (*Apraxine, Senyavine,* and *Oushakoff*).

For a short time the two fleets were steering counter courses, then the Japanese battleships at 3:35 turned together with port helm and steamed again on slightly converging course to Russians, followed by the armored cruisers, except *Nisshin* and *Kasuga*. The *Suvaroff* by this time had suffered so much as to be unmanageable, and with forward turret destroyed and without masts or funnels and in flames fell out of line, to port. From the Japanese fleet the *Nisshin* and *Kasuga* remained behind and continued to fire on *Suvaroff,* while remainder of fighting squadrons proceeded to the southeastward. As *Suvaroff* lay almost helpless under guns of *Nisshin* and *Kasuga* the Japanese made a torpedo attack on her but without result. Russian cruiser division coming up from southward assisted in repelling this attack and handled the Japanese destroyers making it rather roughly. From *Oleg* a running torpedo was seen passing close to ship. *Suvaroff* managed to effect temporary repairs and steamed ahead slowly under fire of *Nisshin* and *Kasuga,* attempting to regain main squadron, while Russian cruiser squadron turned to starboard to cover transports which were again menaced by Japanese cruisers, being joined by *Jemchug* and *Izumrud.*

At this time these cruisers were under fire on both sides, *Nisshin* and *Kasuga* to port and Japanese cruisers to starboard, fire being concentrated apparently on *Oleg* and *Aurora* which suffered more than at any other time. The *Ural* was by this time in distress, and hauled out of line, down by the nose and launching boats. Russian cruisers made letter "S," stopping for a while to clear main squadron, which was then steaming to southward. As main Russian squadron continued on this course, it approached Japanese cruiser squadron and opening fire on it, damaged *Kasagi* and *Naniwa.* Main squadron turned to westward about 4:15, and to northward about 4:45, the main Japanese squadron having lost touch with it, and turning in wide curve at range of about 15,000 yards, no firing going on, and main squadrons not in sight of each other. About 4:00 *Alexander,* damaged, fell out of line temporarily but rejoined main squadron about 5:00 when it was steaming to northward. As battle line and cruisers turned toward *Suvaroff, Nisshin and Kasuga* made off joining main squadron.

At 4:45 the Japanese armored cruisers turned to northward, and at 5:20, the battleships also turned, and went in pursuit of Russians. Japanese were making about 15.5 knots, and rapidly overhauling Russians, sinking the disabled *Ural* as she was passed close aboard. Between 5:00 and 6:00 there was little fighting, though about 5:30 Japanese cruisers again menaced Russian transports and succeeded in sinking *Kamchatka* and *Russ,* but after that time took no further part in the action.

About 6:00 main Russian column was again picked up by main Japanese squadron and active fighting resumed, *Sissoi* being forced out of line with heavy fires aboard but rejoining a little later. About same time Admiral Rojestvensky, having been wounded, was transferred with his staff from *Suvaroff* to *Buini* which passed along the line flying the signal "Admiral entrusts command to Admiral Nebogatoff." Japanese repeated tactics of bearing on head of Russian column, which at 6:20 inclined to port and steered to northwestward, *Borodino* leading, but *Sissoi* and *Alexander* now in bad shape.

Fleets continued on approximately parallel courses, firing going on actively. *Nisshin* and *Kasuga* had rejoined main squadron, and Japanese armored cruisers had been detached to go round Russian rear, the Russian cruisers, destroyers and transports were steaming on parallel course and to left of main squadron. Russian strength now consisted in order of *Borodino, Orel, Nikolai, Senyavine, Alexander, Oushakoff, Sissoi, Navarin,* and *Nakhimoff,* but *Alexander* was again forced out of line under heavy fire of Japanese, and at 7:00 p.m. or just about sunset, the *Borodino* also fell out, and burning fiercely turned over to starboard and sank. The remaining Russian armored ships then turned to the south, followed by the Japanese armored cruisers, while their battleships turned to the northward, the Japanese admiral giving orders to concentrate next morning off Urleung Island.

After 7 p.m., when darkness came on, the Japanese made repeated torpedo attacks on all Russian ships, the torpedo boats coming up from southwestward and acting generally from that direction, while the Japanese destroyers attacked from north to south by way of east. *Alexander* and *Suvaroff* were sunk, and *Navarin, Nakhimoff, Monomakh* and *Sissoi* were damaged. The *Oleg, Aurora* and *Jemchug* continued to southward, until 8:15 p.m. when Admiral Enquist made several attempts to turn to northward but under threatened torpedo attacks, turned again to southward at 10:15 p.m. and continued to Manila. *Bodri* and *Blestyastchi* started for Shanghai, *Blestyastchi* foundering on the way.

Navarin was torpedoed again and sunk at 2 a.m., and *Monomakh* and *Nakhimoff* foundered close to Tsushima Island at 5 a.m. May 28. The *Buini* with Admiral Rojestvensky on board met the *Donskoi* and *Byedovi* early on the morning of the 28th, and after transferring the admiral to the *Byedovi* and the crew to the *Donskoi,* was blown up by the Russians themselves. The *Svietlana* was picked up and sunk by two Japanese destroyers, the *Gromki* was chased and sunk by Japanese destroyers, the *Buistri* was forced to run ashore, and the *Oushakoff* was also sunk after refusing to surrender. The *Byedovi* and *Bravi* were attacked by two Japanese destroyers, the *Byedovi* surrendered with the admiral, and the *Bravi* escaped by superior speed to Vladivostock.

The *Donskoi* was discovered and attacked by three Japanese cruisers and several destroyers about 5 p.m. May 28, and after a most creditable engagement, evaded them but was so damaged that she was run ashore and wrecked the same night on Urleung

Island. The *Almaz* escaped safely to Vladivostock, but the *Orel, Nikolai, Senyavine* and *Apraxine* were surrounded at 10:30 a.m. May 28 and forced to surrender, the *Izumrud,* which was with them, managing to escape the Japanese, but was later wrecked in a bay to the northward of Vladivostock, and blown up by her own crew. The destroyer *Grozni* was probably blown up by her own crew, the converted cruiser *Ural,* transports *Anadir, Kamchatka, Irtish,* and tug *Russ* were sunk during the battle, and the transport *Korea* escaped to Shanghai. The tug *Shir* was met on monring of 28 by squadron of Admiral Enquist and sent in to Shanghai to telegraph Saigon for coal. Hospital ships *Kostroma* and *Orel* were seized by the Japanese, the *Orel* being confiscated for sending a cable while fleet was on its way out, and the *Kostroma* was released.

These notes are compiled principally from reports of Admiral Enquist and of commanding officers of *Bodri* and *Bravi,* and are only an attempt to give a connected story of the great sea battle, the details of which may never be definitely decided, owing to the usual confusion in all official reports of any battle. In this connection it may be as well to state that in all published official reports by either Japanese or Russians, and more particularly the former, there are irreconcilable inconsistencies in each and with each other, in regard to times, distances, names of ships, formation, and in designation of flag officers, more particularly again referring to the Japanese, and this is a fact observed in all of their official reports from the very beginning of the war. The times, as given, are according to time kept by the Russians, which is about 20 minutes earlier than time kept by Japanese.

General Conclusions

The points that seem most worthy of attention during the war and to which attention has perhaps been already directed by many others, are as follows:

First of all was unpreparedness of Russia, and preparedness of Japan. A war, foreseen by every military and naval man, burst on the Russian Government with absolute unexpectedness. Neither the Army in Manchuria, the fleet in the Far East, nor fortresses of Port Arthur and Vladivostock were ready.

In six year's possession of Port Arthur less had been done to defend place from land attack, than was accomplished in first six months after beginning of war. Sea defenses of Port Arthur were good, though there was but one battery of five 10″ long-range guns effective against ships at ranges of 10,000 yards or over, and batteries of 11″ howitzers intended to cover anchorage off entrance had range of only 6,000 yards, and were serviceable only against Japanese land batteries. Vladivostock could not even fire a gun to resent bombardment on March 6, 1904, long-range guns for batteries able to bear on bombarding ships being then on trucks in streets of town.

Official corruption was responsible for much of this unreadiness, government contracts being regarded as sources of private gain. This system of graft was almost officially recognized, not being regarded as at all dishonorable for even generals of divisions, commandants of navy yards or captains of ships, and perhaps also for officials of even higher rank. The percentages received were reduced almost to basis of a tariff, graded down from the head of a department to each clerk in the office. From statements of government contractors, in their opinion, the value received by government varied from 10 to 25 per cent of money expended. Often public works were carried on up to last moment before destruction by military authorities, and again when it was clearly evident that they could never be utilized until conclusion of war.

The dispersion of Russian fleet was inexcusable. Vladivostock was not a closed port in winter, and there was no reason why main fighting fleet should not have been concentrated there, near only dock available for receiving large ships. Even the little antiquated gunboats were scattered about, when if concentrated at Port Arthur might have been of very great assistance to army in holding Nanshan May 26. Indeed it would have been better if entire Russian fleet had been in Baltic at commencement of war, and in any war it would seem better to have entire force concentrated 10,000 miles away from probable scene of action, than to have it divided even in not more than two portions 10,000 miles apart. In case of Russians, unreadiness of government and military organizations was repeated in unreadiness of fleet on night of February 8, and in like unreadiness of single ships, one of which, *Tsésarévitch,* had never fired her guns at target until she went out August 10 to battle.

Admiral in command had never had charge of a fleet underway until he led one against enemy. In other ships maneuvers and target practice had been much neglected, though to be fair, in the beginning there was little difference in proficiency of the two combatants in these respects.

Tactics of both sides seemed bad in beginning, only Japanese improved later, and Russians did not. Demonstration off Port Arthur February 9 was not well handled by Japanese admiral. Leaving entrance unguarded May 14, cost him two battleships, when lesson of *Petropavlosk* was before him. *Bogatyr* lay helpless on rocks near Vladivostock for a month without examination by belligerent controlling the sea, when fact of her predicament was published abroad, and her condition was known even in Port Arthur.

Repeated failure of superior squadron of four armored cruisers of 17 knots speed, assisted by numerous other vessels, to keep in touch with inferior squadron of three weaker armored cruisers steaming 13 knots, after they were once sighted, seems inexplicable. The pursuit after victory was always inefficient until May, 1905. On other hand issue of ussian squadron from blockaded port for purpose of active operations, as on June 23, and its immediate return thereto before a force certainly not superior, showed great irresolution confirmed by manner of sortie and return, and had additional disadvantage of giving enemy information that channel was clear, and damaged ships repaired.

In battle Russians allowed themselves to be obsessed with other ideas than that solely of winning the battle, the final aims of Admirals Vitgeft, Yessen, and Rojestvensky, on August 10–14, 1904 and May 27, 1905, apparently being more to keep their fleets headed for Vladivostock than to properly maneuver with a view to winning the battle. Inactivity of Russian torpedo boats, which might have been made important factor, was deplorable. Only explanation of this inactivity was remoteness of point of attack (Japanese base at Elliott Islands was 64 miles away) and oppressive idea that enemy always confronted Russians with superior force, when as a matter of fact, and considering only numbers, Russians were superior in destroyer strength. The location of Japanese base 64 miles away gave Russians excellent opportunity to avoid fleet action if desired, and escape to Vladivostock, which after fighting was next best thing for them to do.

Systems of information of both sides seemed deficient, though Russians gave Japanese credit for better information than they really had. If Japanese had been acquainted with affairs at Port Arthur, they should have landed and invested place next day after the torpedo attack. Their manner of approaching fortress in the first days of siege showed complete ignorance of strength of individual batteries, and of the strength of fortress as a whole. They believed the channel closed after May 2, and no one was more surprised than they on sortie of entire Russian fleet June 23.

Meantime Russians in Port Arthur were almost daily arresting and executing spies, and suspecting of being spies people who should have been the last to be suspected. The remarkable extent to which this mania extended is evidenced by a statement of Commander Maximof of the *Bezshumni*, who informed me that Japanese were connected up by wireless with Port Arthur through medium of telephone wires, and he knew this from having heard the tapping of their instruments in his telephone!

The torpedo, striking the first sensational blow of the war, exhibits almost the spectacle of a war being decided by a weapon, which came but little short of being discredited during that war. If ever torpedo boats had a favorable opportunity for striking a crushing blow, the Japanese boats had it on night of February 8. That they failed to deliver it was probably due to lack of coolness, judgment of distance, and steadiness, and perhaps to physical deficiencies in eyesight. During the entire war torpedo boats did little in their role as such to justify their existence.

Attacks during night of June 23, July 1, on Vladivostock ships August 10, many times on ships anchored in the entrance, were all without result. Success was finally attained in attacks on the *Sevastopol,* moored off the entrance, and on ships already almost helpless from effects of gun fire on May 27–28, 1905. Though as torpedo boats their success was small, in enforcement of the blockade they were extremely valuable, and it would have been difficult without them to have sustained any sort of blockage of a port with an entrance like Port Arthur. Besides they were of great value in transmitting orders of the admiral to other ships in time of action when signal apparatus was destroyed and were much used as despatch boats, and also, as they probably will in future wars, for cooperation with the Army along the shore, and even bombardments of trenches and field works.

One great advantage of torpedo boats and destroyers is their light draft which besides allowing them to approach closely the shore, usually safeguards them against striking mines. If they are to be used for cooperation with forces ashore or attacks on shore positions they should carry a gun capable of using shrapnel. In this connection and remembering the excellent work of the *Bobr, Chokai,* and *Akagi* at Nanshan, of the Japanese gunboats elsewhere under many circumstances, and of *Gremiastchy, Otvajny,* and *Ghiliak* about Port Arthur, the necessity may be considered as shown for a type of gunboat carrying one or two heavy guns of not less than 8″, lightly armored against reply from field guns, and with draft not over 10 feet to avoid mines.

The losses of Russian destroyers were usually due to inexperienced commanders. Keeping in touch with one's own boats on dark and rainy nights is of course a difficult matter, but what commander of a destroyer would fail to recognize his own boats next morning at daylight, or who would *hoist his flag* as a signal of recognition if in doubt? Keeping the boats together on expeditions at night requires the greatest vigilance and the course considered best with the Russians was to cruise in very close formation. Exposing a light allowed the other boat, if an enemy, to deliver the first fire, as was done in case of *Silnyi*. A call with a dog whistle was also advocated. Judging distances at night is a power most difficult to acquire, and when complicated by flashes of guns and search lights, bursting shells, and spray, seemed impossible for the Japanese, who until after August 10 usually discharged torpedoes at a range of from 2,000 to 3,000 yards. In attacking also the Japanese used boats in small groups and at different times, sometimes single boats making attacks, and approaching their targets with great speed and little judgment. On three occasions they came up from the beam and quarter on ships under way, and when attacking on the night of June 23, needlessly exposed themselves to more of the fire of the shore batteries than was necessary.

For command of torpedo boats young men are necessary, physical defects of older men becoming soon evident. The average age of officers commanding Russian torpedo boats was 40 or over, many of them being commanders. Their eyes became inflamed, their feet swelled, they became exhausted from lack of sleep, and within the first three months of the war there were many changes, and after six months only two boats retained the same commanders with which they began.

Russian officers recommend protection of steam pipes against fragments of bursting shells, or the installation of motive power machinery without pressure pipes. The bows of torpedo boats should be strengthened to prevent twisting in case of slight accident when steaming in close order, and also in order to be able to dispose of an enemy by ramming without giving an alarm by firing a gun, and without disabling one's own boat. The gun armament of Japanese torpedo boats seemed to be a 12-pdr. forward and another aft, with four 6-pdrs., being much superior to Russian boats with one 12-pdr. forward and three to five 3-pdrs. A Russian boat attempting to escape by running away from a Japanese boat was almost helpless, speed being very much inferior, and fire from astern exceedingly weak. The bow gun is useless at night, so blinding the commanding officer and helmsman that in close quarters it is dangerous to use it. Some of the Japanese destroyers were equipped with wireless outfits, and toward the end of the war the new Russian boats coming out with Admiral Rojestvensky also had them.

Mines were much in use, and were responsible for great loss to both sides. About Port Arthur the belt of water between three and six miles off shore was avoided by the large ships of both sides. Japanese often successfully placed mines inside this limit, and the Russians sometimes succeeded in mining outside of the six-mile limit. Between these two distances both sides could and did mine, until about the entrance of Port Arthur there was almost a sea of them. It was rare that the trawlers did not recover a number of mines each day and there always seemed plenty more. The mines that gave the best results were those of the Elia type, mine and anchor let go together, and mine automatically adjusting itself to depth of 10 feet below the surface at low water if intended for the large ships. Smaller mines intended to damage light-draft craft were adjusted to six feet below surface.

Firing mechanism of both Russian and Japanese mines was efficient, but Japanese was much more sensitive, their mines occasionally exploding from motion of the sea when no boats were near, and nearly always exploding when picked up by the trawler. The Japanese lost from mines *Hatsuse, Yashima, Miyako, Kaimon, Heiyen, Saiyen, Chiyoda, Takasago, Hayatori, Ikadsuki,* and torpedo boat No. 48. Russians lost *Yenissei, Boyarin, Petropavlosk, Gremiastchy, Vuinoslivi, Stroini* and damaged *Pobieda, Sevastopol* (2), *Bayan, Serditi* and *Bezshumni.*

The great majority of damages caused by mines were in the forward portions of the ships, and in case of the ships destroyed, blow seemed to have been to some extent directly under the bottom, force of explosion taking its way directly upward into ship, and causing explosion of ship's magazines. To guard in some measure against effect of mines it would be necessary to more thoroughly protect at least the forward underwater portion of the ships, particularly in vicinity of magazines.

Comparing the shooting of the two combatants in their first meeting the Russians seem to have been better, but the Japanese were learning all the time, and in the skirmishes in July, at ranges of 10,000 yards, shot better. In battle of August 10 apparently it was very nearly an even thing as far as the shooting went, damages on both sides being approximately equal. It would still be quite an open question, whether the result would not have perhaps been different if the helm of the *Tsésarévitch* had been jammed to port instead of to starboard.

In battle of Japan Sea Japanese first showed application of a system of fire control, while the Russians never used any. In both these battles it is noteworthy to observe the difficulty and confusion resulting from transferring command while in action.

The propelling powder of the Japanese gave off a light greyish smoke, and seemed fairly constant, the differences in ranges being much smaller than those given by the Russian guns. The explosive used by the Japanese in their shell, shimose, was exceedingly violent, and gave off intense heat. The fuzes seemed very sensitive, shells exploding immediately on impact, most of the fragments going outside. Great heat developed near vicinity of impact, the temperature inside the ships struck being raised very much, and anything inflammable in vicinity set on fire.

Fires were exceedingly numerous on Russian ships, having broken out on board *Peresviet* on August 10, and on both *Rossia* and *Gromoboi* on August 14. Initial cause in these cases was ignition of ready ammunition on deck in vicinity of impact, fire extending to paint work and every article near that was inflammable. These fires died out of themselves after a not extended time for lack of nourishment and not so much on account of fire extinguishing methods. Thick paint is one of the principal factors in a conflagration of this kind, and is a serious danger. A preliminary examination of effects of these shells on unarmored portion of ships led to the conclusion that they were not so dangerous as shells with a delayed action fuze, but in the battle of Japan Sea, splendidly protected ships were sunk by the combination of under-water effect and shattering effect of shells armed with fuzes acting instantaneously. Fragments were exceedingly dangerous, being in large number, and with great velocity and in one case, on *Bayan,* enough getting in through an open 6″ gun port to kill five and wound 30 men. No openings should be left in a ship's side if avoidable. Funnels on all occasions suffered exceedingly from these high explosive shells exploding instantaneously and wrecking funnels, boiler draft being affected, and boilers put out of commission on a number of ships from this character of hit. Funnels of all ships had many marks from fragments, but these were not serious. A plunging hit from these high explosive shells cleared the deck.

The construction of the Russian conning towers was bad, the hood over the tower extending over the sides, with a space all round of about 14″ between lower lip of hood and upper edge of tower. Under this fragments of shells bursting on the deck were collected, and reflected on to the occupants of the tower, as in case of *Tsésarévitch, Gromoboi, Rurik, Aurora* and probably others. Injuries to steering gear were frequent and disastrous, beginning with *Variag,* then *Tsésarévitch, Rurik,* and *Novik.*

Damages to armor were rare and not dangerous until the battle of the Japan Sea when officers testified to having seen armor plates entire fall off *Osliabia,* but this was probably due to faulty construction. There was no record of penetration because Japanese relied usually on their high explosive shells. On *Peresviet* a corner of one plate was cracked off, and on *Rossia* seams between plates opened causing leaks. A character of hit hardly anticipated was initiated on August 8, 1904, when *Retvizan* came very nearly being put out of commission by a hit from a 4.7″ gun at about 10,000 yards. This hit was caused by shell striking near the ship, and not bursting until it brought up against the ship's side underneath the water line and armor belt. *Tsésarévitch* and *Poltava* had similar hits in battle of August 10, and it is probable that some of the ships in that last great naval battle suffered from this character of hit.

Russian cruisers claimed to have exchanged shots with Japanese battleships and to have seriously damaged them. Without questioning the superiority of the big ship and the big gun, the evidence of the battles of February 9, August 10, and 14, 1904, if not also that of May 27, 1905, points rather to a superiority in a volume of fire from guns of 8″ and below, as far as effects on the Russian ships were concerned, and volume of fire was always characteristic of Japanese attack on both sea and land to such an extent, on occasions, that they were prevented from following up success by probable exhaustion of ammunition.

On February 9, 1904, the Japanese used their 12″ guns against the shore batteries and town, and the Russians had only five 10″ modern guns in the shore batteries with which to make effective reply to the Japanese and these fired slowly and deliberately. The Russian ships that fired the oftenest and were nearest the enemy were *Bayan* and *Novik*. At the Russian ships were fired practically only 6″ and 8″ shells, so that in this battle it could hardly be said that the big gun was the weighty factor.

In battle of August 10, a number of the Japanese 12″ guns were unserviceable, and comparing the damages of the Russian ships after this battle with the damages of the Vladivostock fleet after August 14, few of the hits could not be accounted for by 8″ or 6″ guns. In side of *Rossia* were holes very nearly as large as those in *Peresviet* apparently caused by 12″ hits, and in case of *Rossia* and *Gromoboi* there were no larger guns used against them than 8″.

The Russian ships had no telescopic sights, and none had ever been exercised at long-range target practice. Rangefinding was accomplished by "scholl" telemeters, range parties being stationed in the tops, and ranges at first communicated by electric signals. When these were interrupted, messengers were used. The Russian officers advocate two armored rangefinding and fire-control stations, one forward and one aft, with telephonic communications to guns. Every ship employed for military purposes in time of war should have a wireless outfit.

The Russian ships in clearing for action endeavored simply to give a clear arc of fire to the guns, all other gear remaining in place. The boats remained in the cradles or at their davits when not interfering with the fire of the guns, in which case they were stowed on the deck and out of the way. Boats left in place were generally destroyed, boats stowed on the deck were little damaged, and steel boats were quickly repaired. There was no case on record in which torpedoes carried on board ships were found to be useful. *Rurik* fired one, just before she sank, but at extreme range, and not effective. On *Strashni* a torpedo exploded under fire and did great damage about the decks, and on *Rossia*, the warhead of one was struck by fragments of shell, and blown off without any damage to ship or torpedo tube.

Submarines did not enter as a factor in any other way than for moral effect, both sides crediting the other with that method of attack immediately after sinking of their ships on mines.

Of 17 ships sent in to block the entrance not one succeeded, though the expeditions were carried out with great daring. Some of the ships were beached some distance from the entrance, some were blown up and sunk by their crews, and others were stopped by a combination of mines, torpedoes and gun fire. Of those ships that beached close to the entrance, none showed serious effects of gun fire and one Chinese junk under fire of the batteries for 25 minutes finally drifted up on the beach very little injured, so that although it is difficult to block the entrance of a narrow channel at night, it is also difficult to sink by gun fire vessels attempting to do so.

Bombardments from sea, on account of extreme long range and indirect fire, accomplished almost nothing. An effective hit by this method of attack is a pure matter of chance. Bombardments from land are also ineffective, unless the fire can be rectified, but when this can be done, they are extremely dangerous. All the Russian guns of position at Port Arthur were located on the crests of hills and along the sky line. When siege guns were brought up these positions were crushed by the weight of fire and were only held by the infantrymen and machine guns.

The large guns of position in the land defenses at Port Arthur were of little value, particularly the long high-powered naval guns, of which the ships were deprived for the benefit of the batteries. On account of the near approach of the investing army, howitzers were the most useful type of gun employed against the attack by land. The 11″ rifled howitzers of Golden Hill were the only guns to compete with the 11″ howitzers of the besieging forces. In Port Arthur was the usual conflict between the Army and Navy whenever they are required to cooperate, and to the lack of cooperation in a large measure was due the final loss of the fortress.

On June 23 and August 10, the *Peresviet, Pobieda, Pallada,* and *Diana* were sent out to battle, short of some of their guns which had been sent to the land defenses. Previous to this the fleet had been levied on for all sorts of equipment and ammunition, and after August 10, the greater part of the crews and the light guns were also sent ashore to act with the army. General Stessel's idea of the operations could be discerned from his remark after the surrender of the fortress, and when he had asked for news of the Baltic fleet. He was informed that it was still at Madagascar, and he said sadly: "Now since Port Arthur has fallen it is no longer of use for the fleet to come out." There should be some regulation to ensure cooperation of land and naval forces, and to prevent similar catastrophes. If the object of the operations is a naval one, the naval officer should be in charge; if the object is a military one the army man should be in charge. Of all the lessons taught in the war the most important is the value of trained and patriotic personnel, and in the case of the navy, of men who are both fighting men and sailors.

The root of all their disasters is found in the Russian character, of which the government is a natural consequence. Naturally simple, honest, and hard working, through apathy they have developed a government at the head of which is an autocrat whose will is expressed through bureaucrats, and administered by military satraps.

There is no country in which a man is so free personally, and mentally so restricted. It really is a crime for soldier, officer, or civilian to dare to think, while he may be exceedingly lax in many moral relations without suffering any detriment.

As children Russians are subject to little control and grow up with an excellent knowledge of languages and music, but without table manners, careful personal habits, or control over their appetites. One thing they are taught to avoid, and that is any political discussion. Dissipation keeps men's minds from any more serious object than the obtaining of money to gratify it, and it is quite true that a young man who does not dissipate more or less is looked on as a thinker and therefore a latent danger.

With all their splendid physical material, endurance, patience, courage and good temper, the Russians fail because of sluggish and undeveloped mentality. With the bodies and appetities of grown men, they have the mental equipment, the logical and reasoning powers, the faculty of properly estimating the value of facts, and the occasional hysterical excesses of women or seventeen-year-old boys.

Admiral Viren, one of the most admirable Russians I knew, in discussing the loss of the *Petropavlovsk* with me, and comparing it with the loss of the *Maine,* hinted that the latter might have been caused by the Americans themselves to bring on the Spanish war!

The Viceroy, Admiral Alexeieff, a most intelligent Russian, 15 minutes before the Japanese attacked, and with all the information possible for any man to have, informed his captains that negotiations were expected to be resumed in a few days! General Stessel thought when Port Arthur fell that the purpose of Admiral Rojestvensky's squadron was defeated! General Kouropatkin, cool, judicious and most even tempered of men, thought the Japanese armies had seriously deteriorated before Mukden because most of the Samurai had been killed! Vice Admiral Skrydloff makes a speech glorying in the victories of the Russian navy during the war, and reminds his hearers that in doing so they must not forget the victories of the army! Rear Admiral Vitgeft was exceedingly superstitious.

It is almost certain that any Russian however well educated, however much a polished man of the world, however well equipped in technical knowledge, yet in the treatment of some simple, practical question that could be solved by any one with ordinary common sense, he will fall down lamentably. Why could not Admiral Vitgeft or his staff see that Port Arthur was no place for the fleet, after the fortress was once invested? Why could not Admiral Viren, a man whose seamanship and courage no one could question, why could he not have taken out such ships as he had, and made as good a fight as possible or gone to Vladivostock? It is said that after his assumption of command that the affairs of the fleet were still in the hands of a council composed of Admirals Lojinski, Grigorovitch and Viren, and that the council could not agree on a plan of action. From the beginning of the seige there was only one of two things for the Port Arthur fleet to do, and that was to fight or go to Vladivostock. What idea could have impelled sailors to sink their ships under bombardment in order to protect them from falling shells? As regards Admiral Viren, it seemed the case of a man excellent as captain, but not equal to responsibility of directing a fleet under circumstances of great trial.

In closing the report, I wish to mention a few facts relating to the duties of attachés. It seems very doubtful if an attaché can be of much service in operations of war unless both he and his country are sympathetic with the forces to which they are credited.

With the Russians, Americans were no longer in favor, and it was always extremely difficult to get any information, in Port Arthur particularly so. There the authorities made decided distinctions between attachés of France and Germany and myself, giving them many privileges denied to me, failing to receive me properly or to recognize official calls and treating me with marked suspicion, going so far as to include me in a "visite des papiers." Under such circumstances an attaché could accomplish little.

On the Japanese side it seemed well understood that one of the articles of the treaty between the two countries of Japan and Great Britain, provided that in case of war a naval officer of one ally could accompany the fleet of the other in active operation, so that British attachés had exceptional opportunities of observation. Either some agreement of this kind or an understanding that no attachés will be either sent or received in time of war.

This seemed to be also the opinion of the majority of my comrades as attachés with the Russian forces. Of these altogether there were 49, at any one time however not being more than 27.

The transportation of naval attachés in Manchuria was a simple matter usually, as they had little baggage, and no transportation outfits like the military attachés. Each of these latter had, as a rule, a Russian soldier as orderly, and a man as attendant with horses for each, and a spare horse for himself. Another horse hauled the cart with tent and stores, so that the outfit of a military attaché comprised altogether two men besides himself, five horses, a cart, and from 500 to 3,000 pounds of baggage. The attachés of high rank required a separate compartment for themselves on the trains, so that to transport 27 military attachés were required two baggage cars, a dining car, two sleeping cars (or three if they were not to be crowded), 17 box-cars for the horses, three flat cars for carts, a car for the servants, another for the orderlies, and still another for the train servants, or in all 29 cars, or practically a full military train. Under certain circumstances the handling of this train presented embarrassment, and it might have been diverted to more useful purposes. Unless an attaché can be received in the confidential relations of a staff officer on the side to which he is attached, his presence is an embarrassment to the belligerent, and a humiliation to the officer serving with him.

The report has been made out with such information as I was able to obtain without consulting the records of other observers or any of the other reports in the possession of the office, and I have endeavored to mention every incident or fact that might be of any interest whatever. Many facts were obtained by hearsay testimony and these it was always necessary to check and recheck by the evidence of others until perhaps something like the truth was obtained.

No Russian official records or statistics were ever placed at my disposition, and few opportunities were given for personal observation, particularly with the Navy. To a direct question invariably an untrue answer would be given in regard to any point of military information, and only from casual remarks could hints or clues be picked up from which further investigation might develop something.

Under such conditions statements and conclusions in the report must be more indefinite than I should like, and in regard to them I can only say that every effort was made to verify each incident, and that I believe personally all I have stated. With great diffidence the report is closed, with the hope that portions of it, at least, may serve as tracers or clues to guide further investigation of any point desired.

I have the honor to be,
Very respectfully,

Your obedient servant,

Lieutenant Commander, U.S. Navy

Appendix I

Notes on Port Arthur

After return of Russian fleet to Port Arthur it was said there that Admiral Ukhtomsky had been ordered to take it out again immediately, and that he had declined to do so. He was shortly afterward relieved and Captain Viren of *Bayan* promoted to Rear Admiral and assigned to command of the battleship division. Captain Viren was a young captain having received promotion to that rank about one year previous to beginning of war, and on his promotion to Rear Admiral was junior to Rear Admiral Lojinski commanding the shore defense at Port Arthur and Rear Admiral Grigorovitch, Commandant of the navy yard.

From reports of naval officers who escaped to Chefoo in December the decision as to the course of action for the fleet was in hands of a council composed of the three admirals, and it was resolved to wait for the Second Pacific Squadron under Vice Admiral Rojestvensky. Temporary repairs were effected on ships injured in battle of August 10, but the fleet was further weakened by the destruction of the *Gremiastchy* on a mine, August 18, and the injury to *Sevastopol* also by a mine on August 23, and the destruction later on by other mines of destroyers *Vuinoslivi* and *Stroini*.

This completed list of Russian casualties from mines, but fleet was meantime under bombardment of land batteries of Japanese, and it was difficult to get the workmen to effect repairs under bombardment.

The Japanese also suffered further casualties from mines, losing destroyer *Hayatori*, September 3; *Heiyen* September 18; *Saiyen* November 30, and *Takasago* December 12, while gunboat *Atago* was lost on rocks of Pechili Strait. On November 15 destroyer *Rastoropny* was sent to Chefoo with despatches and, taking no chances on a repetition of the *Ryeshitelni* affair, was blown up by the Russians on the same day as arrival. The Japanese gradually approached the town, and on October 1 began the use of 11″ howitzers, of which they finally had 18 in action before December 1. These bombarded the town, navy yard, batteries, and ships which moved about the harbor in the attempt to evade this fire. As the fire could not be rectified the ships were not often hit, but when once damaged repairs were almost impossible due to lack of workmen and difficulty of working under fire.

On November 30 the Japanese captured 203-meter hill and immediately placed five 4.7″ naval guns in little depression between that and lower hill to northward, and December 3 began firing on the ships at 6,000 yards range with direct fire, assisted by the 11″ howitzers, with advantage now of being able to rectify the fire.

The ships suffered so severely from this bombardment, that the Russians sank them with the idea of protecting them by the water, and later of raising them again on arrival of Admiral Rojestvensky. The damages evident on most of the ships in Port Arthur were effected principally by the 4.7″ naval guns, though the ships were not sunk by either these guns, or the 11″ howitzers,—the fleet was sunk by the Russians, and with the intention of being raised again by them.

Before this time, all the crews from the ships, with exception of about 100 men each, had been sent to the batteries along with the smaller RF guns and ammunition. The naval authorities allowed themselves to be persuaded to agree to this plan, by the assurance that the place would never be surrendered. Just prior to the surrender the destroyers *Statni, Serditi, Skori* and *Vlastni* escaped to Chefoo and *Smyeli* and *Boiki* got away to Tsintau. In going out *Serditi*'s screw stream exploded a torpedo which lifted her stern and buckled some deck plates, but she was able to get into Chefoo under her own steam.

Appendix II

Forces in
Port Arthur

On May 8, 1904 the military forces in the Peninsula of Kwantung consisted of the following troops:

3rd Corps East Siberian Rifles

Commanding, Lieutenant General Stessel, in charge of the fortified region of Kwantung, acting independently but subordinate to Commander in chief, General Kouropatkin.
Chief of staff, Colonel Reiss.
Commandant of the Fortress, Major General Smirnoff.

4th Siberian Rifle Division

Commanding Division, Major General Fock
Commanding 1st Brigade, Major General de Bune Gingliat
Commanding 2nd Brigade, Major General Nadiéine
13th Regiment, Colonel Pospieloff
14th Regiment, Colonel Savitzki
15th Regiment, Colonel Griaznoff
16th Regiment, Colonel Monaieff.

2nd Siberian Rifle Division

5th Regiment, Colonel Tretiakoff.

7th Siberian Rifle Division

Commanding Division, Major General Kondratenko
Commanding 1st Brigade, Major General Gorbatofski
Commanding 2nd Brigade, Major General Tserpitzki
25th Regiment, Colonel Sellenin
26th Regiment, Colonel Semenof
27th Regiment, Colonel Petrush
28th Regiment, Colonel Mirman.
Commanding Field Artillery, Major General Nikitine.

4th Siberian Artillery Brigade, 4 batteries, 32 guns.
Commanding Brigade, Colonel Irman.

7th Siberian Artillery Brigade, 3 battalions, 24 guns.
Commanding Brigade, Colonel Mekmendorof
One light battery 57 mm guns.

Kwantung Fortress Artillery.
Commanding, Major General Biélui
Commanding 1st battalion, Colonel Verpritzki
Commanding 2nd battalion, Colonel Stolnikoff
Commanding 3rd battalion, Colonel Mionchurski

Engineers and Sappers.
2 Battalions, Colonel Jerebsoff
1 Mining company, Colonel Borodatoff
1 Field telegraph company, Colonel Globa.

Cavalry—1 Sotnia 4th Verkneudinsk Transbaikal Cossacks.

Reserves—3rd and 7th Reserve battalions.

Volunteers—Commanding, Major General Roznatofski.
1 battalion with mounted detachment.

Police—300 men under Colonel Tautz.

Gendarmes—220 men under Commandant.

Railway Guards—36th Company.

Seamens Barracks—86 officers, 4800 men.

Fleet Personnel—451 officers, 147 warrant officers and 9,400 men.

Recapitulation:

9 regiments infantry full strength 28,800, actual strength	26,100
Field artillery	840
Light battery	120
Fortress artillery	2,200
Cavalry	250
Volunteers	360
Engineers and Sappers	1,200
Mining Company	200
Field telegraph	220
Reserves	2,200
Railway guards	250
Police	300
Gendarmes	220
Seamen in barracks	4,800
Naval personnel	9,990
Total	49,250

Navy	Officers	Men
Fleet personnel	166	3,428
Headquarters staff	3	3
Navy Yard staff	60	29
Seamens barracks	59	2,531
Torpedo mining company	10	142
Civil staff	3	3
	301	6,136
In hospital	420	13,300
Non-combatants		3,645

Or at time of surrender there was a total of 740 officers, 18,740 men able to do duty. Including wounded there were 33,200 military and naval men, so giving a loss between May 8 1904, and time of surrender, of 12,660 men killed and missing, after deducting complements of *Tsérévitch, Askold, Diana, Novik,* and eleven torpedo boats which succeeded in escaping, and making allowance of 250 men for people escaping about the time of surrender.

Appendix III

Defenses
of
Port Arthur*

The defenses of Port Arthur consisted of (1) sea defenses or defense against attack from the sea, and (2) land defenses or defense against land attack.

Sea defenses comprised (a) permanent batteries, (b) semi-permanent batteries, (c) temporary batteries, (d) search lights, (e) mobile land defense, (f) mines, (g) guardships, (h) sunken obstructions, (k) mobile sea defense and (l) signal stations, telephone and telegraph.

(a) Permanent batteries consisted of sea batteries 1, 6, 7, 8, 9, 13, 16, 17, 20, 20 a, 21, of permanent construction, existing before outbreak of war, usually on elevated sites, and armed with guns supposed to be effective against ships at sea at long range. These were all manned by detachments of fortress artillery.

(b) Semi-permanent batteries consisted of sea batteries 2, 3, 4, 14, 18, 19, 22, 76, 77, 78, of semi-permanent construction of practically same strength as permanent batteries, also mounted usually on elevated sites, but constructed subsequent to outbreak of war, armed with guns similar to those of permanent batteries, and manned by detachments of fortress artillery except 76, 77, 78 which were manned by sailors.

(c) Temporary batteries 5, 8a, 9a, 10, 11, 12, 15, 15a, 16a, 23a, 79, 80, and 81, of temporary construction with earth and sand bags, and were either water batteries, or field works, constructed subsequent to outbreak of war, usually near the beach and armed with small guns effective against light craft at short ranges. The water batteries were usually manned by sailors under charge of naval officers, and the field works by detachments from the Army.

(d) The searchlights used in connection with sea defense were placed on elevated positions, but at a lower level than the batteries

* Battery numbers used in the text refer to the tabulation following this appendix.

near at 4, 8a, 16a, and 22. The searchlight on 76 was principally used in connection with land defense. Searchlights were manned by detachments from the fleet.

(e) The mobile land defense consisted of military camps located near batteries 2, 5, 9, 18, 71, 22, 23a, 80 and 81, and constituted first line of defense against attempts at landing. A Chinese earth wall or infantry parapet with revetment connected up batteries 1, 2, 4, 5, 8, 9 and 10 on Tiger Tail Peninsula, spurs ran out from 14 along slopes of Golden Hill, and another from 21 to 20 then to north-westward for about 1,000 yards.

(a), (b), (c), (d) and (e) were under control of the Army, the officer commanding Fortress Artillery being in immediate command.

(f) Mines were partly under the Army, partly under the Navy, the naval officer in charge of shore defense being in immediate control. Observation mines belonged to the Army, automatic and contact mines to the Navy. Trawling for mines was done by the Navy. Near entrance were placed a number of mines to prevent brander attacks or attempts to force the entrance. The trawling steamers endeavored to keep clear an anchorage off the entrance, and three sortie fairways. All ground outside of this, and usually that portion between three and six miles from the beach, was dangerous to both belligerents. Outside of six miles was Japanese ground, except when by neglect they allowed the Russians to mine there.

(g) Guard ships were usually stationed at the entrance, a cruiser being anchored in position "1", and gunboats with a destroyer alongside each at 2, 3, 4.

(h) The Russians sank three large steamers as obstructions at R,R,R,R, while the wrecks of the Japanese branders assisted these to obstruct entrance. Guard ship at "1" acted as a sort of trap, the Japanese torpedo boats repeatedly attacking it, and reporting its destruction, when they saw their torpedoes explode on striking the obstructions outside ot it, being further misled by the occasional sight of the hulls of the sunken ships, as they were uncovered by the swell.

(k) The mobile sea defense was entrusted to gunboats, destroyers, steam launches fitted with torpedo tubes, and mine laying vessels and small boats, under charge of naval officer commanding shore defense. Usually during the night three destroyers were anchored near the shore in Takhé Bay, others stationed near guard ships with steam up ready to get out and others occasionally made expeditions along the shore, but never to a great distance, and not often after April 13. During the day the gun boats accompanied by some destroyers cruised close along shore, and nine dumping steamers converted into mine trawlers assisted by small boats sought for and exploded mines. On May 14 mine vessel *Amur* and some destroyers laid mines successfully 10 miles out, and destroyed *Hatsuse* and *Yashima*, and destroyers also succeeded in laying mines beyond six-mile line.

(l) At 78 was signal station, at 76 a wireless and signal station, near 10 was signal station, at 12a was signal and wireless station, at 20 was signal station and while Kwan Tung shore line was in possession of Russians, signal stations were located on prominent points all round coast, connected up by telephone and manned by sailors under charge of naval officers. Range stations were established on the highest points at 76, 6, 13 and 20.

(2) The land defense composed of 1 outlying positions, 2 main fortress line and 3 interior line, consisted of (a) permanent fortifications, (b) semi-permanent fortifications, (c) temporary fortifications, (d) search light and star shell stations, (e) entrenchments, (f) obstructions as fougasses* or buried mines, barbed wire, military pits, chevaux de frises** and defense by fire.

(1) Outlying positions. These were the temporary fortifications 23, 24, 25, 44, 45, 46, 58, 59, 59a, 60, 61, 61a, and the semi-permanent batteries 76 and 77 of the sea defense, which were also part of the land defense. There were no other semi-permanent fortifications in outer line, no permanent fortifications whatever, and the temporary fortifications were all of the character of field works. All the outlying positions were constructed subsequent to outbreak of the war, some not being completed in August 1904.

(2) Main fortress line consisted of Forts I, II, III, IV, V, VI, all permanent fortifications constructed prior to commencement of

* Fougasses are land mines overlaid with stones or other missiles so laid that the explosion will throw them upward.

** Chevaux de frizes are projecting lines of sharp points, spikes, or nails set firmly into the top of a fence or wall.

war, of masonry and concrete, of great strength, and armed with fortress, small rapid fire, and machine guns, and provided with usual equipment of first-class fortifications, but added to and still further strengthened after commencement of war. In addition to these were the strong semi-permanent works Ia, 28, 33, 35, 40, 49, 50, 56 and 62, little inferior to the permanent fortifications, but constructed or completed after commencement of war. Naval 6-inch guns had been mounted in temporary fortifications 26, 31, 55, 66 in May, June and July, 1904, and smaller shorter range guns in 27, 29, 30, 32, 34, 36, 37, 38, 39, 41, 51, 52, 57, 63, 64 and 65, strong redoubts 44, 45, 46, 47, and 48 completed and armed, while 42, 43, 53 and 54 were field works constructed but not yet armed.

Search light and star shell stations were located at 26, 30, 33, 40, IV, V, 62 and VI. Signal stations were built on high hills along main fortress lines, with others in advanced positions as lookouts, but these constructions being easily distinguishable were of little use when Japanese invested town closely. On the slopes all along main fortress line were trenches with barbed wire obstructions and fougasses. Crossing the valleys and connecting up main fortress line, there were trenches, deep ditches, military pits, fougasses, bombproofs and machine gun stations. Along the crest of the hills from 26 to 41, and from 49 to 51 was the old Chinese earth wall, acting as infantry revetment with banquette* for riflemen, bombproofs, many machine gun stations, communication effected by good military roads.

(3) Interior line of fortress defense surrounding Old Town, consisted of a moat 10′ deep, 12′ across top, 8′ across the bottom, scarped and counterscarped, depth from top of counterscarp to bottom of moat 16′. In rear of moat was infantry parapet with revetment 8′ high, 16′ thick at base, with riflemen's banquette. At 57 in this line was a strong armed redoubt and at 68, 69 and 71 were earth works to receive three field pieces each, but unarmed in August 1904. Besides these earth works were smaller bastions at 70 and 72 for two machine guns each, but also unarmed. Along revetment were emplacements for field guns at average distances of about 200 yards, a few of these guns being in place. Gates in this

* A raised way or foot bank along the inside of a parapet or trench on which soldiers and guns are stationed to fire on an enemy.

interior line were guarded by wire obstructions, fougasses, and chevaux de frise. In advance of the line stones marked with whitewash gave ranges. In rear of the line at various points were bombproofs, consisting of pits in the ground, roofed over with heavy beams covered by earth, top of roof raised very little above general level of ground. It was difficult to see of what value this strong interior line would have been if once the main fortress line were occupied by the enemy, and as a matter of fact it was never used.

Permission was not given to inspect any battery, but many could be approached within 100 or 200 yards, and number, character, and caliber of guns determined with some approach to accuracy in greater number of instances. Contour lines, streams, and Chinese villages obtained from Russian military chart and checked by personal observation, chart in some cases being found slightly in error, particularly in regard to contour lines.

APPENDIX III

DEFENSES OF PORT ARTHUR

Chart No. of Fort.	Armament.	Description.	Russian Designation.	Chinese Designation.	Japanese Designation.	Remarks.
1	3 6″ Krupp, Army model, 2 small.	Sea battery. Mounted in barbette, masonry and cement with glacis of earth. Arc of fire 180°.	Battery No. 1	Chantushan	—	Permanent.
2	2 6″ Krupp.	Sea battery. Earth work. Arc of fire 180°.	Battery No. 2	—	—	Semi-permanent.
3	2 9″ Krupp, old model	Sea battery. Earth work. Arc of fire 180°.	Battery No. 3	Mantoushan	—	Semi-permanent.
4	2 9″ Krupp, old model, one search light	Sea battery. Earth work. Arc of fire 180°.	Battery No. 4	Mantoushan	—	Semi-permanent.
5	2 12 pdrs. long.	Sea battery. Sand bag fort. Arc of fire 180°.	Battery No. 5	—	—	Temporary.
6	9 21 cm howitzers.	Sea battery. Masonry and cement with earth glacis. All round fire. Magazines in traverses.	Battery No. 6 and Suvaroff battery.	Chikwanshan	—	Permanent.
7	4 28 cm howitzers.	Sea battery. Masonry and cement. Magazines in traverses. All round fire.	Battery No. 7	Chikwanshan	—	Permanent.
9	5 6″ long-range modern, with shields.	Sea battery. Masonry and cement emplacement with traverses. Arc of fire 180°.	Battery No. 8	Mantseyin	—	Permanent.
15a	3 12 pdr. RF & one Nordenfeldt mach. gun.	Water battery. Earth work and sand bags.	—	—	—	Temporary. Removed June 1, 1904.

Chart No. of Fort.	Armament.	Description.	Russian Designation.	Chinese Designation.	Japanese Designation.	Remarks.
16	5 10″ BLR hydraulic mounts, long-range with light overhead shields. 2 12 pdr RF	Sea battery. Mounted in barbette in circular pits of masonry and cement open to rear. Magazines in traverses. Heavy glacis of earth. Arc of fire 180°.	Electricheski Utess or Electric cliff Battery No. 16.	—	—	Permanent. This was only battery of heavy long-range guns mounted.
16a	2 field guns and search light.	Earth work.	—	—	—	Temporary.
17	5 6″ Canet, long-range.	Sea battery. Mounted in barbette, masonry and cement with traverses, earth glacis. Arc of fire 180°.	Battery No. 17. Promejutnoi.	—	—	Permanent.
18	4 6″ Army short, 1 12 pdr.	Water battery. Old Chinese earth fort remodeled.	Flat Cape; No. 18 and Laja.	—	—	Semi-permanent.
19	7 9″ old model, using black powder	Sea battery. Earth work and sand bags with traverses. Arc of fire 240°.	Battery No. 19.	—	—	Semi-permanent.
20	4 28 cm howitzers, 1 9.4″ BLR	Sea battery. Earth work and sand bags. All round fire. Signal station.	Battery No. 20. Krestovaya.	Lao li chui	—	Permanent. Old Chinese battery remodeled. 9.4″ mounted in Aug. 1904.
20a	5 6″ Army guns.	Masonry and cement, with traverses. All round fire.	—	—	—	Permanent. Guns transferred May/1904.

Chart No. of Fort.	Armament.	Description.	Russian Designation.	Chinese Designation.	Japanese Designation.	Remarks.
21	2 28 cm howitzers	Sea battery. Earth work and cement. All round fire.	Battery No. 21	Lao li chiu	—	Permanent. Old Chinese battery.
22	5 6″ modern long-range guns in shield, 1 search light.	Earth work and sand bags. Arc of fire 240°.	Battery No. 22.	—	—	Semi-permanent.
23	3 field guns.	Earth work and stones. Field work.	—	Siao-gu-shan	—	Land defense. Temporary.
23a	2 12 pdr. RF, 2 small.	Water battery. Earth work and sand bags.	Battery No. 23.	—	—	Temporary.
24	3 field guns.	Land defense. Earth work and stones.	—	Dagushan	—	Temporary.
25	2 field guns.	Land defense. Earth work and stones.	—	Dagushan	—	Temporary.
26	2 6″ Naval RF, long- range: 1 search light.	Land defense. Earth work and sand bags.	—	—	—	Temporary. Mounted in July 1904.
27	2 6 pdr. RF	Land defense. Small earth work with sand bags.	—	—	—	Temporary.
28	4 86 mm siege guns on field mounts.	Land defense. Earth work and sand bags with overhead bombproof protection.	—	—	—	Semi-permanent.
29	2 field guns, 2 machine guns.	Earth work and sand bags.	—	—	—	Field work.
30	3 6″ Army, short, 2 small R. F.	Earth work and sand bags.	—	—	"Q"	Temporary.
31	2 6″ Naval guns in shields.	Earth work and sand bags.	—	—	—	Temporary. Mounted July, 1904.

Chart No. of Fort.	Armament.	Description.	Russian Designation.	Chinese Designation.	Japanese Designation.	Remarks.
32	3 86 m/m siege guns on field mounts.	Earth work and sand bags.	—	—	"P"	Field work.
33	2 6" naval guns, one search light.	Earth work and sand bags.	Orlina Niezda: or Eagles Nest.	Vantai	—	Semi-permament. Mounted June, 1904.
34	1 field gun, 2 machine guns.	Earth work and sand bags.	—	East Pan-lung	—	Field work. Mounted July, 1904.
35	4 28 cm. howitzers.	Earth work and sand bags.	—	—	"I"	Semi-permanent. Mounted July, 1904.
36	1 field gun, 2 machine guns.	Earth work and sand bags.	—	West Pan-lung	—	Field work, Mounted July, 1904.
37	4 6" howitzers.	Earth work and sand bags.	—	—	"H"	Temporary. Mounted July, 1904.
38	1 field gun, 1 47 mm R. F., 2 mach. guns.	Earth work and sand bags.	—	—	Hachimak-yama	Field work. Mounted July, 1904.
39	2 field guns, 2 machine guns, 1–11" torpedo tube.	Earth work and sand bags.	Advanced work	Erlung lu-nette	—	Field work. Mounted August, 1904.
40	4 120 mm long-range, 9 small RF, one search light	Closed work. Earth, cement and sand bags, with moat, trenches and bombproofs.	—	Sungshushan	—	Semi-permanent. Completed May 1904.

Chart No. of Fort.	Armament.	Description.	Russian Designation.	Chinese Designation.	Japanese Designation.	Remarks.
41	2 86 mm siege, 4 machine guns.	Earth work and sand bags with moat.	—	Sungshushan	—	Semi-permanent. Completed May 1904.
42	2 field guns, 2 machine guns.	Earth work and sand bags.	—	—	—	Field work. Guns not mounted August 1904.
43	3 field guns, 2 machine guns.	do	—	—	—	Field work. No guns mounted August 1904.
44	3 field, 4 machine guns.	Earth work and sand bags. Bombproof, moat and trenches.	Kouropatkin lunette	—	—	Field work. Completed August 1904.
45	1 47 mm RF, 2 machine guns.	Earth work and sand bags, moat and bombproofs.	—	Shiu-shi-yin lunette "D"	—	Field work. Completed August 1904.
46	1 47 mm RF, 2 machine guns, 1 11" torpedo tube.	Earth work and sand bags, moat and bombproofs.	—	Lunette "B"	—	Field work. Completed August 1904.
47	3 86 mm siege on field mounts.	Earth work and sand bags.	—	—	—	Field work. Mounted July 1904.
48	4 12 pdr. naval RF	Earth work and sand bags. Old Chinese fort.	—	—	—	Field work. Mounted July 1904.
49	4 6" Army short, 2 small.	Closed work. Earth work and cement, with moat.	—	Itzushan	—	Semi-permanent. Completed August 1904.

Chart No. of Fort.	Armament.	Description.	Russian Designation.	Chinese Designation.	Japanese Designation.	Remarks.
50	4 6" howitzers.	Masonry and cement. Moat and trenches.	—	—	—	Semi-permanent.
51	4 86 mm siege on field mounts.	Earth work and sand bags.	—	—	—	Temporary. Completed July 1904.
52	2 field guns.	Earth work with moat.	—	—	—	Temporary. Completed July 1904.
53	Intended for field and machine guns.	Earth work and sand bags, with trenches.	—	—	—	Field work. Unarmed August 1904.
54	Intended for field and machine guns.	do	—	—	—	Field work. Unarmed August 1904.
55	2 6" naval guns.	Earth work, and sand bags.	—	—	—	Temporary. Completed July 1904.
56	2 6" naval guns; 6 86 mm siege.	Closed work. Earth work, cement and sand bags, with moat and bombproof.	—	—	—	Semi-permanent. Completed June 1904.
57	4 75 mm field guns.	Earth work and sand bags.	—	—	—	Field work. Completed July 1904.
58	2 machine guns.	Earth work and sand bags with trenches.	—	—	—	Field work. Under construction August 1904.
59	2 field guns, 2 machine guns.	Earth work, bombproof and trenches.	—	—	Akasakayama	Field work. Under construction, August 1904.

Chart No. of Fort.	Armament.	Description.	Russian Designation.	Chinese Designation.	Japanese Designation.	Remarks.
59a	2 12 pdr. RF, 4 machine guns.	Earth work, bombproof and trenches.	—	—	Namaokyama	Field work. Under construction, August 1904.
60–61	2 4.7″, 8 machine guns.	Earth work, sand bags, bomb-proof, trenches and covered ways.	Uglovaya & 203 Meter Hill	—	203 Meter Hill	Field work. Under construction August, 1904.
61a	2 12 Pdr., 5 field, 4 machine guns.	Earth work, bombproof and trenches.	174 Meter Hill	—	174 Meter Hill	Field work. Under construction August, 1904.
62	4 field pieces, 6 machine guns.	Earth work and sand bags, moat, bombproof and trenches.	Valdschnep Hill or Woodcock Hill.	Yahuthwei	—	Semi-permanent. Completed June, 1904.
63	5 86 m/m siege on field mount.	Earth work and sand bags.	—	—	—	Field work, comp'd June '04
64	4 field guns.	Earth work and sand bags.	—	—	—	Field work, comp'd June '04
65	2 field guns.	Earth work.	—	—	—	Field work, comp'd June '04
66	4 6″ naval guns.	Earth work and sand bags.	Peripolich-naya	Peiyushan	—	Temporary. Completed May, 1904.
67	2 86 m/m siege, 3 field guns.	Earth work inside interior line of defense.	—	—	—	Semi-permanent.
68	Intended for 3 field guns.	Earth work inside interior line.	—	—	—	Semi-permanent; closed work.

Chart No. of Fort.	Armament.	Description.	Russian Designation.	Chinese Designation.	Japanese Designation.	Remarks.
69	do	do	—	—	—	do
70	Intended for 1 field; 2 machine guns.	Earth work inside interior line.	—	—	—	Semi-permanent. Lunette.
71	do	do	—	—	—	do
72	Intended for 1 field; 2 machine guns.	do	—	—	—	do
73	Unarmed.	Old Chinese water batteries.	—	—	—	Obsolete.
74	Unarmed.	do	—	—	—	Obsolete.
75	Unarmed.	do	—	—	—	Obsolete.
76	2 6″ Naval guns, 1 search light.	Earth work, stones, and sand bags.	—	Liao-ti-shan	—	Semi-permanent. Completed, April 1904.
77	1 8″ BLR	Earth work and sand bags.	—	—	—	Semi-permanent. Completed August 1904.
78	2 12 pdr., 4 field guns.	Earth work and sand bags.	—	—	—	Semi-permanent. Completed March 1904.
79	4 field guns.	Earth work.	—	—	—	Field work. Completed April 1904.
80	3 field guns.	Earth work.	—	—	—	Field work. Completed April 1904.

Chart No. of Fort.	Armament.	Description.	Russian Designation.	Chinese Designation.	Japanese Designation.	Remarks.
81	2 field guns.	Earth work.	—	—	—	Field work. Completed July 1904.
I	4 6″ Krupp, Army guns; 2 6 pdr., 2 machine guns.	Closed work of masonry and cement, with moat, scarp and counterscarp, caponnieres, galleries, and bombproof.	No. I or Kruglaya	—	—	Permanent.
Ia	6 86 mm siege guns on field mounts.	Earth work, masonry and cement, with bombproofs.	—	South Keekwan.	—	Semi-perma-nent.
II	4 6″ Krupp, Army guns 4 3 pdr. RF, 4 machine guns.	Closed work of masonry and cement, with moat, scarp and counterscarp, caponnieres, galleries, and bombproof.	No. II.	North Keekwan.	—	Permanent.
III	4 6″ Krupp, Army guns 9 machine guns.	Very strong closed work, of masonry and cement, deep moat, scarped and counterscarped, caponnieres, galleries and bombproofs.	No. III.	Erlungshan	—	Permanent.
IV	4 6″ Krupp, Army guns 2 12 pdr., 1 search light.	do	No. IV.	Itzushan		Permanent.

Chart No. of Fort.	Armament.	Description.	Russian Designation.	Chinese Designation.	Japanese Designation.	Remarks.
V	6 6" Krupp, Army guns 2 12 pdr., 1 search light.	do	No. V.	Taiyangkow		Permanent.
VI	4 6" Krupp, Army guns, 2 small RF, 1 search light.	Earth work, masonry and cement, with moat and bombproofs.	No. VI.	—	—	Semi-permanent.

Appendix IV

Defenses
of
Vladivostock*

Defenses of Vladivostock comprised (1) sea defenses or defense from attack from the sea and (2) land defenses or defense from attack by land.

(1) Sea defenses consisted of (a) permanent batteries, (b) semi-permanent batteries, (c) temporary batteries, (d) search lights, (e) mobile land defense, (f) mines,(g) guard ships, (h) mobile sea defense (k) signal stations, telephone and telegraph.

(a) Permanent batteries consisted of sea batteries 1, 5, 6, 7, 9, 42, 48, 49, 50, 51, 58, 63, 66 and 67 of permanent construction existing before outbreak of war, usually on elevated sites, and armed with guns supposed to be effective against ships at sea at long range. Long-range guns in 41, 42, 48 and 49 were not mounted during bombardment of March 6 1904, though guns were on trucks in the streets of Vladivostock. All these batteries were manned by detachments of fortress artillery.

(b) Semi-permanent batteries consisted of sea batteries 2, 10, 23, 41, 45, 52, 55, 56 and 57, of approximately same strength as permanent batteries, but constructed of earth and sand bags, located on elevated sites, armed with guns similar to those of permanent batteries, and also manned by detachments from fortress artillery.

(c) Temporary batteries, list of which is incomplete due to difficulty of finding and examination, consisted of 4, 64, 65, 68, and probably many others around the coasts of Russian Island and the smaller islands to southward of it.

(d) Searchlights were placed at or near 56, 1, 3, 9, 41, 49, 63, 58, 52 and inside harbor near Admiralty Wharf.

(e) Mobile land defense consisted of military camps all round coast of Muravieff Peninsula and Russian Island, exact locations unknown.

---

* Battery numbers used in the text refer to the tabulation following this appendix.

(f) Mines were placed so as to completely block eastern entrance and located approximately as shown on chart. They were placed also off the western entrance in large numbers, but leaving a fairway for entering vessels as indicated on chart. All vessels entering, whether merchant or men of war, reported first at Askold Island and received there a naval officer as pilot who would take the ships in over the mine fields.

(g) Guard ships. A small gunboat of *Aleut*-type was usually on guard just outside boom defenses and a merchant vessel armed with rapid fire guns was stationed near Popoff Island. Occasionally *Gromoboi* or *Rossia* would anchor outside western entrance for a few days.

(h) Mobile sea defense consisted of six torpedo boats, four small gunboats, the submarines after their arrival and the small ice breaker. When ice did not prevent, some of the torpedo boats were usually out on a scout going as far as Possiet Bay to the southward and Olga Bay to the northward. The small gun boats went no further than Askold Island. The submarines began to arrive in December 1904, but could not operate on account of ice until after 1st of April 1905, when their activity was confined principally to exercise in the harbor.

(k) Signal stations were established at 72, 63, 53, 7, Askold Island, and probably at other points on outlying islands, all connected up by telephone. Long distance shore wireless station was constructed during winter of 1904–05, located in the town near the navy yard, and was ready in May 1905.

(2) The land defenses comprised (1) outlying positions, (2) main fortress line, and (3) Russian Island line of defense.

(1) Outlying or advanced positions on side of Muravieff Peninsula consisted of the semi-permanent batteries 28, 29, 30 and 31 in connection with an advanced line of entrenchments extending across the Peninsula from northwest to southeast. No. 30 was on the highest point of the Peninsula and was a very strong work. No. 31 was an intermediate fortified hill between 28, 29, 30, and the main fortress line.

(2) Main fortress line consisted of permanent fortifications 18, 19, 20, 24, 33, 35, 37 and 40, semi-permanent fortifications 21, 22,

23, 25, 26, 32, 34, 36, 38 and 47, and temporary fortifications or field works 11, 12, 13, 14, 15, 16, 17, 27, 39, 43, 44, and 46. This line extended irregularly from two miles northeast of Bobroff Point on west coast to a point on east coast two miles north of Cape Basarghine. Nos. 18, 19, 20 and 24 on crest of ridge and covering easy sloping ground in front were connected by an infantry parapet with wattled revetment, and fronted by a line of military pits in six rows and a line of barbed wire obstruction. The valley of river in rear of this part of line was crossed by five lines of abattis, and one line of wire obstruction, and covered by the field works 11, 12, 13, 14, 15, 39 and semi-permanent battery No. 38. These field works were not yet armed. Nos. 11, 12 and 13 were connected by infantry parapet and fronted by barbed wire obstructions, and from 13 to 31 ran a long abattis, fronted part of the way by wire obstruction. Nos. 34, 35, 36 and 37 were connected up by infantry parapet of earth with wattled revetment. Across the alley from 37 to 40 was a deep moat with wire obstructions in front and infantry parapet in rear with emplacements for machine and field guns. At the strong points in main fortress line, slopes of hills were entrenched and fronted by barbed wire.

(3) Russian Island line of defense consisted of permanent fortification No. 72, semi-permanent fortifications 62 and 70, and temporary fortifications 59, 60, 61, 64, 65, 68, 69 and 71, with a long line of entrenchments, extending practically all round the island, and manned by a large number of troops, toward end of war there being about 20,000 men on Russian Island. Permission was never given to visit this island, and very little could be learned of the system or strength of defense. What is noted here is largely in the nature of guesswork, except that batteries exist on the sites located, and the general idea of the defense of the island.

The existence of this island which makes the harbor difficult to blockade by affording two channels for sortie, creates a weakness to attack by sea, which the Russians fully appreciated, and endeavored to provide against by defense with a large number of men and light guns.

Another method of attack which the Russians did not appreciate until the conditions were on them, was an attack over the ice when the place was frozen in. This condition exists usually from the

20th of December until the 1st of April, the solid ice line covering the bays on both sides of Peninsula and extending usually about five miles outside of Russian Island, though during the winter of 1904–05 ice line did not extend to seaward of the island. The ice is usually 24″ to 28″ thick, strong enough to support large bodies of men and field artillery, but not thick enough to prevent passage of fairly strong merchant vessels or military transports. When the weakness in this direction became evident to the Russian authorities they were exceedingly uneasy, according to the statements of the commandant of the fortress himself, and endeavors were made to guard against it by sending the small ice breaker out each day to keep a channel broken around the Peninsula. An hour after the channel was broken, a man could walk across it, the broken ice floating to the surface again and freezing over. Snow forts and machine gun stations were constructed on the ice about one half mile apart all round the Peninsula, and infantry posts established on the ice. It is easily conceivable that transports with a large number of troops on board could force their way into the ice during the night or thick weather, disembark on it, and make an immediate attack along any part of the coast decided on. As to breaking the ice by artillery fire, this is a question to be determined by experiment, but during the bombardment of March 6 1904, many Japanese 8″ and 6″ shells fell in the ice of the Golden Horn, blowing holes about 6′ in diameter and making so little impression that people driving in sleighs on the ice within a half mile of where the shell fell did not know they were being fired on.

Generally the information as to defenses of Vladivostock is more general and much less complete and accurate than that of the defenses of Port Arthur due to the character of the country which did not permit too close approach to the batteries without exciting suspicion, and to the restriction of the area covered by excursions of attachés. Much of the information was received through the kindness of Major W.V. Judson, U.S. Corps of Engineers, who in October, 1904, was permitted to make a casual inspection of a portion of the lines of defense.

APPENDIX IV

DEFENSES OF VLADIVOSTOCK

Chart No. of battery.	Armament	Description	Designation	Remarks
1	4 6", 6 11" howitzers and 6 RF and machine guns.	Sea battery covering entrance. Earth work and concrete. Guns mounted in barbette.	—	Permanent.
2	4 12 pdr. RF	Sea battery. Earth work and sand bags.	—	Semi-permanent.
3		Large magazine of concrete.	—	
4	4 RF (small probably)	Water battery: earth work under construction.	—	No guns mounted.
5	6 6" long-range, modern.	Sea battery. Concrete, guns in barbette with shields, arc of fire 180°.	—	Permanent.
6	4 10" modern BLR	Sea battery. Concrete, with traverses guns mounted in barbette, with light overhead shields. Arc of fire 180°.	—	Permanent.
7	6 9" howitzers.	Sea battery. Earth work and concrete. All round fire.	Tiger	Permanent.
8	6 small RF (12 pdr.)	Saluting battery.	—	
9	9 9" BLR, old model. 2 12 pdrs. on flank.	Sea battery. Concrete with traverses, guns mounted in barbette, light overhead shields.	—	Permanent.
10	Intended for 4 11" howitzers.	Sea battery. Earth work under construction.	—	Semi-permanent. No guns mounted.
11	6 Emplacements.	Earth work and sand bags, with bombproof.	—	No guns mounted, but intended for 4-field or light-siege guns
12	4 Emplacements.	Earth work.	—	

Chart No. of battery	Armament	Description	Designation	Remarks
13	6 Emplacements for field or machine guns	Earth work redoubt. Unarmed.	—	Field work.
14	4 Emplacements for field or machine guns.	do do	—	Field work.
15	3 Emplacements.	Small closed earth work and block house. Unarmed.	—	Field work.
16	8 Emplacements.	Old earth work. Unarmed.	—	Abandoned, but might be reoccupied.
17	4 Emplacements.	Earth work. Completion apparently abandoned.	—	Temporary.
18	4 fortress, 8 machine guns.	Small closed earth work fort of main line land defense.	—	Permanent.
19	4 fortress, 6 machine guns.	do do	—	Permanent.
20	4 fortress, 4 machine guns.	Small closed earth work of main line land defense.	—	Permanent.
21,22	Machine gun emplacements.	Outlying batteries of Fort Muravieff	—	Semi-permanent.
23	4 8″ BLR	Earth work in connection with both land and sea defenses.	—	Semi-permanent.
24	4 6″ BLR and probably some 11″ howitzers, and one search light.	Large and strong earth work on highest crest of range, forming portion of land defense, with moat outlying batteries, entrenched slopes and obstructions. Overlooked by higher ridges to NE	Fort Muravieff.	Permanent.

Chart No. of battery.	Armament	Description	Designation	Remarks
25	6 fortress guns.	Outlying battery of Fort Muravieff. Earth work.	—	Semi-permanent.
26	4 3″ RF in circular shields.	do do	—	Semi-permanent.
27	6 Emplacements for field or machine guns.	Earth work redoubt unarmed.	—	Field work.
28	Probably 4 fortress and machine guns.	Outlying work in connection with advanced lines.	—	Semi-permanent.
29	do do	do do	—	Semi-permanent.
30	Probably 4 6″, and large number of machine guns.	Closed earth work on highest hill in vicinity of Vladivostock, strong point of advanced line. Constructed with moat, outlying batteries, entrenched slopes and obstructions.	Fort Suvaroff	Semi-permanent. Begun in March 1904; completed October 1904
31	4 fortress & machine guns.	Earth work. Outlying work in main line of defense.	—	Semi-permanent. Completed October 1904.
32	4 RF guns (small).	Earth work. Outlying battery of No. 33.	—	Semi-permanent.
33	4 6″ fortress guns.	Closed earth work in main line land defense.	—	Permanent.
34	Small RF and machine guns.	Earth work. Outlying battery of No. 33.	—	Semi-permanent.
35	4 6″ and a number of small RF and machine guns, one search light.	Closed earth work, with moat, bombproof, entrenched slopes, outlying batteries and obstructions.	—	Permanent.
36	Emplacements for field and machine guns.	Earth work, reinforcing main line.	—	Semi-permanent.

Chart No. of battery.	Armament	Description	Designation	Remarks
37	Probably 4 fortress and number of machine guns.	Closed work with moat, scarped and counterscarped, entrenched slopes and obstructions.	—	Permanent.
38	Emplacements for fortress guns.	Earth work, with redoubts, bombproof.	—	Semi-permanent. Completed October 1904.
39	Emplacements for 6 field or fortress guns.	Earth work, unarmed, but intended to cover valleys to Northwestward.	—	Temporary.
40	Probably 6 6″ and 12 RF or machine guns.	Strong closed work of concrete and earth, with moat scarped and counterscarped, caponnieres and galleries, entrenched slopes and obstructions.	Fort Linievitch.	Permanent.
41	4 6″, 2 small RF & search light.	Sea battery. Earth work.	—	Semi-permanent. Guns mounted in April 1904.
42	4 10″ BLR long-range.	Sea battery. Earth work and concrete.	Fort Ourossoff	Permanent. Completed and guns mounted July 1904.
43	Emplacements for field and machine guns.	Earth work. Auxiliary to main line Unarmed.	—	Field work.
44	Emplacements for 6 light guns.	do	—	Field work.
45	6 11″ howitzers.	Sea battery. Earth work. New.	—	Semi-permanent. Completed July 1904.
46	Emplacements for 4 light guns.	Earth work. Auxiliary to main line. Unarmed.	—	Field work.

Chart No. of battery	Armament	Description	Designation	Remarks
47	No guns visible.	Closed earth work. Said to be disarmed.	—	Semi-permanent.
48	6 6″ long-range guns.	Sea battery. Earth work and concrete.	No. 18	Permanent. Guns mounted April 1904.
49	4 10″ long-range guns, 1 search light.	Sea battery. Earth work and concrete.	Sobab battery.	Permanent. Guns mounted July 1904.
50	4 6″ long-range guns.	Sea battery. Earth work.	—	Permanent.
51	8 9″ and 11″ howitzers.	Sea battery. Earth work and concrete.	—	Permanent.
52	4 6″ long-range, 2 RF small.	Sea battery. Earth work.	—	Semi-permanent.
53	Unarmed.	Old earth work. Signal station.	—	Permanent.
54		High explosive magazines.	—	
55	Armament unknown.	Sea battery. Earth work.	—	Semi-permanent.
56	do	do do	—	do
57	do	do do	—	do
58	6 6″ long-range, 2 RF and search light.	Sea battery. Earth work and concrete.	—	Permanent.
59,60, 61	Emplacements for field guns.	Earth works on line of defense.	—	Field works.
62	4 fortress, 2 machine guns.	Earth work.	—	Semi-permanent.
63	5 11″ howitzers, 6 RF and one search light.	Sea battery. Earth work and concrete.	Skrypleff battery.	Permanent.
64,65	Emplacements for field works.	Earth works.	—	Field works.
66	4 6″, 2 RF	Sea battery. Earth work.	—	Permanent.

Chart No. of battery.	Armament	Description	Designation	Remarks
67	4 11" howitzers.	Sea battery. Earth work.	—	Permanent.
68	Emplacements for field guns.	Earth work. Unarmed.	—	Field work.
69	2 6" guns.	Earth work.	—	do
70	4 11" howitzers, 6 RF	Closed earth work.	—	Semi-permanent.
71	Emplacements for field guns.	Earth work.	—	Field work.
72	2 8", 4 6", 6 11" howitzers, with many small RF and machine guns.	Strong closed work, earth and concrete, with outlying batteries, moat, entrenched slopes and obstructions. On highest hill of Russian Island and the strong point in defense of that island.	Fort Russki	Permanent.

Appendix V

Organization of Japanese Fleet

Combined Fleet—Admiral Togo, commander-in-chief.

First Squadron

1st Division:	*Mikasa* (F), *Asahi, Fuji*
2nd Division:	*Yashima* (lost May 15, '04, mine), *Shikishima, Hatsuse* (F) (lost May 15, '04, mine)
Tender:	*Tatsuta*
3rd Division:	*Chitose* (F), *Kasagi, Takasago* (lost December 12, '04, mine) *Yoshimo* (lost May 15, '04, collision)

After the loss on May 15 of the three ships noted, First and Second Divisions of First squadron retained practically same organization, each one ship less, though *Asama* temporarily filled *Yashima*'s place, the loss of that ship being concealed. *Yakumo* joined 3rd Division and carried flag of Rear Admiral Dewa, continuing to do so until after fall of Port Arthur, when she returned to squadron of Vice Admiral Kamimura. In battle of Japan Sea, May 27, 1905, Vice Admiral Dewa (promoted) carried his flag on the *Kasagi*.

Second Squadron - Vice Admiral Kamimura.

1st Division:	*Idzumo* (F), *Azuma, Asama*
2nd Division:	*Yakumo, Tokiwa, Iwate* (F)
3rd Division:	*Kasuga, Nisshin*
4th Division:	*Naniwa* (F), *Takashiho, Niitaka, Tsushima*

In the beginning of the war *Asama* acted with Rear Admiral Uriu and Fourth Division, and later with Admiral Togo. In May *Yakumo* became flagship of Rear Admiral Dewa commanding 3rd Division of First Squadron replacing *Yoshimo*, but after fall of Port Arthur rejoined Second Squadron, as did also *Asama*.

Third Squadron - Vice Admiral Kataoka.

1st Division: *Matsushima* (F), *Itsukushima, Hashidate, Chen Yen*
2nd Division: *Idzumi* (F), *Akashi, Akitsushima, Chiyoda* (sunk July 26, '04, mine), *Suma*
3rd Division: *Heiyen* (sunk September 18, '05, mine) *Tsukushi, Saiyen* (sunk November 30, '04, mine), *Maya, Udji, Chokai*
4th Division: *Miyako* (sunk May 15, '04, mine), *Yaeyama, Chihaya, Oshima* (lost May 18, '04, collision), *Kaimon* (sunk July 4, '04, mine), *Atago* (ran on rocks Pechili Strait, November 6, '04)

The composition of this squadron is somewhat in doubt, only the 1st and 2nd Divisions being seen often enough to determine the fact that they were operating together. The 1st Division was always together. The 2nd Division was usually together, but in June and July *Asama* was often seen with it. Ships of the 3rd and 4th divisions were seen occasionally only, sufficient to make it probable that they operated in groups of three as bracketed.

The First Squadron was always in the vicinity of Port Arthur. Four ships of the 1st and 2nd Divisions of the Second Squadron, the *Idzumo, Azuma, Tokiwa* and *Iwate,* were always in Japan Sea, operating against the Vladivostock fleet. *Yakumo* was first with these four ships, then in May became flagship of 3rd Division, First Squadron, and remained with it until destruction of fleet in Port Arthur, when she rejoined Second Squadron. *Asama* first operated with 4th Division, Second Squadron, then replaced *Yashima* in battleship squadron, at the same time acting with the 3rd Division of the Third Squadron. Battleship squadron usually remained at anchor in Elliott Islands after May 15. *Kasuga* and *Nisshin* were always off Port Arthur from the time of their first appearance April 15 1904, until end of siege. These two ships usually acted together and, independently, in battle their places in column being next to battleships. The 4th Division of the Second Squadron was never seen off Port Arthur, its duty being apparently to guard Korea Straits, and convoy troops.

The *Matsushima*-Division were always off Port Arthur, working together, and very active about the entire coast of Liao-Tung Peninsula. The 2nd Division of the Third Squadron was also present generally at Port Arthur, the five ships usually being seen together. The gunboat divisions operated along the coasts, covered landings, attacked railways, covered attacks of torpedo boats and destroyers off the entrance to Port Arthur, also the mining operations and blocking attempts, and cooperated with the army along the shores.

Destroyers.

1st Flotilla,	Commander Fujimoto: *Shirakumo, Asaship, Asagiri, Harusame*
2nd Flotilla,	Commanders Ishida and Yoshujima: *Ikadsuchi* (lost May 17, '04), *Akebono, Inazuma, Oboro*
3rd Flotilla,	Commanders Tsuchiua and Yashima: *Akadsuki, Kasumi, Murasame, Hayatori* (sunk September 3, '04, mine)
4th Flotilla,	Commanders Nagai and Hirose: *Shiranui, Ousugumo, Shinanome, Yugiri*
5th Flotilla,	Commanders Mano and Suguki: *Murakumo, Kagiro, Saganami*

Other destroyers were being built in Japan during the war, and some were in commission toward the end, probably the *Fubuki,* and *Arari* which replaced the sunken boats *Ikadsuchi* and *Hayatori,* and filled out the *Sazanami*-division which consisted originally of three boats only. Also it was the practice of the Japanese to rig dummy funnels onto torpedo boats and place them in line with the destroyers in order to prevent the loss of the latter being known and to impose on the enemy.

The torpedo boats were organized in 21 flotillas, four boats in each flotilla, numbers running consecutively.

Appendix VI

Organization of Russian Fleet

Pacific Ocean Fleet

Commander in Chief: Viceroy Alexeieff, Feb. 8—Mar. 8, 1904; Vice Admiral Makaroff, Mar. 8—Apr. 13; Viceroy Alexeieff, Apr. 13—May 5; Vice Admiral Skrydloff, May 24—Jan. 7, 1905; Vice Admiral Rojestvensky, Jan 7—May 25; Vice Admiral Birileff (ordered) May 25.

First Squadron Vice Admiral Bezobrazoff, May 8—Oct. 13; Rear Admiral Yessen, Oct. 13, 1904 to end of war.

1st Division: *Petropavlovsk* (F) Rear Admiral Stark, Feb. 8-26. (sunk April 13, '04, mine), *Tsésarévitch* (F) Rear Admiral Vitgeft, May 5—Aug. 10 (interned Kiao-chau, Aug. 12 '04), *Retvizan* (F) Rear Admiral Viren, Sept. 4—Jan. 2 '05 (sunk Port Arthur), *Pobieda* (sunk Port Arthur)

2nd Division: *Peresviet* (F) Rear Admiral Ukhtomsky, Feb. 8—Sept. 4 '05 (sunk Port Arthur), *Sevastopol* (sunk Port Arthur), *Poltava* (sunk Port Arthur)

Cruiser Division - Rear Admiral Stackelberg until beginning of war; Captain Reitzenstein, Feb. 9—Mar. 5; Rear Admiral Yessen, Mar. 15—Oct. 13 '04.

1st Division: *Rossia* (F), *Gromboi, Rurik* (sunk Tsushima, Aug. 14 '04), *Bogatyr* (wrecked May 15 '04, but repaired)

2nd Division: Commodore Reitzenstein, Mar. 20—Aug. 10 '04. *Askold* (F) (interned Shanghai Aug. 16 '04), *Bayan* (sunk Port Arthur Dec. '04), *Pallada* (sunk Port Arthur Dec. '04),

Diana (interned Saigon Aug. 24 '04), *Variag* (sunk Chemulpo Feb. 9 '04), *Novik* (sunk Korsakovsk Aug. 20 '04), *Boyarin* (sunk Feb. 11 '04, mine)

Coast Defense Division: Rear Admiral Lojinski, Feb. 8, '04—Jan. 2, '05. *Ghiliak* (sunk Port Arthur Dec. '04), *Gremiastchy* (sunk Aug. 18 '04, mine), *Otvajny* (sunk Port Arthur Dec. '04), *Bobr* (sunk Port Arthur Dec. '04), *Mandjour* (interned Shanghai Mar. '04), *Korietz* (sunk Chemulpo Feb. 9 '04), *Sivoutch* (blown up by Russians, Newchwang, July 25 '04), *Amur* (sunk Port Arthur Dec. '04), *Yenisei* (sunk at Dalney, mine, Feb. 11 '04)

Destroyers

1st Division: *Boevoi* (torpedoed July 24 '04), *Boiki* (interned Kiao-chau, Jan. 5 '05), *Burni* (wrecked Shantung, Aug. 11 '05), *Lieutenant Burakoff* (sunk, torpedo, July 24 '04), *Bezstrashni* (interned Kiauchow, Aug. 12 '04), *Bezposhadni* (interned Kiau-Chau, Aug. 12 '04), *Bditelni* (sunk Port Arthur Dec. '04), *Vuineslivi* (sunk, mine, Aug. '04), *Vlastni* (interned Chefoo, Jan. 2 '05), *Vnimatelni* (wrecked May 26 '04), *Grosovoi* (interned Shanghai Aug. 11 '05), *Vnushitelni* (blown up by Russians Feb. 25 '04)

2nd Division: *Smyeli* (interned Kiauchow Jan. 2 '05), *Stroitni* (sunk, mine), *Strashni* (sunk Port Arthur, Apr. 13 '04), *Statni* (interned Chefoo, Jan. 2 '05), *Silnii* (sunk Port Arthur Dec. '04), *Ryeshitelni* (captured Chefoo, Aug. 12 '04), *Steregustchi* (sunk Port Arthur Mar. 10 '04), *Raziastchy* (sunk Port Arthur Dec. '04), *Storojhevoi* (sunk Port Arthur Dec. '04), *Rastoropni* (blown up by Russians, Chefoo, Nov. '04), *Skori* (interned Chefoo Jan. '05), *Serditi* (interned Chefoo, Jan '05)

There were two divisions of 12 boats each, an officer in command of each division. Boats also organized in sub-groups of four each under command of senior officer.

Torpedo Boats - Commander Baron von Baden

201 (sunk Vladivostock, July '04, mine), 202 (sunk Vladivostock, Oct. '04 collision), 203, 204 (wrecked Gensan June 30 '04), 205, 206, 208, 210, 211

Second Pacific Squadron - Vice Admiral Rojestvensky, May 8, '04—May 29, '05.

1st Division: *Kniaz Suvaroff* (F) Vice Admiral Rojestvensky (sunk May '05), *Alexander III* (sunk May '05), *Borodino* (sunk May '05), *Orel* (captured May 28 '05)

2nd Division: *Osliabia* (F) Rear Admiral Felkersam (sunk May '05), *Sissei Veliki* (sunk May '05), *Navarin* (sunk May '05), *Admiral Nakhimoff* (sunk May '05)

3rd Division: *Nikolai I.* (F) Rear Admiral Nebogatoff (captured May 28 '05), *General Admiral Apraxine* (captured May 28 '05), *Admiral Oushakoff* (sunk, May, '05), *Admiral Senyavine* (captured May 28 '05)

Cruiser Division: *Oleg* (F) Rear Admiral Enquist (interned Manila June '05), *Aurora* (interned Manila June '05) *Dmitri Donskoi* (damaged in battle, wrecked May 29 '05), *Vladimir Monomakh* (sunk May '05)

Scout Division: *Jemchug* (interned Manila June '05), *Izumrud* (wrecked, blown up by crew May 29 '05), *Svietlana* (sunk May '05), *Almaz*

Converted cruiser: *Ural* (sunk May '05)

Transports: *Anadir* (sunk May '05), *Irtish* (sunk May '05), *Korea* (interned Shanghai May '05), *Kamchatka* (sunk May '05),

Tugs: *Russ* (sunk May '05), *Sbir* (interned Shanghai May '05)

Destroyers
1st Division: *Byedovi* (captured May 28 '05), *Buini* (blown up by crew May 28 '05), *Buistri* (chased ashore, wrecked May '05), *Bravi*

2nd Division: *Bezupretchni* (sunk May '05), *Grosni* (destoryed May '05), *Gromki* (sunk May '05), *Blestyastchi* (damaged in battle, May '05, foundered), *Bodri* (interned Shanghai May or June '05)

Hospital ships: *Kostroma* (captured and released), *Orel* (captured)

Appendix VII

Changes in Commands in Russian Fleet

Commander in Chief, Land and Naval Forces - Vice Admiral Alexeieff, Feb. 8—Oct. 28, '04; General Kouropatkin, Oct. 27 '04—Mar. 16 '05; Lieutenant General Liniévitch, Mar. 17 'till peace.

Commanding Pacific Fleet - Vice Admiral Makaroff, Mar. 8—Mar. 13; Vice Admiral Skrydloff, May 24—Jan. 7, '05; Vice Admiral Rojestvensky, Jan. 7—May 24 '05; Vice Admiral Birileff ordered May 25.

Commanding Port Arthur Squadron - Rear Admiral Stark, Feb. 8–26; Rear Admiral Ukhtomsky (temporarily); Vice Admiral Makaroff, Mar. 8—Apr. 13; Vice Admiral Alexeieff, Apr. 13—May 5; Rear Admiral Vitgeft, May 5—Aug. 10; Rear Admiral Ukhtomsky, Aug. 10—Sept. 4; Rear Admiral Viren, Sept. 4—Jan. 2 '05.

Commanding Vladivostock Squadron - Rear Admiral Stackelberg, before war 'till Feb. 8; Capt. Reitzenstein, Feb. 9—Mar. 15; Rear Admiral Yessen, Mar. 15—June 12; Vice Admiral Bezobrazoff, June 12—Oct. 15; Rear Admiral Yessen, Oct. 15 to end of war.

Changes in commands, ships:

Tsésarévitch	Capt. Grigorovitch, Feb. 8—Mar. 8; Capt. Vassilief, Mar. 8—Apr. 13; Capt. Eberhardt ordered Apr. 30; Capt. Ivanoff, May 5—Aug. 10.
Retvizan	Capt. Shensnovitch, Feb. 8 to Jan. 2 '05.
Sevastopol	Capt. Chernicheff, Feb. 8 to Mar. 10 '04; Capt. von Essen, Mar. 10 '04 to Jan. 2 '05.
Poltava	Capt. Ouspensky, Feb. 8 '04 to Jan. 2 '05.
Pobieda	Capt. Zatzarenni, Feb. 8 to June 22 '04; Capt. Sarnefski, June 22–24 '04; Capt. Zatzarenni, June 24 '04—Jan. 2 '05.
Peresviet	Capt. Boisman, Feb. 8 '04—Jan. 2 '05.

Bayan	Capt. Viren, Feb. 8 '04—Sept. 4 '04; Capt. Ivanof, Sept. 4 '04—Jan. 2 '05.
Askold	Capt. Grammatchikoff, Feb. 8—Aug. 12 '04.
Diana	Capt. Zalenski, Feb. 8—Mar. 10 '04; Capt. Ivanof, Mar. 10—June 20 '04; Capt. Lieven, June 20—Aug. 24 '04.
Pallada	Capt. Kossovitch, Feb. 8—Mar. 10 '04; Capt. Sarnefski, Mar. 10—June 22, '04; Capt. Ivanof, June 22–24 '04; Capt. Sarnefski, June 24—Jan. 2 '05.
Novik	Cdr. von Essen, Feb. 8—Mar. 10 '04; Cdr. von Schultz, Mar. 10—Aug 20 '04.
Amur	Cdr. Barnatoff, Feb. 8—Mar. 10 '04; Cdr. Ivanoff, Mar. 10—Sept. 4 '04; . . . . . Sept. '04 to Jan. '05.
Ghiliak	Cdr. Alexeieff and Cdr. Stronski.
Gremiastchy	Cdr. Nikolaieff and Cdr. Sveeman.
Otvajny	Cdr. Davidoff, Cdr. Lebedef, Cdr. Lazeref.
Bobr	Cdr. Bubnoff, Cdr. Lieven, Cdr. Shellting Feb. 8—Aug. 14 '04.
Vsadnik	Cdr. Stronski and Cdr. Opatzki, Feb. 8—Aug 14 '04.
Gaidamak	Cdr. Ivanoff and . . . . . Feb. 8—Aug 14 '04.

Torpedo Boats

1st Division:	Capt. Matussievitch, Capt. Bubnoff, Cdr. Elisseieff.
2nd Division:	Cdr. Ginter, Cdr. Lieven, Cdr. Krinitzki.
Boiki	Cdr. Sveeman and . . . . . Feb. 8—Aug 14.
Burni	Cdr. Pogorielski, Lt. Tirkoff
Bezposhadni	Lt. Lukine, Cdr. Rimsky-Korsakoff, Lt. Mikhailoff.
Bezshumni	. . . . . , Cdr. Maximoff
Bezstrashni	Cdr. Zimmerman, Lt. Tegethoff
Silni	Lt. Krinitzki, Lt. Kodorovitch

Serditi	Lt. Kuzmine-Korovaieff, Cdr. Klupfel
Ryeshitelni	Cdr. Kornilaef (wounded), Lt. Travlinski, Lt. Rostshakofski
Smyeli	Cdr. von Schultz, Lt. . . . . .
Storozhevoi	Cdr. Kitkine, Cdr. . . . . .
Rastoropni	Lt. Lepnief, Lt. Bren
Skori	Lt. Komenko, Lt. . . . . .
Stroini	Lt. . . . . ., Lt. . . . . .
Steregustchi	Lt. Kuzmine-Koravaief, Lt. Sergieieff
Raziastchy	Cdr. Simonof, Lt. . . . . .
Grosovoi	Lt. Shellting, Lt. . . . . .
Vlastni	Lt. Kartseff, Lt. Mikhailoff, Lt. Kartseff
Lieutenant Burakoff	Lt. Ivanoff, Lt. . . . . .
Vnushitelni	Cdr. Opatzki, Lt. Podushkine
Vuinoslivi	Lt. Richter
Vnimatelni	Cdr. Simon
Strashni	Cdr. Yurokofski
Statni	Lt. . . . . .

Vladivostock Squadron

Gromoboi	Capt. Dabitch, Feb. 8—Aug. 16; Cdr. Vinogradsky (temporarily); Capt. von Schultz, Oct. 18—Dec. 20; Capt. Broussiloff, Dec. 20 '04—May 25 '05; Capt. Ogoumoff, ordered to command.
Rossia	Capt. Andréef, Feb. 8—Aug 20 '04; Cdr. Kumina (temporarily); Captain Lillier, Oct. 20 to end of war.
Rurik	Capt. Trussof, Feb. 8—Aug. 14 '04.
Bogatyr	Capt. Stemman, Feb. 8 '04—May 15 '05; Capt. Borstrom, May 15 '05 to end of war.

Commanders of torpedo boats were often changed.

Appendix VIII

Pronunciation
of some
Russian names*

"Kh" replaces the Russian "X" and is strongly aspirated, almost like "J" (Spanish) in "José".

"J" replaces the Russian "ж" and is pronounced like the French "J".

The terminal "I" replaces Russian "ы" and has the shortened sound of "ui" or "ooee".

Syllables not accented are slurred.

Aleut	Al-ay-oot′
Alexeieff	Al-lex-ay′-eff
Amur	Ah-moor′
Apraxine	Ah-prak′-seen
Askold	Ass′-kold
Aurora	Ow-ro′-rah
Bayan	Bai-yan′
Bditelni	Behdee′-tle-nooee
Bezposhadni	Bez-posh-chad′-nooee
Bezshumni	Bez-shoom′-nooee
Bezstrashni	Bez-strash′-nooee
Bezupretchni	Bez-oo-pretch′-nooee
Byedovi	Beeay-do′-vooee
Blagoveshchensk	Blag′-o-vay′-shensk
Blestyastchi	Bless-tee-ast′-schee
Bobr	Bo′burh
Boevoi	Boee-voi′

*Names have been listed in alphabetical order; in original report they appeared in no discernable order.

Bogatyr	Bo-gah-teer′
Boiki	Boy′-kee
Bravi	Brah′-vooee
Boyarin	Boee-yar′-rin
Buistri	Booeest′-trooee
Burni	Boor′nooee
Chita	Chee′-tah
Diana	Dee-ah′-nah
Djidjit	Djee′-ghit
Dmitri Donskoi	Demmee′try Don′-skoee
Gaidamak	Gai-da-makk′
General Admiral	Ghay-nay-rall′ Ad-mee-rall′
Ghiliak	Ghee-ly-akk′
Gremiastchy	Grem-my-ast′-schee
Grigorovitch	Gree-go-ro′-vitch
Gromiastchy	Grom-mee-ast′-schee
Gromki	Grom′-kee
Gromoboi	Grom′-mo-boee
Grosovoi	Grozo-voy′-ee
Izumrud	Ee′-zoom-rood
Jemchug	Zhem′-choog
Kamchadal	Kam-cha-dall′
Khabarovsk	Khah-bah′-rovsk
Kharbine	Khar′-been
Kiakta	Kee-akh′-tah
Kniaz Potemkim Tavritchesky	Knee′asz Potty-ome′-kin Ta-vreetch-ess-ky′
Kniaz Suvaroff	Knee′asz Soo-vah′-roff
Korietz	Ko′-reeaytz
Kouropatkin	Koo-ro-pat′-kin
Lieutenant Burakoff	Lieut. Boo-rah′-koff
Linievitch	Leen-yay′-vitch
Makaroff	Mah-kah′-roff
Manjour	Man′-choor
Mistchenko	Mist′-shen-ko

Mukden	Mook′-den
Nadiojhnik	Na-dee-ozh′-neek
Nakhimoff	Nah-kee′-moff
Navarin	Nav-va-reen′
Nebogatoff	Nay-bo-gat′-off
Nikolai	Nee-ko-lai′-ee
Novik	Nov′-vik
Oleg	Ol′-leck
Orel	Ah-ree-ole′
Osliabia	Ose-lee-ah′-beea
Otvajny	Ott-vazh′-nee
Pallada	Pal-lah′-dah
Peresviet	Perress-vee-ett′
Petropavlosk	Pet′-ro-pav′-losk
Pobieda	Po-bee-yay′-da
Poltava	Pol-tah′-vah
Rastoropni	Rass-to-rop′-nooee
Razboinik	Raz-boy′-neek
Raziastchy	Raz-ee-ast′-schy
Retvizan	Ret-vee′-zan
Rojestvensky	Ro-zhes′-ven-sky
Rossia	Ros-see′-yah
Rurik	Reeoo′-reek
Ryeshitelni	Ree-ess-sheet′-el-nooee
Senyavine	Sen-yah′-veen
Serditi	Sere-dee′-tooee
Sevastopol	Say-vass′-to-poll
Silni	Seel′-nooee
Sissoi Veliki	Sis′-soee Vel-lee′-key
Sivoutch	See′-voutch
Skori	Skore′-ee
Skrydloff	Skruid′-loff
Smirnoff	Smeer′-noff
Smyeli	Smee-ay′-looee
Statni	Stat′-nooee

Steregustshi	Ster-ry-goost'-schee
Stessel	Stes'-sle
Storozhevoi	Sto-rozh'-ay-voee
Strashni	Strash'-nooee
Stroini	Stro'-ee-nooee
Sungari	Soon'-ga-ree
Tsésarévitch	Tses-sar-ray'-vitch
Tungus	Toon-goose'
Ukhtomsky	Ook-tom'-sky
Variag	Vah-re-akk'
Verkhneudinsk	Vairk-new'-dinsk
Viren	Vee-renn'
Vitgeft	Veet'-geft
Vladivostock	Vlad'-di-vos-tock'
Vlastni	Vlast'-nooee
Vnimatelni	Vhnee-mat'-tle-nooee
Vnushitelni	Vhnoo-sheet'-tle-nooee
Vunoslivi	Vooee-noss'-lee-vooee
Vzadnik	Vez-zad'-nik
Yakut	Yah-koot'
Yenisei	Yen-ny-say'-ee
Zabiaca	Zah-bee-ah'-kah

Appendix IX

Decision of Vladivostock Prize Court in case of Steamship *Allanton*

Steamer was apprehended June 18 '04, by the Russian squadron consisting of *Rossia, Gromoboi, Rurik.* An officer with armed boats crew was sent form *Rossia* to inspect the steamer, which turned out to be the British steamer *Allanton* with a cargo of 6,500 tons Japanese coal. Besides the Captain, Henry Motyer, and the crew consisting of 30 men of different nationalities, was a young Japanese who declared he had embarked in Mororan for purpose of going to America, which statement was confirmed by the Captain. Examination of the ship's documents showed that the *Allanton* was going to Singapore with coal from Mororan, nevertheless the officer requested the captain to take all documents and accompany him on board the cruiser, for the purpose of giving more exact information. To this the Captain demurred, but sent on board his mate, Henry Mitchell, with the documents. At the second examination of the documents it turned out that the official log book and chief officer's log book were missing, and these were immediately ordered to be sent for examination. The official log book was not in order, being kept up only until May 2–15, '04.* According to remarks in chief officers log and also other documents it became evident that in May the *Allanton* brought to Sasebo a full cargo of Cardiff coal. After having discharged this contraband in Sasebo, the steamer went to Mororan where she took a new cargo of Japanese coal according to documents destined for Singapore and addressed to Messrs. Patterson, Simon & Co. The Admiral being doubtful as to the genuineness of steamer's destination, gave orders to have her taken to Vladivostock. On June 19 steamer arrived in Vladivostock under command of Lieutenant Petroff, and the case was given to the Prize Court for trial. At trial Captain

* The two dates are New Style and Old Style.

stated that steamer was registered at Glasgow, owned by W. Rea, resident in Belfast. On Feb. 8–21, she left Cardiff with coal bound for Hong Kong, by way of Cape of Good Hope. Upon her arrival at Hong Kong the Captain received orders to proceed to Sasebo with cargo. Having discharged her cargo there she proceeded to Mororan, where new cargo of coal was taken for Singapore. On her way to this port she was detained by the Russian cruisers in the Japanese Sea.

The Japanese, Tatiki Miachara, declared that he embarked on the *Allanton* in Mororan intending to go to America for the purpose of completing his education, but neither a passport nor any other document to prove his identity were in his possession.

Examination of ship's documents as examined by the Court gave evidence of the following facts:

According to ship's charter party, concluded on Dec. 23–Jan. 5 in London, between the owner and Lambert Brothers, the *Allanton* had to take full cargo of Cardiff coal, proceed to Hong Kong via Suez canal, with instructions to discharge in Hong Kong or Sasebo, loading coal to be began January 19– Feb. 1. Regarding these terms the owner wrote from Belfast Feb. 3–16, to the Captain as follows "Take maximum cargo (6,500 tons), fill up bunkers to Lloyds mark, renewing your coal supply when necessary at Malta, Port Said, and Colombo. In case you will have to go further than Hong Kong, be very careful not to come within the war region, and to avoid all danger".

On Feb. 6–19, owner telegraphed to Captain. "Call at Gibraltar for orders whether ship shall go through Canal or round the Cape".

From the bill of lading issued Feb. 7–20 at Cardiff, it is to be seen that the *Allanton* took 6,500 tons of coal for Hong Kong to be discharged at Hong Kong or Sasebo. By a letter of Feb. 9–22, addressed to Gibraltar, the owner informed the Captain that he had decided to send ship around Cape instead of through the Canal. This decision apparently coincides with the fact that the squadron of Admiral Wirenius was cruising in the Mediterranean at this time. After this letter on Feb. 11–24 the owner of the ship telegraphed to Gibraltar to the Captain "Go round the Cape take coal Gibraltar, Palmas or Vincent, further Natal, Labuan or other ports if necessary." On Feb. 14–27 Captain Motyer wired from Gibraltar to owner asking for orders whether to go to Hong Kong or Sasebo, in reply being directed to go to Hong Kong. Captain Motyer on April 27–May 10 received instructions from the firm of Carmichail Clark to proceed to Nagasaki and Sasebo, cargo to be discharged at latter port. According to instructions given by the owner of the ship, the Captain when in Sasebo applied to Messrs. Dodwell & Co. of Yokohama, from whom he received instructions, after discharging to go to Mororan, at disposal of Japanese Industrial Company—Hokkaido Tauko Tetsudo Kaisha. Said company loaded *Allanton* with 6,500 tons Japanese coal, consigning same to Messrs. Patterson Simon & Co., Singapore. On May 31–June 13 steamer left Mororan with this cargo. Having taken into consideration all circumstances of the case, referred to, the Court decided:-

1. That the SS *Allanton* was arrested correctly, under observance of the rules in paragraphs 2, 3, 15, and 17 of the statutes of Maritime prizes, and on the basis of fully satisfactory reasons justifying the steps taken. Such reasons are:

    a. The irregularity of the ship's log.

    b. Indisputable proof of the ship having delivered recently at Japanese port a full cargo of contraband of war with full knowledge and sanction of owner.

    c. The chartering of the steamer by a Japanese trading company and the fact that [she] was loaded exclusively with coal, being contraband of war, in case the real destination were not Singapore but a hostile port or squadron.

Proceding to consider the question of the owner's standpoint with regard to the obligations of neutrality, the Court found that:

2. This question dissolves itself through the correspondence between the owner and Captain concerning the first trip referred to. This correspondence gives evidence that the character and real destination of the cargo sent February last were perfectly well known to the owner of the ship. The double destination of the cargo, Hong Kong and Sasebo, shows that the probability of a rupture between Russia and Japan had been foreseen by the owner at the time his ship was chartered, and that he took active measures that the cargo should not be exposed to detention on its way to

Japan. To that effect when the rupture had already taken place the owner, on the Captain's inquiry as to what would be the final port of destination, stated Hong Kong, and further in order to ward off all kinds of risks, ordered the Captain instead of going through the Canal, as originally stipulated in charter party, to go round the Cape. On arrival of the steamer in Hong Kong, as was to be expected, received orders to go to Sasebo, which he did. It appears from the above that the steamer *Allanton* played no passive role, bringing to a hostile port in seat of war, the maximum of cargo consisting exclusively of contraband of war, and that the owner had taken an indubitable and very active part in the transaction.

With regard to the second trip, during which the *Allanton* was arrested by the Russian cruisers in the Japanese Sea, this time the Court also turned its attention to the following important circumstances:

a. The course the steamer kept on her way from Mororan passed through the whole theatre of present war, and besides the general dangers necessarily connected with the immediate vicinity to the belligerent fleets, this course was very disadvantageous as the steamer was exposed to the obvious risk of being retained by Russian cruisers on account of circumstances as aforesaid in Point No. 1 which could be very easily avoided by taking the way through the ocean, so much the more as the last mentioned way to Singapore, if this were the destination, would have been only a trifle longer, about 100–120 miles.

b. The statement given by the young Japanese Tatiki Miachara embarked in the *Allanton* at Mororan for the purpose of going to America to finish his education is apparently invented as Miachara had no document whatever in his possession to prove his identity, whereas taking into consideration the utterly strict passport rules in Japan and with regard to Asiatics in America, its appears impossible for a Japanese subject, not having served his time in the army, and not having in his possession a certificate stating his being released from the same, to leave Japan without permission from the local authorities, and without a passport in his possession.

c. The discontinuance of remarks of arrivals at ports in the official log, from the moment the ship left Hong Kong, and further the fact that even after the first illegal trip was finished no such remarks have been made, seem to prove that on the second trip Singapore was no more the destination of the *Allanton* than Hong Kong was on the first.

3. Concerning the cargo the *Allanton* carried when arrested, the fact that the steamer was chartered directly by the Japanese company for taking a full cargo of coal from Mororan and the nonexistence of any statement whatever showing that the coal had become the property of a neutral proves that the cargo in question was still the property of and in the possession of the Japanese company, consequently being hostile property, accompanied by the Japanese Miachara presumably in the capacity of agent.

A combination of all details and circumstances mentioned above and the character of the cargo convinces the Court that the real destination of this hostile cargo was by no means Singapore but a Japanese or Korean port, or even the enemy's fleet maneuvering in the open sea, on account of which the cargo in question was declared by the Court to be contraband of war in accordance with paragraph 6, clause 8 of HIM order of February 14, 1904.

The Court considers it proved that illegal actions have been exercised by the owner of the ship and Captain of the same for the strengthening of the enemy's military store by bringing him coal, necessary for carrying on naval war, and that the steamer *Allanton* has thereby forfeited the rights of neutrality.

Considering the circumstances in this case in connection with state of affairs in the theatre of war, the Court finds—even independent of the proved fact that the *Allanton* was about to bring contraband of war to the enemy—that the facts referred to are so much the more important, as ships of neutrals serving in the place of the Japanese merchant service, and thus enabling the Japanese Government to utilize the latter for furtherance of war operations, exercise a great influence on the results of the war, disadvantageous to Russia, not speaking of the fact that such actions on the part of neutrals, being left unpunished, would make it almost impossible for Russia to follow up one of the most important and natural objects in naval war: to cut off the enemy from the possibility of availing himself of the sea as a means of communication.

From such a point of view, or still a stricter one, these matters are looked upon by English authors of maritime law. Sir Robert Phillimore in his works says: "but if a neutral acts in a fraudulent manner dishonestly or against the interests of the belligerent parties, he can in specially clear cases be punished by confiscation of his vessel."

Thus, guided by the facts aforesaid in this matter, foreseen in paragraphs 5, 18, 13 of the statutes re Maritime Prizes, and by the considerations emanating from same, applicable according to paragraph 4 of same, the Prize Court considered the *Allanton* as well as her cargo, fully legal prizes, and accordingly decided to confiscate the same in favour of the Imperial Government.

Translation by Mr. Schuster of the Great Northern Telegraph Company at Vladivostock from original documents of the Court.

Appendix X

Decision of
Vladivostock Prize Court
in case of
steamship *Knight Commander*

By order of HIM the Prize Court of Vladivostock met on July 27–August 6,* 1904 and listened to the case of the seizure of the British steamer *Knight Commander.*

Present: Major General Knipper, Chairman; Captain 2d rank Simonoff; Lieutenant Colonel Egerman; Public Councillor Stein, Collegiate Secretary Cheborenko; Procurator Titular Councillor Lazarevsky; Collegiate Secretary Engelhardt, Secretary.

The facts of the case are as follows: On July 11/25 about 6 a.m. a separate detachment of cruisers of the Pacific Ocean squadron under command of Rear Admiral Jessen consisting of cruisers *Rossia* (flagship), *Gromoboi* and *Rurick* while in latitude 34° 21′ N., Longitude 138° 53′ .5 E., to southwest of entrance to Gulf of Tokio, perceived a merchant steamer. *Rossia* gave chase, and when within 15 or 20 cables hoisted signal "stop" and then sent one after another two blank shots, then two projectiles under her bow as steamer continued on her course at full speed for entrance of Tokio Gulf. The steamer then stopped and hoisted British commercial flag. By order of commander of detachment *Rossia* hoisted signal "Master come on board with papers," but as this order was not obeyed, a party headed by Lieutenant Favrishenko and Sublieutenant Aminoff was sent aboard to examine steamer's papers and cargo. Examination showed that J. R. Durant was master, that she was on voyage to Japan with cargo consisting of railway material, bridge material, machinery, and various articles. The master of the steamer was not able to present any documents of his cargo, but examination of the holds showed that they were filled with contraband exclusively, the other articles constituting an unimportant portion.

After examination the officers returned to the cruiser bringing

* The two dates are New Style and Old Style.

the master and papers along. Having inquired of the master why there were no bills of lading amongst the papers, and learning there was aboard coal for four days only Rear Admiral Jessen informed the master that steamer was subject to confiscation, and as she had not sufficient coal to take her into a Russian port, she would be destroyed. Half an hour was given for removal of the crew. After removal of crew she was sunk by explosion of cartridges at 9.15 a.m.

On return of cruiser division to Vladivostock, the matter of sinking of steamer was submitted to the Prize Court. Examination of master's papers showed that steamer was British register, built in Yarrow in 1890, of 9,620 displacement, 4,305, and 2,716 registered tonnage, and speed of 11.0 knots. Her registry was from Liverpool No. 97801, and steamer belonged to Robert Low Greenshields of Liverpool. From entries in log and testimony of master it was learned that until December 1903 the vessel made voyages between Calcutta and other East Indian ports. In December she was chartered by the Austrian Lloyd for a trip to Trieste and Venice. From Venice steamer chartered by an Austrian firm in Trieste to carry coal for machinery and private cargo to Messina, then to Palermo to load 25,000 cases of lemons and general cargo for New York, where the charter lapsed.

In New York the steamer was not chartered by any one but gradually received various cargo, and was sent by orders of the agents of the ship's owner to Singapore, Manila, Shanghai, Yokohama and Kobe, where this voyage was to end. In regard to the cargo for which the master Durant presented no bills of lading or even manifest, the Court could only form a certain notion of that portion addressed to Japanese ports of Yokohama and Kobe, which was in the steamer at time of capture.

Ship's papers being missing, the Court took the evidence of the two boarding officers, Lieutenant Favrishenko and Baron Aminoff in two private memorandum books, presented by the latter. From the data, when carefully confronted one side with the other, we may conclude that the cargo at moment of seizure of ship consisted of the following articles: rails, bridge materials, various railway material, steel, steel sheets, nails, wire, pipes, wheels, tar, acids, shovels, and a small quantity of assorted cargo consisting of paint, clothing, leather, sail cloth, tin, hardware, wood, and small articles as ink, perfumery, soap. Thus it may be considered as fully proven that the *Knight Commander* was arrested by the Russian cruisers while carrying contraband of war into the enemy's ports.

When asked by the Court to give an explanation why there were no manifest or bills of lading, the captain answered that in New York he had only given a power of attorney to agents of the ship's owner to sign the bill of lading and manifest. That some of the manifests he saw only in Shanghai in the office of Arnold, Carberry, but that he himself had never received copies of bills of lading or manifests, nor had signed any bill of lading. Captain Durant could not remember whether he had or had not sworn to the ship's manifest and the absence among the papers of the New York port passport he could not explain otherwise than by having lost it.

Whereas the Court is aware that certain formalities must be attended to before a ship receives permission to leave a port; that on board of a vessel there should be copies of bills of lading, and in any event the manifest of the cargo taken on board; that in America the fulfilment of similar formalities are enforced with special strictness which Captain Durant confirms in his letter to his ship's owner from Messina, March 3, 1904, and that consequently without his signature on the manifest with the established testimony under oath certifies that the said cargo is exactly that which was actually received on board and consigned to the ports mentioned in the manifest. He could in no way have been allowed such "pratique" is proven by the fact of his having landed at Manila from the *Knight Commander,* that part of his cargo assigned to that port. That he could not have been allowed "pratique" without signing a manifest is corroborated by the fact that in Manila he had to sign under oath a manifest that merely declared that in that port he took no cargo. That a manifest signed by the Captain in New York and a passport from that port should be with him is apparent from the circumstances firstly that the Manila manifest and passport were found among the documents presented by the Captain and secondly that in the leather case bearing the inscription "Steamer *Knight Commander*" as a guide and memorandum for a master, there is a list printed of documents that are unconditionally obligatory to be on board, and among them are precisely mentioned bills of lading, manifests, and port passports. In this way Captain Durant could not help remembering whether in New York he signed a manifest or did not; could not help possessing a passport from said port, and could not help possessing a manifest of the cargo signed by himself. The plea of Captain Durant of a slip of memory and of a probable loss of these documents as the cause of their absence cannot be passed over as sound. The destruction by Captain Durant of these documents that were compromising his vessel or at least their intentional suppression is the only explanation that may be accepted. The insincerity of Captain Durant's explanations may be inferred from his business correspondence with the shipowner, that the Court found in a copy book, delivered to the Court with the other documents. From this book, that Captain Durant acknowledges to have belonged to him, and that contains copies of letters written in his own hand, the following quotations deserve attention, for they disclose especially vividly both the true character of the voyages of the vessel, and the relations to the obligations of neutrality on the part of the shipowner and master.

(1) Page 422 of the copy book "New York, April 15, 1904—the work of loading is going very slow with us owing to the character of the cargo, for nearly two entire days we have been loading parts of bridge material, weighing each from 6 to seven tons. Our Agent telegraphed to Chemulpo to have adjustments prepared there for discharging them, but until now no answer was received. Thus I shall have to get the heavy tackle and beams in order to unload this part of the cargo and to have done with it. I shall probably even sell it at a profit. For our ship the bother with the cargo is exceedingly costly for we are short both of suitable pulleys and of ropes".

(2) Page 424, "New York, April 22, 1904—I regret to be compelled to advise you that we are still loading very slowly owing to the character of the cargo we have to handle. We are putting the bridge material into No. 1 which is designated for Chemulpo".

(3) Page 443, "Shanghai, July 19—as much as I could learn from Messrs. Arnold Carberry, the attempt to go to Chemulpo at the present time is dangerous. They earnestly advised me that if I should still attempt it to go first southerly, then turn directly westward before approaching. I have no intention to remove responsibility, but I cannot see why we should go to face a catas-

trophe. Until the receipt of your letter yesterday, I was under the impression that we were to land cargo at Chemulpo. Our late (?) safe port on leaving here will be Kobe. You may feel confident that I have carefully considered this circumstance, as well as whether it shall be safe to go further or not. I am afraid that the ship will sink by the bow considerably after discharging the (present) cargo for Kobe, for when we were loading the No. 2, 4 and 1 holds were the only ones where we stowed away the main part of the bridge material."

The above quotations from the correspondence show firstly that the vessel was far from being passively an instrument for the transportation of military contraband to the enemy's ports, but on the contrary, that her owner took in this operation the most active part; secondly that the final destination of the steamer *Knight Commander* so carefully dissimulated, was not Yokohama or Kobe but Chemulpo; or in other words the active Japanese army; and thirdly that the true character of the cargo as well as its own and the steamer's destination were positively known to Captain Durant. Whereas being ignorant of the fact that among the papers presented to the Court was his own copy book, Captain Durant made the declaration, that the bridge material was consigned to Kobe, and that he was not aware that railroad materials constituted contraband of war. In view of such indubitable insincerity of Captain Durant in his testimony before the Court, as well as the proven suppression by him of a whole file of very important papers on ship and cargo, led the Court to conclude that it would be impossible to avail themselves of Captain Durant's testimony in the matter of deciding what ratio the contraband articles bore to the bulk of the cargo in the steamer when she was seized.

The two memorandum books Nos. 4 and 5, contain only the names and commercial marks of packages addressed to Yokohama and Kobe, without any mention of their weight or bulk, but they do not contain any notice whatever of rails or railroad material in general that were in the ship and alleged to be consigned to Kobe; among the documents and records presented to the Court there was nowhere found the slightest mention of these materials, and finally the memorandum books Nos. 4 and 5 represent only private memoranda, being at the same time manifestly incomplete and insufficient; so that the only reliable and faith inspiring data for the Court to determine the relative quantity of the contraband cargo "that had been in the steamer *Knight Commander*" present themselves in the depositions of Lieutenant Favrishenko and Sub-lieutenant Baron Aminoff who had examined the entire vessel. When examining the holds in the fore part of the ship, the more spacious ones, the former saw that the cargo in them consisted of railroad material in the form of disjointed parts of a bridge, of rails, pipes for boilers, waggonets, on springs, cogged wheels, corner iron, telegraph wire and barrels of cement. In the holds at the stern examined by both officers together, railroad materials were in predominance too. Iron pipes in great quantities occupied one third of the holds, and there were also parts of some machinery and their adjustments; and lastly in the central hold there were seen various iron parts in form of waggonets or platforms.

Lieutenant Favrishenko, upon examining the steamer jointly with Sublieutenant Aminoff, came to the conclusion that her cargo consisted of railroad material, and if there were any private cargo, then only in a very insignificant quantity. Therefore the Court feels convinced that the following is indubitably proven.

(1) The fact that the owner of the steamer *Knight Commander* having performed illegal acts, directed to make more effective the resources of our antagonist, by carrying to him at Chemulpo, the theatre of war directly, articles of military contraband.

(2) The suppression by the master of said steamer of an entire file of important documents relating to his vessel and to his cargo as well as his undoubted knowledge that he was conveying articles of military contraband to the enemy, and

(3) The presence on the said steamship at the moment of being seized, of military contraband, in quantity indubitably far exceeding one half of her entire cargo.

On these grounds and taking into consideration the actual facts of the present case as provided for by Articles 5, 8, 13 of the statutes of naval prizes the Prize Court finds:

(1) That the *Knight Commander* was arrested in a legal manner in compliance with the rules enacted in articles 2, 3, 15–17 of the statutes, and

(2) That the said steamer having been caught conveying military contraband to the enemy in quantity exceeding one half of

the cargo, as well as the mentioned contraband, appear to be legal prizes and decrees to adjudge the steamer *Knight Commander* and the contraband cargo that was in her at the time of her seizure as subject to confiscation as legal prizes.

Original duly signed by Chairman and Secretary of Court. Translation verified by R. T. Greener, Vice Consul and Commercial agent, U. S., at Vladivostock.

APPEAL IN CASE OF *KNIGHT COMMANDER*

To the Higher Prize Court.

From the attorney for the owners of the steamer *Knight Commander*, and for owners of the sunken cargo, Attorney John Romanovitch Bagenoff.

The Prize Court of Vladivostock after examining the case of the arrest and sinking by the Russian cruisers on July 11/24 near Yokohama of the British steamer *Knight Commander* decided to adjudge said steamer and contraband cargo in her as prizes legally taken.

This view I consider illegal in view of the Court having permitted a series of violations, as regards form as well as the essential character of the case. In the statutes on Naval Prizes one can easily see that it does not lay down any special rules for trial by the Prize Court, but as to the nature of the case which when we compare articles 80 to 86 with each other we find the rules of procedure are those of civil trials, with some inconsiderable changes. This conclusion is fully confirmed by the contents of Article 59, in which it is stated that in case any difficulties are met with during the trial, they should be decided in accordance with the statutes of Civil and Penal Law.

Applying myself now in particular to the trial in the present case, I consider it necessary to call attention merely to the following more important violations of form.

(1) Article 36 was not strictly complied with so far as it relates to the examination and arrest of vessel i. e. on the protocol of the examination of the steamer and on the act of sinking there is no resolution of Rear Admiral Jessen, ordering the destruction of the steamer, with the statement under what point of the said instruction the steamer should have been arrested; though in the protocol there is a resolution of the commander of the cruiser *Rossia;* but in

the presence of the Admiral it can have no pertinence; for the Admiral did not by his signature approve the reference in the Commander's orders.

Also the act of sinking the steamer was not signed by the Admiral, though the latter was on board the cruiser. A punctual performance of the said instructions is the only guaranty for the examination of the vessel for the correct acts of the naval and military administration. For the sake of which for the better understanding of instructions the whole process of arresting is divided into paragraphs and each of them has a special heading. Such underscoring by the lawgiver clearly indicates the necessity of punctually and unconditionally complying with them. Paragraph 86 appears to be the most important and decisive for it represents the first result of the examination, and expresses a definite final decision allowed only to the highest Naval chief.

Captain Durant was examined not under oath but simply as a witness, which appears to be a violation of article 64 according to which, being an accessory, he could not be examined as a witness.

As to the grounds on which the ship was condemned as prize, the fact of the illegal acting on the part of the owner of the *Knight Commander* of causing to be transported to Chemulpo, the theatre of war, articles of military contraband. This circumstance the Court extracts from the business correspondence of Captain Durant with the shipowner. As a matter of fact, the court had only the letters of Captain Durant, while the letters of the shipowner were not at its disposal. Not to mention that from simple answers and one-sided letters it is difficult to form a correct judgment of the essence of the correspondence, and the Court out of a mass translated only three quotations that were more favorable to the decision rendered. Even when we apply to these three quotations we cannot agree with the decision rendered. From the first and second quotations we can only conclude that the loading of the bridge material was going on very slowly, and the Captain supposed this cargo was intended for Chemulpo, but the third quotation shows directly that the Captain was mistaken in his supposition, as is clearly seen from his words "until I received your yesterday's letter, I was entirely under the impression we had to discharge cargo at Chemulpo". But the phrase in the second letter "we put the bridge material with No. 1 which is intended for Chemulpo", does not indicate at all that the material was designated for Chemulpo, for the words "which is intended for Chemulpo", do not refer to the bridge material but to No. 1 hold which was assigned to cargo going to Chemulpo. But according to the regulations for loading cargo it was evidently found necessary to change the disposition of the holds; what cargo was intended for Chemulpo can be seen from the letters. What refers to remarks in the letters about the dangers of the voyage, appear perfectly natural for it is not without danger to be subjected to examination by a warship even if having an entirely neutral cargo; for the least casual misunderstanding may lead to the arrest of the steamer, consequently to material loss. That is why every merchant desirous of not meeting trouble seeks to avoid such meetings. Therefore the conclusion of the Court from this correspondence of the insincere testimony of the Captain, and his reference to the duties of neutrality, can scarcely be accepted as convincing.

2. The concealing by the Captain of a whole file of very important documents relating to his vessel and cargo, as well as his undoubted knowledge of transporting to the enemy articles of military contraband. To elucidate that question it is necessary to know the meaning of ship's papers and documents and which of them are to be considered of the most importance. The answer we find in the appendix I to the 2d paragraph of instructions, where in the list of the ship's chief documents for Great Britain are mentioned eight (8). Of this number Captain Durant failed to present only:

(1) The charter party.

(2) The bills of lading on cargo for Kobe and Yokohama.

Whereas the list of cargo for these ports with the marks was in the memorandum books of the steamer, Nos. 4 and 5, which in the judgment of the Court were for some reasons called "private." The first of these documents was not necessary if the steamer was not chartered by any one, but was working for her owner and in this case there is no indication that she was chartered. With reference to the bills of lading, it certainly would have been more convenient for Captain Durant to have had them or copies of them, in which case the steamer would have scarcely been arrested. But the absence of these documents can in no way place blame on the Captain for (the loss of) the bills of lading and their copies. In view of the delay in loading the steamer at New York they had most likely been sent forward by mail signed by the agent as attorney for the Captain. And such documents he did see in Shanghai and Manila, after delivery of the cargo, receiving copies of them in hand. The absence of these documents can have no import in the law of this case can be seen from the contents of Article 18 of the Instructions which points out that the law considers "in particular the most important documents are those by which it is possible to define the nationality of the vessel, and verify the circumstances of the voyage." A bill of lading is a document about the cargo. When the vessel is suspected of carrying contraband, it may be considered a suspicious document. In particular as Article 20 says in such cases when the vessel "is going to an enemy's port" and therefore, even in the presentation of bills of lading the steamer could scarcely have been released without examination. Finally the absence of bills of lading gives only the right to examine the vessel in order to obtain the assurance that among the goods there are no articles of military contraband. The foregoing shows that the accusation against Captain Durant of hiding documents appears to be a conjectural one on the part of the Court, and not founded on any actual data.

(3) The finding on the said steamer, at the time of seizure of military contraband, in quantity indubitably far exceeding one half of the total cargo.

From the conclusion stated in the decision of the Court it is seen that the Court not having sufficient documents to determine the quality and quantity of the cargo, and considering the testimony of the officers Favrishenko and Aminoff, sent on board to examine the whole steamer, are data worthy of absolute trust in the determination of the relative quantity of the contraband cargo on board the steamer *Knight Commander.* Without doubting the truthfulness of the testimony of the officers named, let us see what conclusions one can arrive at on the basis of these testimonies, and how the examination was made. Sublieutenant Aminoff testified that he examined the hold in the stern from the upper hatchway and saw in it a large quantity of iron pipes about three inches in diameter and

15 to 20 feet long, which occupied one third of the hold. In the back part of the hold he saw some cast iron, and parts of some machine; in the middle hold a large space was occupied by long articles of cylindrical form, encased in planks, 2 1/2 arching in diameter; one of the crew told witness it was some kind of a pipe. In the middle hold witness saw different iron parts and as it appears to him parts of carts or moving platforms. Further the witness looked in the front hold in the bow, where he saw only iron, and as it appeared to him again springs for cars; besides, on both sides of the hold were some closed wooden boxes unopened. From this examination it appeared to the witness that the steamer was carrying iron cargo exclusively.

The testimony of Lieutenant Favrishenko appears to be more circumstantial. He says there were five holds in the steamer, in which he, also looking from the upper hatchway, saw the following: in the two forward holds, as far as he could see, were railroad articles, parts of bridges, rails, pipes for boilers, carts with springs and wheels, cogged wheels, bars of corner iron, telegraph wire, barrels of cement. The middle contained many closed boxes, packed, of which not one had been opened. In the same way he continued the examination of the other holds, from which he came to the conclusion (from looking at them) that railroad cargo predominated. Comparing these two testimonies, we observe that first witness did not see in the same holds those articles which were seen there by the other; whereas the method of examination by looking into the holds through the hatchway, by both witnesses was the same. Generally speaking one found that hardware cargo predominated, the other railroad cargo. Both witnesses agree that they saw many boxes and many barrels among which not a single one had been opened. In one of the holds they saw some immense articles boarded up, which to one of the witnesses seemed to be a pipe, and to the other a boiler.

Without considering it necessary to enumerate all the contradictions in these testimonies, one cannot help concluding, that the examination of the steamer was incontestably superficial, the witnesses paying attention only to such articles as in their opinion could be considered military contraband. At the same time one of them ascribed as such all hardware, and the other all railroad material which character he appeared to see in each package of hardware. Meanwhile neither of them paid attention to the other cargo of which there was a considerable quantity, as is evident from the memorandum books Nos. 5 and 6 which are in the case. Only a superficial examination could lead to similar results, and indeed examining from above through a hatchway, a loaded hold 35 to 40 feet deep one can see only the uppermost articles; that the examination was superficial is indicated by that part of the testimony of Lieutenant Favrishenko that "he had not time to open the boxes for from the cruiser he was signalled to "make haste." Referring to the Imperial edict of February 14, 1904 we see in paragraphs 6, 7, and 9 that "military contraband constitutes all kinds of ship's machinery and boilers, both completed or in parts, and articles and materials suitable for the erection of telegraphs, telephones, and railroads. From this it is clear that not every kind of machinery and iron constitute military contraband, but only those specially designated.

Among the testimonials of these witnesses one fact only may be considered as more or less established, that among the cargo there were rails and parts of bridges; and that seen by the eye they occupied about 2/3 of the two forward holds out of five, and the remainder of the cargo consisted of a considerable quantity of hardware boxes, barrels etc. the destination of which could not be defined by the witnesses, and has not been defined. Taking all this together it gives in no manner a basis on which to consider the cargo as contraband, even should we ascribe to the rails and parts of bridges such a character, in a quantity exceeding half the cargo, and the conclusion unsupported by any exact figures more or less, or documentary data, appears entirely arbitrary. Therefore the only action that should have been taken in this case, was to arrest the ship and bring her into the nearest Russian port to land the contraband, but in no case to sink the steamer. Under the circumstances when the steamer was arrested, taking her into a Russian port presented scarcely any difficulty whatever; for (1) because there was on the steamer as seen from the record, about 120 tons of coal which allowing for a 10 knot speed would have been sufficient for four days—distance of nearly 1000 miles. Whereas the distance to the nearest Russian port, Korsakovsk or Saghalin, from Yokohama is considered 750 miles, and (2) though the vessel was stopped 15.0 miles off the entrance of the gulf of Tokio, no enemy was seen nor was there any evidence of his proximity, whereas these circumstances exactly were deemed extraordinary and the steamer was sunk. The Prize Court in its decision with reference to the quantity of the cargo was guided by the same data as the Naval authority, whereas had they acted in conformity with Article 71 Statutes on Prizes, by virtue of which in similar cases the skipper must be summoned by publication, in such case most probably there would have been at the disposal of the Court a sufficient number of proofs of the faulty character of the decision regarding the quantity of cargo adjudged military contraband.

Relying upon all of the above statements, I have the honor to ask the Highest Prize Court to revoke the decision of the Vladivostock Prize Court as incorrect, and to decree that the sinking of the *Knight Commander* was unjustifiable and that the owners both of the steamer and cargo are entitled to receive remuneration for the sinking of the one and the other.

Signed by attorney.

Translation by Mr. Schuster of the Great Northern Telegraph Company at Vladivostock from original documents of the Court.

Appendix XI

Decision of Vladivostock Prize Court in case of steamship *Calchas*

Officers present at the session: Chairman, Major General Knipper; Member, Captain 2d rank Stratanevitch; Member, Lieutenant Colonel Egerman; Councillor at Court, Stein; Collegiate Assesor, Karminsky; Collegiate Secretary, Cheborenko; Procurator Titular Councillor, Lazarevsky; Collegiate Secretary Engelhardt, Secretary.

Circumstances of case are as follows:—On July 12, present year, in Pacific Ocean about 7.30 a.m., lat. 34° 53′, long. 140° 13′ E, the cruiser *Gromoboi,* while in company with a detachment of cruisers perceived a two-masted steamer with one funnel under the English flag, which after a hoisted signal and two warning shots, stopped. A party under Lieutenant Bolotnikoff sent on board for examination, which disclosed that steamer was the *Calchas,* British, bound with cargo from Tacoma to Liverpool via Japanese and Chinese ports and had besides the crew, 9 passengers.

On inspection of the ship's papers it became clear that among the articles consigned to Japan there were different machines and appurtenances, flour, cotton, and lumber; and in addition a large quantity of mail addressed to Japanese and Korean ports, and for this reason the commander of the detachment of cruisers gave orders to take the steamer to Vladivostock. During the above proceedings neither captain nor any of the crew offered resistance. A prize crew from *Rurik* took charge, Lieutenant Stackelberg in command. The bills of ladings and passengers certificates were turned over to Captain Dabitch of *Gromoboi,* but the other documents and the mail were left on board in charge of Lieutenant Stackelberg. The *Calchas* kept along in view of *Rossia* but on 15/28* July became

* The two dates are New Style and Old Style.

lost in fog and made her own way to Port Korsakovsk. Upon arrival at Korsakovsk a supply of coal was taken on board (200 tons), and in view of the scarcity of flour at that place, and with permission of the Commander-in-Chief of the fleet, Vice Admiral Skrydloff, and consent of master of *Calchas* 2,000 sacks of flour were left there, after which steamer continued her course to Vladivostock, where her case was taken up for consideration by the Vladivostock Prize Court.

From the documents presented to the Court it was made clear that the steamer *Calchas* under command of a British subject, Captain W. T. Hannah, was built at Greenock, 1899, in Scott & Co.'s shipyard, registered at the Port of Liverpool, No. 110586 and belonged to the Ocean Steamship Company, India Building, Liverpool: extreme length 441.7 feet; beam 52.6; displacement 12,530; gross tonnage 6,748.3; registered tonnage 4,278.99. Machinery consisted of one triple expansion engine of 13 knots. Crew consisted of 73 persons, including Captain Hannah, and composed of 33 Europeans, 40 Chinamen. There were besides 9 passengers. From entries in log book supplemented by testimony of Captain, learned that *Calchas* left Birkenhead, England for Glasgow consigned to Victoria, B.C., (March 16/29, present year.) Vancouver, Seattle and Tacoma, calling on her way at Port Said, Suez, Jedda, Penang, Singapore, Hong Kong, Nagasaki, Moji, Kobe, and Yokohama. Steamer commenced her last voyage at Tacoma where she took in part of the cargo adding other at Vancouver and Victoria and left for Liverpool, making calls for delivery of parts of her cargo at Yokohama, Kobe, Hong Kong, Singapore and purposed a call at Colombo. During this voyage and not far from Yokohama steamer was arrested by Russian cruisers. Besides cargo mentioned, the *Calchas,* though not a regular mail steamer, received 122 bags of sundry mail matter put on board by the American Postal authorities at Tacoma, by virtue of which circumstance, the Captain had no choice but to accept. Upon examination of the cargo documents, in order to determine the character of the voyage, the Court found that the cargo was divided as follows:

The cargo consigned to Japan at time of seizure consisted of the following articles: 651,700 pounds flour = 13,300 sacks; 36 packages cotton weighing 19,264 pounds; 97 pieces girders weighing

472,420 pounds; and 77 packages sundry machinery weighing 120,000 pounds; in addition consigned to Tokio and Yokohama was a considerable quantity of varnish and leaf tobacco. The flour and girders as composing articles of military contraband, by decision of the Court were immediately discharged from the vessel as well as 77 packages of machinery with regard to which the Court decided to invite expert opinion in regard to the nature and purpose of said machinery and lumber. Examination of these articles gave following results: The machinery consisted of a horizontal steam engine; different appurtenances of a steam motor with adjustments; dynamo machines and parts; electrical transmitters; anchors; brush holders; blackmith's furnaces; lathes; pipes; appurtenances for turbine motors, and a large quantity of separate parts of these articles. The experts came to the conclusion that the major portion of the machinery examined was for the production and transfer of energy, both for labor and electricity; for the regulation of the quantity of water in hydraulic works for lighting buildings by electricity, etc; but altogether they would not furnish a complete outfit for a manufactory or workshop. In the opinion of experts not one of the articles named bore the character of being specially adapted for military use, though if used for lighting purposes for arsenals, or for the transfer of power for movable lathes used in preparing war supplies, they could undoubtedly be used for war needs. The experts could not give any definite opinion with reference to the true purpose of said machines; and limited their declarations by the statement that the articles of machinery could according to circumstances, serve equally for the needs of peace or war. In view of the fact that according to the declarations of the experts, there was no sufficient data as to the purpose of the above mentioned 77 packages of machinery and electrical appliances, and because Captain Hannah, who was present during the hearing of the matter, could not supply any information in this regard, the Court is deprived of the possibility of rendering a decision in this instance, and therefore by virtue of articles 71–73 of the statutes on Naval Prizes, has decided to issue a summons by publication to the original owners of said property to show proof to the Court that it was not intended for military purposes of Japan; and to grant a term of three months from the date of last publication; and meanwhile to postpone decision on the 77 packages of machinery and electrical appliances. In regard to the 97 pieces of girders in accordance with the declaration of the experts, this material is fit for ships and bridge building not excepting bridges for broad gauge railways.

(2) The cargo consigned direct or by reloading to neutral ports at Tientsin, Hong Kong, Shanghai, Colombo, Glasgow, Liverpool, Southampton, London, Woolwich, or Capetown, weighing 3,423,413 pounds of the dimensions of 41,610 cubic feet, consists mainly of lumber besides a certain quantity of assorted merchandise, as hardware, preserves, machinery, liquors, furs, hard-tack, and personal effects. Among the cargo according to the declaration of Captain Hannah there was received on board at Tacoma one 12-pd cannon addressed to Woolwich, and at Victoria about 30 parcels, with outfits for the English Navy addressed to the different Government Departments in London.

On July 31, the Court examined the mail matter taken from the *Calchas,* and presented to the Court. It consisted of 122 sacks and two envelopes, addressed to Japanese and Korean ports. The Court selected 16 bags of letters addressed from Tacoma—4 sacks to Tokio, 11 sacks to Yokohama, and 1 sack to Korea, out in accordance with the statutes 2, 3, 15, 17 on Naval Prizes.

(2) That the articles carried for the ports of Japan; flour to the amount of 651,700 pounds; 36 packages cotton; 97 packages girders; by virtue of Paragraph VI, pp. 9 and 10 of the Imperial Edict of February 14 and April 8 of present year comprehended military contraband.

(3) That the official Japanese mail matter on the steamer has no direct reference to military actions of the Army or Navy.

(4) That the cargoes on the steamer addressed to the neutral ports to the amount of 3,423,413 pounds do not come under the definition of military contraband.

Therefore, and upon the basis of articles 5, 8, 13, 27, 28 of the Statutes on Naval Prizes it is decided:

(1) That the cargo consigned to Japanese ports and consisting of 13,300 sacks (651,700 pounds) flour, 36 packages of cotton and 97 girders are confiscated as a legal prize in favor of the Govern-

ment and must be handed over to the Port authorities to be taken charge of by them in accordance with article 33 of the Statutes:

(2) The cargo addressed to neutral ports consisting of 3,423,413 pounds not being contraband, is to be released immediately:

(3) The steamer *Calchas* since it was seized while carrying to the enemy military contraband in a quantity less than half of the cargo at the time of seizure, and while carrying official Japanese correspondence but having no direct reference to military affairs, is also released. But the decision to release the steamer in accordance with Article 80 of the Statutes, does not go into effect until the decision becomes of legal force; nor can there be returned to Captain Hannah any of the ship's documents until the expiration of the above named term.

(4) The manifests and bills of lading for the released cargo are to be returned to the said Captain Hannah.

(5) With reference to the 77 packages of machinery and electrical appliances to postpone the decision of their military purpose by summoning their original owners to appear in Court in three months time.

(Signed) KNIPPER, Major General.
ENGELHARDT, Secretary—and verified
by U.S. Consul.

PROTEST OF PROCURATOR

Upon examination of the decision of the Prize Court, August 31 (September 13), 1904 in the matter of the arrest by the cruiser *Gromoboi* of the British steamer *Calchas* on July 12, I find that the decision is not founded upon the principles of the regulations of February 14 as confirmed by the Czar, according to which Russia was to guide herself during the war with Japan, as follows:

First. As seen in the protocol of the Prize Court to the question whether the electrical machinery on the *Calchas* was fit for searchlights in sea battles, the answer was "the electrical appliances on the steamer though they are not adapted for it, may serve for searchlights". Notwithstanding this, the Court decided "With regard to the 77 packages of machinery and electrical appliances, the discussion as to their intention for military used is postponed." By this action the Court may be said to have acknowledged that articles suitable for electric searchlights can not be used for military purposes.

Second. As is seen from the protocol of the examination of the 15 packages of enemy's correspondence, some of them were addressed by Japanese official persons residing in America to official persons in Tokio, leaving out of consideration the character of the correspondence, the conclusion can not be avoided that in releasing the steamer, the Court paid no attention to the 7th article of the regulations confirmed by Imperial sanction "in like manner as in the trade in contraband articles the following acts forbidden to neutrals must be considered: transportation of enemy's troops, of the enemy's despatches and correspondence— Neutral vessels caught with similar kind of military contraband may according to circumstances not only be arrested, but also confiscated."

In my opinion, in case cited, the act of seizing the *Calchas* occurred at such a time when so far as the enemy was concerned, it was specially important to have information on questions of finance, and envelope No. 10 contains such intelligence.

Taking all these things into consideration, I respectfully petition the Highest Prize Court to overrule the decision of the Vladivostock Prize Court of August 31, 1904—that portion relating to points above stated.

(Signed) LAZAREVSKY, Procurator—Sept. 18-Oct. 1, 1904.

Protest of Admiral Jessen, chief of the separate detachment of cruisers of Pacific squadron.

On examination of the decision of the Vladivostock Prize Court of August 31 of this year, in the matter of the arrest by the *Gromoboi* of the *Calchas* on July 12, I find that the decision does not correspond with the exact principles of the regulations confirmed by the Czar on February 14, that Russia intended to use as a guide during the war with Japan. As is seen in the protocol of the examination, among the 15 envelopes of the enemy's correspondence, some were addressed by Imperial Japanese Consuls in America to the

Ministry of Foreign Affairs of the Japanese Empire. Among them were:

First. Envelope No. 3 contains secret information or intelligence on commercial relations with Belgium, and on the establishment of a Japanese Bank in the said kingdom.

Secondly. Envelope No. 4 contains slips from the American newspapers with reference to the present war action.

Thirdly. Envelope No. 31, a secret one of political character, has immediate relation to the present war between Japan and Russia.

Fourthly. Envelope No. 11 is also of a political character.

During the discussion of the present case Lieutenant Gervais who was my representative, called the attention of the Prize Court to the political character of the correspondence.

Notwithstanding this the Court ignored in its decision the political character of the said correspondence and failed to apply Article 7 of the above named regulations confirmed by the Czar, which reads "Alike with the commerce in military contraband, the following forbidden acts of neutrals should be included; transportation of the enemy's troops; of the enemy's despatches and correspondence. Neutral vessels caught with such military contraband may be according to circumstances not only seized but confiscated."

Considering that the estimate of the political character of an enemy's correspondence is the business of experts, consisting of officials from the Ministry of Foreign Affairs of War and of the Navy, and since I do not agree with the estimate of this correspondence as made by the Court in its decision, I ask the Highest Prize Court to cancel the decision of the Vladivostock Prize Court of August 31, 1904.

(Signed) Jessen (Rear Admiral of the suite of HIM)

Translation by Mr. Schuster of the Great Northern Telegraph Company at Vladivostock from original documents of the Court.

NOTE: In reference to cargo on board *Calchas* it was learned from reliable sources that the machinery was in 20 different lots, from various firms, to different consignees and intended for various purposes, the largest lot of 26 packages consisting of material for refrigerating plant. The 97 packages girders were 97 heavy wooden beams. Of the mail, until December 2, there were 49 bags unaccounted for by the Russian authorities, among them 5 bags letters addressed to U.S. Consul Shanghai, one bag letters to Manila Post Office, two bags letters to Hong Kong, one bag letters to Canton, and the rest newspapers to the same addresses. All this was American mail put on board in Tacoma, and a considerable portion presumably for the U.S. ships in Asiatic Station. On making inquiry at the office of Staff of Vice Admiral Skrydloff, I was informed that this mail had been sent to its address via St. Petersburg.

N. A. McCully.

Sources to Footnotes

[1] Ambassador Robert S. McCormick to Secretary of State, February 27, 1904. Diplomatic Despatches, "Russia" 624–626 1–94. Records of the Department of State, National Archives, Washington, D.C.

[2] Deck Log of USS *Vicksburg,* 9 February 1904. Records of the Bureau of Naval Personnel, National Archives, Washington, D.C.

[3] Tupper, Harmon, *To the Great Ocean: Siberia and the Trans-Siberian Railway* (New York: Little, Brown & Company, 1965), p. 98.

[4] Tupper, *op. cit.,* pp. 122–133.

[5] Tupper, *op. cit.,* pp. 225–233.

[6] *Voennaia Entsiklopediia* (St. Petersburg: 1909–1916), IV, pp. 618–620.

[7] Brassey, T.A., ed., *The Naval Annual* (Portsmouth: J. Griffin and Co., 1905), pp. 119–120.

[8] *The Russo-Japanese War: Reports From British Officers Attached to the Japanese and Russian Forces in the Field* (London: Eyre and Spottiswoode, 1908), II, pp. 357–359.

[9] *Cassell's History of the Russo-Japanese War* (London: Cassell & Co., Ltd., 1905), II, 43.

[10] Robertson, Captain D.S., "The Battle of Mukden: Operations of the 8th Division, Second Japanese Army," *The Russo-Japanese War: op. cit.,* pp. 181–218.

INDEX

Prepared by Newton A. McCully,
Lieutenant Commander, U.S. Navy

INDEX